Adaptive Behavior Assessment System-II: Clinical Use and Interpretation

Adaptive Behavior Assessment System-II: Clinical Use and Interpretation

Editors

Thomas Oakland
and
Patti L. Harrison

ELSEVIER

AMSTERDAM • BOSTON • HEIDELBERG • LONDON • NEW YORK • OXFORD
PARIS • SAN DIEGO • SAN FRANCISCO • SINGAPORE • SYDNEY • TOKYO
Academic Press is an imprint of Elsevier

Academic Press is an imprint of Elsevier
525 B Street, Suite 1900, San Diego, CA 92101-4495, USA
30 Corporate Drive, Suite 400, Burlington, MA 01803, USA
84 Theobald's Road, London WC1X 8RR, UK

First edition 2008

Library of Congress Cataloging in Publication Data
A catalog record for this book is available from the Library of Congress

British Library Cataloguing in Publication Data
A catalogue record for this book is available from the British Library

ISBN: 978-0-12-373586-7

For information on all Academic Press publications
visit our website at books.elsevier.com

Typeset by Charon Tec Ltd (A Macmillan Company), Chennai, India
www.charontec.com

08 09 10 10 9 8 7 6 5 4 3 2 1

CONTENTS

SECTION I

INTRODUCTION

1

ADAPTIVE BEHAVIORS AND SKILLS: AN INTRODUCTION 3

THOMAS OAKLAND AND PATTI L. HARRISON

2

PROFESSIONAL AND LEGAL ISSUES IN ADAPTIVE BEHAVIOR ASSESSMENT 21

THOMAS OAKLAND AND PATTI L. HARRISON

3

ABAS-II ASSESSMENT METHODS 37

PATTI L. HARRISON AND THOMAS OAKLAND

SECTION II

ABAS-II AND ADAPTIVE SKILL AREAS

4

COMMUNICATION SKILLS 53

G. RICHMOND MANCIL AND BETSY VINSON

5

ADAPTIVE BEHAVIOR AND SKILLS IMPORTANT TO COMMUNITY USE 71

STACY K. DYMOND

7

SCHOOL AND HOME LIVING ADAPTIVE SKILLS 115

DANIEL E. STEERE, HEATHER GARRISON, AND JOYCE BURGENER

8

HEALTH AND SAFETY ADAPTIVE SKILL AREA 137

MARTIN AGRAN, FRED SPOONER, AND TRACIE-LYNN ZAKAS

9

THE USE OF LEISURE TIME 159

ROBERT BELAND

10

PROMOTING SELF-CARE SKILLS 179

MONICA A. WALLACE AND MARISA W. SHUBERT

11

SOCIAL SKILLS 197

KRISTY LEE PARK, SHELDON LOMAN, AND MELISSA A. MILLER

12

ABAS-II AND WORK SKILLS AND ATTITUDES 219

KAGENDO MUTUA

13

MOTOR FUNCTIONING AND ADAPTIVE BEHAVIOR 245

SARAH A. SCHOEN AND LUCY JANE MILLER

SECTION III

ABAS-II AND ASSESSMENT ACROSS AGE RANGES

14

USING THE ABAS-II WITH INFANTS, TODDLERS, AND PRESCHOOLERS 269

TINA SMITH-BONAHUE

15

USING THE ABAS-II WITH ELEMENTARY AND MIDDLE SCHOOL STUDENTS 293

RANDY G. FLOYD AND RENEE BERGERON

16

USING THE ABAS-II WITH ADOLESCENTS AND YOUNG ADULTS 313

S. CRAIG RUSH, MICHELLE MAJOR-SANABRIA, AND STEPHANIE CORCORAN

SECTION IV

ABAS-II AND ASSESSMENT FOR SPECIAL POPULATIONS

17

18

PREFACE

Mature persons can be expected to be responsible for meeting their personal needs as well as for responding effectively to responsibilities that arise through their family, school, work, social settings, and community involvement. Centuries ago these qualities were thought to constitute intelligence. They now are considered to be adaptive behavior.

During the 20th century, adaptive behavior assessment first became important when diagnosing mental retardation and developing interventions for persons with mental retardation. Its importance has expanded, given increased recognition that adaptive behavior is important for all persons and may constitute the ultimate developmental outcome. Thus, professionals need to be alert to possible detriments in adaptive behavior and skills as a result of disabilities, disorders, and impairments, including those associated with attention disorders, auditory and visual acuity impairments, autism spectrum disorders, behavioral and emotional disorders, brain injury, dementia, developmental disorders, learning disabilities, psychotic disorders, stroke, and substance-related disorders.

In 1992, the American Association on Mental Retardation (AAMR; now named the American Association on Intellectual and Development Disabilities or AAIDD), a leader in defining adaptive behavior, broadened and sharpened its concept of adaptive behavior by underscoring the importance of adaptive skills. "Mental retardation refers to substantial limitations in present functioning. It is characterized by significantly subaverage intellectual functioning, existing concurrently with related limitations in two or more of the following applicable adaptive skill areas: communication, self-care, home living, social skills, community use, self-direction, health and safety, functional academics, leisure, and work. Mental retardation manifests before age 18." (AAMR, 1992, p. 5). This emphasis on adaptive skills enables clinicians to narrow their focus from the broader concept of adaptive behavior to one on critical and functional behaviors in one or more of the ten adaptive skill areas, thus increasing the linkage between assessment and intervention efforts.

We have been committed to the principle of linking assessment and intervention efforts for some time. We first recognized the need to develop a test of adaptive behavior consistent with current notions of adaptive behavior based on ten adaptive skills. This led to the development of the Adaptive Behavior Assessment System (ABAS) for ages 5–89 and later its revision, the Adaptive Behavior Assessment System-II (ABAS-II) for ages 0–89. We then saw the need for a book that helps clinicians and others better understand current theory and research on adaptive behavior and skills as well as to use this information to inform comprehensive assessment and intervention efforts. We trust you and others will find this book, *Adaptive Behavior Assessment System-II:* Clinical Use and Interpretation, assists your ability to use the ABAS-II in your work with infants, children, youth, and adults.

We, along with colleagues at Harcourt Assessment, saw the need to assist clinicians further by providing a computer-assisted method that helps identify strengths and weaknesses and that links ABAS-II item data and needed interventions. This lead to the *ABAS-II Intervention Planner and Scoring Assistant.* It determines scaled and standard scores, identifies score differences, assists in drafting reports, suggests item-level interventions for school and home based on test results, and enables professionals to track children's progress over time. We hope these two additions assist professionals in their use of the ABAS-II.

The completion of this edited book was possible due to the professional commitment of the 35 chapter authors who share our view to provide content that enable those who use the ABAS-II to improve their professional skills in assessment and planning interventions. We also appreciate the support and encouragement with the ABAS and ABAS-II from our colleagues at Harcourt Assessment, including Dr. Aurelio Prifitera, Dr. Larry Weiss, Dr. Jianjun Zhu, Dr. David M. Schwartz, Yvonne Elias, and Dr. Judith Treloar. The contributions of Mary Sichi to the ABAS, ABAS-II, and the *ABAS-II Intervention Planner and Scoring Assistant* have been instrumental and thus particularly noteworthy. We thank our colleagues at Elsevier, including Nikki Levy, Barbara Makinster, and other staff. We also express our gratitude to Nicholas Longo, graduate research assistant at the University of Alabama, for his assistance.

Thomas Oakland
Patti L. Harrison
February 2008

American Association on Mental Retardation (1992). *Definitions, classifications, and systems of supports* (9th ed.). Washington, DC: Author.

List of Contributors

Martin Agran Department of Special Education, University of Wyoming, Laramie, WY 82071, U.S.A.

Kathleen Armstrong Department of Pediatrics, University of South Florida, Tampa, FL 33612, U.S.A.

Robert Beland Department of Tourism, Recreation and Sport Management, University of Florida, Gainesville, FL 32611, U.S.A.

Renee Bergeron Hawaii Department of Education, Waipahu, HI 96797, U.S.A.

Joyce Burgener Department of Special Education and Rehabilitation, East Stroudsburg University, East Stroudsburg, PA 18301-2999, U.S.A.

Stephanie Corcoran Shelby County, Alabama Public School System, Alabaster, AL, 35007, U.S.A.

Ann W. Cox Chapel Hill, NC 27516-5587, U.S.A.

Heather Curtiss Department of Pediatrics, University of South Florida, Tampa, FL 33612, U.S.A.

Stacy K. Dymond Department of Special Education, University of Illinois, Champaign, IL 61829, U.S.A.

Nicole Fenty Department of Teaching and Learning, University of Louisville, Louisville, KY 40292, U.S.A.

Randy G. Floyd Department of Psychology, University of Memphis, Memphis, TN 38152, U.S.A.

Heather Garrison Department of Special Education and Rehabilitation, East Stroudsburg University, East Stroudsburg, PA 18301-2999, U.S.A.

Patti L. Harrison Department of Educational Studies in Psychology, Research Methodology, and Counseling, University of Alabama, Tuscaloosa, AL 35487-0231, U.S.A.

Carol Lilly Department of Pediatrics, University of South Florida, Tampa, FL 33612, U.S.A.

Sheldon Loman University of Oregon, Eugene, OR 97403-1235, U.S.A.

Michelle Major-Sanabria Department of Psychology, Barry University, Miami Shores, FL 33161-6695, U.S.A.

G. Richmond Mancil, Department of Child, Family and Community Sciences, University of Central Florida, Orlando, FL 32816, U.S.A.

Lucy Jane Miller, Greenwood Village, CO 80111, U.S.A.

Melissa A. Miller, University of North Carolina at Chapel Hill, Chapel Hill, NC 27599-3500, U.S.A.

Kagendo Mutua, Department of Special Education and Multiple Abilities, University of Alabama, Tuscaloosa, AL 35487, U.S.A.

Thomas Oakland, University of Florida, Gainesville, FL 32061-8405, U.S.A.

J. Gregory Olley, Center for Development and Learning, University of North Carolina at Chapel Hill, Chapel Hill, NC 27599-7255, U.S.A

Kristy Lee Park, University of Louisville, Louisville, KY 40292, U.S.A.

Kyle Popkave, Department of Pediatrics, University of South Florida, Tampa, FL 33612, U.S.A.

S. Craig Rush, School Psychology Program, The University of Alabama, Tuscaloosa, AL 35487-0231, U.S.A.

Sarah A. Schoen, Greenwood Village, CO 80111, U.S.A.

Marisa W. Shubert, Psychology Department, Middle Tennessee State University, Murfreesboro, TN 37132, U.S.A.

Tina Smith-Bonahue, University of Florida, Gainesville, FL 32611-7047, U.S.A.

Fred Spooner, Department of Special Education and Child Development, University of North Carolina at Charlotte, Charlotte, NC 28223-0001, U.S.A.

Daniel E. Steere, Department of Special Education and Rehabilitation, East Stroudsburg University, East Stroudsburg, PA 18301-2999, U.S.A.

Betsy Vinson, Department of Communication Processes and Disorders, University of Florida, Gainesville, FL 32611, U.S.A.

Monica A. Wallace, Psychology Department, Middle Tennessee State University, Murfreesboro, TN 37132, U.S.A.

Christine Woolf, Capella University, Minneapolis, MN, U.S.A.

Steven Woolf, Beacon Services, Milford, MA 01757, U.S.A.

Tracie-Lynn Zakas, Department of Special Education and Child Development, University of North Carolina at Charlotte, Charlotte, NC 28223-0001, U.S.A.

SECTION

I

Introduction

1

ADAPTIVE BEHAVIORS AND SKILLS: AN INTRODUCTION

THOMAS OAKLAND* AND PATTI L. HARRISON**

*University of Florida, Gainesville, FL 32611-7047, U.S.A.
**University of Alabama, Tuscaloosa, AL 35487-0231, U.S.A.

Envision a person who cares for his or her health, engages in community activities, attends school or has suitable employment, effectively applies what he or she learned in school, sustains meaningful relationships and communicates regularly with family and friends, enjoys leisure activities, is self-directed, and cares for his or her daily living needs (e.g., cleaning, toileting, dressing, and eating). Those who display these qualities may be said to have suitable adaptive behavior and skills.

This chapter provides a historical background for adaptive behavior and its use, traces changes in the definitions of adaptive behavior, reviews the development of tests of adaptive behavior, discusses age and demographic differences in adaptive behavior, and concludes with a discussion as to ways information from the Adaptive Behavior Assessment System-II (ABAS-II) (Harrison & Oakland, 2003a) may be used.

Adaptive behavior refers to the ways individuals meet their personal needs as well as deal with the natural and social demands in their environments (Nihira et al., 1993). One may think of adaptive behavior as a constellation of skills that allow a person to function effectively every day at home, school, work, and in the community.

An understanding of the importance of adaptive behavior requires some knowledge of its history and evolution, including its close association with assessment and identification of individuals with mental retardation. The following section provides this background information by drawing on information from events in Europe and the United States.

SOME HISTORIC BACKGROUND FOR ADAPTIVE BEHAVIOR AND ITS USE

Ancient Greek society provides the first recorded writings on adaptive behavior and its association with mental retardation. The term *idiot*, used somewhat commonly until the 20th century to describe persons with mental retardation, is derived from a Greek word that signifies persons who do not engage in the public life of the community. Persons whose self-care and community engagement are similar to others their age were thought to be normal. Those whose self-care and engagement are considerably less were thought to have mental retardation. Both Greek and Roman societies generally treated those with mental retardation with disdain, often either killing them or maintaining them for their amusement (Barr, 1905).

During the Middle Ages, the concept of mental retardation broadened to include persons with various emotional, medical, mental, and physical disorders. Persons who displayed these disorders typically were treated harshly, given the belief that their conditions were due to witchcraft. Their treatment did not improve during Protestant Reformation, given prevailing beliefs that they were illegitimate prodigies of the Devil and filled with Satan.

During the Enlightenment period, Christian humanitarian efforts together with the emergence of the scientific study of mental retardation lead to various improvements. Some European countries enacted legislation to protect those with mental retardation and to provide for their basic needs through institutions. In addition, efforts to distinguish mental retardation from emotional disorders gained ground, including efforts by Locke (1689) who drew distinctions between idiots and madmen. A foundation for efforts to improve educational and social skills of persons with mental retardation was laid during this period.

In 1838, Itard published the first in-depth study of a child with mental retardation. He and his wife took a child found wandering outside their city, Aveyron, France, into their home with the goal to socialize and educate him. Although these efforts with this "Wild Boy of Aveyron" were unsuccessful, they sparked interests in other scholars and educators to continue efforts that could lead to methods that promote the development of those with mental retardation.

Another Frenchman, Esquirol, published a book in 1838 that proposed three somewhat revolutionary ideas. He noted that mental retardation exists on a continuum, with at least two classes: the weak-minded and the idiot. He also suggested that language ability may successfully distinguish people with mental retardation from those with normal functioning. Esquirol also recognized the need for objective methods to distinguish levels of mental retardation and set about, through the use of anthropomorphic measures (e.g., skull measurements), to objectify this assessment.

Also, in 1838, Seguin, Esquirol's student, established a school in Paris to educate children with mental retardation. His school helped foster the commitment of others to help those with mental retardation and other biologically based disorders (e.g., those who were blind or deaf), leading to the establishment of more than 80 private and state-supported residential institutions within Australia, Canada, Europe, and United States for people with these disorders by the 1870s (Goodenough, 1949). In 1848, Seguin came to the United States and opened a school for children with mental retardation.

The American Journal of Insanity, the first scientific journal devoted to mental disease and deficiency, was established in 1844. A number of scientific studies of mental retardation were published in this journal, including those that examined the nature of mental deficiency, efforts to measure it, differences between those with mental retardation and other disorders, and methods to educate or at least ensure the basic needs of those with mental retardation.

1848: THE IMPACT OF AN ORGANIC THEORY OF EVOLUTION

Darwin's 1848 publication of the Origin of Species marked the beginning of the debate as to the relative impact of nature (i.e., the biological basis of behavior) and nurture (i.e., the environmental impact on behavior). This debate continues. Those who first endorsed Darwinian theory saw mental retardation as a form of social deviance and, for some, fostered the eugenics movement in the United States and elsewhere. Later, those who favored eugenics would rely heavily on data from intelligence tests to support their beliefs. The use of measures of intelligence became standard when assessing mental retardation.

Opposing views thought of mental retardation as a form of social incompetence that could be remedied through education. Before tests of adaptive behavior were available, persons holding this view relied heavily on clinical observations of a person's adaptive behavior. Much later, as the measures of adaptive behavior became available, reliance on them became more common.

Among psychologists interested in mental testing, some but not all were dedicated to a Darwinian theory that emphasized the hereditarian nature of mental retardation. Examples include the work of Galton (1914) in England and Fernald (1912) in the United States.

The work by Binet and his colleagues took a different course, one that was more pragmatic and beneficial. He and his colleagues attempted to understand the nature and development of intelligence and to differentiate children who could and could not benefit from schooling. Their quest to develop objective measures of intelligence first used anthropomorphic measures, including palmistry and handwriting. Finding little value in these methods, Binet sought the advice of educators, fellow members of the Societe Libre pour L'etude Psychologique de L'enfant who recommended they focus on cognitive development (e.g., judgment, reasoning, and comprehension).

Binet's views as to the importance of adaptive skills often are overshadowed by this monumental work in developing the first practical intelligence tests in 1905 and 1911. He thought intelligence to be a quality needed in order to competently engage in important daily life activities (Binet & Simon, 1905). In his *Development of Intelligence of Children*, Binet wrote that "An individual is normal if he is able to conduct his affairs of life without having need of the supervision of others, if he is able to do work sufficiently remunerative to support his own personal needs, and finally if his intelligence does not unfit him for the social environment of his parents" (p. 88). Parallels between Binet's views as to the importance of adaptive behavior and those expressed 18 centuries earlier by the Greeks are obvious. Moreover, we continue to use similar standards in the assessment of adaptive skills in the 21st century.

As noted above, private and public supported institutions began to be established to care for those with mental retardation. In 1879, superintendents and other leaders in these institutions within the United States formed the Association of Medical Officers of American Institutions for the Idiotic and Feebleminded. Its name was changed to the American Association for the Study of the Feebleminded in 1906, to the American Association on Mental Deficiency in 1933, and later to the American Association on Mental Retardation (AAMR). The American Association on Mental Retardation changed its name to American Association on Intellectual and Developmental Disabilities in 2007. The former name generally is used throughout this chapter.

Many members of the earliest association were leaders in the eugenics movement (Hallar, 1963) and ascribed to the notion of morbid heredity (e.g., protoplasmic defects in the germ plasma in the family stock caused mental retardation). Association members commonly wrote about the social and economic burden imposed on society by those with mental retardation, including those who became orphans, prostitutes, drunkards, and criminals.

Some social policy planners became disturbed by the vision of a permanent and large class of persons with mental retardation. The thought that waves of new immigrants from southern Europe, countries identified through studies of ethnic differences in intelligence (Brigham, 1923), would bring thousands of additional persons with mental retardation into the United States also was very alarming. Some added fuel to the fire by suggesting that, "one feeble-minded person left at large five generations ago is responsible for seventy-five feeble-minded persons living at the present time" (Sessions, 1917). These fears lead to strong racial, ethnic, and social class biases, given the belief that most persons with mental retardation were members of minority groups or, due to their diminished mental abilities, were economically impoverished.

Thus, efforts to restrict the interaction of people with mental retardation with society, to promote sterilization, and prohibit marriage were thought to be in the public interest. Fernald (1912), superintendent of the Massachusetts School for the Feebleminded and then President of the Medical Officers Association, recommended the creation of a national census of all persons with mental retardation.

1920s: CHALLENGES TO EUGENICS AND EFFORTS TO IMPROVE METHODS USED WITH PERSONS WITH MENTAL RETARDATION

During the 1920s new voices began to be heard that challenged the more narrow views of those who favored eugenics. These new voices generally were not from psychologists or those working with persons with mental retardation and instead were from parents of children and adults with mental retardation and their legislative advocates. Their expressions generally focused on three related issues: the eugenics movement, with its emphasis on heritability, was not scientifically based; the care and education of those with mental retardation was substandard; and the diagnosis of those with mental retardation, if established only on one score from an intelligence test, was flawed (see Porteus [1941] and Hollingsworth [1920] for more details).

Intelligence test data acquired on more than one million men inducted in the army during World War I suggested that, if the then current definition of feeble-minded were used, 30% of white men and 79% of non-white men would be classified as feeble-minded. Upon the release of this information, the public was appalled by these interpretations because they were inconsistent with other evidence (Porteus, 1922; Davies, 1923). For example, virtually all recruits had lived normally in their communities and surely did not deserve a diagnosis as being feeble-minded.

The Stanford-Binet and other measures of intelligence generally were used to diagnose mental retardation. Adults with mental age scores below 12 commonly were thought to have mental retardation. People increasingly began to question the accuracy of this standard to diagnose mental retardation, the narrowness of basing decisions on a single IQ, and the prognostic accuracy of this information.

The results from a study of 1537 adults who had been first diagnosed at being feeble-minded, then institutionalized, and later released against the recommendation of the institutions added to this debate. Some adults did not function well outside the institution while others became self-supporting, married, and became integrated in their communities (Fernald, 1920). These findings and those from other studies underscored the importance of education, challenged the accuracy of diagnosis as a reliable predictor of a person's ability to adapt to his or her environment, and suggested a need to consider a person's adaptation to his or her environment when diagnosing mental retardation.

DEFINITIONS OF MENTAL RETARDATION AND THE INCREASING IMPORTANCE OF ADAPTIVE BEHAVIOR AND SKILLS

The AAMR has had a long history of leadership in defining adaptive behavior. This leadership is consistent with AAMR's efforts to underscore the importance of adaptive behavior to the diagnosis, treatment, and care of person with mental retardation. Nine definitions of mental retardation and its various definitions of adaptive behavior and skills are reviewed below.

The AAMR's first two definitions of mental retardation emphasized the incurability of cognitive deficiencies associated with mental retardation. Its third definition (Doll, 1937, 1953) emphasized the incurability of the condition's social incompetence.

The British had taken the lead earlier in establishing a broader definition of mental deficiency when, in 1929, the Mental Deficiency Committee of England (1923) adopted a social definition of mental retardation. Those who were unable to adapt socially to one's environment and required external care, supervision, and control were thought to have mental retardation. Again, the similarities between this view and those held by the Greeks centuries earlier are remarkable. Furthermore, evidence of a person's adaptive behavior was thought to be more important than scores from an intelligence test.

World War II and its aftermath in the United States and Western Europe drew the public's attention away from many domestic social issues. Interest in issues important to the diagnosis and care of persons with mental retardation resurfaced in the 1950s, resulting in federal, state, and private funds being used to investigate these issues. Efforts spearheaded by President John F. Kennedy to prevent mental retardation and to better address the needs of those with mental retardation reflected national interests in these issues.

The AAMR's Committee on Nomenclature assumed the challenge of examining ways to better describe and classify persons with mental retardation. Its fifth definition[1], in 1959, defined mental retardation as subaverage general intellectual functioning that originates during the developmental period and is associated with impairment in one or more of the following: (1) maturation, (2) learning, (3) social adjustment (Heber, 1959). AAMR offered its first approved definition of adaptive behavior (Heber, 1959) as "... the effectiveness with which the individual copes with the natural and social demands of the environment. It has two major facets: (a) the degree to which the individual is able to function and maintain himself or herself independently, and (b) the degree to which he or she meets satisfactorily the culturally imposed demands of personal and social responsibility" (AAMR, 2002, p. 21).

The AAMR's sixth definition of mental retardation makes specific reference to adaptive behavior: "mental retardation refers to subaverage general intellectual functioning which originates during the developmental period and is associated with impairment in adaptive behavior" (Heber, 1959). Adaptive behavior was defined as the "effectiveness of the individual to adapt to the natural and social demands of his or her environment as reflected in maturation, learning, and social adjustment" (AAMR, 2002, p. 21). Heber acknowledged that, although no suitable measure of adaptive behaviors existed, the Vineland Social Maturity Scale may be of some value.

AAMR's seventh definition of mental retardation, in 1973, continued its emphasis on assessing adaptive behaviors when diagnosing mental retardation. It extended Heber's 1961 definition of adaptive behavior by adding that adaptive

[1] Information on AAMR's fourth definition could not be located.

behavior "... may be reflected in the following areas: (a) early years: sensorimotor skills, communication, self-help, socialization; (b) childhood and early adolescence: application of basic academics in daily life, application of reasoning and judgment; (c) later adolescence and adult life: vocational and social responsibilities and performances" (AAMR, 2002, p. 21).

AAMR's eighth definition of mental retardation, in 1983, continued its emphasis on assessing adaptive behaviors and offered new views as to qualities associated with adaptive behavior: "Significant limitations in an individual's effectiveness in meeting the standards of maturation, learning, personal independence, or social responsibility that are expected for his or her age level and cultural group" (AAMR, 2002, p. 22).

AAMR's ninth definition of mental retardation, in 1992, underscored the importance to adaptive skills, not merely adaptive behavior. "Mental retardation refers to substantial limitations in present functioning. It is characterized by significantly subaverage intellectual functioning, existing concurrently with related limitations in two or more of the following applicable adaptive skill areas: communication, self-care, home living, social skills, community use, self-direction, health and safety, functional academics, leisure, and work. Mental retardation manifests before age 18" (AAMR, 1992, p. 5). The AAMR identified four levels of support (i.e., intermittent, limited, extensive, or pervasive) that may be needed by persons with mental retardation.

This 1992 AAMR definition also continued a tradition of redefining adaptive behavior. It focused on adaptive skills by defining them as "... an array of competencies that reflect both the ability to fit into a given niche as well as the ability to change one's behavior to suit the demands of the situation. Ten adaptive skills were specified with the requirement that an individual evidence sufficiently comprehensive limitations, interpreted as being limitations in 2 or more skills areas applicable to his or her age" (AAMR, 2002, p. 22). See Table 1.1 for a description of 10 adaptive skill areas.

Thus, adaptive behavior is characterized as a broad construct that is composed of a number of specific, important skills. This 1992 AAMR definition diminished an emphasis of the broader construct of adaptive behavior and focused attention on the ten adaptive skill areas. An emphasis on adaptive skills, not merely adaptive behavior, is important when confirming a person has functional limitations that may warrant a diagnosis of mental retardation. Furthermore, the identification of functional skill limitations can be linked to needed interventions and other services. Efforts to improve specific adaptive skills are likely to be more effective than efforts to improve general adaptive behavior.

The AAMR's tenth definition of mental retardation, in 2002, states: "Mental retardation is a disability characterized by significant limitations both in intellectual functioning and in adaptive behavior as expressed in conceptual, social, and practical adaptive skills. This disability originates before age 18" (AAMR, 2002, p. 1).

The 2002 AAMR definition of adaptive behavior and skills is the most extensive. "Adaptive behavior is the collection of conceptual, social, and practical skills

TABLE 1.1 American Association on Mental Retardation's Ten Adaptive Skills and Three Adaptive Behavior Domains

Adaptive Skills	
Communication	Speech, language, and listening skills needed for communication with other people, including vocabulary, responding to questions, and conversation skills
Community Use	Skills needed for functioning in the community, including use of community resources, shopping skills, and getting around in the community
Functional Academics	Basic reading, writing, mathematics, and other academic skills needed for daily, independent functioning, including telling time, measurement, as well as writing notes and letters
Home Living	Skills needed for basic care of a home or living setting, including cleaning, straightening, property maintenance and repairs, as well as food preparation and performing chores
Health and Safety	Skills needed for protection of health and to respond to illness and injury, including following safety rules, using medicines, and showing caution
Leisure	Skills needed for engaging in and planning leisure and recreational activities, including playing with others, engaging in recreation at home, and following rules in games
Self-Care	Skills needed for personal care including eating, dressing, bathing, toileting, grooming, and hygiene
Self-Direction	Skills needed for independence, responsibility, and self-control, including starting and completing tasks, keeping a schedule, following time limits, following directions, and making choices
Social	Skills needed to interact socially and get along with other people, including having friends, showing and recognizing emotions, assisting others, and using manners
Work	Skills needed for successful functioning and holding a part-time or full-time job in a work setting, including completing work tasks, working with supervisors, and following a work schedule
*Motor Skills	Basic fine and gross motor skills needed for locomotion, manipulation of the environment and the development of more complex activities such as sports, including sitting, pulling up to a standing position, walking, fine motor control, and kicking
Three Adaptive Behavior Domains and Associated Adaptive Skill Areas	
Conceptual	Includes Communication, Functional Academics, Self-Direction, and Health and Safety skills
Practical	Includes Social Skills and Leisure skills
Social	Includes Self-care, Home/School Living, Community Use, Health and Safety, and Work skills

*Although fine and gross motor development is not included as one of the ten skills identified by the American Association on Mental Retardation, it is included in some scales of adaptive behavior.

that have been learned by people in order to function in their everyday lives. Limitations in adaptive behavior affect both daily life and the ability to respond to life changes and environmental demands, and should be considered in light of four other dimensions: Intellectual Abilities; Participation, Interaction, and Social Roles; Heath; and Context. Significant limitations in adaptive behavior can be established only through the use of standardized measures normed on the general population including people with disabilities and people without disabilities, and are defined as performance that is at least two SDs [standard deviations] below the M [mean] of (a) one of the following three types of adaptive behavior: conceptual, social, or practical, or (b) an overall score on a standardized measure of conceptual, social, and practical skills" (AAMR, 2002, p. 23).

Conceptual skills include receptive and expressive language, reading and writing, and self-direction. Social skills include responsibility, obeying rules and laws, naiveté, and competence in interpersonal interactions. Practical skills include personal and instrumental self-care activities such as toileting, taking medication, dressing, preparing meals, eating, using the telephone, managing money, and using transportation, as well as occupational skills and maintaining a safe environment (AAMR, 2002).

The 2002 AAMR definition makes some assumptions pertinent to adaptive skills. Adaptive skills must be considered in light of the environments in which a person functions, Thus, skill limitations must be evaluated in light of community opportunities and standards typical of the person's age and culture. This includes consideration of cultural and linguistic diversity together with a person's communication, sensory, motor, and behavioral characteristics. Persons typically display a pattern of both strengths and limitations. A focus on limitations directs attention to needed and appropriate personalized support that, over time, will improve the life functioning of persons with mental retardation.

THE DEVELOPMENT OF TESTS TO ASSESS ADAPTIVE BEHAVIOR

Test development and use began during the early part of the 20th century. Tests typically are developed to meet clinical needs. Until about 30 years ago, professionals generally relied on data only from measures of intelligence when assessing mental retardation. The use of measures of adaptive behavior became more prominent after the 1970s as the importance of adaptive behavior received more recognition. The evolution of their development is outlined below.

Porteus, an early proponent of intelligence tests, later recognized the need to construct parallel tests that assess social behaviors and to better diagnose mental retardation (Porteus, 1922). His early efforts focused on fifty anti-social qualities. He also developed a scale that assessed a person's knowledge of local information (e.g., name of the mayor, size of the community). Porteus' work was important in underscoring the need for tests that asses more practical and applied behaviors that are important to a person's daily functioning.

In 1926, Porteus left his post as director of research at the Vineland Training School and was replaced by Edgar Doll, a young professional with eugenic beliefs who also was interested in the social effects of mental retardation. Doll's efforts lead to the publication of the Vineland Social Maturity Scale (Doll, 1937, 1953). The scale was designed to assess a person's ability to care for himself or herself and others and, with age, to display increasing social competence and independence. Skills included self-help, locomotion, occupation, communication, self-direction, and social relationships. Unlike the commonly used Stanford-Binet to measure intelligence by assessing a child directly, the Vineland Social Maturity Scale relied on reports from others who knew the child well (e.g., parents and other care givers).

The use of the Vineland Social Maturity Scale was limited. Its critics identified various flaws, including the following three. The test assumed persons able to display a particular skill *will* display the skill (Starr, 1938). A person's ability to display skills measured by this test require him or her to be raised in an environment that nurtures the skills (Porteus, 1941). The scale measured social behaviors more accurately at the lower end than at the upper end.

The first criticism warrants the need to distinguish skills that have not been acquired (i.e., displays a *skill* deficit) from those that have been acquired and are not used (i.e., displays a *performance* deficit), and those that have been acquired and are used somewhat often or almost always. Furthermore, the second criticism underscores the importance of understanding the development of a person's adaptive behavior in light of environmental demands and opportunities. In reference to the third criticism, current measures of adaptive behavior also can be criticized for not being sufficiently sensitive when assessing the skills of those who display the highest level of skill development.

A team of researchers from Parsons Kansas, lead by Leland, developed one of the first viable scales of adaptive behavior primarily for use by institutions when assessing persons with mental retardation. One form assessed the adaptive behavior of persons 12 and under and another for persons older than 12. In its original form, the scale carried the title Scale of Adaptive Behavior. Its revised title is the AAMR Adaptive Behavior Scale (Lambert et al., 1993; Nihira et al., 1993).

National and state concerns about the over-identification of children, especially African American children, diagnosed as having mental retardation lead to increased emphasis on adaptive behavior. Mercer's (1974) proclamation that most children labeled in the category of mental retardation show signs of academic delay at school yet function well in their communities led to the use of the term "six hour retarded child" to describe this group.

Mercer also was critical of the process used to diagnose mental retardation, given her belief that mental retardation is an achieved status, not one that is ascribed. That is, a person has mental retardation when his or her inability to function well in society is apparent. A classification of mental retardation should not be based on scores from intelligence tests. Her views highlighted the importance of understanding the social systems in which a person functions and the roles he or she plays in them. Again, similarities between her beliefs and those of the ancient Greeks are apparent. Mercer's Adaptive Behavior Inventory for Children was developed to be sensitive to differences among children and youth and to be used in schools (Mercer, 1972).

Other scales of adaptive behavior also became available during the latter half of the 20th century and early 21st century: AAMR Adaptive Behavior Scale, Second Edition (Lambert et al., 1993; Nihira et al., 1993); ABAS-II (Harrison & Oakland, 2003), Scales of Independent Behavior-Revised (Bruininks et al., 1996); and Vineland Adaptive Behavior Scales-Second Edition (Sparrow et al., 2005).

MODELS AND CONCEPTS OF ADAPTIVE BEHAVIOR AND SKILLS

We enter the 21st century with the benefit of history that emphasizes the following principles. Adaptive behavior is important to everyone. Limitations in adaptive behavior may indicate underlying deficits. Adaptive behavior may be important in the assessment of mental retardation. Adaptive behavior must be evaluated within the contexts of the environments in which persons were raised and now live. Adaptive behavior may be improved through education.

AGE AND DEMOGRAPHIC DIFFERENCES ON ADAPTIVE BEHAVIOR SCALES

As noted earlier in this chapter, adaptive behavior assessment is viewed as an important method of assessing development of individuals across all age and cultural groups. The AAMR (2002) emphasized the importance of adaptive behavior assessment within a developmental and sociocultural context because expectations may differ based on the age of an individual and within different settings and contexts. Most widely used assessments of adaptive behavior were designed to reflect the acquisition, expansion, and growth of adaptive skills across childhood and adolescence, with most adaptive skills well developed by early adulthood for typical adults. Norm-referenced scores on adaptive behavior scales typically emphasize a person's performance in relation to age-based peers.

Items of most adaptive behavior scales were selected to include basic skills that would be expected to be developed by individuals from various cultural groups. Research related to cultural, race, and ethnic group differences on adaptive behavior scales is of increasing importance, given concerns about disproportionate placement of minority students in special education programs, especially in the category of mental retardation (Donovan & Cross, 2002). Reschly et al. (2002) concluded that "There seems to be little evidence that adaptive behavior assessment is as prone to cultural, racial, and ethnic bias as other areas of psychological testing" (p. 157). Research summarized below suggests that age is highly related to adaptive behavior, as would be expected, and that gender, race/

ethnicity, and socioeconomic status generally make small contributions, although statistically significant in some cases, to the variance in adaptive behavior scores.

AGE

Scores on adaptive behavior scales generally increase with age, as is true for other measures of developmental constructs (e.g., Harrison & Oakland, 2003; Sparrow et al., 2005). However, because some adaptive skill areas have different developmental progressions (e.g., development of basic motor adaptive skills tends to occur before middle childhood), specific adaptive skill areas on adaptive behavior instruments may be characterized by floor and ceiling effects or variations in item sampling and density at different age levels (Reschly et al., 2002).

Craig and Tasse (1999) described differing cultural expectations for age-based adaptive skills of children. For example, parents in some sociocultural contexts may not expect developmental milestones to occur at later ages or may be more permissive than other parents. Some parents may respond more immediately to children's needs and have different expectations for their children's independent functioning.

GENDER

Research investigating gender differences on adaptive behavior scales typically has shown that, although gender differences may exist, these differences explain only small amounts of variance in scores on adaptive behavior scales. For example, Keller (1986, 1988) found that gender was related to parent and teacher ratings of children's scores on the Adaptive Behavior Inventory for Children and Mercer's Teacher Questionnaire. Lambert (1986) and Huberty (1987) also found that gender contributed to scores on the school version of the Adaptive Behavior Scale, yet did not explain meaningful amounts of variance. However, Sparrow et al. (2005) reported similar scores for males and females on the Survey Form of the Vineland Adaptive Behavior Scales (2nd edition).

Boney (2002) analyzed the standardization data for the school age Parent Form and Teacher Forms of the ABAS. Although girls scored significantly higher than boys on the General Adaptive Composite (GAC), the effect sizes for gender were only .6% and 2.7% for the ABAS Parent Form and ABAS Teacher Form, respectively. Similarly, Boney also found significant gender differences for the adaptive skill areas, again with small effect sizes.

RACE/ETHNICITY AND SOCIOECONOMIC STATUS

Research investigating race/ethnic and socioeconomic group differences on adaptive behavior scales has shown some group differences and small effect sizes. Keller (1986, 1988) found that ethnicity was related to parent and teacher ratings of children's adaptive behavior as measured by the Adaptive Behavior Inventory for Children and Mercer's Teacher Questionnaire. Lambert (1986) and Huberty (1987) also found ethnic differences on the school version of the Adaptive Behavior Scale yet did not explain meaningful amounts of variance. However, Sparrow et al. (2005) reported similar scores by ethnicity on the Survey Form of the Vineland Adaptive Behavior Scales (2nd edition) after controlling for parental education level (a measure of socioeconomic status) and age.

Using the standardization data for the school age Parent and Teacher forms of the ABAS in a comprehensive analysis, Boney (2002) analyzed both interactions and main effects for ethnicity and parental education level. On the ABAS Parent Form, the interaction between the two demographic variables was not significant while the main effects for both ethnicity and parental education level were significant. White children scored higher than Hispanic children on the GAC. Other ethnic group differences were not significant. Ethnicity had a small effect size of 2.1%. Differences were found in children's GAC scores from parents with less than high school or a high school diploma compared to parents with some college; however, parent education had a small effect size, .8%. Multivariate analyses of the specific adaptive skill areas also showed no significant interactions, yet the main effects for ethnicity and parental education were significant. Effect sizes were small.

On the ABAS Teacher Form's GAC, the interaction between the two demographic variables as well as the main effect for ethnicity were not significant. The main effect for parental education was significant. The Teacher Form GAC for children whose parents reported a high school diploma was higher than for children whose parents reported less than a high school diploma; children of parents that report some college received higher scores than both other groups on the ABAS Teacher Form. However, the effect size was small (i.e., 3.2%). Multivariate analyses of the specific adaptive skill areas also showed that interactions were not significant, yet main effects were, with small effect sizes for ethnicity and parental education.

APPLICATIONS OF ADAPTIVE BEHAVIOR INFORMATION

The ABAS-II provides comprehensive assessment information to assist professionals in making diagnoses and classifications, identifying a person's strengths and limitations, planning, and monitoring intervention programs, and in their research and evaluation activities. The information from the ABAS-II can assist professionals in better understanding persons from all ages, from infants through the elderly. The various forms of the ABAS-II may be used alone or in combination. Acquiring information from two or more independent sources often provides a clearer and more accurate understanding of one's adaptive behavior and skills. The ABAS-II is used in various programs and settings, including schools, other public and private agencies, clinical settings that provide psychological and social services, medical and other health facilities, residential facilities and group homes, community programs and agencies, vocational and occupational training programs, and prisons.

As noted previously, measures of adaptive behavior typically have been used when providing services for persons with mental retardation. The ABAS-II often is used in this way. In addition, information from the ABAS-II can assist professionals when working with persons who display Alzheimer's type and other forms of dementia, Asperser's or an autistic disorder, attention deficit/hyperactivity disorder, developmental delays, depressive and mood disorders, emotional/behavioral disorders, language disorders, learning disabilities and disorders, physical impairments, sleep disorders, substance abuse, or Tourette's disorder as well as those who are hearing or visually impaired.

Diagnosis and classification: Disability and special education policy and regulations set forth by local, state, federal, and international agencies often require the use of a measure of adaptive behavior. Professional and legal issues associated with the use of adaptive behavior are reviewed in some detail in the following chapter and thus are not reviewed here. The ABAS-II commonly is used to assist professionals in diagnosing and classifying disorders. Research and clinical experiences with the ABAS-II underscore its value when working with children who display Asperser's or an autistic disorder, attention deficit/hyperactivity disorder, emotional/behavioral disorders, language disorders, learning disabilities and disorders, physical impairments, sleep disorders, or Tourette's disorder as well as those who are hearing or visually impaired. Research and clinical experiences with the ABAS-II also underscore its value when working with older adolescents and adults, including the elderly diagnosed with Alzheimer's type and other forms of dementia, depressive and mood disorders, or substance abuse. Additionally, ABAS-II data may be useful when working with adults who continue to display disorders commonly diagnosed first during childhood or adolescence (see above for examples).

Identify strengths and limitations: Most if not all persons display differences in their cognitive and adaptive skills. When the scores are examined normatively (i.e., compared to others their age), the pattern may show some to be high, most to be average, and others may be low. When the scores are examined ipsatively (i.e., compared to a person's own mean), some will be higher, some average, and others lower.

Knowledge of a person's strengths and limitations is important to diagnosis and program planning. Diagnoses often require clinicians to document the presence of limitations in a person's General Adaptive Composite (GAC), one of the three adaptive domains, or in two or more skills. Program planning typically can be assisted when information from the three adaptive domains and nine or ten adaptive skill areas is considered.

Knowledge of a person's strengths often is important in program planning. Clinicians use this information to identify qualities that are supporting more normal development, given their desire to utilize similar strategies to help promote limitations. In addition, the utilization of strengths in one or more adaptive skill areas may help propel development in needed skills.

The ABAS-II provides a profile of scores that include three domain composites and ten adaptive skill areas: Conceptual (including adaptive skill areas of Communication, Functional Academics, and Self-Direction), Social (including adaptive skill areas of Leisure and Social Skills), and Practical (including adaptive skill areas of in Community Use, Home or School Living, Health and Safety, Self-Care, and Work). A motor adaptive skill area is included for children under age 6. Thus, clinicians may examine strengths and limitations in reference to the three adaptive domain composites and the ten adaptive skills, in addition to an overall GAC.

Identify service needs: The identification of functional adaptive skill limitations can be linked to a person's needs for interventions and other services. Although a score profile may suggest many limitations, not all skill limitations are equally important to address. Some are more important than others. For example, limitations in health and safety are likely to deserve priority over limitations in leisure activities.

In addition, clinicians increasingly are reviewing a person's profile of adaptive skill strengths and limitations in light of environmental requirements. For example, among young children, limitations in self-direction and functional academics may be less important than those associated with in feeding and toileting. Among children with autism, limitations in community use and school living may be less important than those associated with communication and social skills. Among the elderly living with family members, limitations in use of community resources and work may be less important than those associated with self-care and communication.

Educators, occupational and physical therapists, psychologists, social workers, and other service providers increasingly are identifying service needs in light of the functional implications of a person's strengths and limitations. When identifying service needs, score profiles from the ABAS-II should be evaluated in light of the functional impact the skills have in sustaining or reducing needed behaviors.

Program planning and monitoring: A goal of program planning and monitoring is to increase one's ability to independently display functional skills important to one's environment. Attainment of this goal is increased by conducting a comprehensive assessment that includes a thorough analysis of a person's adaptive behaviors, conducting an analysis of critical environments (e.g., those in one's home, school, and workplace) to identify skills that are most needed to function effectively in them, evaluating skill strengths and limitations in light of these critical needs, and finally identifying skill limitations that most need to be improved in order to function more effectively at home, school, and work.

Research in the behavioral sciences underscores the importance of focusing on small and well-defined behaviors needed to function effectively in one's home, school, work, or other environment when developing needed intervention. A person's adaptive skills are likely to improve following interventions that are suitably tailored, personalized, and sustained over a period of time; focus on important skill limitations that need to be improved in order to function in one or more environments; and when the environments utilize and reward the display of the newly acquired skills.

The ABAS-II enables clinicians to focus on twenty or more behaviors reflected in the various items for each of the 10 adaptive skill areas. Thus, information from the ABAS-II enables a clinician to focus on small and well-defined behaviors needed to function effectively in one's home, school, work. The ABAS-II Intervention Planner and Scoring Assistant (2008) assists clinicians in this process by suggesting item-level interventions, tracks a child's progress overtime, and helps identify skills that require additional attention.

However, these item data are likely to constitute a starting point. Intervention efforts also should consider critical companion skills that may warrant intervention efforts. As noted above, an analysis of a person's environment may identify skills that are most needed to function effectively.

Programs, once implemented, need to be monitored to determine their effectiveness. One should not assume the initial program will result in achieving desired goals. Various methods exist to advance important adaptive skills. Readers are encouraged to see the various chapters in this book to gain further understanding of various ways to promote their development.

Research and evaluation: The ABAS-II has a number of excellent features that favor its use in research. It assesses various and important adaptive skills in persons ages 0–98. It is easy to administer (e.g., does not require an interview) and score. Its five separate forms (e.g., two for parents: 0–5 and 5–21; two for child care workers and teachers: 2–5 and 5–21; and one for adults: 16–89) enable the collection of information from multiple informants. Its norms are current. Its psychometric features are very strong.

EXTERNAL REVIEWS OF THE ABAS-II

The ABAS-II has had two reviews in the authoritative Mental Measurement Yearbook. Both reviews were very positive. For example, Burns' (2005) review concluded with the following remarks.

> The ABAS-II was developed from sound theory and empirical methodology, and provides a norm group that is sufficiently representative and large. Scores from the GAC [General Adaptive Composite] are adequately reliable to make eligibility and entitlement decisions, and domain scores are stable enough for clinical and intervention utility. Skill area scores should be interpreted cautiously. Data to support the tool's reliability and validity are impressive and the authors should be commended for employing the usefulness of the data for intervention planning and progress monitoring. Although the assessment of adaptive behavior should not be limited to norm-referenced testing, the ABAS-II provides data that could strengthen most comprehensive assessments of adaptive behavior and/or mental retardation in general. Further, many commercially prepared norm-referenced measures already exist, and at first glance the ABAS-II does not significantly differ from the usual approach. However, the ABAS-II appears technically superior to most of its competitors and it is recommended for use with few reservations.

REFERENCES

ABAS-II Interventional Planner and Scoring Assistant (2008). San Antonio, TX: Harcourt Assessment.

American Association on Mental Retardation (AAMR) (1992). *Definitions, Classifications, and Systems of Supports*, 9th edn., Washington, DC: AAMR.

American Association on Mental Retardation (AAMR) (2002). *Mental retardation: Definition, Classification, and Systems of Support*, 10th edn., Washington, DC: AAMR.

Barr, A. (1905). Heredity: Its influence for good and evil. *Alienism and Neurology*, *26*, 509–918.

Binet, A. & Simon, T. (1912). *A Method of Measuring the Development on Intelligence of Young Children*. Lincoln, IL: Courier.

Boney, T. L. (2002). *Race, Gender, and Parental Education Differences in Children's Scores on the Adaptive Behavior Assessment System*. Unpublished doctoral dissertation, The University of Alabama, Tuscaloosa, AL.

Bruininks, R., Woodcock, R., Weatherman, R., & Hill, B. (1996). *Scales of Independent Behavior – Revised*. Chicago, IL: Riverside Publishing.

Brigham, P. (1923). *A Study of American Intelligence*. Princeton, NY: Princeton University Press.

Burns, M. K. (2005). Review of the Adaptive Behavior Assessment System. In R. Spies, & B. Plake (Eds.), *The Sixteenth Mental Measurements Yearbook*, 2nd edn., Lincoln, NE: Buros Institute of Mental Measurements.

Craig, E. M. & Tasse, M. J. (1999). Cultural and demographic group comparisons of adaptive behavior. In R. L. Schalock, (Ed.), *Adaptive Behavior and its Measurement*, pp. 119–139. Washington, DC: American Association on Mental Retardation.

Davies, S. (1923). *Social Control of the Feebleminded*. Washington, DC: National Committee for Mental Health.

Doll, E. (1937). The inheritance of social competence. *Journal of Heredity*, *28*, 37–53.

Doll, E. (1953). *The Measurement of Social Competence*. New York: Educational Test Bureau.

Donovan, M. S., & Cross, C. T. (Eds.) (2002). *Minority Students in Special and Gifted Education*. Washington, DC: National Academy Press. This text explores many topics related to special education and minority children. The assessment chapter includes a discussion of conceptual and practical issues in adaptive behavior assessment.

Fernald, W. (1912). *Burdon of Feeblemindedness*. Massachusettes Medical Society Publication, 23, 1–14.

Fernald, W. (1920). After-care study of patients discharged from Waverly over the period of twenty-five years. *Mental Hygiene, 4*, 695–704.

Galton, F. (1914). *Heredity Genius*, 2nd edn., London: Macmillan.

Goodenough, H. (1949). *Mental Testing: Its History, Principles, and Applications*. New York: Rinehart.

Harrison, P. & Oakland, T. (2003a). *Adaptive Behavior Assessment System*, 2nd edn., San Antonio, TX: Harcourt Assessment.

Harrison, P. & Oakland, T. (2003b). *Technical Report: Adaptive Behavior Assessment System*, 2nd edn., San Antonio, TX: The Psychological Corporation.

Hollingsworth, L. (1920). *The Psychology of Subnormal Children*. New York: Macmillan.

Heber, R. (1959). A decade of research in the behavioral sciences. *Proceedings of Two Conferences on Research Opportunities in Mental Retardation*. Langhorne, PA: Wood School and Residential Treatment Center.

Huberty, Thomas J. (1987). Factor analysis of the WISC-R and the Adaptive Behavior Scale – School Edition for a referral sample. *Journal of School Psychology*, *25*, 405–410.

Keller, H. R. (1986). In-school adaptive behavior: Assessment domains of behavior rating scales and child characteristics. *Journal of Psychoeducational Assessment*, *4*, 1–12.

Keller, H. R. (1988). Children's adaptive behaviors: Measure and source generalizability. *Journal of Psychoeducational Assessment*, *6*, 371–389.

Lambert, N. M. (1986). Evidence on age and ethnic status bias in factor scores and the comparison score for the AAMD Adaptive Behavior Scale-School Edition. *Journal of School Psychology*, *24*, 143–153.

Lambert, N., Nihira, K., & Leland, H. (1993). *AAMR Adaptive Behavior Scale-School*, 2nd edn., Austin, TX: PRO-ED.

Locke, J. (1689). Essays concerning human understanding, In M. Rader's (1969) *The Enduring Question*. New York: Rinehart & Winston.

Matthews Media, LLC. (2005). Section 504 & the ADA articles & resources. Retrieved September 10, 2006, from http://www.reedmartin.com/section504articlesandresources.htm.

Mental Deficiency Committee of England (1923). Report of the Mental Deficiency Commission of England. In S. Davies (Ed.), *Social Control of the Feebleminded.* Washington, DC: National Committee for Mental Hygiene.

Mercer, J. (1972). *Adaptive Behavior Inventory for Children. The Psychological Corporation: San Antonio, TX.*

Nihira, K., Leland, H., & Lambert, N. (1993). *AAMR Adaptive Behavior Scale-Residential and Community*, 2nd edn., Austin, TX: PRO-ED.

Ninety-fourth Congress of the United States (1975). Public laws 91-696, 93-650, 93-651 and the laws and concurrent resolutions enacted during the first session of the 94th congress of the United States of America 1975 and proclamations. *United States Statutes at Large*, *89*(48). Washington, DC: U.S. Government Printing Office.

Porteus, S. (1922). *Studies in Mental Deviation.* Vineland, NJ: Vineland Training School.

Porteus, S. (1941). *Practice of Clinical Psychology.* New York: American Book Co.

Reschly, D. J., Myers, T. G., & Hartel, C. R. (Eds.) (2002). *Disability Determination for Mental Retardation.* Washington, DC: National Academy Press.

Rust, J. O. & Wallace, M. A. (2004). Test review: Adaptive Behavior Assessment System – Second Edition. *Journal of Psychoeducational Assessment*, *22*, 367–373.

Salvia, J. & Ysseldyke, J. (2001). *Assessment.* Boston, MA: Houghton Mifflin.

Sattler, J. (1998). *Clinical and Forensic Interviewing of Children and Families: Guidelines for the Mental Health, Education, Pediatric, and Child Maltreatment Fields.* San Diego, CA: Author.

Sessions, M. (1917). Feeblemindedness in Ohio. *Journal of Heredity*, *8*, 291–298.

Sparrow, S., Cicchetti, D., & Balla, D. (2005). *Vineland Adaptive Behavior Scales*, 2nd edn., Circle Pines, MN: AGS Publishing.

Starr, A. (1938). Discussion of the Vineland Social Maturity Scale. *Mental Measurement Yearbook* Rutgers. NJ: Rutgers University.

2

Professional and Legal Issues in Adaptive Behavior Assessment

Thomas Oakland[*] and Patti L. Harrison[**]

[*]University of Florida, Gainesville, FL 32611-7047, U.S.A.
[**]University of Alabama, Tuscaloosa, AL 35487-0231, U.S.A.

The use of measures of adaptive behavior is guided by four sets of standards: (a) those governing test development and use, (b) those informing diagnoses and classifications of individuals, (c) those guiding ethical behaviors of professionals, and (d) those established by laws and related legal policies and practices, including case law. This chapter reviews some of the more important standards that pertain to the use of adaptive behavior assessments.

Professional Standards Governing Test Development and Use

STANDARDS GOVERNING TEST DEVELOPMENT AND USE

The development and use of standardized tests may represent psychology's most important technical contribution to the behavioral sciences. Tests are used within the behavioral sciences with persons of all ages to describe current behaviors and other personal qualities, estimate future behaviors, assist guidance and counseling services, plan and monitor interventions, evaluate progress, screen for special needs, diagnose disabling disorders, help place persons, and assist in determining whether persons should be credentialed, admitted/employed, retained, or promoted. Tests also are used widely in research and for various administrative, planning, and forensic purposes.

STANDARDS FOR EDUCATIONAL AND PSYCHOLOGICAL TESTING

The *Standards for Educational and Psychological Testing* (American Educational Research Association, American Psychological Association and the National Council on Measurement in Education, 1999; hereafter referred to as the *Standards*) constitutes the most authoritative industry standard for ways tests should be developed and used. The issues discussed in this 194-page book address test construction, evaluation, and documentation; fairness in testing, and test applications. Assessment specialists can be expected to know and adhere to these *Standards* when performing their work. The *Standards* also can guide the formation of public policy governing assessment services.

Definition of a test: A test is "an evaluation devise or procedure in which a sample of an examinee's behaviors in a specified domain is obtained and subsequently evaluated and scored using standardized procedures" (American Educational Research Association et al., 1999, p. 183). Tests may be administered to groups or individually. Group tests are less costly to use, typically acquire information about group characteristics or are used to screen an individual's qualities, and generally have a low stakes impact. Individually administered tests such as the Adaptive Behavior Assessment System-II (Harrison & Oakland, 2003) typically are used to make high stakes personal decisions as well as to help control conditions that otherwise may impact test performance adversely.

Standardized tests: Most tests used in clinical practice are standardized. Standardized tests require test users to administer and score them in a uniform fashion. Most standardized tests also are normed on a sample of persons representative of those for whom the test is designed to be used. For example, tests designed to be used with children and youth typically are normed on a representative sample of children and youth stratified by age, gender, the region of the country in which they reside, and their parent's education. Children and youth who display various diagnoses (e.g., mental retardation, learning disabilities, attention-deficits) generally are sampled relative to their incidence in the population. In addition, members of these and other clinical groups are likely to be sampled in even larger numbers when a test is designed for use with them. Their larger numbers facilitate clinical studies with members of clinical groups

Assessment: The *Standards* defines assessment as a comprehensive examination undertaken to answer specific questions about a client's functioning during a particular time interval or to predict a client's functioning in the future (American Educational Research Association et al., 1999, p. 119).

Thus, assessment practices typically are guided by referral questions. Some referrals ask test specialists to address narrow and low stakes issues (e.g., vocational interests) while others request broader and high stakes issues. Low stakes issues are those that are unlikely to have a material impact on one's life. In contrast, high stakes issues are those that are likely to have a high impact on one's life. Assessment practices that lead to diagnoses clearly occur in high stakes arenas.

Thus, assessment practices that lead to high stakes decisions require utmost care and attention to professional standards. When engaged in high stakes testing, the *Standards* emphasizes the importance of acquiring information from multiple sources (e.g., the person being evaluated, family members, teachers, supervisors) through the use of multiple assessment methods (e.g., interviews, observations, tests) that allow professionals to assess various personal qualities (e.g., adaptive behavior, intelligence, personality) in ways that lead to a description of behaviors as they occur in various settings (e.g., home, work, school) over some period of time (e.g., during the past 5 years). High stakes decisions never should be based only on data from one test.

Test validity: Validity – the accuracy with which a test measures a construct – is a test's most important quality. Validity is judged in light of evidence that supports the manner in which test data are interpreted and used. Strictly speaking, a test does not have validity. Thus, the question, "How valid is the test?" needs to be reframed into "To what degree do research and/or theory support the ways the data are being interpreted and used?" Test validation requires the test user to develop a scientifically sound argument that supports the intended interpretation of test scores and their relevance to the proposed uses.

Two broad qualities that may jeopardize test validity: Issues associated with validity figure prominently when developing a standardized test. Efforts are made to help insure a test measures a desired construct adequately and that qualities irrelevant to the construct do not attenuate its measurement. Thus, efforts that avoid *construct under-representation* (i.e., when a test fails to measure important aspects of the construct) and *construct irrelevance* (i.e., when qualities extraneous to the construct attenuate its measurement) are critical when developing tests (American Educational Research Association et al., 1999).

In reference to the assessment of adaptive behavior, clinicians should determine whether the test they use is consistent with current theory and research that help define the construct (e.g., adaptive behavior) being assessed. The American Association of Mental Retardation (AAMR[1]) has been an authoritative source for defining adaptive behavior (AAMR, 2002). Thus, when selecting a measure of adaptive behavior, clinicians should insure the measure they use assesses adaptive behavior consistent with the manner in which the AAMR or other authoritative sources defines it.

Clinicians also should review proposed tests to determine whether they have sufficient depth so as to adequately measure the construct (i.e., the test they use

[1] The American Association on Mental Retardation changed its name to American Association on Intellectual and Developmental Disabilities in 2007. The former name generally is used throughout this chapter.

should not under-represent the construct of adaptive behavior). In general, tests with more items are better than those with fewer items because they generally provide a more complete assessment of adaptive behavior. Additionally, the selected measure should assess only adaptive behavior, not extraneous qualities. For example, some tests of adaptive behavior assess behavior pathology, qualities that clearly fall outside the scope of current definitions of adaptive behavior.

Test reliability: Reliability refers to the consistency of scores. The *Standards* defines reliability as "the degree to which test scores for a group of test takers are consistent over repeated applications of a measurement procedure and hence are inferred to be dependable, and repeatable for an individual test taker; the degree to which scores are free of errors of measurement for a given group" (American Educational Research Association et al., 1999, p. 180). Reliability typically is estimated by examining the degree to which test items correlate with their total score (i.e., reflect a test's internal consistency) or the degree the rank order of scores is consistent over two or more test administrations (i.e., a test's stability). Tests that have higher reliability measure a construct with less error than do tests with lower reliability. Estimates of internal consistency close to or above .90 generally are considered to be sufficiently error-free to use when making important decisions about an individual.

DIAGNOSTIC STANDARDS

Professionals can be expected to know and conform their practices to professionally established protocols for services, including diagnoses. The public can expect consistency within and between professions in the ways in which behaviors are classified. For example, professionals in psychiatry, psychology, education, and social work can be expected to use a somewhat uniform standard when diagnosing mental retardation, attention-deficit/hyperactivity, Asperger's, and other disorders.

Diagnostic and Statistical Manual of Mental Disorders, Text Revision: Health care providers, including psychologists, as well as social workers, educators, and others engaged in assessment typically rely on the *Diagnostic and Statistical Manual of Mental Disorders, Text Revision* (DSM; American Psychiatric Association, 2000) when making diagnoses. The DSM is the most authoritative source for use in clinical practice within the United States. The *International Statistical Classification of Diseases and Related Health Problems, Tenth Edition* (ICD-10; World Health Organization, 1992), a companion to and virtually identical to the DSM content, has been one of the most authoritative sources for use in clinical diagnostic practice outside of the U.S.

STATE BOARD OF EDUCATION STANDARDS FOR DIAGNOSING SCHOOL-BASED DISORDERS

Professionals working in public schools typically rely on rules and policies established by state education agencies when diagnosing disorders. These rules and policy generally reflect prevailing federal laws, including the Individual with

Disabilities Education Improvement Act (United States Department of Education, 2006; United States Code Service, 2007). Although the DSM is known and may be considered by school-based professionals, diagnostic criteria approved by its state board of education constitute a protocol to be used in public schools.

APPLICATIONS OF ADAPTIVE BEHAVIOR TO THE ABOVE DIAGNOSTIC STANDARDS

Measures of adaptive behavior are used most routinely in the diagnosis of mental retardation. Virtually all diagnostic manuals define mental retardation as a condition that has its onset before age 18 and includes significantly subaverage intellectual functioning with concurrent deficits in adaptive functioning.

Additionally, measures of adaptive behavior may be used to better understand the impact of other disorders on a person's daily life activities. For example, children diagnosed with other disorders usually first diagnosed in infancy, childhood or adolescence also are likely to display impairments in their functional daily living skills. These include those diagnosed as displaying disorders associated with attention, autism, communication, conduct, elimination, feeding and eating, learning, motor skills, and pervasive developmental disorders. Adults diagnosed as displaying a disorder associated with anxiety, acute stress adjustment, bipolar, depression, mood, psychosis, Parkinson's, postpartum, substance abuse, schizophrenia, sleep, and other disorders – to name a few – also are likely to display impairments in their functional daily living skills. Older adults diagnosed as displaying Alzheimer's, dementia, and other disorders whose onsets typically occur later in life will display impairments in their functional daily living skills. Thus, although adaptive behaviors may not be important to the diagnosis of these disorders, those with these disorders are likely to display deficits in adaptive behaviors that warrant professional attention during assessment and planning of interventions.

Research reported by Harrison and Oakland (2003) indicates persons with autism, attention-deficit/hyperactive disorder, developmental delays, emotional and behavioral disorders, hearing and motor impairments, language disorders, learning disabilities, neuropsychological disorders, and pervasive developmental disorders also displayed deficits in adaptive behaviors and skills. Although data about adaptive behavior of these persons may not have been critical to the diagnosis of these and other disorders, these data are likely to be critical to efforts to describe and promote their daily lives, especially the degree to which they can function independently in important live activities. Information on an individual's ability to perform functional life skills independently is likely to have a greater practical and beneficial impact of their lives than knowledge of their diagnosis.

The World Health Organization's International Classification of Functioning, Disability, and Health: The International Classification of Functioning, Disability, and Health (ICF) is emerging as an important international standard for classifying human functioning and disability (World Health Organization, 2001). The ICF model replaces its predecessor, the International Classification of Impairments, Disabilities, and Handicaps – a medically based model designed to assist in identifying disorders (World Health Organization, 1980). The ICF is not an assessment system. Instead it is designed to enable health care providers to classify health and disability and to identify how facilitators and barriers in the environment interact with and influence health and functioning, including a person's ability to participate in desired personal and social activities. Thus, the ICF model emphasizes the importance of a person's adaptive behaviors. Within the ICF model, disability is defined as a broad term for impairments, activity limitations, and participation restrictions. Behaviors are viewed as an interaction between personal and environmental qualities.

The ICF's emphasis on a person's participation in meaningful daily activities underscores the importance of adaptive behavior within this model. For example, the ABAS-II is designed to evaluate whether an individual displays various important functional skills needed for a person's daily living – including his or her participation in meaningful daily activities. Its focus on the degree to which an individual displays needed independence in the display of these skills allows professionals to classify health and disability and to identify how facilitators and barriers in the environment interact with and influence the person's health and functioning, including the person's ability to participate in desired personal and social activities.

TEST ETHICS

The American Psychological Association's (2002) *Ethical Principles and Code of Conduct* also addresses test use. Issues addressed include the bases for assessments, use of assessments, informed consent, release of test data, test construction, interpreting assessment results, assessment by unqualified persons, use of obsolete tests and outdated test results, test scoring and interpretation services, explaining assessment results, and maintaining test security. Readers are encouraged to consult Appendix A, for more detailed information on text ethics.

LEGAL ISSUES THAT IMPACT ADAPTIVE BEHAVIOR ASSESSMENT

FEDERAL LEGISLATION AND RELATED POLICIES AND PRACTICES

Legislation, legal policy, and regulations set forth by local, state, and federal agencies often require the use of test data, including adaptive behavior. In addition, although adaptive behavior assessment may not be mandated, its use may be critical to the desired impact of the legislation. Three important federal legislative efforts are reviewed below.

INDIVIDUALS WITH DISABILITIES EDUCATION IMPROVEMENT ACT

The 2004 Individuals with Disabilities Education Improvement Act (IDEIA; One-hundred eighth Congress of the United States, 2004) generally is consistent with prior legislation (i.e., Individuals with Disabilities Education Acts) that addressed the needs of infants and toddlers and older students with disabilities. IDEIA offers assistance to states to provide services to infants and toddlers with disabilities under Part C and to children and youth with disabilities under Part B.

Part C addresses the needs of infants and toddlers under age 3 who are at risk of experiencing a substantial developmental delay if early intervention services were not provided to them. Early intervention services are designed to meet the developmental needs of an infant or toddler who displays a disability in physical, cognitive, communication, social/emotional, and/or adaptive development. The ABAS-II can be used as a comprehensive measure of adaptive behavior through the use of two forms: the Parent/Primary Caregiver Form for age: 0–5 and the Teacher/Daycare Provider Form for age: 2–5. School districts or other community agencies are responsible for providing services designed to meet the developmental needs of an infant or toddler qualifying for services at no cost to the parents. An Individualized Family Service Plan is developed for each infant or toddler that designates one or more of the following services: family training, counseling, and home visits; special instruction; speech-language pathology and audiology services; occupational therapy; physical therapy; psychological services; service coordination services; medical services for diagnostic or evaluation purposes; early identification, screening, and assessment services; health services necessary to enable the infant or toddler to benefit from the other early intervention services; social work services; vision services; assistive technology devices and services; and/or transportation services.

Part B establishes the right to a free public education in the least restrictive environment to eligible students ages 3 through 21 who, due to their disability, need special education and related services. Thus, eligible students must display a need for these services, including an academic deficiency, and demonstrate one or more of the following 13 disorders: autism, blind/deaf, deaf/hearing impairment, developmental delay, mental retardation, multiple disabilities, orthopedic impairments, other health impairments, serious emotional disturbance, specific learning disabilities, speech or language impairments, traumatic brain injury, and/or visual impairments. Students are ineligible for special education services if their disability results from a lack of instruction in reading or math or their limited English proficiency. After qualifying for services, an education program must be proposed, guided by an individual education plan (IEP) that is agreeable to members of the IEP team, including educators and parents, responsible for making assessment, diagnostic, placement, and programming decisions.

Although IDEIA requires use of a measure of adaptive behavior only for the diagnosis of mental retardation, many if not all students who demonstrate one or more of the other 12 disorders are likely to display deficits in adaptive behavior and skills. ABAS-II data can be especially helpful in identifying strengths and weaknesses in students' daily living skills, including those that need to be addressed through interventions. Assessment data should have utility when developing interventions intended to promote a student's functional skills and abilities, including his or her ability to independently assume responsibility for his daily life skills. ABAS-II data can assist in this process.

Assessment practices: According to IDEIA, assessment practices must reflect the following characteristics. A variety of assessment tools and strategies to gather relevant functional, developmental, and academic information including information provided by parents, are to be used. The results of any single measure or assessment should not be used as the sole criterion for determine a disability or for educational programming. Technically sound instruments that may assess relative contributions of cognitive, behavioral, physical, and developmental qualities shall be used. The assessments and other evaluation materials are to be selected and administered so as not to be racially or culturally discriminatory; are provided and administered in the language and form most likely to yield accurate information on what the child knows and can do academically, developmentally, and functionally (unless it is not feasible to so provide or administer); are used for purposes for which the assessments or measures are valid and reliable; are administered by trained and knowledgeable personnel; and are administered in accord with any instructions provided by the test publisher. The child is to be assessed in all areas of suspected disability. The assessment tools are to provide relevant functional information that directly assists persons in determining the educational needs of the child.

IDEIA places added emphasis on the importance of acquiring functional information – that is, information that can be used to establish interventions that are reasonably calculated to have a practical impact on important life skills. The emphasis on acquiring information important to functional intervention planning and evaluation may warrant the use of measures of adaptive behavior. The qualities they assess, including those assessed by the ABAS-II, are likely to have practical applications, leading to improvements in daily life functions.

Due process provisions: For years, school districts provided services consistent with privileges associated with the concept of *en loco parentus* that held that schools retained ultimate authority for decisions pertaining to a student's education while at school. Thus, parents had limited authority for governing their children's education. Current practice has displaced this concept with one in which parents and educators are viewed as holding joint responsibility for children's education.

Parents who object to services provided to their children under IDEIA retain various due process rights, including the right to object to assessment, diagnostic, placement, and programming decisions. If the dispute between parents and educators cannot be resolved amicably among them, disputed issues may be resolved through mediation or a due process hearing. During a due process hearing, parents retain the following rights: to have legal council and to present evidence, to examine all documents, to receive written notices of all meetings and proposed changes in one's written language, and to appeal the decision of the hearing officer.

MEDICAID

Medicaid is a federally initiated program, funded by both federal and state sources, that provides health insurance to children, low-income families, the elderly, and the disabled (U.S. Public Law 89.97, 1965; U.S.A. gov., 2007). The program serves more than 50 million people, slightly more than 50% of whom are children and another 16% who are elderly.

Medicaid is by far the nation's largest public provider of children's health insurance. Covered services include those that are medically necessary, including physician and hospital visits, health screening, vision and dental services, and well-child care. The use of measures of adaptive behavior, especially those designed for a broad age range, including infants and young children, can assist health care providers in assessing normal development and deficits.

SUPPLEMENTAL SECURITY DISABILITY AND SUPPLEMENTAL SECURITY INCOME

The federally supported Supplemental Security Disability and Supplemental Security Income program provides financial assistance to persons who meet eligibility criteria due to a disability (Social Security Administration, 2006). These criteria include an inability to perform one's previous work or to adjust to new work due to one's medical, physical, or mental condition. For example, a person who displays severe functional limitations for at least 1 year, including impairments in one's ability to work and in the independent performance of their daily needs (e.g., health and safety, self-care, home living needs) may be eligible for financial support under this program.

Information provided by measures of adaptive behavior, including the ABAS-II, is critical to determining program eligibility. The documentation of skill or performance deficits in the ten skills assessed by the ABAS-II, together with other information, can assist persons applying for assistance, their attorneys, hearing officers, and government employees responsible for administering this program to determine eligibility.

ASSESSMENT OF PERSONS ON DEATH ROW: DO THEY DISPLAY MENTAL RETARDATION?

The United States is wresting with issues as to whether mental illness or mental retardation are mitigating factors that should be considered when persons are charged with a capital offense and later when sentenced. The U.S. Supreme Court in Atkins versus Virginia (U.S. Case No. 8452, 2002) ruled that persons with mental retardation should not be executed. This 2002 ruling has focused considerable attention on various issues, including whether state or federal standards are used to determine mental retardation, how to conduct a retrospective evaluation of mental retardation (in that almost all prisoners on death row are older than age 18 – the age before which mental retardation typically is determined), and the adversarial nature of the decisions (with state officials often wanting to find the prisoner not to have mental retardation and thus can proceed with his or her execution). The use of measures of adaptive behavior assessment figure prominently in the process of determining whether the prisoner displayed mental retardation prior to age 18 (and possibly currently). The importance of these issues warranted a special chapter in this book. Thus, see Olley and Cox's chapter for a more thorough discussion of these and other issues.

TO WHOM DO PROFESSIONALS RELEASE TEST DATA?

Clinicians often wrestle with questions as to whom and under what circumstances they can and must release test data, including data from measures of adaptive behavior. Unfortunately, authoritative sources that address the release of test data are not uniform in their opinions. Thus, answers to clinician's questions may not be consistent and thus unclear. Ethical and legal standards that address this issue are reviewed below.

ETHICAL STANDARDS GOVERNING RELEASE OF TEST DATA

The American Psychological Association (APA) (2002) *Ethical Principles of Psychologists and Code of Conduct* addresses this issue under Section 9.04 Release of Test Data. It first begins by defining *test data.*

> The term *test data* refers to raw and scaled scores, client/patient responses to test questions or stimuli, and psychologists' notes and recordings concerning client/patient statements and behavior during an examination. Those portions of test materials that include client/patient responses are included in the definition of *test data* (p. 1071).

Having defined test data, the APA ethical code then describes their release.

> Pursuant to a client/patient release, psychologists provide test data to the client/patient or other persons identified in the release (p. 1071).

This policy governing the release of test data differs somewhat from prior ethical standards that required psychologists to release test data only to others who are qualified to interpret them or under court order. However, as noted below, the clinician may decide to not release test data.

> Psychologists may refrain from releasing test data to protect a client/patient or others from substantial harm or misuse or misrepresentation of the data or the test, recognizing that in many instances release of confidential information under these circumstances is regulated by law. (b) In the absence of a client/patient release, psychologists provide test data only as required by law or court order (p. 1071–1072).

LEGAL STANDARDS GOVERNING RELEASE OF TEST DATA

Three federal sources also developed policy governing the release of test data: the Family Education Records Privacy Act (FERPA), Individuals with

Disabilities Education Act (IDEA) of 1997, and the Office of Special Education Programs (from 1979 until May 2005). These sources generally were consistent in stating that parents may request and receive access to all educational records that identify their child. The term *access* refers to the right to review the information, not to obtain copies of the records.

In May 2005, the Office of Special Education Program, in response to a request for information from Harcourt Assessment, issued a revised statement. This statement generally is consistent with FERPA and does not expand the scope of information available to parent examination beyond those records to which they have access under FERPA. Educational records were defined as those records related to a student and maintained by an educational agency or institution. Records that are not directly related to a student and maintained by an agency or institution are not "educational records" under FERPA, and parents do not have aright to inspect and review such records (e.g., a test protocol or question booklet which is separate from the sheet on which a student records answers and which is not personally identifiable to the student).

An educational agency or institution shall respond to reasonable requests for explanations and interpretations of educational records. If a school maintains a copy of a student's test answer sheet, a parent has the right to request an explanation and interpretation of this record. The explanation and interpretation by the school could entail showing the parent the test question booklet, reading the questions to the parent, or providing an interpretation for the responses in some other adequate manner that would inform the parent. FERPA was said to exempt the school from providing *raw data and notes* (i.e., they are not considered to be educational records). A clinician's notes are considered to be memory joggers maintained by the school official unbeknownst to others.

Public agencies are required to comply with the provisions of IDEA and FERPA and must ensure that state law and other contractual obligations do not interfere with compliance of IDEA and FERPA (i.e., the violation of copyright laws may be considered to be of secondary importance to the violation of IDEA and FERPA). Federal copyright law protects against the distribution of copies of the copyrighted documents, such as a test protocol. IDEA and FERPA generally do not require the distribution of copies of an educational record, only parental access to inspect and review. Thus, copyright law generally should not be implicated under these provisions.

Case law that addresses this issue: There is little case law that addresses issues pertaining to access of data. However, in Newport-Mesa Unified School District versus State of California Department of Education (43, IDELR 161 (C.D. Cal. 2005)), the California Department of Education alleged a school district was out of compliance with the California Education Code for failure to provide parents of special education students with requested copy of copyright achievement test protocols. Thus, the California Department of Education ordered the district to revise its policies and procedures on student record requests. The district refused, leading to the adjudication of this issue.

The U.S. District Court, Central District, State of California ruled that a statute requiring copies of test protocols to be provided to parents of special education students falls within acceptable fair use under federal copyright laws and that federal copyright law does not preempt state statute. The Court held that the school district can distribute copies of test protocols to parents of special education students without violating federal copyright laws, in accord with California Education Code Section 56504. Such distribution is fair use under copyright law because it is noncommercial – that is, a test protocol given to a parent had been purchased, used, and cannot be reused. The receipt of test data broadens parents' understanding of their child's education needs. The court found no evidence that the limited release of test protocols to parents of special education students, which has been the department's policy since 1983, resulted in any adverse market effect.

This decision, if implemented nationally, would have strong and possibly adverse impacts on test security. Thus, this decision is being appealed. In the meantime, this decision is directly applicable only to the Central District in California (the location in which the case was adjudicated).

CONCLUSION

The present chapter described a number of professional standards, standards for diagnosis and classification, ethical principles, and legal issues that impact assessment practices of professionals. Implications of these for adaptive behavior assessment, including assessment with the ABAS-II, were summarized. Professionals that engage in adaptive behavior assessment are encouraged to apply these standards to their practices.

REFERENCES

American Association of Mental Retardation (2002). *Mental Retardation: Definition, Classification, and Systems of Support.* Washington DC: Author.

American Educational Research Association, American Psychological Association, & National Council for Measurement in Education (1999). *Standards for Educational and Psychological Testing.* Washington DC: American Psychological Association.

American Psychiatric Association (2000). *Diagnostic and Statistical Manual of Mental Disorders: Text Revision.* Washington DC: Author.

American Psychological Association (2002). Ethical principles of psychologists and code of conduct. *American Psychologist, 57,* 1060–1073.

Harrison, P. & Oakland, T. (2003). *Adaptive Behavior Assessment System-II.* Harcourt Assessment: San Antonio, TX.

Olley, J. G. & Cox, A. W. (in press). Assessment of adaptive behavior in adult forensic cases: The use of the adaptive Behavior Assessment System-II. In T. Oakland, & P. Harrison (Eds.), *Adaptive Behavior Assessment System-II: Clinical Use and Interpretations.* New York: Elsevier.

Social Security Administration (2006). SSA Publication Number 64-039 ICN 468600: Disability evaluation under Social Security. Retrieved 6/14/2007 from http://www.ssa.gov/disability/professionals/bluebook/.

United States Code Service (2007). *20 USCS § 1400: Individuals with Disabilities Education Act.* Retrieved 6/12/2007 from http://web.lexis-nexis.com/universe/document?_m=6af9d78cf01c007d8151e26c38f4192d&_docnum=1&wchp=dGLbVlz-zSkVb&_md5=412bb646231d76b75426f221f837233a.

United States Department of Education (2006). The Individuals with Disabilities Education Improvement Act of 2004. Retrieved 6/13/2007 from http://www.ed.gov/about/offices/list/osers/osep/index.html.

USA.gov. (2007). Social Security online: Disability programs. Retrieved 6/14/2007 from http://www.ssa.gov/disability/.

World Health Organization (1980). *ICIDH: International Classification of Impairments, Disabilities, and Handicaps. A Manual of Classification Relating to the Consequences of Disease.* Geneva:

Word Health Organization (1992). *International Statistical Classification of Diseases and Related Health Problems, Tenth Revision (ICD-10).* Geneva, Switzerland: World Health Organization.

World Health Organization (2001). *ICF: International Classification of Functioning, Disability, and Health.* Geneva: Word Health Organization.

APPENDIX A

The following section is from the American Psychological Association's (2002) *Ethical Principles of Psychologists and Code of Conduct.* Copyright © 2002 by the American Psychological Association. Reprinted with permission. The official citation that should be used in referencing this material is American Psychological Association (2002). Ethical principles of psychologists and code of conduct. *American Psychologist, 57,* 1060–1073.

9. ASSESSMENT

9.01 BASES FOR ASSESSMENTS

(a) Psychologists base the opinions contained in their recommendations, reports, and diagnostic or evaluative statements, including forensic testimony, on information and techniques sufficient to substantiate their findings. (See also Standard 2.04, Bases for Scientific and Professional Judgments.)

(b) Except as noted in 9.01c, psychologists provide opinions of the psychological characteristics of individuals only after they have conducted an examination of the individuals adequate to support their statements or conclusions. When, despite reasonable efforts, such an examination is not practical, psychologists document the efforts they made and the result of those efforts, clarify the probable impact of their limited information on the reliability and validity of their opinions, and appropriately limit the nature and extent of their conclusions or recommendations. (See also Standards 2.01, Boundaries of Competence, and 9.06, Interpreting Assessment Results.)

(c) When psychologists conduct a record review or provide consultation or supervision and an individual examination is not warranted or necessary for the opinion, psychologists explain this and the sources of information on which they based their conclusions and recommendations.

9.02 USE OF ASSESSMENTS

(a) Psychologists administer, adapt, score, interpret, or use assessment techniques, interviews, tests, or instruments in a manner and for purposes that are appropriate in light of the research on or evidence of the usefulness and proper application of the techniques.
(b) Psychologists use assessment instruments whose validity and reliability have been established for use with members of the population tested. When such validity or reliability has not been established, psychologists describe the strengths and limitations of test results and interpretation.
(c) Psychologists use assessment methods that are appropriate to an individual's language preference and competence, unless the use of an alternative language is relevant to the assessment issues.

9.03 INFORMED CONSENT IN ASSESSMENTS

(a) Psychologists obtain informed consent for assessments, evaluations, or diagnostic services, as described in Standard 3.10, Informed Consent, except when (1) testing is mandated by law or governmental regulations; (2) informed consent is implied because testing is conducted as a routine educational, institutional, or organizational activity (e.g., when participants voluntarily agree to assessment when applying for a job); or (3) one purpose of the testing is to evaluate decisional capacity. Informed consent includes an explanation of the nature and purpose of the assessment, fees, involvement of third parties, and limits of confidentiality and sufficient opportunity for the client/patient to ask questions and receive answers.
(b) Psychologists inform persons with questionable capacity to consent or for whom testing is mandated by law or governmental regulations about the nature and purpose of the proposed assessment services, using language that is reasonably understandable to the person being assessed.
(c) Psychologists using the services of an interpreter obtain informed consent from the client/patient to use that interpreter, ensure that confidentiality of test results and test security are maintained, and include in their recommendations, reports, and diagnostic or evaluative statements, including forensic testimony, discussion of any limitations on the data obtained. (See also Standards 2.05, Delegation of Work to Others; 4.01, Maintaining Confidentiality; 9.01, Bases for Assessments; 9.06, Interpreting Assessment Results; and 9.07, Assessment by Unqualified Persons.)

9.04 RELEASE OF TEST DATA

(a) The term *test data* refers to raw and scaled scores, client/patient responses to test questions or stimuli, and psychologists' notes and recordings concerning client/patient statements and behavior during an examination. Those portions of test materials that include client/patient responses are included in the definition of *test data*. Pursuant to a client/patient release, psychologists provide test data to the client/patient or other persons identified in the release. Psychologists may refrain from releasing test data to protect a client/patient or others from substantial harm or misuse or misrepresentation of the data or the test, recognizing that in many instances release of confidential information under these circumstances is regulated by law. (See also Standard 9.11, Maintaining Test Security.)

(b) In the absence of a client/patient release, psychologists provide test data only as required by law or court order.

9.05 TEST CONSTRUCTION

Psychologists who develop tests and other assessment techniques use appropriate psychometric procedures and current scientific or professional knowledge for test design, standardization, validation, reduction, or elimination of bias, and recommendations for use.

9.06 INTERPRETING ASSESSMENT RESULTS

When interpreting assessment results, including automated interpretations, psychologists take into account the purpose of the assessment as well as the various test factors, test-taking abilities, and other characteristics of the person being assessed, such as situational, personal, linguistic, and cultural differences, that might affect psychologists' judgments or reduce the accuracy of their interpretations. They indicate any significant limitations of their interpretations. (See also Standards 2.01b and c, Boundaries of Competence, and 3.01, Unfair Discrimination.)

9.07 ASSESSMENT BY UNQUALIFIED PERSONS

Psychologists do not promote the use of psychological assessment techniques by unqualified persons, except when such use is conducted for training purposes with appropriate supervision. (See also Standard 2.05, Delegation of Work to Others.)

9.08 OBSOLETE TESTS AND OUTDATED TEST RESULTS

(a) Psychologists do not base their assessment or intervention decisions or recommendations on data or test results that are outdated for the current purpose.

(b) Psychologists do not base such decisions or recommendations on tests and measures that are obsolete and not useful for the current purpose.

9.09 TEST SCORING AND INTERPRETATION SERVICES

(a) Psychologists who offer assessment or scoring services to other professionals accurately describe the purpose, norms, validity, reliability, and applications of the procedures and any special qualifications applicable to their use.

(b) Psychologists select scoring and interpretation services (including automated services) on the basis of evidence of the validity of the program and procedures as well as on other appropriate considerations. (See also Standard 2.01b and c, Boundaries of Competence.)

(c) Psychologists retain responsibility for the appropriate application, interpretation, and use of assessment instruments, whether they score and interpret such tests themselves or use automated or other services.

9.10 EXPLAINING ASSESSMENT RESULTS

Regardless of whether the scoring and interpretation are done by psychologists, by employees or assistants, or by automated or other outside services, psychologists take reasonable steps to ensure that explanations of results are given to the individual or designated representative unless the nature of the relationship precludes provision of an explanation of results (such as in some organizational consulting, pre-employment or security screenings, and forensic evaluations), and this fact has been clearly explained to the person being assessed in advance.

9.11 MAINTAINING TEST SECURITY

The term *test materials* refers to manuals, instruments, protocols, and test questions or stimuli and does not include *test data* as defined in Standard 9.04, Release of Test Data. Psychologists make reasonable efforts to maintain the integrity and security of test materials and other assessment techniques consistent with law and contractual obligations, and in a manner that permits adherence to this Ethics Code.

3

ABAS-II ASSESSMENT METHODS

PATTI L. HARRISON[*] AND THOMAS OAKLAND[**]

[*]*University of Alabama, Tuscaloosa, AL 35487-0231, U.S.A.*
[**]*University of Florida, Gainesville, FL 32611-7047, U.S.A.*

The Adaptive Behavior Assessment System-Second Edition (ABAS-II) is a comprehensive norm-referenced rating scale that measures adaptive behavior and skills displayed by individuals ages birth through 89 years. The five forms of the ABAS-II provide tools that can be used for a variety of assessment purposes, including for individuals experiencing difficulties with daily skills needed for effective functioning in their environments. The use of the ABAS-II, in conjunction with other assessment methods in a multi-dimensional and multi-method approach, assists professionals with diagnoses, identifying strengths and weaknesses, and planning and evaluating interventions. The purpose of this chapter is to provide a description of the ABAS-II, including its administration, scoring, and interpretation, and to summarize information found in the ABAS-II manual (Harrison & Oakland, 2003). The present chapter is intended to serve as a foundation for later chapters in this book.

OVERVIEW OF THE ABAS-II

ABAS-II FORMS

The five forms of the ABAS-II provide an opportunity for respondents to rate the adaptive behavior and skills of an individual targeted for an assessment.

Each item on the five rating forms describes a specific functional adaptive skill. Respondents provide a rating to indicate if an individual is able to perform the skill and, if so, the frequency with which the individual performs the skill when needed (i.e., always, sometimes, or never). Although information from one respondent may be used, the use of multiple respondents is recommended, when possible, leading to an assessment that acquires information from multiple sources that describe behavior displayed in multiple settings in which the individual displays adaptive skills. The use of multiple informants is especially useful when making high stakes decisions.

The five rating forms of the ABAS-II, the age range of individuals targeted for the assessment, possible respondents, and number of total items are summarized below:

- The *ABAS-II Parent/Primary Caregiver Form* is used for children whose ages range from birth through 5 years. Respondents include parents and other primary caregivers living with the child and who are familiar with the child's daily activities (e.g., grandparents and other adult relatives). The form includes 241 items. This form is also available in Spanish and French Canadian, in addition to English.
- The *ABAS-II Parent Form* is used for children ages 5 through 21 years or children in kindergarten through grade 12. Respondents include parents and other primary caregivers living with the child and familiar with the child's daily activities (e.g., grandparents and other adult relatives). The form includes 232 items. This form also is available in Spanish and French Canadian, in addition to English.
- The *ABAS-II Teacher/Daycare Provider Form* is used with children ages 2 through 5 years. Respondents include teachers, teacher aides, daycare providers, and others familiar with the child's daily activities in daycare, preschool, or school settings. The form includes 216 items.
- The *ABAS-II Teacher Form* is used for children ages 5 years through 21, or children in kindergarten through grade 12. Respondents include teachers, teacher aides, and others familiar with the child's daily activities in school settings. The form includes 193 items.
- The *ABAS-II Adult Form* is used for adults ages 16 through 89 years. Respondents include family members, supervisors, close friends, aides, caregivers, and others familiar with the adult's daily activities in home and community settings. The Adult Form also may be completed by the individual himself or herself in a self-rating provided the person's mental and emotional qualities permit a valid response to the items. The form includes 239 items.

ABAS-II CONTENT

Each of the five ABAS-II forms includes an assessment of 10 specific adaptive skill areas that are broadly categorized in three adaptive domain composites.

The adaptive skill areas and domains measured by the ABAS-II are based on the conceptual foundation of adaptive behavior defined by the American Association on Mental Retardation (AAMR; 1992, 2002). (*Note*: The AAMR has changed its name to the American Association on Intellectual and Developmental Disabilities or AAIDD). In addition, the ABAS-II provides a general score, the General Adaptive Composite (GAC) that summarizes performance across all adaptive skill areas. The 10 adaptive skill areas, three domains, and General Adaptive Composite are outlined below:

General Adaptive Composite: A general score that is a composite of all adaptive skill areas.

- Conceptual Domain
  - *Communication Adaptive Skill Area*: Items include speaking, listening, engaging in conversations, and responding.
  - *Functional Academics/Functional Pre-Academics Adaptive Skill Area*: Items include functional academic skills (Parent Form, Teacher Form, and Adult Form) or functional pre-academic skills (Parent/Primary Caregiver Form and Teacher/Daycare Provider Form) in reading, writing, math, and other areas needed for daily, independent functioning.
  - *Self-Direction Adaptive Skill Area*: Items include completing tasks, keeping schedules, meeting time limits, following instructions, and other activities related to responsibility and self-control.
- Social Domain
  - *Leisure Adaptive Skill Area*: Items include participation in play and recreation activities, following game rules, and planning leisure and other fun activities.
  - *Social Adaptive Skill Area*: Items include engaging in social interactions, getting along with others, making and maintaining friendships, and displaying manners and emotions.
- Practical Domain
  - *Community Use Adaptive Skill Area*: Items include using community resources, shopping, navigating the community, and other skills displayed in community settings.
  - *Home Living Adaptive Skill Area/School Living Adaptive Skill Area*: Items include skills in caring for the home environment (on the Parent/Primary Caregiver Form, Parent From, and Adult Form) or school setting (on the Teacher/Daycare Provide Form and Teacher Form), such as straightening, cleaning, repairing, and caring for possessions.
  - *Health and Safety Adaptive Skill Area*: Items include protecting one's health, responding to health and safety concerns, using medicines, and demonstration of caution.
  - *Self-Care Adaptive Skill Area*: Items include eating, dressing, bathing, hygiene, and other personal care activities.

- *Work Adaptive Skill Area*: This adaptive skill area is included only for the Parent Form (ages 5–21 years), Teacher Form (ages 5–21 years), and Adult Form (ages 16–89 years) and is completed for an individual if he or she has a part-time or full-time job. Items measure functional skills important to successful job performance, including completing tasks, following schedules, and following instructions.
- *Motor Adaptive Skill Area*: This adaptive skill area is included only for the Parent/Primary Caregiver Form (ages birth to 5 years) and Teacher/Daycare Provide Form (ages 2–5 years) and contains items related to fine and gross motor adaptive skills needed for movement, locomotion, manipulation of objects, and other motor functions of daily living. The motor adaptive skill area is included in the General Adaptive Composite and is not included in the Conceptual, Social, or Practical domains.

ABAS-II USES

The ABAS-II has a number of uses and applications in settings and agencies that provide services for children and adults, including daycare programs, public and private schools, colleges and universities, community agencies, assisted living facilities, rehabilitation agencies, and medical settings. Data from the ABAS-II are useful when working with individuals who display various disabilities, disorders, and injuries, including those with declining mental and physical health, and who may display limited daily living skills due to other acute or chronic problems. Subsequent chapters in this book discuss the use of the ABAS-II with those who display a range of disorders. Case studies illustrate many of its uses across a number of settings and for various purposes.

The ABAS-II is used as part of comprehensive assessment for determining diagnoses, classification, and eligibility for services. Disability and special education regulations typically require a comprehensive adaptive behavior assessment along with assessment of intelligence, achievement, and other personal qualities, when working with individuals who may display mental retardation (now identified as intellectual and developmental disabilities by AAIDD). However, the use of the ABAS-II is not limited to individuals with mental retardation or intellectual and developmental disabilities.

Standards established by federal and state law and policy as well as commonly used diagnostic criteria (e.g., Diagnostic and Statistical Manual of Mental Disorders) often require a comprehensive assessment of adaptive skills and other areas of functioning for various types of disabilities and problems as well as for program eligibility (e.g., federal funds for children with various disorders supported through the Social Security administration). For example, the ABAS-II may be included as part of the comprehensive assessment for the following types of disabilities and problems: Alzheimer's type dementia, attention deficits, autism spectrum disorders, behavior disorders, developmental delay, emotional disorders, learning disabilities, physical and sensory impairments and disorders, and neuropsychological disorders. Thus, the ABAS-II has wide application with children and adults who may have, or are suspected of having, many types of problems. The ABAS-II manual summarizes the results from a number of validity studies with various clinical groups. The remaining chapters in this text, especially those in Section III (ABAS-II and Assessment Across Age Ranges) and Section IV (ABAS-II and Assessment for Special Populations) include summaries of ABAS-II validity studies with various clinical groups, guidelines and case studies that describe diagnosis and classification, use of multiple sources of information about various areas of development and functioning of individuals, and the use of the ABAS-II in a comprehensive, multi-method assessment.

The ABAS-II assists in the identification of strengths and weaknesses in adaptive skills. The ABAS-II focuses on life skills that impact important daily functions needed by everyone to effectively take care of themselves and to interact with others. The ABAS-II provides a comprehensive assessment of adaptive skills and its results may be integrated with information from other assessment tools to determine if an individual displays required skills to meet demands in different environments (e.g., one's home, school, work, and community). The remaining chapters in this book include guidelines and case studies that describe the use of the ABAS-II for identifying strengths and weaknesses, including ways to integrate ABAS-II results with information from additional assessment tools.

The ABAS-II provides a foundation for planning intervention and treatment programs, including the identification of other needed services and supports. The comprehensive information provided by the ABAS-II and its identification of strengths and weaknesses in adaptive skills are helpful for planning programs to improve individuals' independent daily functioning. Professionals are provided a wealth of information to assist them in planning programs designed to increase specific adaptive skills and general daily functioning of individuals when ABAS-II results are examined in light of one's self-expectation or expectations others have for the display of daily living skills in different settings (e.g., home, residential facility, community agency, work, school). The remaining chapters in this text, especially those in Section II (ABAS-II and Adaptive Skill Areas), include a detailed examination of conceptual foundations and interventions for adaptive skill areas, guidelines, and case studies that illustrate interventions based on comprehensive assessment with the ABAS-II and other instruments.

Finally, the ABAS-II is an instrument useful for research and evaluation. The ABAS-II provides a comprehensive assessment of adaptive behavior and skills and encompasses a wide age range and thus is useful for research and program evaluation across the lifespan.

ABAS-II ADMINISTRATION, SCORING, AND INTERPRETATION

RESPONDENTS' COMPLETION OF THE ABAS-II FORMS

The ease of the administration and scoring of the ABAS-II is an important feature. An ABAS-II form should be completed in its entirety, and respondents are instructed to rate every item. Respondents may complete the various rating forms independently by personally reading the items and marking their ratings on the questionnaire booklet. Although the ABAS-II items require a sixth grade reading level or less, professionals may read the ABAS-II items to respondents who do not have the necessary skills for reading and rating the items independently. Professionals may also elect to read ABAS-II items to respondents who have the necessary reading skills if the respondents are anxious, lack self-confidence in their ability to complete the scale independently, or have a number of questions about the assessment or if the professional is using the ABAS-II as part of an overall interview about several aspects of the individual's adaptive skills.

Respondents for the ABAS-II must be selected carefully. Respondents should have sufficient opportunity to observe the daily adaptive skills of the individual being assessed as well as recent and frequent contacts of somewhat long duration with the individual. On occasion, respondents have detailed information about the display of important adaptive skills in some but not all skill areas. For example, a supervisor may have detailed information about a person's adaptive skills associated with work and self-direction, yet lacks information about the other eight adaptive skills. Their information should be obtained and amalgamated with that acquired from other respondents.

The value of the ABAS-II may be enhanced when information is obtained from multiple respondents who know the person well. The use of several respondents, instead of a single respondent, provides a more comprehensive and possibly valid assessment. Validity may be enhanced when information about a person's adaptive skills is obtained from multiple respondents, across multiple settings, and in response to demands of different environments. Multiple respondents provide important information about the degree of consistency an individual displays in his or her daily living skills in various settings as observed by different respondents. The use of multiple sources of information can improve decision-making about diagnoses, service needs, strengths and weaknesses, and interventions. Sample case studies found in the other chapters of this book illustrate the value of using multiple informants for the ABAS-II during a comprehensive assessment.

When using the ABAS-II, professionals strive to establish and maintain rapport and communication with respondents to yield a valid assessment. Professionals are encouraged to explain the purpose of the general assessment as well as reasons for administering the ABAS-II. Professionals should review the expectations for respondents and determine if the respondent understands the directions and has the knowledge and skills needed to complete the rating form. Professionals should describe the instructions for completing the rating form and verify that the respondent understands them. Finally, professionals should solicit and answer a respondent's questions before, during, and after administration and provide instruction that will promote the respondent's reliable and valid information.

Respondents rate each item on a scale from 0 to 4. A rating of 0 indicates that the person is not able and cannot perform the skill described by the item. If the individual being assessed can perform the skill, the respondent is instructed to select a rating of 1, 2, or 3 to indicate the frequency of the individual's performance – 1: never or almost never when needed; 2: sometimes when needed, or 3: always or almost always when needed. In addition, the respondent is asked to evaluate whether he or she has directly observed the individual in performance of the activity or if he or she is guessing; if the respondent's rating of 0, 1, 2, or 3 is a guess, the respondent is asked to check a column under the heading "Check If You Guessed" in the rating form booklet.

The ABAS-II uses a rating scale format. Although rating scales are common and useful assessment techniques, they have a number of limitations. For example, rating scales reflect the perspectives of respondents. These perspectives may differ depending on respondents' expectations, standards, and settings. The rating of each item reflects an overall summary, not an exact frequency, of an individual's behavior in reference to the behavior assessed by that item. In addition, the items on rating scales sample behaviors and cannot measure the display of every behavior by an individual in all situations. Thus, professionals who use rating scales should select respondents carefully, establish and maintain proper rapport and communication with them, work to solicit complete and valid responses, and use multiple respondents when needed. These characteristics apply to all rating scales.

ABAS-II SCORING

Following the completion of the ABAS-II by a respondent, professionals are instructed to check the items to insure all are answered. Confer with the respondent to complete all unanswered items. Professionals are also instructed to check the guessing factor. Professionals are instructed to count the total number of items checked in the "Check if you Guessed" box for each adaptive skill area. During the norming of the ABAS-II, few respondents guessed on more than three items for each skill area. Thus, the results from respondents who guess on four or more items in a skill area should be evaluated carefully before the ABAS-II is scored and results are used. Professionals are encouraged to discuss guessed items with the respondent to identify reasons for them. Items often can be assigned clear scores following this discussion. Professionals who decide to continue with scoring and use of the results despite having more than three guessed items should communicate this possible limitation in all reports, team meetings, and decision-making activities. If a professional determines that a respondent did not have sufficient knowledge about the individual, new respondents with more knowledge should be identified and asked to complete the ABAS-II.

Scoring the ABAS-II consists of a series of steps to determine norm-referenced scores for the nine or ten adaptive skill areas, the three domains (i.e., Conceptual, Social, and Practical) and the General Adaptive Composite. Six ABAS-II normative samples provide the basis for the norm-referenced scores. Norms tables are based on one normative sample for each of the following: Parent/Primary

Caregiver Form (ages 0–5 years), Parent Form (ages 5–21 years), Teacher/Daycare Provider Form (ages 2–5 years), and Teacher Form (ages 5–21). The Adult Form has two types of normative samples: Adult-Form-Ratings by Other and an Adult Form Self-Report. The age-based norm-referenced scores allow professionals to compare one individual with his or her age peers.

After rating all adaptive skill items, these ratings are then summed to obtain a raw score for each adaptive skill area. Adaptive skill area raw scores are converted to *scaled scores* with a mean of 10 and standard deviation of 3. Scaled score distributions for adaptive skill areas are skewed due to the natural ceiling that is reached as skills are acquired throughout the lifespan. Thus, scaled scores above 13 are somewhat rare.

The adaptive skill area scaled scores are summed to determine composite *standard scores* for the Conceptual, Social, and Practical domains as well as the General Adaptive Composite. These standard scores have a mean of 100 and standard deviation of 15. Unlike the adaptive skill area scaled scores, standard score distributions for the Conceptual, Social, and Practical domains and the General Adaptive Composite closely approximate a normal distribution. Interpretation of these composite standard scores is enhanced by knowledge of *confidence intervals* based on the standard error of measurement. Confidence intervals at the 90% and 95% confidence level are provided. Additional norm-referenced scores for the three domains and the General Adaptive Composite include age-based *percentile ranks* that indicate an individual's standing relative to others of the same age.

The adaptive skill areas scaled scores, the three domain composite standard scores, and the General Adaptive Composite standard score may also be interpreted using *descriptive classifications* of Very Superior, Superior, Above Average, Average, Below Average, Borderline, and Extremely Low. The descriptive classifications represent general characterizations of an individual's performance and are based on broad ranges of norm-referenced scores. The descriptive classifications for the three domains and General Adaptive Composite standard scores follow:

Standard Scores	*Percentile Ranges*	*Classifications*
130 or more	98 or more	Very Superior
120–129	91–97	Superior
110–119	75–90	Above Average
90–109	25–74	Average
80–89	9–24	Below Average
71–79	3–8	Borderline
70 or less	1–2	Extremely Low

Several optional and supplementary procedures may be used in *ipsative analyses* of the ten adaptive skill area scaled scores and the three domain composite standard scores. In contrast to a norm-referenced score (e.g., scaled score, standard score, percentile rank) that compares a person's score with those from same age peers in the normative sample, ipsative analyses enable professionals to determine the significance and frequency of score fluctuations *within* an individual's ABAS-II scores – that is, compared to one's mean performance, not compared to one's same age peers. *Scatter* between the adaptive skill areas, including the difference between the individual's highest and lowest scaled scores across all adaptive skill areas, or the differences between the individual's highest and lowest scaled scores for the adaptive skill areas within each of the Conceptual, Social, or Practical domains, may be calculated to determine if scatter is statistically significant (0.5 and 1.5 levels) and rare (derived from base rates from the normative samples reflecting scatter obtained by only 25%, 10%, 5%, 2%, or 1% of the sample).

Adaptive skill area strengths and weaknesses can be calculated by comparing each obtained skill area scaled score with the individual's mean of all scaled scores or with the individual's mean of the scaled scores within a domain. This information enables the professional to identify the degree to which an adaptive skill area scaled score is higher (a strength) or lower (a weakness) than the person's average scaled score. Adaptive skill area strengths and weaknesses represent statistically significant or rare differences from the person's average scaled score. Similarly, *comparisons between the composite standard scores* of the Conceptual, Social, and Practical domains determine if the pair-wise differences between composite scores are statistically significant and rare.

An optional norm-referenced score for the ABAS-II, the *test-age equivalent*, should be used with caution if at all. Test-age equivalents indicate the age in years and months at which an individual's raw score was the average raw score for that age. For example, on the Teacher Form, a raw score of 59 on the Communication Skill Area corresponds to a test-age equivalent of 10:8–10:11 (i.e., 10 years 8 months through 10 years 11 months). This means that a raw score of 59 was the average raw score of children in the normative sample ages who were 10:8 to 10:11. Although test-age equivalents are widely used, they have numerous limitations. Test-age equivalents may not be comparable across skill areas, do not have equal intervals of measurement, and provide no information about an individual's relative standing in comparison to others his or her same age. Due to the risk of misinterpretation and psychometric limitations of test-age equivalents, they should not be used or should be used cautiously with appropriate explanations of their limitations. These caveats apply to the use of test age equivalent scores on all tests.

ABAS-II INTERPRETATION AND APPLICATIONS

Professionals are instructed to verify the administration and scoring before interpreting and using the ABAS-II results. Respondents' questions should be answered. If guessing rates are higher than average, respondents should be interviewed about the guessed items and work to resolve them. If needed, information from other respondents more familiar with the person should be acquired. The accuracy of the ABAS-II data should be reviewed and evaluated, including calculating the summed scores, recording of scores, and determining scaled and standard scores. Many professionals who use the ABAS-II also use the ABAS-II Scoring Assistant or the more recent ABAS-II Intervention Planner and Scoring Assistant (2008) to help insure the accuracy of transforming raw scores to scaled scores.

Although multiple respondents generally are recommended, they may rate the individual differently and thus their ABAS-II scores will differ. The resolution of these differences is important in order to obtain accurate descriptions of a person's adaptive skills – a prerequisite to accurate decision-making. Professionals must be vigilant to differences between respondents and possible reasons for these differences. Finally, interpretation of ABAS-II results should take into account the information from additional sources (e.g., obtaining a history of the individual, examining existing documents, interviewing others) to help verify the data and to interpret this information within a person's environmental context. The case studies included in later chapters illustrate interpretations of the ABAS-II that includes analysis of conflicting data and use of information from additional sources.

Interpretation of ABAS-II scores generally begins with interpretation of the General Adaptive Composite. The General Adaptive Composite represents the most global estimate of an individual's adaptive functioning across all adaptive skill areas. The General Adaptive Composite standard score and percentile rank provide a quantitative description of relative standing of an individual's general adaptive behavior compared to one's age peers. The General Adaptive Composite generally provides the most comprehensive, reliable, and accurate measure of an individual's adaptive behavior. However, the General Adaptive Composite may be a less accurate summary of a person's general adaptive functioning if there are significant and/or rare differences between the Conceptual, Social, and Practical domain composite standard scores or wide scatter in adaptive skill area scaled scores.

After focusing on the General Adaptive Composite, interpretation typically shifts to the Conceptual, Social, and Practical domain standard scores and finally to the adaptive skill area scaled scores. Both provide a quantitative description of the relative standings of more specific components of an individual's adaptive behavior compared to his or her same age peers. The composite standard scores and adaptive skill area scaled scores enable the professional to determine any strengths or deficits (e.g., more than two standard deviations below the normative mean) compared to the scores of their same age peers. Scores reflecting deficits may be used to determine if an individual meets state or national criteria for diagnoses and eligibility for services.

For example, the AAMR manual (2002) provides an operational definition for limitations in adaptive behavior: "For the diagnosis of mental retardation, significant limitations in adaptive behavior should be established through the use of standardized measures normed on the general population, including people with disabilities and people without disabilities. On these standardized measures, significant limitations in adaptive behavior are operationally defined as performance that is at least two standard deviations below the mean of either (a) one of the following three types of adaptive behavior: conceptual, social, or practical, or (b) an overall score on a standardized measure of conceptual, social, and practical skills" (p. 76).

Information from additional assessment results, background information, and personal qualities of the individual being evaluated should guide an understanding of the individual's capabilities and should be compared to and integrated with the ABAS-II results. Data from a *single* assessment tool never should be used alone to develop diagnoses, determine services, or target interventions. Comprehensive evaluations are preferable, including the use of various assessment methods to acquire information on various traits and abilities from various sources so as to enable the professional to understand a person's multiple traits, including adaptive behavior and skills, displayed in various settings and over some period of time. These methods promote valid decision-making about an individual. Although comprehensive ABAS-II data provide information for valid decision-making about diagnoses or disorders and need for interventions, these results should be used in conjunction with information from other tests and sources about an individual's functioning.

Interpretations of ABAS-II results and those from other methods and sources should focus on intervention planning. Norm-referenced standard scores for the three domains, as well as scaled scores from the adaptive skill areas, that are higher or lower than same age peers can assist in targeting intervention for individuals with disabilities and other disorders. Ipsative comparisons of these domain standard scores and adaptive skill area scaled scores can also highlight strengths and weaknesses and can assist in prioritizing skill areas for interventions.

For example, norm-referenced adaptive skill area scaled scores may identify that a person has a large number of skill areas that are well below the mean derived from the national standardization sample – information that may be useful in planning interventions. In addition, an ipsative analysis that compares these scores with the person's own average scaled scores for adaptive skill areas may help identify the one, two, or more adaptive skill areas that represent significant and rare relative weaknesses and thus may constitute intervention priorities. Additional sources of information (e.g., from interviews, direct observations, record reviews, results from other assessment methods) should be integrated with ABAS-II results to provide additional support to prioritize needs for interventions.

Professionals using the ABAS-II for program planning and monitoring may include information from ratings on specific items and scores from adaptive skill areas, adaptive domains, and the General Adaptive Composite, as well as results from additional test instruments and assessment techniques to provide a basis for developing interventions and identifying benchmarks or goals for monitoring interventions. For example, each item of the ABAS-II identifies an essential daily living skill important for independent functioning that can represent a target area for intervention. Professionals may select items of the ABAS-II that are of primary importance and plan intervention activities relevant for the activity described by the item.

The ABAS-II manual suggests several steps for interventions. First, identify the skills needed in the individual's current environment or setting, or in an environment or setting to which an individual is transitioning. Second, determine the individual's adaptive skill strengths and weaknesses relevant to the needed skills. Third, prioritize objectives for the intervention by noting any discrepancy between environmental demands and the person's current skills. Fourth, plan interventions to achieve the objectives. Finally, implement and monitor interventions to determine whether desired skills are acquired and used.

The ABAS-II Intervention Planner and Scoring Assistant (2008) is available to assist professionals in their use of the ABAS-II. This report provides an interpretative written report that professionals can download and, if needed, modify when preparing their written reports and providing ABAS-II information in other forms. The report assists in interpreting ABAS-II results by providing information on the General Adaptive Composite as well as comparisons between it and the three domain composite standard scores. In addition, the report provides comparisons between the adaptive skill areas, thus identifying adaptive skill strengths and weaknesses. Importantly, the report facilitates interventions by enabling professionals to identify adaptive skills that require interventions and to receive suggestions for their promotion. Thus, this report assists professionals in linking assessment and intervention.

The remaining chapters of this present book provide extensive information about interpretation and use of the ABAS-II within a comprehensive assessment, including additional tests and other techniques for assessing adaptive skills as well as assessing skills in other areas (e.g., intelligence, achievement, social, and emotional behavior). These chapters also provide information about using results from multiple instruments and other techniques for assessing many areas of functioning as well as integrating information to assist in decision-making about diagnoses, strengths and weaknesses, and intervention needs. The ABAS-II generally should be administered in its entirety because an individual may have a number of strengths and weaknesses across adaptive skill areas that may suggest intervention needs in several specific areas. Reliance on two or more respondents may be needed to acquire information needed for a compete ABAS-II. The chapters in Section II (ABAS-II and Adaptive Skill Areas) examine adaptive skill areas included in a comprehensive assessment of adaptive behavior, summarize conceptual foundations, discuss methods to obtain information, and provide guidelines for interpretation and interventions based on comprehensive assessment using the ABAS-II and multiple methods and sources of information.

SUMMARY

This chapter summarizes the basic information about administering, scoring, and interpreting the ABAS-II. This information is intended to provide a foundation for information discussed in subsequent chapters and illustrates possible uses of the ABAS-II. Section II highlights adaptive skill areas included in a comprehensive ABAS-II assessment. Section III emphasizes the assessment and interventions of individuals in different age groups. Section IV addresses assessment and interventions for special populations.

REFERENCES

American Association on Mental Retardation (1992). *Mental Retardation: Definition, Classification, and Systems of Supports*, 9th edn., Washington, DC: AAMR.

American Association on Mental Retardation (2002). *Mental Retardation: Definition, Classification, and Systems of Support*. Washington, DC: AAMR.

Harrison, P. L. & Oakland, T. (2003). *Adaptive Behavior Assessment System Manual*, 2nd edn., San Antonio, TX: PsychCorp.

SECTION

II

ABAS-II and Adaptive Skill Areas

4

COMMUNICATION SKILLS

G. RICHMOND MANCIL* AND BETSY VINSON**

*Department of Child, Family and Community Sciences, University of Central Florida, Orlando, FL 32816, U.S.A.

**Department of Communication Processes and Disorders, University of Florida, Gainesville, FL 32611, U.S.A.

The Adaptive Behavior Assessment System-II (ABAS-II) is designed to provide a comprehensive assessment of adaptive functioning (Harrison & Oakland, 2000). The ABAS-II provides an assessment of the degree to which individuals, ages 0–89, independently display functional skills in everyday living. The ABAS-II assesses 10 adaptive skill areas, including communication. Because communication is a skill that influences the adaptive ability of an individual in every facet of life, the ABAS-II emphasizes the importance of this adaptive skill area.

The ability to communicate is necessary for almost every life function, from asking for basic needs to sharing thoughts and feelings. Communication is "the process participants use to exchange information and ideas, needs and desires" (Owens, 2001, p. 11). Without the ability to communicate, individuals are more likely to become frustrated, isolated, and engage in maladaptive behaviors, including screaming and hitting. These frustrations are not limited to the ability to speak and hear. Communication also includes such skills as looking at individuals who are talking, understanding facial cues such as frowns and squinted eyes, and knowing when and how best to begin and to terminate conversations. Persons who are successful communicators are better able to meet their needs and desires and to respond to those of others – the hallmark of a mature person – and thus are able to navigate a complex world and have a greater chance of living an independent and rewarding life.

The ABAS-II may be used to assist in assessment of communication skills. The communication items of the ABAS-II allow evaluators to assess the areas of receptive language, expressive language, and nonverbal communication and the use of these adaptive skills in everyday situations. This chapter will provide a discussion of the ABAS-II as it relates to communication. First, a brief discussion of the definition and measurement of the communication adaptive skill area of the ABAS-II will be covered. Second, a discussion of additional communication assessments will be provided. Third, a discussion of interventions connected to the ABAS-II and other assessments will be provided. Finally, a case study example using the ABAS-II will be discussed.

ABAS-II MEASUREMENT

The ABAS-II measures adaptive behavior and skills by utilizing information provided by teachers, parents, or other care providers following their completion of a comprehensive rating scale that consists of 10 adaptive skill areas that comprise three adaptive behavior composites (conceptual, social, and practical) and a General Adaptive Composite. Adults with pre-requisite skills (e.g., the ability to read, understand, and evaluate the rating scale items) also may complete the ABAS-II about themselves. All skills assessed by adaptive behavior measures must be performed independently and thus with no help from others. A Likert type scale, ranging from zero to three, is used by respondents to rate the ABAS-II items. The rating is a measure of behavior frequency. That is, the measure indicates approximately how often the individual engages in the behavior. For example, a rating of zero indicates an individual is unable to perform the skill due to a skill deficit. A rating of one indicates an individual has the skill yet never or almost never displays the behavior when needed. A rating of two indicates an individual has the skill and sometimes displays the behavior when needed. A rating of three indicates an individual has the skill and always or almost always displays it when needed.

Communication is one of the 10 adaptive skill areas measured on the ABAS-II. When completing the ABAS-II communication adaptive skill area items, the respondent focuses on a person's behaviors associated with receptive and expressive language skills and nonverbal communication skills displayed independently in daily activities. Behaviors include, at the lowest levels, looking at another's face when talking as well as laughing in response to another's laugh. Those at the higher levels include talking about future goals and engaging in conversation.

The ABAS-II identifies a number of communication adaptive skills important for school success. A teacher or clinician may observe an individual in his or her environment to determine if these skills are displayed. For example, while observing a child at school, an observer could determine whether the child listens closely for at least 5 minutes when the teacher talks, takes turns during conversations with peers, and gives verbal instructions that involve two or more steps. Information from this direct observation could be compared with data provided by a teacher who completed the ABAS-II Teacher Form for children ages 5–21.

As aforementioned, the ABAS-II measures the triad of communication adaptive skills in receptive language, expressive language, and nonverbal communication. Thus, the ABAS-II can be used to assess receptive language, expressive language, and nonverbal communication skills demonstrated by individuals in daily situations.

RECEPTIVE LANGUAGE

Receptive language involves the input language system (Kuder, 2003), information acquired largely by what we see and hear. Receptive language relies on one's ability to comprehend information presented through language. Receptive language includes one's ability to recognize the names of objects, people, and pets, as well as action verbs together with one's ability to comprehend information from stories and to follow directions.

One may assess receptive language informally by observing whether an individual understands when others speak and is able to follow directions. However, these observations should be considered a starting point to their evaluation. Furthermore, if an individual has difficulty with expressive language as measured by having the individual speak, gesture, or write a response ("Tell me what to do with a spoon"), the assessor may provide such directions to which the client can respond gesturally or by performing them. Examples of these directions are, "Point to the door" or "Touch your nose and clap your hands three times." The ABAS-II assesses an individual's receptive language in the communication adaptive skill area. For example, the ABAS-II questions whether an individual listens responsively to directions, stories, and conversations. In addition, the ABAS-II assesses whether an individual follows simple and multiple-step directions. Assessment of receptive language further with the ABAS-II includes items that assess whether an individual interrupts others when speaking and ends conversations appropriately, both which require an individual to recognize facial expressions and other body language (e.g., slouched shoulders, folded arms).

EXPRESSIVE LANGUAGE

Expressive language involves the output language system (Kuder, 2003), the use of language to communicate and/or express one's thoughts and feelings. Expressive language includes spoken (oral), written, and gestural (signing) communication.

One may assess expressive language informally by observing an individual's speech, writing, or use of gestures, including their effectiveness in naming objects, asking questions, and engaging in conversations. The ABAS-II assesses an individual's expressive language in the communication adaptive skill area. Several items on the ABAS-II analyze expressive language. For example, one item asks if an individual says hello and goodbye to others, while another item asks if an individual says irregular pronouns such as knives and mice. Additional items assess conversational skills such as ending conversations appropriately, speaking in sentences of six or more words, and discussing a topic for more than 3 minutes.

NONVERBAL COMMUNICATION

Nonverbal communication includes both input and output language systems (Kuder, 2003). It requires the ability to interpret what we see and understand without using receptive or expressive language (e.g., body language and other means of expression such as shaking ones head yes or no).

One may assess nonverbal communication informally by observing whether an individual understands another's intentions expressed nonverbally as well as whether an individual's body movements are suitable socially and help support communication (e.g., whether an individual stands too far or too close to another speaker and whether he or she recognizes nonverbal cues signaling an end to conversations). The ABAS-II assesses an individual's nonverbal communication abilities. For example, one ABAS-II item asks if the individual takes turns during conversations with people. That is, the item questions whether the individual is too talkative or too quiet. This particular skill requires an individual to notice nonverbal communication of others to signal when to talk and when not. Similarly, an ABAS-II item assesses whether a person ends conversations appropriately. Although this addresses expressive language, it also addresses nonverbal communication because it requires an individual to assess the nonverbal cues of others such as facial expressions that may indicate the person is in a hurry or is bored with a topic.

ADDITIONAL ASSESSMENTS

In conjunction with the use of the ABAS-II, additional assessments completed by a speech-language pathologist and other specialists may be warranted for individuals with significant communication deficits. Recall that the primary purposes of a language assessment process are to describe a person's language behaviors, to identify strengths and weaknesses in their comprehension and use of language and other important communication methods, and to acquire data useful for proposing interventions. A person's language and communication skills often are evaluated in light of three standards: the person's age, the person's intellectual ability, and the environmental needs.

A careful review of a person's strengths may point to pathways that help support the development of skills in a deficient area. For example, a clinician may work with a child who is able to name specific objects to develop skills in demonstrating their use, to categorize items based on their function, and to explain similarities and differences between a set of objects.

Task analysis may be useful in determining a person's core skill strengths and deficits. Task analysis is a process in which a complex task is broken down into its component tasks in order to identify the different skills needed to correctly complete the task. For example, if a child is learning to pronounce specific sounds, the clinician may need to break down the sound into its components (such as teaching lip closure and build up intra-oral pressure in order to have the child eventually articulate a /p/). Task analysis becomes important, in part, because it provides direct links between diagnosis and interventions. The abilities the person demonstrates must be examined in order to build a task-analyzed program to help him or her develop the areas that are revealed as deficits in the assessment process.

As part of the analysis of a person's responses on a test, the clinician should break down the tasks the child could not do to determine at what level the child can and cannot succeed. Likewise, the items the child could do should be task analyzed to see what skills exist in the child's repertoire that can be used as pathway to achieve those skills that need further development. Interventions should focus on needed and functional outcomes, with interventions provided in the most efficient and effective manner possible.

In addition to the aforementioned informal methods, some more direct measurements should be used to assess complex, symbolic, and generative language processes (Erickson, 1981). Also, language use varies based on the communication setting, the listener(s), and the topics. Language assessment requires the use of tests, direct observation, and information from parents and other caregivers as well as teachers (e.g., through the use of the ABAS-II). Furthermore the involvement of parents, teachers, and other team members facilitates the formation and application of interventions to achieve needed functional behaviors.

DIRECT OBSERVATIONS

Direct observations of individuals may provide additional information about their communication and other adaptive skills. The observer selects natural environments in which to observe. Some environments should be structured (e.g., classrooms) while others should be non-structured (playgrounds, interaction that occurs while eating) (Bentzen, 1997).

DIRECT TESTS OF SKILLS

Both receptive and expressive language should be assessed. Receptive tests measure a child's linguistic understanding: what persons understand as a result of what they hear or see. Examples of standardized receptive tests include the Peabody Picture Vocabulary Test – IV (Dunn & Dunn, 2007), The Receptive One-Word Picture Vocabulary Test (Brownell, 2000b), and the Test for Auditory Comprehension of Language, 3rd Edition (Carrow-Woolfolk, 1998).

Expressive tests measure expressive linguistic performance: how well persons use their knowledge of language. Examples of standardized expressive language tests include the Expressive One-Word Picture Vocabulary Test (Brownell, 2000a) and the Structured Photographic Expressive Language Test (Dawson, Stout & Eyer, 2003). These examples of tests of receptive or expressive language narrowly measure only one of these two skills.

In contrast, other tests assess language more broadly by assessing both receptive and expressive skills together with other communication skills. Examples of these more broadly focused standardized tests include the Test of Language Development – Primary, 3rd Edition (Newcomer & Hammill, 1997), the Test of Early Language Development, 3rd Edition (Hresko et al., 1999), the Clinical Evaluation of Language Function, 4th Edition (Semel et al., 2003), the Detroit Tests of Learning Aptitude (Hammill, 1998), the Utah Test of Language Development (Mecham, 2002), and the Oral and Written Language Scales (OWLS; Carrow-Woolfolk, 1996).

Developmental checklists often are used with infants and preschool children. The child's score may be described in reference to a developmental age based on the number of items passed on the checklist. For example, a child who displays 14 skills may be similar to a normally developing child who is 4 years 7 months. Developmental checklists can be used to record observations, as a guide during a parent interview, or as a formalized method of assessing a child's developmental level based on behaviors and skills exhibited by the child. Checklists can be completed by observation, by interaction with the child, or interactions with the primary caregivers. Some examples are found below.

The *Receptive–Expressive Emergent Language Scale – 2* (Bzoch & League, 1991) can be used to guide the interview of parents about their child's speech and language abilities. The Vineland *Social-Emotional Early Childhood Scale* (Sparrow et al., 1998) allows the clinician to identify behaviors described by the primary caregiver as typical of the child's communicative behaviors.

The *Communication and Symbolic Behavior Scales Developmental Profile* (Wetherby & Prizant, 2002) provides a normed developmental checklist for use in a parent interview and observation of the child in his everyday settings. This Profile is designed to assist in the assessment of language and communication functions of children 8–24 months of age. It also can be used to assess the language and communication skills (e.g., gaze shifts, use of gestures, positive affect, and rate of communicating) of children up to 72 months who have developmental delays.

The *MacArthur Communicative Development Inventories* (CDI) (Fenson et al., 2007) provide two normed checklists parents can complete: words and gestures and words and sentences. The words and gestures checklist is used with 8–16 month old infants, whereas the words and sentences checklist is used with 16–30 months of infants. The MacArthur Communicative Development Inventory: Words and Sentences (CDI) (Fenson et al., 2007) is a parent report test tool that measures vocabulary development. The CDI includes an "extensive vocabulary checklist containing words that children typically produce in the second and third years of life" (Miller et al., 1995, p. 1037).

One final note of consideration is warranted prior to looking at communication interventions that stem from the ABAS-II. That is, prior to, during, and after conducting the ABAS-II and other assessments, the assessor should consider a few possibilities. Clinicians should recognize language and communication delays and deficits may be attributable to various causes. For example, persons with diminished auditory acuity are less capable of hearing and thus less able to acquire language and to communicate. Persons with diminished visual acuity may be less able to discern facial cues and thus appear awkward in their communication patterns. The adequacy of one's exposure to language at home and/or school will have a sizable impact on their language development. Persons for whom English is a second language also may show diminished communication skills in an environment in which English is used exclusively or predominantly. Persons who are shy or lack self-confidence may display performance deficits, not skill or knowledge deficits.

Clinicians should consider too that persons who display language disorders also may display other disorders. For example, the individual may display an autism spectrum disorder, with associated deficits in social and communication skills. Persons who are cognitively challenged also may display diminished language skills.

Additionally, cultural differences may account for communication deficits. For example, a culture may promote the belief that children should not make direct eye contact with adults or speak without first being spoken to. Professionals are encouraged to determine whether a person displays a skill deficit (i.e., does not know how to perform the skill) or performance deficit (i.e., knows how, but does not do it).

INTERVENTION METHODS

Before identifying particular interventions connected to the ABAS-II, it is important to identify and discuss the primary communication intervention methods. Two commonly used intervention methods to promote language and communication skills include applied behavior analysis and naturalistic approaches. Each is discussed below.

Applied behavior analysis involves an analysis of the events surrounding behavior, both antecedent events (i.e., those occurring prior to a behavior) and consequence events (i.e., those occurring after a behavior), and the manipulation of these variables to produce behavior change in the desired direction (Baer et al., 1968, 1987). Applied behavior analysis acknowledges that many behaviors are learned through an individual's interactions with his or her environment through operant conditioning (i.e., a process that involves the relationship between a stimulus and the consequences of a response; Skinner, 1953). A discriminative stimulus is one type of antecedent factor that establishes the occasion for a behavior to occur and signals the availability of a reinforcer (or consequent event). The consequence that follows the behavior determines the probability of the behavior reoccurring in the presence of the same or a similar stimulus. Therefore, the individual's environment must be assessed to determine the antecedents and consequences surrounding the target behavior in order to understand their effects on that behavior (Baer et al., 1968). Behavior analysis procedures also should identify and investigate ways that reliably produce significant behavior change (Bailey & Burch, 2002). Applied behavior analysis includes such approaches as functional communication training (FCT) and verbal behavior therapy.

Some interventions use more naturalistic approaches such as milieu therapy (Kaiser, 1993a). These interventions often align more closely with the theoretical framework of most speech-language pathologists. Milieu therapy involves teaching children new skills and behaviors within their natural environments (Kaiser, 1993b). The natural environment may refer to any setting in which a person would naturally spend time regardless of his or her disability, including the home, school, or an inclusive educational setting (Schwartz, 2003). These approaches involve using the individual's interest to guide the intervention in natural environments such as the home and school. Further, students typically are provided with choices, and their language and communication skills are shaped by reinforcing each behavior that more closely approximates the desired behavior.

As mentioned, both applied behavior analysis and naturalistic interventions use reinforcement to enhance learning. Reinforcement occurs if the event following the behavior (e.g., communication) increases the future probability of the behavior occurring. Reinforcers may be tangible items, praise, and tokens (see Bailey and Burch, 2002, for further detail). FCT and milieu therapy use reinforcement to promote change in behavior. These and other interventions for persons with communication problems will be selected in light of a person's receptive language, expressive language, and nonverbal communication strengths and limitations.

RECEPTIVE LANGUAGE

Interventions designed to promote receptive language (e.g., understanding words) typically focus on improving such skills as paying attention, comprehending, and following directions. One broad intervention involves communicating directions using multiple formats (i.e., using spoken and written language or pictures if needed). Many teachers and clinicians use a nonverbal cue to engage the individual in communication (e.g. pulling on the adult's ear or touching his or her nose, holding up a blue chip, or somewhat more intrusively, clapping their hands. The use of such a cue will signal a child to attend and thus to be receptive to what is being said.

The playing of games also may be used to promote receptive language. For example, play *Simon Says* without tricking the individual (i.e., always say, "Simon says"). After the individual's receptive language improves, consider changing the game. For example, say, "Touch your feet" or "Touch the TV." This may help improve such skills as following directions, behaviors assessed by ABAS-II items on the form for ages 2–5.

Communication can be enhanced by having a person look at another's face when speaking, a behavior assessed by the ABAS-II. Thus, an intervention may stress the reinforcement of an individual for looking at your face and the faces of others when talking. Although this typically is used for individuals ages 2–5, it can be used with persons from all ages, when needed. Similarly, individuals may be reinforced for paying attention during classroom discussion or other forms of communication. Methods that successively shape the desired behaviors may be required (i.e., provide reinforcement for increasingly closer approximations to the final goal).

EXPRESSIVE LANGUAGE

Interventions designed to improve expressive language differ from those designed to improve receptive language. Expressive language interventions typically target skills associated with personal needs. The interventions typically involve teaching interaction skills, conversation skills, and telephone skills.

Interaction skills: An intervention intended to promote turn taking may involve selecting one or more personally preferred and shared activities (e.g., coloring, board games, and legos for younger children) that will provide opportunities for communication. During these activities the individuals practice using others' names (e.g., Mrs. Johnson, my turn), which is tied to the first communication item (C[1]-1) on the ABAS-II for ages 5–21. Further, the individual can practice asking questions such as, "Is it my turn?" Individuals also may practice raising his or her voice for attention and repeating others words. Also, when working with persons over age 5, provide practice in their both giving and following verbal instructions that involve two or more steps (e.g., Pick up the red logo and put it on the top), a behavior assessed by ABAS-II item C-17.

Persons older than age 5 can be expected to know their home address, including the zip code and phone number, behaviors assessed by ABAS-II items C-18 and C-22. Thus, those who do not engage in these behavior should acquire them. Those who are nonverbal yet able to write should practice writing their address and phone number. Further, teach them to whom they may give the address (e.g., police officers and good friend, not strangers).

Conversational skills: Conversational skills need to be acquired by those who lack these skills. Begin by modeling and practicing saying *hello* and *goodbye*, behaviors assessed by ABAS-II items C-3. When the individual says *hello* or *goodbye*, respond with the same response.

Persons over age 8 can be expected to converse with others for a few minutes about a topic of personal interest. For those who display a performance deficit in this skill, arrange an intervention that promotes it, perhaps through shaping (i.e., gradually increase the length of the conversation as well as the reinforcement for it, starting first with 30 seconds, and gradually progress to 3 minutes). Select

[1] C is used to refer to the communication adaptive skill area of the ABAS-II.

topics of mutual interest. Later, the individual should practice using a topic that interest other persons in the conversation, a behavior assessed by ABAS-II item C-19. This process is intended to promote a person's ability and willingness to talk about his/her own interests and those of others – qualities key to developing and maintaining personal relationships.

Another conversational intervention involves giving the individual a series of topics of interest and have him or her practice talking about and giving their opinions about it, behaviors assessed by ABAS-II items C-22 of the parent form for ages 0–5 and C-23 of the parent form for ages 5–21. Have the target individual ask questions about the topic. Similarly, conversational skills can be promoted at home by having the person discuss events associated with school, work, or other daily activities with a family member who models language and conversational styles, including the use of the past and future tenses while reinforcing the individual for doing the same.

Select preferred toys or other objects that provide opportunities to make plurals. For example, while playing with toy cars or observing real cars, encourage the individual to refer to a car and then to cars. Use a favorite hobby such as models or baseball cards for older persons. This practice will help address the skill assessed by ABAS-II item C-14.

Engage in a series of discussions about your prior or current future educational and career goals to serve as a model. Encourage the person to discuss possible goals and to create short-term goals that support the attainment of long-term goals. This practice will address any deficit noted on ABAS-II item C-20.

Telephone skills: Our telephones increasingly provide a lifeline to others. Thus, all persons need to be able to use the telephone. The ABAS-II considers it important to the extent it has three specific items related to telephone use (i.e., ABAS-II items C-10, C-18, and C-21). One approach to address telephone skill deficits is to promote its use by having the person memorize his or her phone number. They should practice dialing their phone numbers and those of family members and emergency response providers. After reaching a family member or friend, they should practice discussing their intent to make the call. This practice may start by sitting next to another. Then, move to another room. Finally, the individual should call a friend or relative to talk. They also may need practice in answering the phone properly and talking on it. For example, the individual could answer the phone by saying, "Hello, this is the Johnson residence."

NONVERBAL COMMUNICATION

Interventions that address nonverbal communication skills focus on important qualities that facilitate or impede conversation (e.g., facial expressions, body movements, and gestures). Interventions may be needed to perform them, including how to correctly recognize and interpret the nonverbal communications of others. Several examples are provided below that demonstrate how to enhance nonverbal communication.

We often communicate by shaking our head to indicate "yes" or "no", behaviors assessed by ABAS-II item C-2. If needed, promote this activity by selecting preferred and shared activities that will provide opportunities for communication. During these activities, both you and the person should take turns asking questions and having the other person answer them by shaking his/her head yes or no. Note that, although shaking one's head from side to side may indicate to many that the person is saying "no", in some cultures this is a sign for saying "yes".

The ability to listen when another person is talking by phone or in person is important to acquire. This skill is assessed by the ABAS-II with items 8, 9, 11, and 12. Listening 1 minute for younger children and up to 5 minutes for older individuals may be suitable. This behavior may be developed best by shaping it (i.e., reinforce it first for 10 seconds, then 20 seconds, up to a minute).

Voice volume (e.g., soft or loud) and other voice qualities (e.g. high or low pitch, soft or harsh tones) also comprise important communication quality, which is assessed on the ABAS-II form for ages 2–5 through items 3 and 5. Interventions may be needed to promote an understanding between the volume of one's voice used and different feelings and needs. For example, model how to raise the tone of one's voice when hurt and to lower one's voice to provide comfort. Similar instruction can be offered for sadness, happiness, anger, and other feelings. Have them practice these qualities. Teach anger using appropriate responses (i.e., raised voice, but not screaming or the use of foul language).

The use of humor constitutes another important communication skill, a behavior assessed by item 13 on the ABAS-II parent form for ages 5–21. Humor typically involves language and thus may require considerable receptive and expressive language sophistication. Humor can be troublesome for those who lack these language skills or needed intellectual abilities (Kruder, 2003). Practice the promotion of humor by telling a joke and then laughing. In addition, explain what types of things are funny (i.e., may want to consider teaching others how to laugh appropriately). Reinforce the individual for laughing.

CHILD CASE STUDY

Deidre, a 5 year 5 month old girl, was referred following a diagnosis of displaying expressive and receptive language delays secondary to mild mental retardation.

FAMILY AND MEDICAL BACKGROUND

Deidre's mother reports she did not experience complications during her pregnancy and that Deidre was a full-term baby. Deidre achieved most of her developmental milestones at a lower than normal rate. She lives at home with her mother, father, grandmother, and three older brothers (ages 12, 10, and 7). Family history is significant for one of her brothers also receiving speech-language therapy. Although English and Spanish are spoken in the home, Deidre's primary language is English. Her mother has a bachelor's degree, and her father has a master's degree. Deidre's parents first became concerned about Deidre's speech and language skills as well as her fine and gross motor skills when Deidre was approximately 2½ years old.

SPEECH AND LANGUAGE HISTORY

Deidre failed a hearing screening at school. However, a follow-up visit with an audiologist found Deidre's hearing to be normal. Deidre's mother notes several concerns when completing a speech and language case history form for a local university's speech and hearing clinic, For example, although Deidre combines more than 3 words to communicate with others, she does not give directions well or express herself in a coherent manner that is understood by others, including family members. Occasionally Deidre resorts to whining or crying when frustrated in her communication efforts.

EDUCATION BACKGROUND

Deidre attends a public school kindergarten program for children with cognitive delays, where she receives special education services and attends speech-language therapy 1 hour a week at school. Deidre's mother is most concerned about Deidre's pronunciation skills and her not speaking in a manner consistent with others her age. Deidre is receiving clinic services 1 hour a week to help address these deficiencies.

RESULTS OF PREVIOUS TESTING

At age 4 years 11 months, a local psychologist evaluated Deidre after Deidre's pediatrician referred her for academic, motor, and language testing. At that time, Deidre's mother reported that Deidre's learning was slow, that she did not know her numbers and colors, and that she generally seemed behind other children Deidre's age. The psychologist administered the *Wechsler Preschool and Primary Scale of Intelligence – Revised* (WPPSI-R) (Wechsler, 2000), the *Child Development Inventory* (CDI), and *Behavior Assessment System for Children*, 2nd Edition (BASC-2) (Reynolds & Kamphaus, 2004). Deidre's full scale IQ on the WPPSI-R was 68, which corresponds to the extremely low range. The psychologist made the following conclusions based on the WPPSI-R results.

Deidre's nonverbal, perceptual reasoning ability is within a Borderline range; this means she performs moderately below other children her age. Her persistence, perception of a whole from parts, and spatial visualization are low average. However, visual recognition, attention to details, and eye-motor coordination were very low. Deidre's verbal comprehension abilities are very deficient. Her recognition of words, concept formation, and language expression skills are somewhat higher. Her long-term memory, intellectual curiosity, practical knowledge, social judgment, and logic-abstract thinking are moderately low. Finally, her arithmetic reasoning ability is very deficient.

Her mother completed the *Child Development Inventory*. Deidre's developmen tal functioning was estimated to be in the 2 to 3 year level. She displays delays in her social development, self-help, gross and fine motor, expressive language, language comprehension, and knowledge of letters and numbers.

Deidre's mother's responses on the *Behavior Assessment System for Children*, 2nd Edition suggest that Deidre is at risk for hyperactivity and depression, and lacking in social skills. She was average in aggression, anxiety, externalized somatization, withdrawal, adaptability, and attention problems. Activities of daily living and functional communication were clinically significant.

Deidre's speech and language abilities were evaluated at the beginning of the school year by a speech-language pathologist employed by the public schools. Deidre's performance on the *Kaufman Brief Intelligence Test* (Kaufman & Kaufman, 1990) resulted in a score of 84 (14th percentile). Deidre's performance on the *Test of Language Development – Primary (TOLD-P: 3)* resulted in a speech-language quotient of 84 (14th percentile), a level consistent with her general intellectual ability. Her language quotient, 112, corresponds to the 79th percentile. Other scores on the TOLD-P: 3 included her organizing quotient of 70 (2nd percentile) and a speaking quotient of 76 (5th percentile). The organizing quotient reflects her performances on the sentence imitation task and relational vocabulary (the child's ability to comprehend and express the relationships between two words such as how a pencil and a pen are alike. The speaking quotient reflects her oral vocabulary and grammatical completion abilities (i.e. recognition, understanding, and usage of morphological forms). At the conclusion of her testing, the public school clinician noted that Deidre's expressive and receptive overall language skills fall in the below average range, more than 2 standardized deviations below the mean. Her ability to organize her thoughts and to speak are below average by more than 1½ standard deviations.

SPEECH-LANGUAGE ASSESSMENT AT THE UNIVERSITY SPEECH AND HEARING CLINIC

Deidre was 5 years and 2 months when she began receiving therapy from the university speech clinic. One articulation and two language tests were administered at that time to help establish a basis for therapy and to help evaluate progress.

Deidre's mother completed the *ABAS-II* (Parent/Primary Caregiver Form: Ages 0–5 (see Table 4.1). Deidre's adaptive behavior and skills are consistent with information we have on her prior and current language development. Her ABAS-II General Adaptive Composite of 57 was lower than the 1st percentile, compared to other children her age and classifies her general adaptive behavior as extremely low. Her scores on the three ABAS-II composites ranged from extremely low, with standard scores of 55 and 65, respectively, on the practical and conceptual composite to a borderline score of 77 on the social composite. Her adaptive skill area scaled scores ranged from a low of 1 in the motor adaptive skill area to a high of 8 in the social adaptive skill area. Deidre's scaled scores in the motor, home living, health and safety, and self-care adaptive skill areas are classified as extremely

TABLE 4.1 Scores on the ABAS-II Parent/Primary Caregiver Form for Diedra, age 5 years 2 months

	Adaptive Skill Area Scaled Scores			
Adaptive Skill Areas	General Adaptive Composite	Conceptual	Social	Practical
Communication	6	6		
Community use	4			4
Functional academics	5	5		
Home living	3			3
Health and safety	3			3
Leisure	5		5	
Self-care	2			2
Self-direction	4	4		
Social	8		8	
Motor	1			

Adaptive skill area scaled scores have a mean (average) of 10 and a standard deviation of 3.

Composites	Standard Score	Percentile Rank	Standard Score Confidence Interval (90%)
General Adaptive Composite	57	0.2	54–60
Conceptual Composite	65	1.0	59–71
Social Composite	77	6.0	71–83
Practical Composite	55	0.1	49–61

Composite standard scores have a mean (average) of 100 and a standard deviation of 15.

low. Scaled scores for the community use and functional academic adaptive skill areas are in the borderline range, while the scaled score of 6 in the communication adaptive skill area is in the below average range. Clinical observations also show her social adaptive skills, which fell into the average range on the ABAS-II, to be a relative strength for Deidre, compared to other adaptive skill areas.

Deidre's speech also was evaluated using the *Structured Photographic Articulation Test – Dudsberry II*. At the single word level, although Deidre's speech is within normal limits (i.e., her errors were age appropriate), her intelligibility declined with increasing length of utterances.

In addition to the ABAS-II, Deidre was assessed with the Test of Language Development-P: 3. Her standard scores on the Test of Language Development-P: 3 indicate average receptive language as measured by the Picture Vocabulary subtest (pointing to one of four pictures named by the clinician), expressive language as measured by the Oral Vocabulary subtest (defining words spoken by the clinician), and language comprehension as measured by the Grammatical Understanding subtest (comprehending sentences with emphasis on syntax as indicated by pointing to the picture described by the clinician). She displayed below average concept formation ability as measured by the Relational Vocabulary subtest (describing how two words are similar), as measured by the Sentence Imitation subtest (imitates sentences spoken by the clinician), and as measured by the Grammatical Completion subtest (understanding morphological forms). Her spoken language quotient indicates below average language abilities. Her speaking and semantic skills are below average. Deidre's listening and syntax skills are average. If one were to average Deidre's language development, it is equivalent to a child 3 years 8 months old. A summary of Deidre's performance on the six subtests indicates the test areas from highest to lowest as follows:

Picture Vocabulary (50th percentile)
Oral Vocabulary (37th percentile)
Grammatic Understanding (25th percentile)
Relational Vocabulary (5th percentile)
Sentence Imitation (5th percentile)
Grammatic Completion (5th percentile)
Her composite scores ranged as follows (again from highest to lowest)
Listening abilities (Picture Vocabulary and Grammatic Understanding)
Understanding the use of syntax (Grammatic Understanding, Sentence Imitation, Grammatic Completion)
Understanding the use of semantics (Picture Vocabulary, Relational Vocabulary, Oral Vocabulary)
Speaking ability (Oral Vocabulary and Grammatic Completion)
Spoken Language ability (comprised of all 6 subtests)
Organizing ability (Relational Vocabulary and Sentence Imitation)

Specific examples of items missed and achieved on the subtests include the following:

Subtest	Correct Items	Incorrect Items
Picture Vocabulary	Mirror, tray, bulb, lizard, anchor, explosive, stump, winged	Dental, afloat, monument, surgeon, medical, emerald, salmon, weep
Relational Vocabulary	Glass/cup, book/newspaper	Kite/bird, couch/chair, oven/grill, penny/dime
Oral Vocabulary	Bird, apple, rest, brown	Cow, poor, ocean, face, bed, sugar, zoo, baby
Grammatic Understanding	They sat up and listened The leaves had fallen to the ground	She went quickly She stood between them The dog waited for its owner.
Sentence Imitation	Her friends walked to school My new kitten is spotted	After the party, the boys fixed the car Have the people been helped by the king?
Grammatic Completion	Lorena is a girl. Irene is a girl. They are both _____.	The shoes belong to the boy. Whose shoes are they? They are the _________.

Deidre's ability to express herself using one word, as assessed by the *Expressive One-Word Picture Vocabulary Test*, is comparable to a child age 3 years 8 months, with a score of 81 (10th percentile). This test requires children to answer questions based on pictures they see. Examples include "What's he doing?", "What word names all of these?", and "What are these?" Her performance on this test generally is consistent with her performance on the Test of Language Development-P: 3.

RECOMMENDATIONS

After examining the data from the ABAS-II and other assessments, it is evident Deidre needs some intensive interventions. Overall, she should continue in therapy at both her school and the university clinic. Goals for therapy are selected based on clinical observations, responses on the ABAS-II, and results on the Test of Language Development-P: 3. Emphasis will be placed on increasing conceptual development, the mean length of her utterance, sequencing (including following two-step directions in order), pre-literacy skills, and her ability to answer questions. The speech-language pathologists at school and the clinic should coordinate goals with her teacher to facilitate applications of skills learned in the clinic to her daily settings.

As aforementioned, the therapist should focus several interventions on the area of communication. Results from the ABAS-II and the Test of Language Development-P: 3 suggest what interventions to be targeted. Deidre requires interventions that address her expressive language deficits. Particularly, interventions should focus on deficits that relate to items 10, 15, and 17–24 of the ABAS-II parent form for ages 0–5. The interventions should be conducted with the methodologies outlined in the intervention methods section of this chapter. Several of the targeted interventions will be detailed in the following paragraphs.

Deidre needs practice repeating words others say. The therapist could accomplish this task in game formats. For example, the therapist could say, "Let's play pirates. I will be the pirate and you can be the parrot." During the game, Deidre would repeat the words the therapist speaks. When Deidre correctly performs the task, she could be given a *cracker*. However, in this case, since food items result in quick satiation, the *cracker* would be a token that looks like a real cracker and later exchanged for rewards. This could be referred to as the *Parrot Game*.

Deidre also needs work on making plurals of words by adding an -s, such as shoes and cats. In addition, Deidre needs help using sentences with a noun and a verb. To best accomplish this task, the therapist first should focus on topics that interest Deidre, which may be reinforcing. For example, Deidre may say, "Play with doll" or other statements related to items she enjoys. When the therapist notices improvement, Deidre then can start referring to other topics such as, "Do work." This intervention will help lay the foundation for her to begin using longer sentences.

While practicing using nouns and verbs, Deidre also should improve speaking in sentences of six or more words. The therapist could shape this behavior. That is, Deidre could practice three word sentences and gradually increase the amount of words used per sentence. Also, she should practice using past tense to talk about prior events. For example, Deidre may say, "I ate hamburgers last night."

The sentences she practices should include both statements and questions. For example, Deidre could practice asking, "Will you play with me?" with the therapist. This role-play activity could prepare her to ask her peers these questions. The teacher would then need to observe Deidre in the classroom, playground, and other appropriate areas for occurrence of this behavior. The teacher may need to provide prompts and should provide praise and other reinforcement for correct responses.

A final recommendation involves engaging in conversations. The aforementioned interventions should help in giving Deidre a repertoire for practicing these conversations. While having a conversation, Deidre needs to engage in a topic for more than 3 minutes, refrain from interrupting others when they are talking, and end conversations appropriately. This could begin by having Deidre choose a topic of interest and then taking turns speaking about the topic. At first, a timer may need to be used to indicate when turns should be exchanged. Later during the intervention sessions, the timer may be faded out. Deidre could be reinforced for closer approximations to each of the conversation goals. That is, the closer she gets to 3 minutes, the longer and more frequent she refrains from interrupting others, and the more often she ends conversations appropriately should be reinforced. Also, the teacher should look for these skills occurring in the classroom and provide reinforcement and prompts as needed. Note here that the best form of reinforcement in the classroom for generalization to occur may need to be intermittent reinforcement, which tends to have the greatest success with generalization and sustainability.

REFERENCES

Baer, D. M., Wolf, M. M., & Risley, T. R. (1968). Some current dimensions of applied behavior analysis. *Journal of Applied Behavior Analysis*, *1*, 91–97.

Baer, D. M., Wolf, M. M., & Risley, T. R. (1987). Some still-current dimensions of applied behavior analysis. *Journal of Applied Behavior Analysis*, *20*, 313–327.

Bailey, J. S. & Burch, M. R. (2002). *Research Methods in Applied Behavior Analysis.* London, England: Sage Publications.

Bentzen, W. R. (1997). *Seeing Young Children: A Guide to Observing and Recording Behavior*, 3rd edn. Albany, NY: Delmar Publishers.

Brownell, R. (2000a). *Expressive One-Word Picture Vocabulary Test – 2000.* Novatno, CA: Academic Therapy Publications.

Brownell, R. (2000b). *Receptive One-Word Picture Vocabulary Test – 2000.* Novatno, CA: Academic Therapy Publications.

Bzoch, K. & League, R. (1991). *The Receptive–Expressive Emergent Language Scale – 2.* Los Angeles, CA: Western Psychological Services.

Carrow-Woolfolk, E. (1996). *Oral and Written Language Scales.* Bloomington, MN: Pearson Assessments.

Carrow-Woolfolk, E. (1998). *Test for Auditory Comprehension of Language*, 3rd edn. Austin, TX: Pro-Ed.

Dawson, J. I., Stout, C. E., & Eyer, J. A. (2003). *Structured Photographic Expressive Language Test*, 3rd edn. DeKalb, IL: Janelle Publications.

Dunn, L. M. & Dunn, L. M. (2007). *The Peabody Picture Vocabulary Test – IV*. Circle Pines, MN: American Guidance Services.

Erickson, J. G. (1981). Communication assessment of the bilingual cultural child: An overview. In J. G. Erickso & Dr. R. Omark (Eds.), *Communication Assessment of the Bilingual Bicultural Child*, pp. 1–24. Austin, TX: Pro-Ed.

Fenson, L., Marchman, V. A., Thal, D., Dale, P. S., Reznick, J. S., & Bates, E. (2007). *MacArthur Communicative Development Inventories: User's Guide and Technical Manual*, 2nd edn. San Diego: Singular Publishing Company.

Hammill, D. (1998). *Detroit Tests of Learning Aptitude*, 4th edn. San Antonio, TX: Psychological Corporation.

Harrison, P. L. & Oakland, T. (2003). *Adaptive Behavior Assessment System*, 2nd edn. San Antonio, TX: The Psychological Corporation.

Hresko, W. P., Reid, K., & Hammill, D. D. (1999). *Test of Early Language Development – 3*. Austin, TX: Pro-Ed.

Kaiser, A. P. (1993a). Functional language. In M. E. Snell (Ed.), *Instruction of Students with Severe Disabilities*. New York: Macmillan.

Kaiser, A. P. (1993b). Parent-implemented language intervention: An environmental system perspective. In A. P. Kaiser & D. B. Gray (Eds.), *Enhancing Children's Communication: Research Foundations for Intervention*, pp. 63–84. Baltimore: Paul H. Brookes Publishing Co.

Kaufman, A. S. & Kaufman, N. L. (1990). *Kaufman Brief Intelligence Scale*. Boston, MA: Pearson.

Kruder, S. J. (2003). *Teaching Students with Language and Communication Disabilities*, 2nd edn. Boston: Allyn & Bacon.

Mecham, M. J. (2002). *Utah Test of Language Development – 4*. Itasca, IL: Riverside Publishing.

Miller, J. F., Sedey, A. L., & Miolo, G. (1995). Validity of parent report measures of vocabulary development for children with down syndrome. *Journal of Speech and Hearing Research, 38*, 1037–1044.

Newcomer, P. L. & Hammill, D. D. (1997). *Test of Language Development – 3*. Austin, TX: Pro-Ed.

Owens, R. E. (2001). *Language Development: An Introduction*. Boston: Allyn & Bacon.

Reynolds, C. R. & Kamphaus, R. W. (2004). *Behavior Assessment System for Children*, 2nd edn. Boston, MA: Pearson.

Schwartz, I. S. (2003). Social validity assessment: Voting on science or acknowledging the roots of applied behavior analysis? In K. S. Budd & T. Stokes (Eds.), *A Small Matter of Proof: The Legacy of Donald M. Baer*, pp. 53–61. New York: Context Press.

Semel, E., Wiig, E. H., & Secord, W. A. (2003). *Clinical Evaluation of Language Fundamentals*, 4th edn. San Antonio, TX: Psychological Corporation.

Skinner, B. F. (1953). *Science and Human Behavior*. New York: Free Press.

Sparrow, S. S., Balla, D. A., & Cicchetti, D. V. (1998). *Vineland Social-Emotional Early Childhood Scales*. Circle Pines, MN: American Guidance Services.

Wechsler, D. (2000). *Wechsler Preschool and Primary Scales of Intelligence – 3*. San Antonio, TX: Psychological Corporation.

Werner, E., & Krescheck, J. D. (1983). *Structured Photographic Expressive Language Test—II*. Sandwich, IL: Janelle Publications.

Wetherby, A. M. & Prizant, B. M. (2002). *Communication and Symbolic Behavior Scales: Developmental Profile*. Baltimore, MD: Brookes.

5

Adaptive Behavior and Skills Important to Community Use

STACY K. DYMOND

Department of Special Education, University of Illinois, Champaign, IL 61829, U.S.A.

The term *community* means different things to different people. For some, community refers to the geographic area in which they live. Others see community as locations outside the home where they travel to do business, obtain services, or engage in leisure activities. Still others use the term to convey a sense of belonging and a shared role for making a neighborhood (or other location) a better place for all involved. This chapter encompasses all of these varied definitions of community and provides strategies for helping individuals develop adaptive skills that increase their involvement, participation, and independence in the community.

DESCRIPTION OF COMMUNITY USE ADAPTIVE SKILL AREA

Community skills typically have been conceptualized as falling into several distinct goal areas. For example, Renzaglia and Aveno (1986) defined the goal areas of the community as restaurants, stores/shops, services, and health and safety. Ford et al. (1989) expanded these goal areas to include travel, community safety, grocery shopping, general shopping, eating out, and using services. More recently, Dymond (2004) re-conceptualized the goal areas according to activities in the general community (i.e., restaurants/eateries, grocery stores, retail stores, services, public facilities, recreation facilities, volunteer work, transportation) and the school community (i.e., special events, clubs/organizations, school jobs, athletics, arts). Although the school typically is not identified as a community setting, some have argued that, for school-aged children, the school constitutes their community and thus should be considered as a community setting in which they should learn to function (Sands et al., 2000).

The Adaptive Behavior Assessment System-II (ABAS-II; Harrison & Oakland, 2003) is a comprehensive measure that includes 10 adaptive skill areas, including a community use adaptive skill area. The community use adaptive skill area measures a range of skills that cut across the broad goal areas identified in the literature. These skills generally cluster into four areas: travel, using services, community safety, and appropriate behavior in the community.

- *Travel* consists of the skills needed to orient and move around in the community, including the use of various forms of transportation.
- *Using services* focuses on knowledge and use of businesses, services, and resources.
- *Community safety* encompasses skills needed to participate in the community without undue risk to oneself as well as knowledge of what to do when emergencies arise.
- *Appropriate behavior* refers to acting in ways that are socially appropriate and conform to the norms of each environment.

Examples of the types of community use adaptive skills measured in the ABAS-II for each goal area are listed in Table 5.1. Skills listed in the ABAS-II are samples of the broad array of adaptive skills needed to function successfully in various community settings.

IMPORTANCE OF COMMUNITY USE ADAPTIVE SKILL AREA

A primary purpose of education is to prepare individuals to be productive citizens (Egan, 2003). This purpose is reinforced in the Individuals with Disabilities Education Improvement Act (IDEA, 2004) which states that special education services should prepare students for independent living and employment. The Americans with Disabilities Act (1990) furthers the expectation for community participation for individuals with disabilities of all ages by ensuring access to public accommodations, employment, and transportation. While some individuals develop skills needed to function in the community as a result of their participation in the general education curriculum, guidance from parents, or involvement in community activities, more intensive and structured instruction may be warranted for those who do not develop these skills through typical means.

TABLE 5.1 Sample community use adaptive skills from the ABAS-II measured within each goal area.

Travel	Using services	Community safety	Appropriate behavior
Looks both ways before crossing a street or parking lot	Identifies services provided by professionals in the community	Informs parents when someone comes to the door	Obeys authority of community officials
Uses public transportation, bicycle, or car	Recognizes the need to pay for an item before leaving a store	Carries personal Identification	Shows respect for school or public property
States which bus is taken to school	Uses the school or local library	Describes procedures for contacting community services in case of emergency	Refrains from talking loudly in a public place
Follows another's directions to nearby places	Mails letters at post office	Recognizes own home in his/her immediate neighborhood	Refrains from touching items in a store
States general address of a travel destination	Orders own meals when eating out		
	Finds restrooms		

One may question why children and adults who struggle to participate in the community should receive instruction in this area. Consider the many benefits that accrue as a result of knowledge and skills associated with community participation. Knowing how to use the community increases self-sufficiency by enabling individuals to acquire goods and services needed to live independently (e.g., grocery shop, visit the doctor). This knowledge reduces dependence on others to meet basic needs. Individuals who possess community skills are able to make a meaningful contribution to their community through participation in volunteer work, service clubs, or voting. Understanding how to behave appropriately in community settings may increase the number of opportunities individuals have to participate in settings outside the home, thus expanding the environments to which they have access to develop relationships with others. Freedom to come and go from home when desired exists when individuals learn how to travel safely. In summary, possession of community skills enhances overall quality of life by increasing an individual's participation, independence, freedom, and choices.

CONDITIONS THAT IMPACT DEVELOPMENT AND PERFORMANCE OF COMMUNITY SKILLS

Several factors may influence an individual's acquisition of community skills. Some of these include access to community settings, type of community in which the individual lives, individual or family preferences, age appropriateness of the skills, and the instructional context. With appropriate planning, those responsible for delivering instruction can address these factors to maximize the impact of instruction.

Access to community settings: For some, lack of skill development is due to insufficient opportunities to access and participate in the community. Lack of transportation or concerns about safety may impact the extent to which individuals have physical access to the community. Likewise, for individuals with significant disabilities, parents or support staff may believe it is easier (i.e., less time consuming, less work) to leave the individual at home while they conduct business in the community. The acquisition of community skills requires an individual to have frequent access to the settings in which the skills are to be developed, mastered, and maintained.

Type of community: The skills needed to function in the community depend on the community in which one lives (Falvey, 1989; Dymond, 2004). For example, when living in a large city, individuals need to know how to use public transportation and cross double lane highways at a light. However, those living in a rural community are unlikely to have access to public transportation. Their travel skills may emphasize the importance of navigating unmarked intersections. The community must be carefully assessed to determine the skills that are needed by individuals who reside there. In addition, instruction should focus on teaching skills that enable the individual to function in both current and future settings (Brown et al., 1979). Thus, if an individual currently lives in a rural community and intends to travel or move to an urban area in the near future, instruction should focus on skills needed in both types of communities.

Individual or family preferences: The types of activities in which one participates in the community are affected by a number of variables. Location of one's home, prior relationships with particular businesses, recreational interests (e.g., sports, clubs), and perceived safety of various environments are just some of the many factors that affect one's choice about how, when, and where to participate in the community. Instruction on community skills should reflect the natural routines of the individual and his/her family. For example, teaching an individual to use the post office to purchase stamps when the family purchases them electronically through the internet or at the grocery store does not reflect the family's natural routine. Thus, instruction on using the post office to purchase stamps may not be useful if the individual is unlikely to use the post office for this function. In addition, instruction should take into account the priorities of the individual and his/her family. Skills targeted for instruction should be those that are likely to make the greatest impact on the individual's quality of life and promote self-determination (Browder et al., 1997; Hughes et al., 2006).

Age appropriateness: Expectations for the types and complexity of skills demonstrated across settings generally increase with age. When possible, skills selected for instruction should match the individual's chronological age (Falvey, 1989; Dymond, 2004). For example, a preschool or elementary school child may be expected to accompany an adult to the laundromat and participate in that setting by reading at a table, playing an arcade game, purchasing a snack from the vending machine, or using the bathroom. Beginning in middle and high school, and continuing through adulthood, an individual may be expected to wash, dry, and fold the laundry. Although some individuals may function cognitively at a level much lower than their chronological age, teaching age-appropriate skills enhances participation in settings alongside same-age peers without disabilities. Instruction that focuses only on skills commensurate with cognitive level may prevent some individuals from progressing to a point where they are provided the opportunity to learn age-appropriate skills, thus curtailing their access to and use of the community (Wilcox, 1987).

Instructional context: Instructional context refers to the conditions under which a skill is learned (e.g., setting, activity, type of instruction). In order for instruction to be effective, the individual must perceive what they are learning and the way in which they are learning it to be meaningful. The information or skill learned must serve a purpose (Browder et al., 1997; Dymond, 2004). What is meaningful to one individual may not be meaningful to another. Instruction may adversely affect motivation to participate or learn when the intervention focuses only on an individual's deficits and does not consider the skills he/she is most interested in learning. For example, if skills are practiced only under simulated conditions and never practiced or tested in the community, an individual may lose interest in the activity or fail to understand its relevance to his/her life.

ISSUES WITH SPECIAL POPULATIONS

There are some in the field who would argue that individuals must achieve certain prerequisite skills before they are *ready* to participate in the community (Wilcox, 1987; Dymond, 2004). This line of thinking is often present when discussing individuals with challenging behaviors. Those subscribing to this view believe that individuals with challenging behaviors need to learn how to behave appropriately at home or at school prior to using the community. They may also believe that access to the community should be contingent on good behavior.

The problem with making community access dependent on the presence of appropriate behavior is twofold. First, some individuals may spend their entire lives *getting ready* without ever having opportunities to participate in the setting for which they are preparing. Second, evidence exists that challenging behaviors are often connected to environmental contexts, thus behaviors displayed at school or home may not be as prevalent in natural community settings when individuals are engaged in preferred activities and are taught appropriate behavior for the setting (Carr & Carlson, 1993; Inge & Dymond, 1994; Alberto et al., 2002). Spending more time in the community may improve overall quality of life and actually eliminate or diminish some challenging behaviors.

Another group of individuals for whom instruction on community skills is often questioned are those with severe multiple disabilities. Because these individuals often require extensive support in all aspects of their lives, complete independence is rarely a reasonable goal. Yet to suggest that they cannot benefit from instruction in community settings is also a fallacy. The primary goal of instruction is independence. An equally valuable and worthy goal is partial participation (Baumgart et al., 1982; Ferguson & Baumgart, 1991). With partial participation, an individual learns to complete a portion of the task independently and receives assistance from another person to complete the remainder of the task. For example, when cleaning up after lunch at a fast food restaurant, the individual may place all of his/her materials on the lunch tray and another person may carry the tray to the trash can and empty it. Partial participation increases self-esteem and control over one's environment.

SPECIAL CONSIDERATIONS FOR CHILDREN

Emphasis within the last decade on inclusive education and participation in the general curriculum has had an impact on the extent to which community skills are addressed at school by students with disabilities. IDEA (2004) requires almost all students will participate in the general curriculum and in statewide assessments. It also acknowledges that special education services should enable students to pursue other types of curriculum that meet their individual needs. Many in the field define the general curriculum as an academic curriculum that is aligned with a state's learning standards (Browder et al., 2006; Nolet & McLaughlin, 2005) although some have suggested that the general curriculum needs to be expanded to include attention to both academic and life skills (Dymond et al., 2007; Turnbull et al., 2003; Wehmeyer et al., 2003). As schools strive to help students with disabilities access the general curriculum and participate in high stakes testing, there is concern that attention to important life skills, such as community skills, may receive diminished attention.

A second factor that affects the extent to which school-age students address community skills is the emphasis placed on inclusive education. In recent years, leaders in special education have debated the appropriateness of removing students with disabilities from school settings to provide instruction in the community. Those who oppose instruction outside the school setting believe that the community is not an age-appropriate setting for instruction because peers without disabilities do not access that setting during school hours (Tashie et al., 1996; Schuh et al., 1998; Fisher & Sax, 1999). They feel that instruction in community settings should occur after school or on weekends when peers are likely to access those same settings.

Those who support instruction in community settings believe that instruction in the community can occur alongside peers without disabilities during the school day. This form of instruction is needed to teach priority skills that cannot be simulated easily or realistically in a school setting. It is also beneficial for students who do not learn well under simulated conditions (i.e., they have difficulty generalizing what they learn in one setting to other settings) (McDonnell, 1997; Agran et al., 1999; Dymond & Orelove, 2001; Dymond, 2004).

Clearly the needs and priorities of students should dictate the type of curriculum they receive and where they receive it. Academics and community skills can be blended to simultaneously address both curriculum areas. Likewise, instruction in community settings can occur alongside peers without disabilities who may be pursuing different goals (Beck et al., 1994; Burcroff et al., 2003). Choices about the amount of emphasis placed on teaching community skills to school-age children should consider the overall importance of learning community skills in relation to the student's current goals and the potential impact not learning such skills may have for the student in the near future.

ADDITIONAL TECHNIQUES TO ASSESS COMMUNITY USE IN COMBINATION WITH THE ABAS-II

The ABAS-II measures a wide variety of adaptive skills related to community use. Additional forms of assessment, when used in combination with the ABAS-II, can assist with the selection and prioritization of skills for intervention. Gathering additional data is particularly important when an individual demonstrates limited abilities across the adaptive skill area (i.e., community use), performs some steps of a skill but not the entire skill (e.g., carries money to make purchases but does not understand how much money to give the cashier when making a purchase), or when it seems questionable as to whether a skill is appropriate for intervention (i.e., due to age of individual, family/individual preferences, need for skill in the individual's community). Areas to assess include the community, individual/parent preferences and priorities, and the individual's skills.

COMMUNITY

Skills selected for instruction from the ABAS-II should be tailored to the community in which the individual lives. Additional skills (not listed on the ABAS-II) may also be targeted to increase the individual's participation in the targeted environments. One method for assessing the types of skills needed to function in a particular community is to conduct an ecological inventory (Brown et al., 1979; Burcroff et al., 2003; Dymond, 2004). Conducting an ecological inventory begins with identifying the environments that exist within a community. An environment is any building or defined space within the community (e.g., grocery store, video arcade, subway station, football field). Developing a list of environments may help determine additional settings (beyond those currently accessed) in which the individual would like or need to participate in the near future. Environments identified as priorities can be further inventoried to determine the sub-environments, activities, and skills needed to participate in that setting.

With some items on the ABAS-II, it may be necessary to inventory an environment to determine more precisely how an individual will participate. For example, one community use adaptive skill identified in the ABAS-II is using the public library. In order to determine the skills needed in the library, an ecological inventory could be conducted. Sub-environments within the public library may include the book section, video section, computer area, reference desk, check-out area, reading area, and bathrooms. Activities within the sub-environment of the check-out area may include obtaining a library card, renewing a book, returning a DVD, checking out materials, picking up a book from inter-library loan, paying a fine for an overdue book, signing up for a book club, or reporting a problem with a damaged CD. Skills needed to check out materials (one activity in the check-out area sub-environment) may include locating the check-out desk, waiting in line, interacting with the library employee, using a library card, and exiting the check-out line. An ecological inventory, in this circumstance, could be used to identify the range of skills needed to use the library. Skills for instruction could be chosen based on the types of activities in which the individual would like to participate.

Other skills identified in the ABAS-II identify the actions an individual will perform but leave the context (i.e., environment) unspecified. In this case, an ecological inventory could be used to determine the environments within the community where the skill is needed. For example, one of the skills on the ABAS-II is "carries enough money to make small purchases". An ecological inventory could help determine the settings accessed by same-age peers and the types of items that might be purchased in each location. Decisions about where to teach the skill and what to purchase would be made based on the environments available within the community and the types of items the individual needed or wanted to purchase. The inventory also would identify additional skills to teach that would enhance participation in the setting. For example, the primary goal might be to purchase items, but instruction also could focus on locating items in the store, comparing prices of different brands, or using revolving doors safely.

The ABAS-II samples skills needed for community use. An ecological inventory allows additional information to be collected about the types of skills needed to function in a particular community. These skills extend beyond those identified on the ABAS-II and should be considered when decisions are made about instructional priorities. Conducting an ecological inventory helps ensure that the range of skills needed to function in a particular setting are considered and that the goal of instruction focuses on increased participation in community activities as opposed to acquisition of isolated skills.

INDIVIDUAL/PARENT PREFERENCES AND PRIORITIES

Decisions about the types of skills targeted for intervention from the ABAS-II should consider the preferences and priorities of the individual and his/her family. Information about preferences and priorities can be gathered by sharing the findings from the ecological inventory and ABAS-II with the individual and his/her family and then asking them to identify their priorities. For some individuals who are unable to clearly communicate their preferences, it may be necessary to assess preferences by sampling the community (Dymond, 2004). This method involves taking individuals to various settings in the community and observing their reactions to participating in the environment. Community sampling is typically employed when the goal is to identify new environments to access in the community and information about the individual's experience with or preference for the proposed settings is limited.

INDIVIDUAL'S SKILLS

Many ABAS-II items require an individual to perform multiple steps in order to demonstrate the ability to perform the skill. For example, finding and using a payphone involves the steps of locating a telephone (e.g., using a store directory, asking someone for directions, following verbal directions or a store map, orienting within a building) and using the telephone (e.g., knowing how much a call costs, identifying coins, inserting the correct amount of money in the tele-phone, knowing the number to call, dialing the number, having a conversation). For individuals who are deemed "not able" to perform skills on the ABAS-II, additional information should be gathered to determine the specific steps of the skill that the individual can perform independently and those that are not yet mastered. This type of assessment is frequently referred to as a discrepancy analysis (Brown et al., 1984; Udvari-Solner et al., 2004). To conduct a discre-pancy analysis, list the steps of the task in accordance with how a person without a disability typically performs the task. Allow the individual to perform the task without assistance in the setting where the task is normally performed. Note the steps that he/she can do independently and those that are not yet mastered. Information from the discrepancy analysis will help to determine which steps of the task should be targeted for intervention and adaptations needed to the task or materials.

INTERVENTION METHODS

Information gathered from the ABAS-II and other assessment methods (discussed in the previous section) can provide direction as to the types of skills that should be targeted for instruction and the community settings in which the skills are or will be needed. Development of an effective intervention should take into account the prioritization and selection of skills for instruction, location of instruction, type of instruction, generalization strategies, instructional prompting strategies, and methods for providing instruction alongside same-age peers.

PRIORITIZATION AND SELECTION OF SKILLS FOR INSTRUCTION

If community use has been identified as an area of weakness on the ABAS-II, it is likely that the individual experiences difficulty completing numerous activities

TABLE 5.2 Issues to consider when prioritizing and selecting community skills for instruction.

Matches priorities of the individual/family
Skill occurs within a preferred activity
Skill can be taught in a way that is meaningful to the individual
Skill is needed in current and future environments
Skill acquisition will increase participation and independence in the community
Frequent opportunities to practice, acquire, and maintain skill are available
Skill is chronologically age appropriate
Skill is part of the natural routines of the individual or family

within this adaptive skill area. One of the most critical tasks involved with developing an intervention is determining where to focus initial skill instruction. That is, given the wide array of skills that *could* be taught, what skills *should* be targeted initially for intervention?

One method is to select the skill items rated lowest on the ABAS-II and target those skills for instruction. Although this method might seem reasonable, it is not the best method for selecting skills for instruction. The ABAS-II provides a sample of skills representative of those needed for community use. It is not intended to provide a comprehensive list, nor does it reflect all skills needed in every community or by every individual. Decisions about the skills to target and the order in which they should be taught need to take into consideration data gathered from ecological inventories, inventories of parent/individual preferences, and observations of the individual's skills, as well as the wide array of issues discussed thus far in this chapter (see Table 5.2).

LOCATION OF INSTRUCTION

Instruction can be provided in a variety of settings, including the home, school, or community. Choice of location depends on the learning style of the individual and the type of skill to be learned. If an individual is able to apply what is learned in one setting to other settings, he/she may be able to acquire skills through instruction that occurs at home or school. The types of skills that lend themselves to instruction in these settings are ones that are needed in both community and non-community settings (e.g., using the restroom/bathroom), and/or can be simulated in ways that approximate the actual community (e.g., money usage).

Some individuals have difficulty applying skills outside the setting in which they have been taught or fail to acquire skills at all under simulated conditions. These individuals benefit from instruction in the actual setting where the skill is needed (i.e., the community). In addition, some skills are difficult to simulate realistically in non-community settings (e.g., crossing streets, using an elevator, riding the subway), thus making instruction in community settings the most appropriate location for instruction. Many individuals benefit from instruction that is provided across multiple settings (i.e., home, school, community).

TYPE OF INSTRUCTION

Skills important to community use are generally taught through simulations, community-referenced instruction, community-based instruction (CBI), or a combination of these techniques.

Simulations: Simulations occur in non-community settings (e.g., home, school) and seek to approximate the materials and conditions of the community environments in which the skills are typically needed. Some of the many skills that have been taught effectively through simulations include locating items in a grocery store (Mechling & Gast, 2003), using a cell phone (Tabor et al., 2002), purchasing (Xin et al., 2005), banking skills (Davies et al., 2003; Cihak et al., 2006), and laundry skills (Taylor et al., 2002).

Research on the use of simulations has found that they are most effective when the materials employed are the same or nearly the same as those used in the community (Westling & Floyd, 1990). In other words, the more *real* the materials and conditions under which the simulation takes place, the more likely individuals are to learn through this type of instruction. Many simulations discussed in the recent literature focus on the use of computer technology to teach skills (Davies et al., 2003; Mechling & Gast, 2003; Cihak et al., 2006), thus extending the types of materials typical of simulations in the past (e.g., mock grocery stores, flashcards, slides, cardboard replicas of laundry machines). As Westling and Floyd point out, many investigations involving simulations involve the development of complex materials, thus making it questionable whether it is easier and more efficient to provide instruction in the actual community setting.

Although simulations are frequently employed to teach community skills, care must be taken to ensure that skills learned under simulated conditions can also be performed in the actual community settings where the skill is needed. Skills should not be considered mastered until they can be performed under the natural conditions that exist in the community. For example, if an individual is able to pay to the next whole dollar when a teacher verbally communicates the cost for an item in the classroom, the skill should not be considered mastered until the individual demonstrates the ability to pay to the next whole dollar when purchasing items at various locations in the community.

Community-referenced instruction: Community-referenced instruction involves teaching skills in the home or school that have joint applicability in the community (Dymond, 2004). Using the restroom, running errands, or following directions to a nearby location are examples of skills important to community use. They are also important skills needed to function at home or at school. Whenever possible, instruction in non-community settings should seek to teach skills that reference those needed in the community. Teaching skills across settings increases the number of opportunities available to learn the skill and apply it across environments.

In some instances, skills that are deemed a priority for instruction in the community may not be naturally available in the home or school setting. It may be necessary to create new routines in these settings that make it necessary for the skill to be performed or increase the number of opportunities to use the skill. For example, mailing letters may be a skill that is typically performed at school by the secretary but a job could be created for a student to deposit the school's mail in the mailbox outside. Likewise a student who is learning to order food at a restaurant could order his/her lunch at school. An additional activity might include ordering lunch for the school nurse and delivering it to her office on days when she is caring for a sick child and cannot leave to obtain lunch.

Community-referenced skills can also refer to activities that include a portion of a skill or task that is needed in the community. Suppose an individual is learning to use a picture list to identify items to purchase at a store. The pictures prompt the individual to obtain a series of items that need to be purchased for use at home. This skill (using a picture list) could be used simultaneously at home for different tasks not related to shopping, thus making it a form of community-referenced instruction. For example, the individual could have a picture list that prompts her to select clothing to wear the next day (e.g., underpants, brassiere, blouse, slacks, hosiery, and shoes) or lists chores to complete at home (e.g., sweep, vacuum, take out garbage, replace plastic bag in garbage can). The skill of using a picture list remains the same across each of these activities, thus providing the individual with more opportunities to apply the skill across different contexts (i.e., shopping, selecting clothes, completing chores) and settings (i.e., store, home).

Community-based instruction: Instruction provided in the community is known as community-based instruction (CBI). The primary benefit of CBI is that it allows skills to be taught in the natural settings where they will be used. Factors within the environment (e.g., different cashiers, items moved from traditional location, length of time spent waiting in line, outdoor weather) are not always easily replicated in simulated conditions. These factors have the potential to influence skill acquisition and performance in the setting. By teaching in the community, these factors become part of the natural context under which the skill is learned. Additional benefits of CBI are that it allows the individual to actively participate in community settings as they learn new skills and engage in activities that serve a purpose. Despite the many benefits of CBI, some of the reasons why the community is not selected as the setting for instruction are due to barriers related to staffing, transportation, expenses, and liability (Dymond, 2004). Table 5.3 provides a variety of methods for overcoming these barriers.

CBI typically occurs in the community settings frequented by the individual and his/her family. If instruction must occur in settings other than those normally used by the individual, skills learned in those settings should not be considered mastered until they can be performed in the settings typically used by the individual and his/her family. Just because the individual is able to perform a new

TABLE 5.3 Steps for addressing barriers to CBI*.

Barrier	Steps for addressing barrier
Transportation	Walk to community sites Use school buses Use school cars and driver education vehicles Use private vehicles Use public transportation (e.g., buses, trains) Share transportation with other agencies (e.g., The Arc, vans used by the parks and recreation center or YMCA)
Staffing	Change the job of teaching assistants to include CBI Have therapists provide therapy in the context of CBI Recruit volunteers, college students, and peer tutors Share roles with general education teachers
Liability	Include community skills on the individual's IEP or IHP Develop procedures and policies for CBI Train staff in CPR, basic first aid, and how to handle other types of emergencies Make sure each individual is covered by health insurance Obtain written parent permission for each individual's participation Ensure the school/organization's insurance will cover staff and students/clients engaged in CBI
Expenses	Use a portion of the classroom budget to fund CBI Purchase items needed by the individual or his/her residence Identify individuals in the community for whom the individual can purchase items (e.g., senior citizens, home-bound individuals) Conduct fund raisers

*Steps for overcoming barriers are from Dymond (2004).

skill in one setting (e.g., check out books at the public library near school) does not mean that he/she will be equally competent when using a similar facility used by the family (i.e., a different library in the individual's neighborhood).

Instruction in community settings should be provided individually or in groups of 2–3 (Dymond, 2004). This allows the instructor to provide effective instruction to each individual. It also reduces attention to the group and allows them to blend in with others who are also using the community. In some instances, limited transportation may require that all individuals from a group home or special education class travel together to the community. One method for addressing this problem is to divide into smaller groups and have each group participate in a different location of the community.

The frequency and duration of instruction in community settings depend on the needs of the individual. CBI is not a one-shot trip into the community or a monthly outing. In order for individuals to benefit from this form of instruction, access to the community must occur on a regularly scheduled basis where specific skills are targeted and repeatedly taught. It is often more helpful to provide multiple trips of short duration to the community across a week than it is to provide one long trip once a week, simply because it provides the individual with more opportunities to learn and practice the skill.

GENERALIZATION STRATEGIES

Generalization refers to the ability to apply a skill learned in one setting to other settings where the skill is needed. Many individuals are able to learn skills at school or home and immediately apply them in the community. This is often not the case for individuals with cognitive disabilities. In their review of empirical research on successful strategies for promoting generalization in community settings, Westling and Floyd (1990) identified support for several strategies briefly described below. These strategies continue to be demonstrated as effective:

- The most complex method for promoting generalization is general case programming (Horner et al., 1982). By incorporating the range of instructional variables present in the community into the instructional routine, the individual learns to perform the skill across a variety of contexts. This method can be used to enhance simulations, community-referenced instruction, and CBI (Frederick-Dugan et al., 1991; Gumpel & Nativ-Ari-Am, 2001; Taylor et al., 2002).
- Generalization is more likely when simulations are used in combination with instruction in the community and not used as the sole method of instruction. Methods for combining these forms of instruction include alternating simulations with CBI and using concurrent scheduling (i.e., teaching through simulation just prior to providing CBI) (Branham et al., 1999; Morse & Schuster, 2000; Xin et al., 2005; Cihak et al., 2006).
- When using CBI, generalization is more likely when skills are taught across multiple community settings (Haring et al., 1995; Branham et al., 1999; Gumpel & Nativ-Ari-Am, 2001). In some cases, instruction in only one community setting may be effective if general case programming is used (Horner et al., 1982).
- Sequential modification is effective when the range of environments needed for generalization is known. With this method, instruction occurs in one community environment until the skill is mastered. Once mastered, the skill is tested in other settings where it is needed. Additional instruction is provided in each subsequent setting until the skill is mastered.

INSTRUCTIONAL PROMPTING STRATEGIES

Community skills typically are taught through the use of systematic instructional procedures. For skills that involve multiple steps (e.g., using a cell phone) a task analysis is developed that lists each step of the task to be performed. The prompts (e.g., verbal, modeling, picture, gesture, physical) provided to teach each step and the sequence in which they are provided depend on the individual and how he/she learns best. Most prompting strategies involve pre-determined methods for preventing and correcting errors as well as fading dependence on prompts. Some of the types of prompting strategies found to be effective in teaching community skills include constant time delay, progressive time delay, and least to most prompts (for descriptions of these strategies see Frederick-Dugan et al., 1991; Morse & Schuster, 2000; Taylor et al., 2002).

The strategies employed to teach skills in community settings should not call undue attention to the individual or involve methods that are perceived negatively by others (Browder et al., 1997; Alberto et al., 2002). Wolfe (1994) found that the types of instructional strategies perceived to be least appropriate included the use of food, exclusionary time-out, overcorrection, and repeated practice. Care should be taken to select strategies that respect the dignity of the individual and promote participation in the community.

METHODS FOR PROVIDING INSTRUCTION ALONGSIDE SAME-AGE PEERS

One of the concerns about CBI mentioned previously is that individuals of school age who participate in CBI during school hours do not have access to same-age peers while they are in the community. There are several strategies that have been used successfully to engage students with and without disabilities in CBI. Three strategies include using community-referenced instruction in school settings, including peers in CBI, and developing volunteer work or service learning projects (Dymond, 2004). With community-referenced instruction, students with and without disabilities can engage in school-based projects that reference the community. For example, students could work together to operate a school store or run a school post office for internal mail. With CBI, students without disabilities apply skills learned in class while out in the community. The student with a disability works simultaneously on a related goal in the same setting (Beck et al., 1994; Burcroff et al., 2003). Finally, service learning provides an opportunity for students with and without disabilities to complete a service project that meets a community need and augments academic learning (Dymond et al., 2008; Gent & Gurecka, 1998).

CASE STUDY: BRIAN

Brian is 16 years old and a sophomore at Whitely High School. He has severe cognitive disabilities and mild cerebral palsy that affects his left side. He walks independently and relies on his right hand to complete most fine motor tasks. Brian's greatest strength is his social skills. He initiates greetings and interactions, and responds eagerly to interactions from others. He talks in two to three word phrases to make requests, comment, and ask questions. At times he also uses gestures and pictures to augment his speech. Because of his strong social skills, he appears to understand much more than he actually comprehends. Some of Brian's preferred activities include helping his father with his construction business (e.g., handing his father tools, holding a board while his father cuts it with a saw), running errands to the school office, hanging out with others (i.e., being part of the group), watching TV, and going out for pizza or hamburgers.

Brian spends half of his school day learning life skills and functional academic skills in a self-contained class for students with severe multiple disabilities. He attends lunch with his peers and also participates in a general education building trades class and an automotive maintenance class. He has an in-school job this year that involves sampling various types of jobs with the custodian (e.g., sweeping, putting up chairs in the cafeteria, polishing the floor). Once a week he travels with his class to eat at a nearby restaurant where he is learning to order a meal. Since Brian's academic skills have not progressed and he is preparing to transition into adulthood, the emphasis of his curriculum has become increasingly focused on life skills. Academic skills are addressed within the context of life skills activities.

PURPOSE AND RESULTS OF THE ABAS-II

In preparation for Brian's Individual Education Program and transition plan meeting, the ABAS-II was used to obtain information on Brian's adaptive behavior and skills. The ABAS-II was completed by Brian's special education teacher, teaching assistant, and father. These individuals were selected because they were the most knowledgeable about Brian's skills.

The ABAS-II General Adaptive Composite (GAC) standard scores across respondents (i.e., special education teacher, teaching assistant, father) ranged from 40 to 42 (see Table 5.4). Compared to other individuals of the same age, Brian is functioning in the ≤1st percentile. His overall adaptive behavior is considered to be extremely low.

Scores across the composites were fairly consistent across respondents. The greatest range in scores was evident in the practical composites. Because the scaled scores for each of the four adaptive skill areas that make up this composite were the same across respondents, it is unlikely that substantial differences exist in Brian's skills within this composite. In fact, respondents' scaled scores across all 10 adaptive skill areas were uniform except for the area of social skills. The social adaptive skill area scaled score from Brian's father was higher than those from the special education teacher and teaching assistant; the social adaptive skill area scaled score was the highest adaptive skill area scaled score across all respondents and clearly indicates that social skills are Brian's greatest strength.

RESULTS OF ADDITIONAL ASSESSMENT DATA

Because participation in the community is an important skill Brian will need in adulthood and results of the ABAS-II signified serious deficits in the community

TABLE 5.4 Results of the ABAS-II for Brian, age 16 years.

	Teacher form ages 5–21[1]			Teacher form ages 5–21[2]			Parent form ages 5–21[3]		
	Adaptive skill area scaled score	Composite standard score	Composite percentile rank	Adaptive skill area scaled score	Composite standard score	Composite percentile rank	Adaptive skill Area scaled score	Composite standard score	Composite percentile rank
Conceptual		50	<0.1		45	<0.1		49	<0.1
• Communication	1			1			1		
• Functional academics	1			1			1		
• Self-direction	1			1			1		
Social		61	0.5		61	0.5		66	1
• Leisure	1			1			1		
• Social	3			3			5		
Practical		45	<0.1		50	<0.1		40	<0.1
• Community use	1			1			1		
• Home living	–			–			1		
• School living	1			1			–		
• Health and safety	1			1			1		
• Self-care	1			1			1		
General Adaptive Composite		42	<0.1		42	<0.1		40	<0.1

[1]Completed by the special education teacher
[2]Completed by the teaching assistant
[3]Completed by Brian's father

Note: Adaptive skill area scaled scores have a mean (average) of 10 and a standard deviation of 3. Composite standard scores have a mean (average) of 100 and a standard deviation of 15.

use adaptive skill area, it was determined that community skills should receive increased attention in the coming year. In order to determine where to focus instruction, the Individualized Education Program (IEP) team decided to collect additional information by talking with Brian and his parents about the types of skills that were most important to learn. When asked where he liked to go in the community Brian said "pizza", "tools" (i.e., home improvement stores where he shops for tools with his father), "store", and "church". Brian's parents indicated that the family likes to eat out in a casual restaurant once a week and attends church weekly. Brian often accompanies his parents on errands to various stores (e.g., grocery store, home improvement store, post office, drug store). When asked what their priorities were for instruction, Brian's parents expressed concern for his safety in the community. In particular, they indicated that he is often oblivious to traffic in parking lots and would not know what to do if he became lost while shopping with his parents. They thought Brian would enjoy being more involved in each of the community settings they frequent (e.g., helping to locate items to purchase, pushing a cart, ordering meals at a restaurant).

As a result of this information, the IEP team decided to inventory three of the settings used by the family on a weekly basis to determine how they could increase Brian's participation in those settings. These settings included the grocery store, the drug store, and the home improvement store. Information was gathered about the types of activities and skills that were needed across all three settings. Since school staff were unfamiliar with Brian's skills in these settings, they took Brian into each setting and observed his participation and interest in various activities.

PRIORITIZATION OF SKILLS FOR INSTRUCTION

Findings from the inventory and observations of Brian were shared with Brian and his family to determine which skills should be targeted for instruction. Skills chosen included walking safely in the parking lot, using a cell phone to communicate when lost in a store, using a picture list to obtain items, and carrying a basket/pushing a cart. These skills were chosen because they were needed across multiple settings now and in the future, they were priorities of the family, they involved activities preferred by Brian, and they could be addressed at least twice a week by both parents and school staff.

RECOMMENDATIONS FOR INTERVENTION

Since Brian is 16 years old, it is important that his curriculum is designed to prepare him to function as independently as possible in adulthood. Community skills must receive increased attention. Instruction might initially focus on crossing the parking lot safely and using a cell phone to communicate when lost. If too many skills are targeted for instruction at once, it will be difficult to provide instruction of sufficient quality to lead to skill acquisition. Once these two skills are mastered, instruction could begin on the other two skills and data could be taken once a week to make sure that Brian continues to maintain the two skills previously learned.

High school is a time when all students begin to make choices that will prepare them for adulthood. Some leave school early to obtain a job while others take additional advanced placement classes in preparation for college. As such, it is natural for someone like Brian to leave school for a portion of the day to receive instruction in community settings. CBI should be provided individually or with 1–2 other students at least 2–3 times a week and supplemented with community-referenced instruction. Since Brian experiences difficulty learning under simulated conditions it is not recommended that simulations be used to teach these skills.

Community-referenced instruction can be used to teach all four skills at school. Examples are provided below:

- *Carrying a basket/pushing a cart*: To perform in-school jobs, Brian could push a cart to carry soda to refill the soda machines, carry a basket to the office to deliver mail, or use a basket in the home economics room to carry laundry to the laundry machines for washing.
- *Using pictures to locate items*: Pictures could be used across the school day to provide prompts for Brian to locate items needed to complete his work. In his building trades and automobile maintenance classes he could use pictures to obtain the tools needed for the day, and in his self-contained classroom he could have a picture list indicating materials needed to complete classroom tasks.
- *Crossing the parking lot*: Brian could naturally address this objective when exiting the bus in the morning and locating the bus in the afternoon.
- *Cell phone*: Instruction on using a cell phone when lost or not in the presence of an adult could be taught at school in the same way it is taught in the community.

Prior to beginning instruction, information should be gathered from the literature about effective ways to teach the targeted skills. For example, Tabor et al. (2002) have developed an effective method for teaching cell phone usage that might be appropriate for Brian.

Past instruction with Brian has used a constant time delay procedure (for a description, see Morse & Schuster, 2000). In addition, instruction has focused on teaching the whole task at once. This method (i.e., constant time delay and teaching the whole task) should be employed to teach the targeted skills. Information about this method should be shared with the parents since they have indicated a willingness to provide additional instruction twice a week to Brian when they are running errands in the community. Demonstrating the technique for the parents and providing feedback on their implementation of the technique in the community will ensure that Brian is receiving consistent instruction from everyone.

Finally, consideration should be given to involving peers in instruction that occurs in non-general education classrooms and in the community. In school, jobs could be performed with a peer if Brian were to serve as an office aide or sign up to assist a particular teacher with other students during a free period. In the community, the teachers of the building trades and automobile maintenance classes may want to arrange for small groups of students to go to the home improvement store each week to obtain supplies or check out the equipment available. Although the goals of these students may be different than those for Brian, they could still travel together and engage in similar activities. There may also be a service club at school that shops for home-bound senior citizens or performs other service tasks that require usage of stores. It may be possible for Brian's instruction to occur in conjunction with peers who are engaged in these activities.

REFERENCES

Agran, M., Snow, K., & Swaner, J. (1999). A survey of secondary level teachers' opinions on community-based instruction and inclusive education. *Journal of the Association for Persons with Severe Handicaps, 24*, 58–62.

Alberto, P., Heflin, L. J., & Andrews, D. (2002). Use of the timeout ribbon procedure during community-based instruction. *Behavior Modification, 26*, 297–311.

Americans with Disabilities Act (ADA) (1990). PL 101-336, 42 U.S.C. §12101 *et seq.*

Baumgart, D., Brown, L., Pumpian, I., Nisbet, J., Ford, A., Sweet, M., et al. (1982). Principle of partial participation and individualized adaptations in educational programs for severely handicapped students. *Journal of the Association for the Severely Handicapped, 7*, 17–27.

Beck, J., Broers, J., Hogue, E., Shipstead, J., & Knowlton, E. (1994). Strategies for functional community-based instruction and inclusion for children with mental retardation. *Teaching Exceptional Children, 26*(2), 44–48.

Branham, R. S., Collins, B. C., Schuster, J. W., & Kleinert, H. (1999). Teaching community skills to students with moderate disabilities: Comparing combined techniques of classroom simulation, videotape modeling, and community-based instruction. *Education and Training in Mental Retardation and Developmental Disabilities, 34*, 170–181.

Browder, D. M., Bambara, L. M., & Belfiore, P. J. (1997). Using a person-centered approach in community-based instruction for adults with developmental disabilities. *Journal of Behavioral Education, 7*, 519–528.

Browder, D. M., Spooner, F., Wakeman, S., Trela, K., & Baker, J. N. (2006). Aligning instruction with academic content standards: Finding the link. *Research and Practice for Persons with Severe Disabilities, 31*, 309–321.

Brown, L., Branston, M. B., Hamre-Nietupski, S., Pumpian, I., Certo, N., & Gruenewald, L. (1979). A strategy for developing chronological age appropriate and functional curricular content for severely handicapped adolescents and young adults. *Journal of Special Education, 13*(1), 81–90.

Brown, L., Shiraga, B., York, J., Zanella, K., & Rogan, P. (1984). The discrepancy analysis technique in programs for students with severe handicaps. In L. Brown, M. Sweet, B. Shiraga, J. York, K. Zanella, P. Rogan, & R. Loomis (Eds.), *Educational Programs for Students with Severe Handicaps*, Vol. XIV, pp. 43–47. Madison, WI: Madison Metropolitan School District.

Burcroff, T. L., Radogna, D. M., & Wright, E. H. (2003). Community forays: Addressing students' functional skills in inclusive settings. *Teaching Exceptional Children, 35*(5), 52–57.

Carr, E. G. & Carlson, J. I. (1993). Reduction of severe behavior problems in the community using a multicomponent treatment approach. *Journal of Applied Behavior Analysis, 26*, 157–172.

Cihak, D., Alberto, P. A., Taber-Doughty, T., & Gama, R. I. (2006). A comparison of static picture prompting and video prompting simulation using group instructional procedures. *Focus on Autism and Other Developmental Disabilities*, *21*, 89–99.

Davies, D. K., Stock, S. E., & Wehmeyer, M. L. (2003). Utilization of computer technology to facilitate money management by individuals with mental retardation. *Education and Training in Developmental Disabilities*, *38*, 106–112.

Dymond, S. K. (2004). Community participation. In P. Wehman & J. Kregel (Eds.), *Functional Curriculum for Elementary, Middle, and Secondary Age Students with Special Needs*, 2nd edn., pp. 259–291. Austin: Pro-ed.

Dymond, S. K. & Orelove, F. P. (2001). What constitutes effective curricula for students with severe disabilities? *Exceptionality*, *9*, 109–122.

Dymond, S. K., Renzaglia, A., & Chun, E. J. (2008). Inclusive high school service learning programs: Methods for and barriers to including students with disabilities. *Education and Training in Developmental Disabilities*, *43*, 20–36.

Dymond, S. K., Renzaglia, A., Gilson, C. L., & Slagor, M. T. (2007). Defining access to the general curriculum for high school students with significant cognitive disabilities. *Research and Practice for Persons with Severe Disabilities*, *32*, 1–15.

Egan, K. (2003). Testing what for what? *Educational Leadership*, *61*(3), 27–30.

Falvey, M. A. (1989). *Community-based Curriculum: Instructional Strategies for Students with Severe Handicaps*, 2nd edn. Baltimore: Paul H. Brookes.

Ferguson, D. & Baumgart, D. (1991). Partial participation revisited. *Journal of the Association for Persons with Severe Handicaps*, *16*, 218–227.

Fisher, D. & Sax, C. (1999). Noticing differences between secondary and postsecondary education: Extending Agran, Snow, and Swaner's discussion. *Journal of the Association for Persons with Severe Handicaps*, *24*, 303–305.

Ford, A., Schnorr, R., Meyer, L., Davern, L., Black, J., & Dempsey, P. (Eds.). (1989). *The Syracuse Community-Referenced Curriculum Guide for Students with Moderate and Severe Disabilities.* Baltimore: Paul H. Brookes.

Frederick-Dugan, A., Test, D. W., & Varn, L. (1991). Acquisition and generalization of purchasing skills using a calculator by students who are mentally retarded. *Education and Training in Mental Retardation*, *26*, 381–387.

Gent, P. J. & Gurecka, L. E. (1998). Service learning: A creative strategy for inclusive classrooms. *Journal of the Association for Persons with Severe Handicaps*, *23*, 261–271.

Gumpel, T. P. & Nativ-Ari-Am, H. (2001). Evaluation of a technology for teaching complex social skills to young adults with visual and cognitive impairments. *Journal of Visual Impairment and Blindness*, *95*, 95–107.

Haring, T. G., Breen, C. G., Weiner, J., Kennedy, C. H., & Bednersh, F. (1995). Using videotape modeling to facilitate generalized purchasing skills. *Journal of Behavioral Education*, *5*, 29–53.

Horner, R. H., Sprague, J., & Wilcox, B. (1982). General case programming for community activities. In B. Wilcox & T. Bellamy (Eds.), *Design of High School Programs for Severely Handicapped Students*, pp. 61–98. Baltimore: Paul H. Brookes.

Hughes, W., Wood, W. M., Konrad, M., & Test, D. W. (2006). Get a life: Students practice being self-determined. *Teaching Exceptional Children*, *38*(5), 57–63.

Individuals with Disabilities Education Improvement Act (IDEA) Amendments (2004). P.L. 108-446, 118 Stat 2647.

Inge, K. J. & Dymond, S. (1994). Challenging behaviors in the workplace: Increasing a student's access to community-based vocational instruction. *Journal of Vocational Rehabilitation*, *4*, 272–284.

McDonnell, J. (1997). Isn't it about achieving a balance? *TASH Newsletter*, *23*(2), 23–24, 29.

Mechling, L. C. & Gast, D. L. (2003). Multi-media instruction to teach grocery word associations and store location: A study of generalization. *Education and Training in Developmental Disabilities*, *38*, 62–76.

Morse, T. E. & Schuster, J. W. (2000). Teaching elementary students with moderate intellectual disabilities how to shop for groceries. *Exceptional Children, 66*, 273–288.

Nolet, V. & McLaughlin, M. J. (2005). *Accessing the General Curriculum: Including Students with Disabilities in Standards-Based Reform*, 2nd edn. Thousand Oaks, CA: Corwin.

Renzaglia, A. & Aveno, A. (1986). *Manual for the Administration of an Individualized, Functional Curriculum Assessment Procedure*. Charlottesville, VA: University of Virginia.

Sands, D. J., Kozleski, E. B., & French, N.K. (2000). *Inclusive Education for the 21st Century*. Stamford, CT: Wadsworth.

Schuh, M. C., Tashie, C., Lamb, P., Bang, M., & Jorgensen, C. M. (1998). Community-based learning for all students. In C. M. Jorgensen (Ed.), *Restructuring High Schools for all Students: Taking Inclusion to the Next Level*, pp. 209–231. Baltimore: Paul H. Brookes.

Tabor, T. A., Alberto, P. A., Hughes, M., & Seltzer, A. (2002). A strategy for students with moderate disabilities when lost in the community. *Research and Practice for Persons with Severe Disabilities, 27*, 141–152.

Tashie, C., Jorgensen, C., Shapiro-Barnard, S., Martin, J., & Schuh, M. (1996). High school inclusion strategies and barriers. *TASH Newsletter, 22*(9), 19–22.

Taylor, P., Collins, B. C., Schuster, J. W., & Kleinert, H. (2002). Teaching laundry skills to high school students with disabilities: Generalization of targeted skills and nontargeted information. *Education and Training in Mental Retardation and Developmental Disabilities, 37*, 172–183.

Turnbull, H. R., Turnbull, A. P., Wehmeyer, M. L., & Park, J. (2003). A quality of life framework for special education outcomes. *Remedial and Special Education, 24*, 67–74.

Udvari-Solner, A., Causton-Theoharis, J., & York-Barr, J. (2004). Developing adaptations to promote participation in inclusive environments. In F. Orelove, D. Sobsey, & R. K. Silberman (Eds.), *Educating Children with Multiple Disabilities: A Collaborative Approach*, 4th edn. (pp. 151–192). Baltimore: Paul H. Brookes.

Wehmeyer, M. L., Lattin, D. L., Lapp-Rincker, G., & Agran, M. (2003). Access to the general curriculum of middle school students with mental retardation: An observational study. *Remedial and Special Education, 24*, 262–272.

Westling, D. & Floyd, J. (1990). Generalization of community skills: How much training is necessary? *The Journal of Special Education, 23*, 386–406.

Wilcox, B. (1987). Why a new curriculum? In B. Wilcox & G.T. Bellamy (Eds.), *A Comprehensive Guide to the Activities Catalogue: An Alternative Curriculum for Youth and Adults with Severe Disabilities*, pp. 1–10. Baltimore: Paul H. Brookes.

Wolfe, P. S. (1994). Judgment of the social validity of instructional strategies used in community-based instructional sites. *Journal of the Association for Persons with Severe Handicaps, 19*, 43–51.

Xin, Y. P., Grasso, E., Dipipi-Hoy, C. M., & Jitendra, A. (2005). The effects of purchasing skill instruction for individuals with developmental disabilities: A meta-analysis. *Exceptional Children, 71*, 379–400.

6

Functional Academic Adaptive Skills

MELISSA A. MILLER[*] AND NICOLE FENTY[**]

[*]*University of North Carolina at Chapel Hill, NC 27599-3500, U.S.A.*
[**]*Department of Teaching and Learning, University of Louisville, Louisville, KY 40292, U.S.A.*

INTRODUCTION

The ability to display basic academic skills, including the ability to read, write, and perform math, is needed to for adaptive functioning in society – at home, in school, at work, and in the community. This need has been present for more than a century. However, given our technologically advancing society, the need for these skills has increased and at higher standards (Browder, 2001). Some students acquire these skills more slowly than others, and a few lack the cognitive ability to successfully master them. Persons who are delayed in acquiring functional academic adaptive skills may require special services, including how they are taught and what content is taught (Clark, 1994). Thus, assessment of functional academic adaptive skills typically is included as part of a comprehensive assessment of adaptive behavior. This chapter provides guidelines for instruction and interventions for functional academic adaptive skills and methods for assessing these skills, including the Adaptive Behavior Assessment System-II (ABAS-II).

The need for a functional academics curriculum that enables individuals with disabilities or other types of learning and behavioral difficulties to succeed in society is apparent. The term *function* implies fulfilling a purpose or having usefulness to something or someone. Thus, functional academics are adaptive skills developed sufficiently to allow persons ages 5 and older to be successful in daily activities in and outside the school environment, to increase their independence, and to promote their ability to succeed in a less restrictive environment (Slaton et al., 1994).

A functional academic program utilizes instruction that results in the acquisition of reading, writing, and math adaptive skills at least at a basic level that enables a person to perform daily routines, including reading signs, making change, writing one's name and, at older ages, writing checks and completing job applications. Academic skills, to be functional and adaptive, must be relevant to an individual's lifestyle needs – including their specific responsibilities and expectations from those with who they interact. Thus, functional academic adaptive skills may display a degree of uniqueness. What is functional for one individual may not be functional for others. In addition, the focus of instruction should consider what is needed now and in the foreseeable future. Thus, functional academics adaptive skills include those that are pre-requisite to acquiring functional skills (e.g., functional pre-academics skills) together with enduring functional skills based on an individual's lifestyle needs, environmental expectations, age, current level of skill acquisition, and future needs.

MEASUREMENT OF FUNCTIONAL ACADEMIC ADAPTIVE SKILLS USING THE ABAS-II

The ABAS-II provides an assessment of the degree to which individuals independently displays adaptive skills in everyday living for ages 0–89. The ABAS-II consists of 10 adaptive skill areas, including the functional pre-academic adaptive skill area for young children and the functional academic adaptive skill area for school age children and adults. For ages 0–5, one of the ABAS-II adaptive skill areas is functional pre-academics adaptive skills, including pre-reading, basic math concepts, and pre-writing skills. For ages 5–89, one of the ABAS-II adaptive skill areas is functional academics adaptive skills, including basic reading, writing, and math needed for daily, independent functioning.

The ABAS-II includes an adaptive skill area of functional pre-academic skills on the Parent/Primary Caregiver Form for children ages 1–5 and on the Teacher/Daycare Provider from for children ages 2–5. Children below age five typically are unable to read, do math, or write. Thus, an assessment of their functional pre-academic adaptive skills requires attention to qualities that provide a foundation for later-developing skills. The functional pre-academic adaptive skills measured by the ABAS-II include foundational skills necessary for the later acquisition of functional reading, mathematics, and writing adaptive skills. The acquisition of these skills increases young children's personal independence and provides the building blocks for learning sight words, basic mathematics computations, and functional writing. Pre-reading skills, as measured by the ABAS-II functional pre-academics adaptive skill area, are those skills that younger individuals need prior to reading instruction. Examples include pointing to pictures in books, singing the alphabet song, recognizing one's name in print, and reading common signs. Examples of pre-math skills include stating one's age, counting, sorting, and stating the time and day of one's favorite TV shows. Examples of pre-writing skills include holding a crayon, drawing recognizable pictures, writing numbers, and printing first and last names.

The ABAS-II Parent Form (ages 5–21), Teacher Form (ages 5–21) and Adult Form (ages 16–89) include an adaptive skill area of functional academic skills. Functional academic adaptive skills are those needed by children, youth, and adults to successfully navigate through their daily responsibilities and experiences. Examples of functional reading adaptive skills, as measured by the ABAS-II, include reading his or her name, reading menus, using a dictionary, and reading important documents. Examples of functional math skills include measuring length and height, using scales to weigh items, and using money (Browder, 2001). Examples of functional writing skills include writing his or her name, writing letters or e-mails, taking notes, and completing application forms. These skills are important during an individual's daily routine.

IMPORTANCE OF FUNCTIONAL ACADEMICS

IMPLICATIONS FOR GENERAL FUNCTIONING

Virtually all segments of U.S. society recognize the importance of teaching academic skills to students with and without disabilities. Responsibility for education typically starts at home. Although parents and other family members must remain engaged in the education process, educators commonly assume primary responsibility when children are in preschool or kindergarten. Public education has had a long-standing commitment to educate all children regardless of their abilities and disabilities. Thus, as the numbers of students with special needs, some at severe levels, increase, educators often face challenges when educating them. Efforts initially focus on developing basic educational skills that are age-appropriate and enable persons to engage successfully in daily life activities (Valletutti et al., 1996).

Ryndak and Alper (1996) suggested three advantages for adopting a functional-skills approach for students with severe disabilities. First, students can obtain age-appropriate skills that increase school and community functioning that, when performed independently, raise the expectations that caregivers and teachers place on the individual. Second, the importance of teaching skills that are commonly performed by age peers is underscored, thereby increasing the individual's opportunities for inclusion and social interactions. Finally, skills are individualized based on student strengths and weaknesses, making it more likely for skills to be used in a variety of settings that are useful to the individual. Without comprehensive assessment of needed skills, development of a functional academics curriculum and instruction would be fruitless.

The development of functional academic adaptive skills requires attention to instructional methods, curricular planning, and comprehensive assessment. The selection and use of instructional methods and curriculum require knowledge of a student's needs and the degree to which current skills meet these needs. Without comprehensive assessment of skill need, however, functional skills instruction cannot take place. Thus, the first step in offering a viable academic program is to identify a student's academic needs in light of the student's immediate environment and those into which he or she may be transitioning (e.g., a higher grade, another school, an employment setting). Having determined his or her needs, the next steps are to assess the student's academic skills and identify the extent to which existing skills meet existing or forthcoming needs.

The term *functional* has become important in education. Education is expected to have practical applications and serve useful purposes. Thus, the functionality of both the instructional methods and curriculum should be considered when designing a functional education program (Browder, 2001). The importance of newly acquired skills can be determined by evaluating whether they are required by and foster independence within a person's home, school, or community (Gast & Schuster, 1993; Slaton et al., 1994). For example, assessment should determine whether a person seeking work as a cashier displays the ability to make change and count money as well as display needed socials skills. Instruction then is directed to areas of deficiency.

CONDITIONS THAT IMPACT DEVELOPMENT AND PERFORMANCE OF FUNCTIONAL ACADEMICS

Individuals with disabilities may display deficiencies in one or more skills pre-requisite to instruction. Students with severe disabilities may display fewer academic skills than 99% of their non-disabled peers (Brown et al., 1983). Thus, the selection of instructional method and content should be based on the needs of that individual. What is deemed functional for one person may be irrelevant for another (Clark, 1994). Additionally, the acquisition of functional academic skills increases their use, maintenance, and generalization (Slaton et al., 2001). The functional value of proposed academic skills acquisition should consider the following seven questions (Clark, 1994): The environments in which skills are first acquired and later applied should be highly similar. (a) Thus, is the instructional environment appropriate for meeting the student's social, daily living, and vocational training needs? (b) What are the positive and negative effects of providing instruction in a classroom? (c) Does the instructional content focus on knowledge and skills necessary for independent home, school, and community functioning? (d) Does the instructional content address a student's future academic, social, and vocational needs? (e) Do the parents/caregivers view the instructional content to be useful? (f) Does the recipient of the educational services (e.g., child, youth, or adult) view the instructional content to be useful? (g) To what extent does the instructional content reflect the recipient's age and abilities?

Academic instruction that has a functional impact considers four phases of learning (Wolery et al., 1988): skill acquisition (i.e., a new skill or behavior is learned), fluency (i.e., the skill is practiced to mastery), maintenance (i.e., the skill is performed in the absence of instruction), and generalization (i.e., the skill is used in various settings and circumstances). Functional skill acquisition increases when individuals personally see the value of their newly acquired skills in their daily lives (e.g., receive self-reinforcement) and receive reinforcement from others (Slaton et al., 2001).

As noted above, the environment in which functional academic skills are taught and acquired can have an impact. Skill acquisition, maintenance, and generalization often are most successful when the environments in which skills first are acquired and later applied are similar (Slaton et al., 2001). Classroom environments that are designed and equipped similarly to the natural setting may be used successfully to acquire and maintain needed skills (Gast & Schuster, 1993; Nietupski et al., 1986; Wolery et al., 1986). Classrooms may provide relevant instructional settings.

IMPACT ON AND ISSUES WITH SPECIAL POPULATIONS

The reauthorized Individuals with Disabilities Education Acts (IDEA) of 1997 and 2004 both support the education of students with mild and moderate levels of disabilities in more inclusive environments (Thomas & Rapport, 1998; Mastropieri & Scruggs, 2000). Despite efforts by general education teachers (Heller, 2001), many teachers express difficulty with creating ways to include students with severe disabilities within the general education setting. Given the difficulty that general education teachers experience in providing needed services on their own, they often collaborate with special education teachers to facilitate the academic and social success of students with severe disabilities (Jackson et al., 2000; Snell & Janney, 2000; Salisbury et al., 1997).

General education classrooms are becoming home to more students with severe disabilities, supported by evidence that their participation in the general education curriculum has long term benefits for them and their non-disabled peers (Katsiyannis et al., 1995; Kennedy et al., 1997; U.S. Department of Education, 2000). Efforts by educators to serve students with special needs in separate self-contained classrooms, even in inclusive settings, have had limited success because typical academic curriculum offered to students with severe disabilities does not foster the adaptive behavior, skill development, and independence required for daily living (Slaton et al., 2001). Students often need a more functional curriculum, one that emphasizes independent functioning and quality of life.

Although the education of students with moderate and severe disabilities poses challenges, the education of students with multiple or severe cognitive, motor, or sensory disabilities poses greater challenges. Attempts to identify successful interventions with these populations generally have not been successful (Browder & Cooper-Duffy, 2003). However, research does stress that, despite an individual's level of functioning, pre-requisite skills may not always be needed to learn new skills. Support for a partial-participation approach to skills instruction allows for individuals with disabilities to participate, doing those skills they can master so that they may have more choices and independence within their daily routines (Snell et al., 1989; Ferguson & Baumgart, 1991; Kennedy & Haring, 1993).

Consistent with prior comments about working with those with multiple or severe disabilities, the provision of functional academic instruction also presents additional challenges for educators and caregivers when working with students who display severe visual and hearing impairments (Miller & Thompson, 2005). The inclusion of students with severe visual and hearing impairments in general education requires additional individual assistance when promoting skills acquisition (Jorgenson-Smith & Lewis, 2004). Instructional models that emphasize community academic instruction and focus on acquiring pre-requisite skills needed for daily routines have been proposed (Cronin & Patton, 1993; Wehman, 1996). Students with visual impairments and multiple disabilities between age 12 and 20 were trained to assist in a lunch delivery business that provided local lunch delivery to businesses within a three-block radius (Miller & Thompson, 2005). Students developed skills related to communication, customer relations, taking and placing orders, math, and language arts/reading. Additionally, students' knowledge of science and nutrition increased as they learned more about healthy foods and the impact of weather on their deliveries.

POSSIBLE AGE AND GENDER ISSUES

Efforts to promote functional academic adaptive skills in individuals with disabilities should consider both their developmental and chronological ages (White, 1980; Browder, 1987; Giangreco et al., 1998). Although their developmental age is likely to be lower than their chronological age, is important that functional academics instruction focus on the chronological age of the student as much as feasible to foster independence within home, school, work, and community settings (Slaton et al., 2001). Chronological age is the most important aspect to focus on for functional academic instruction because the goal of instruction is to provide the student with opportunities to participate in activities that are age appropriate and are necessary for the student to interact in social situations with same-aged peers.

As noted previously, skill selection should identify those skills that are functional and needed. For example, although their developmental age may limit their acquiring higher-level reading and math skills, adolescent students beginning life skills training may benefit from acquiring basic functional skills in reading and mathematics (Browder, 2001). For example, sight words were taught to students even though they did not possess phonics or decoding skills, qualities normally thought to be pre-requisite to reading (Schoen & Ogden, 1995). Students with severe disabilities whose daily routines required reading signs, simple directions, and product labels were taught these skills using peer tutoring (Wolery et al., 1994). Peer tutoring involves peer helpers or tutors assisting in the learning process and helping each other learn by teaching (Goodlad & Hirst, 1990; Topping, 2001). Traditionally, peer tutoring has focused on academic instruction. Students who struggle in specific content areas are paired with a higher performing peer to supplement teacher-led instruction.

Gender-related issues generally are not discussed in literature on functional academic acquisition. Functional reading, writing, and math skills are needed regardless of gender. The students' environment-based needs reveal adaptive skills needs for participation in specific activities (Gast & Schuster, 1993). Skills for both males and females should be selected and prioritized based on how frequently the individual will need to use the skill, how soon the skill will be used, and the likelihood the additional skills will lead to participation in a less restrictive environment and increased independence (Slaton et al., 2001).

ADDITIONAL TOOLS USED FOR ASSESSMENT OF FUNCTIONAL ACADEMIC ADAPTIVE SKILLS

The reauthorization of IDEA of 1997 and 2004 also provided for the use of alternative assessments to measure students' progress (Thompson & Thurlow, 2001). State policies generally acknowledged a need to align alternate assessments with the functional curriculum. Thus, states began to include academic (e.g, reading and math), and functional life skill domains (e.g., personal health and communication skills) (Thompson et al., 2001; Browder et al., 2002). Most states align their functional academic curriculum with their learning standards for general education. Prior to their placement in special education classrooms, students' functional needs should be determined to assist in skill planning efforts.

Thus, comprehensive adaptive behavior assessments should identify the social and functional academic adaptive skills most needed to function effectively at school, home, work, and the community as well as the pattern of skill strengths and weaknesses a student currently displays in relation to those that are needed. Assessments help identify skill deficiencies in light of adaptive skills needed by a student to function effectively in environments within which a student is likely to study, work, and live. This information helps guide teachers and caregivers as they identify instructional skills that are likely to foster greater independence in those environments and is critical for developing individualized education plans (IEP) (Campbell et al., 1998; Slaton et al., 2001).

INFORMATION FROM THE ABAS-II

Information from the ABAS-II helps evaluate an individual's adaptive behavior in 10 important adaptive skill areas, including adaptive skill areas to evaluate skill deficiencies related to functional pre-academic adaptive skills (for younger children) and functional academic adaptive skills (for school-age children and adults). Each of the 23 Functional Academics/Functional Pre-Academics adaptive skill area items on each of the two Parent Forms (for children ages 0–5 years and 5–21 years), the 24 Functional Pre-Academics adaptive skill area items on the Teacher Daycare Provider Form (for children ages 2–5 years), and the 22 Functional Academics adaptive skill area items on the Teacher Form (for children age 5–21 years) assesses adaptive, pre-academic or academic skills likely to be found to be functional. In addition, the ABAS-II Adult Form includes 27 items on the Functional Academics adaptive skill area. Individuals with item scores of 0 (i.e., unable to perform the skill) or 1 (i.e., has the ability yet does not perform the skill when needed) on relevant items provide evidence of the need either to develop the skills or to increase their performance frequency. An item score of 2 (i.e., has the ability to perform the skill and displays it some of the time when needed) suggests the need to find occasions when this skill is needed and to reinforce its display so as to promote its maintenance and use. An item score of 3 indicates that an individual has the ability to perform the skill and always performs it as needed.

ECOLOGICAL INVENTORIES

Ecological inventories are assessments that assist teachers and caregivers in evaluating the student's environment and then customizing instruction based on the specific adaptive skills needed by a student within his or her current home, school, work, or community environment (Slaton et al., 1994; Browder, 2001). Assessment specialists and important stakeholders (e.g., parents/guardians) complete the ecological inventory to determine the specific skills most important to be successful in each domain (Overton, 1996; Downing & Perino, 1992). Ecological inventories are useful in developing specific curricula for students to be successful in work, leisure, or school settings.

However, ecological inventories may be time-consuming and require input from various sources. Therefore, community catalogs are often completed in place of ecological inventories (Gast & Schuster, 1993). Although community catalogs and ecological inventories are both community focused curricular planning assessments, community catalogs are created within each school district or community and are based on the specific community supports and resources provided within each individual The catalog lists all activities and settings available for students, such as locations for shopping, restaurants, community services, and transportation, thus making the catalog easy to complete for all caregivers. The targeting of specific settings and activities the student will encounter daily enables teachers to identify a specific set of skills necessary to foster independent use of those resources.

PERSON-CENTERED PLANNING

Person-centered planning is used to assess a student's functional academic adaptive skills. Its goal is to improve participation within preferred activities for students with severe disabilities (Miner & Bates, 1997; Browder, 2001). Rather than the environment driving instructional planning, person-centered planning puts the needs of the individual first, resulting in greater autonomy and decision making for students throughout the process (Hagner et al., 1996; Marrone et al., 1997).

A specific agenda may be followed when conducting a person-centered planning meeting (Miner & Bates, 1997). First, the student's support circles are drawn to include those involved in the student's support system. Secondly, a community map is drawn to indicate the settings the student uses regularly. Third, the committee lists the student's preferences, including both likes and dislikes. Fourth, the student's strengths are described, including others' perceptions of the student. Future settings or activities the student desires then are listed. Finally, an action plan is devised along with listings of those responsible for teaching specific tasks and making system changes needed take to help ensure success. A blending of both ecological inventories and person-centered planning provides an opportunity for teachers and caregivers to create a curriculum that mirrors individual preferences as well as meaningful and useful skills that a person needs to function independently at home, school, work, and in the community (Giangreco et al., 1993; Browder, 2001).

STANDARDIZED TESTS

In addition to rating scales of adaptive skills, such as the ABAS-II, commercially available tests also are used commonly to directly assess functional academics skills. One widely used direct assesment is the Kaufman Functional Academics Skills Test (K-FAST; Kaufman & Kaufman, 1994). The K-FAST is an individually administered assessment of functional reading and math skills for persons between the ages of 15 and 85. Whereas many measures rely on informant ratings to assess functional skills, the K-FAST assesses an individual's actual skill performance directly in reading and math. The availability of various methods to assess functional academics enables professionals to evaluate an individual's skills acquisition and develop instructional plans based on his or her needs.

INTERVENTION METHODS THAT PROMOTE AND ACCOMMODATE FUNCTIONAL ACADEMIC ADAPTIVE SKILLS

FUNCTIONAL READING

Functional reading refers to a person's ability to successfully use sight word recognition knowledge to recognize and understand verbal and nonverbal written messages found in the environment. This ability allows persons to be independent members of the community (Slaton et al., 1994; Valletutti et al., 1996). Goals for functional reading curriculum differ somewhat for preschool and school age children. The primary goals for preschool age children include the acquisition of certain pre-reading skills: alphabet recognition (e.g., recognizing letters in the student's own name), receptive vocabulary (e.g., points to pictures in a book on request), and knowledge of nursery rhymes (Valletutti et al., 1996). Acquisition of these skills will provide a solid foundation for students to succeed in later curriculum. The primary goals for school age children include using knowledge of the printed word to access personal information written on formal or informal documents (e.g., recognize own name on a list of names) to make choices (e.g., using a menu), to understand written directions (e.g., signs), and to access general information (e.g., using a dictionary) (Valletutti et al., 1996). Before engaging in intervention strategies for preschool or school age students who appear to be struggling in any or all of the aforementioned categories, professionals should determine that reading problems are not due to vision, hearing, or language problems.

FUNCTIONAL PRE-ACADEMICS FOR READING

Intervention strategies for preschool age children who struggle with functional pre-reading adaptive skills should focus on three key categories: alphabet recognition, receptive vocabulary, and knowledge of nursery rhymes. Alphabet recognition includes the following skills: naming the letters in his or her own name, naming written letters of the alphabet, and singing the alphabet song. Receptive vocabulary includes the following skills: pointing to pictures in a book when requested to do so by an adult and recognizing a target picture among other distracters. Knowledge of nursery rhymes includes the following skills: completing nursery rhymes when prompted with a beginning phrase and reciting entire nursery rhymes from memory.

The ability to visually discriminate between the features of letters of the alphabet is a necessary pre-requisite to successful word recognition (Pinnell & Fountas, 1998). Teachers may develop letter recognition with young children by having them recognize letters in their own names. Children usually are very interested in the letters in their names. Below are several instructional strategies that can be used to help increase student interest and knowledge of letters in their names.

- Point out the features of the letters in students' written names. For example, provide students with and encourage students to provide verbal descriptors of the features of the letters in their names.
- Provide students with opportunities to manipulate the letters in their written name. For example, allow students to use their fingers to write their initials or perhaps the letters in their first name in shaving cream, sand, dirt, or paint. Also allow students to manipulate magnetic letters to spell parts of their name.

- Play games that draw attention to the letters in students' names. For example, have students form a line in alphabetical order by first or last initial or have students group themselves according to first or last initial.
- Post student names so that they are visible. For example, teachers can post student names for daily attendance, birthdays, and job charts. Allow students to find and place a star next to their name to indicate their daily attendance. Also, write students' names on cardboard cut outs. Allow students to find and place the cardboard cut out containing their name next to their daily classroom job or duty.

The promotion of students' knowledge of the letters in their own names should be coupled with instruction of other letters of the alphabet, including the letters used in the names of family members and friends. The instructional strategies above can be adapted to accomplish this. Teachers may provide students with and encourage students to provide verbal descriptors of the features of various letters in the alphabet. For example, when demonstrating how to write the letter "t", verbalize the process by telling students that the letter consists of a line going down and a line going across.

Receptive vocabulary refers to the ability to understand spoken words. Receptive vocabulary has a significant impact on listening comprehension skills. Below are some instructional strategies that can be used to help increase students' receptive vocabulary.

- Use picture books to assist in the instruction of new vocabulary words. Be very explicit by matching written vocabulary words with the illustrations that accompany them.
- Play games that require students to discriminate between a target picture and a group containing other pictures. Students can start off by playing on teams during whole class instruction and then they may play individually within the entire group.

Rhyming also is an important pre-reading skill (Kenney, 2005; Beer, 2007). A student's ability or inability to rhyme is a significant indicator of his or her future reading ability (Kenney, 2005). Several instructional strategies can be used to help increase students' opportunities to manipulate the letters in their own names.

- Read literature to children that rhymes (e.g., Dr. Seuss books, Mother Goose rhymes, and children's poetry).
- Also, read nursery rhyme tales such as *Old Mother Hubbard* and *Hey Diddle Diddle*. Practice these nursery rhymes with students and encourage then to complete nursery rhymes when prompted with a beginning phrase. Encourage students to recite rhymes as a group and individually.
- Dissect nursery rhymes by discussing the parts that rhyme. For example, after reading the sentence, "I know a cat named Pat" to students. Emphasize that the words Pat and cat rhyme because of the /at/ sound that both words share.

FUNCTIONAL ACADEMICS FOR READING

Intervention strategies for school age children who struggle with functional reading adaptive skills should focus on three key goals: the ability to access personal and general information from various written documents, to make choices when provided with written documents, and to understand written directions (Browder, 2001). The ability to access general and personal information can follow success in acquiring the ability to recognize and differentiate one's own name from other names on a list, to use reference resources such as dictionaries and encyclopedias, to recognize store names, and to recognize products in stores. The ability to make choices when provided with written documents can follow success in acquiring the ability to choose food and/or drink from a menu and choose from among a variety of bus routes. The ability to understand written directions can follow success in acquiring the ability to read and follow signs in the community, follow directions to complete a task, and follow directions printed on a prescription or other medical product.

The ability to locate general and personal information on written documents is essential to functioning in the community (Browder, 2001). Whether a student plans to seek employment or simply take a trip to the grocery store, he or she must be able to receive and navigate the different kinds of information. Below are several instructional strategies that can be used to help facilitate a student's ability to gain access to personal and general information. Some intervention strategies for school age children are similar to the strategies that were described earlier for preschool age children (see the chapter on Community Use Adaptive Skills in the present text for additional intervention suggestions).

- Provide students with opportunities to use references and other types of resources. For example, require students to use references such as an encyclopedia to complete a class project. Be sure to provide direct instruction using think aloud methods on how to use different kinds of references. For instance, in whole or small groups model reading the names of a list of animals that must presented in the form of a class project. Think out loud for students while searching for the animals in the encyclopedia and while deciding the kinds of information to include in the report.
- Provide opportunities for students to read and recognize the names of various stores in the community. Students must learn to identify products they plan to purchase frequently. Allow students to role play by setting up the classroom to resemble a shopping plaza. Have students examine several products commonly found in the different stores. Provide exposure to the types of stores students experience in the community. Take trips into the community. Allow students to look at and choose items from store shelves. Be sure to talk with students afterwards about the kinds of things they saw and how those things compare to their experiences while role playing. Encourage students to compare and contrast their simulated community experience with their real world experience.

The ability to make choices also is essential to being a successful member of the community (Browder, 2001). For example, the selection of wrong items on a menu or on a store shelf could have dire consequences if a student is allergic to a certain food. Below are several instructional strategies that can facilitate a student's ability to make choices based on written information.

- Provide students with opportunities to make choices based on information on written documents. Post the daily or monthly lunch schedule. Engage students in conversation about what they will choose to eat.
- As with the aforementioned skill, allow students to role play and actually experience labeling different products they see in stores. Develop sight word recognition of words that appear often on store products (Slaton et al., 1994).
- Many students must rely on public transportation. Students should be provided with explicit directions on how to determine which method of public transportation to use and how to go about using it. Role-playing will be a helpful start followed by providing students with actual experiences.

The ability to follow written directions is essential to being successful at school, work, and in the general community. The intervention strategies below can assist students in following directions.

- Allow students to follow written directions when performing simple tasks. For example, provide students with directions to how to access a specific page on a website. Provide students with a small number of steps in a set of directions to start and increase the steps as students become more comfortable.
- Allow students to both role play and actually experience using community signs. Be sure to discuss the meaning of each sign. Develop sight word recognition of words that appear often on community signs. Some important community signs include: *do not enter*, *pedestrian crossing*, *bus stop*, *walk*, and *don't walk*.
- Expose students to directions that accompany different medications. For example, bring in empty bottles of over the counter and prescription medicines. Discuss the purpose of each kind of medicine. Help students role play following the directions on various medications. Discuss the importance of following certain specifications such as dosage. Discuss the importance of taking medication only when medically needed.

FUNCTIONAL WRITING

Functional writing refers to the ability to convey and record information in written form (Slaton et al., 1994). Functional writing differs from creative writing by deemphasizing self-expression and writing for pleasure.

The primary goals of the functional writing curriculum for preschool age children include the acquisition of prewriting skills such as using writing instruments (e.g., pencils and crayons) and forming individual letters of the alphabet (e.g., writing letters in the student's own name). Additionally, the primary goals of the functional writing curriculum for school age children include the student's ability to produce personal information (e.g., his/her own name and address) and convey information to others (e.g., letters, e-mails, and lists) (Slaton et al., 1994).

Children need to acquire mastery of writing instruments such as pencils and crayons. Much of the information students produce is handwritten or drawn. The intervention strategies below can assist students to learn to how to grip writing tools.

- Model how to hold the writing tool. Initially emphasize holding it, not necessarily producing actual letters.
- Allow many opportunities to practice. Again, the focus should be more on drawing and less on producing letters. This allows students to produce something meaningful in non-threatening ways.

The ability to form letters is pre-requisite to more sophisticated forms of writing (Graham et al., 2006). The intervention strategies below can assist students to learn to form individual letters of the alphabet.

- In addition to providing students with a variety of multisensory experiences, provide students with alphabet tracing tools. Students can be expected to stamp and then trace the letters or they can be provided with pre-stamped letters. Letter tracing printables are also available free online in both capital and lower case and also in denelian and zaner bloser formats.

Adaptive behavior at school, work, and the community requires persons to be able to write personal information (Slaton et al., 1994). The intervention strategies below can assist students to learn to write personal information such as their names and addresses on formal and informal documents.

- Insist that students write their names on all papers and worksheets. Alter expectations for students who are just learning so that the youngest children are expected to write their initials, then their first name followed by their last initial, and finally their full name.
- Provide students with opportunities to write their home address. For example, when teaching students to write letters, include their address on the heading. Also allow students to include the address on the envelope.
- Provide students with the opportunity to complete various forms that require their written name and address (e.g., on a library card or job application form).

One primary purpose for functional writing adaptive skills is to convey information to others (McCarrier et al., 2000). The intervention strategies below can assist students to learn to convey information through writing.

- Provide students with opportunities to make lists. For example, require them to make lists of materials needed for a class projects as well as items they plan to purchase at a store.
- Encourage students to communicate in written form, using paper or electronic means. Students can exchange information through instant messenger, e-mails, or by hand messages. Establish a purpose for students' writing.

FUNCTIONAL MATHEMATICS

Functional mathematics refers to the ability to apply mathematical concepts that are relevant to everyday life. Thus, a functional mathematics curriculum focuses on adaptive skills related to understanding and applying the basic aspects of money, measurement, and time (Valletutti et al., 1996). The goals of a functional mathematics curriculum differ for preschool and school age children.

Functional mathematics goals for preschool age children include basic counting skills (e.g., counting using fingers or counting objects), calendar math (e.g., days of the week), and producing numbers in written form. The primary outcomes of the functional mathematics curriculum for school age children include knowledge of time (e.g., tells time on a clock correctly) and knowledge of money (e.g., counts and combine coins).

The ability to count is pre-requisite to learning basic math skills needed to be successful in daily living (Browder, 2001). The strategies below can assist students to learn to count using various objects and tools.

- Encourage students to use their fingers to assist them in counting a number of objects. Do not limit counting to classrooms. Look for objects to count on the playground, in the hallway, in the lunchroom, and at home (e.g., count the number of parents, siblings, and bedrooms).
- Provide opportunities for students use objects such cubes and chips to help count the total number of a given set. Allow students to witness this being done before expecting them to perform the tasks.

Calendar math provides young children with a foundational understanding of the concept of time (Ethridge & King, 2006). Teaching calendar math goes beyond simply exposing students to the days of the week and the months of the year. Calendar math also can be use to teach other math concepts such as counting, graphing, and place value (Ethridge & King, 2006). The intervention strategies below can assist students to learn about the calendar.

- Set aside some time each day to discuss the different concepts that relate to the calendar. For example, reinforce counting the number of days in a week or the months left in the school year.
- Graph the number of rainy days in a given month or add the number of vacation school days in a given month.

As with letters, the ability to write numbers also is critical to success in school, work and community. The intervention strategies below can assist students to learn to write numbers.

- As with letters, provide students with opportunities to write numbers with their fingers in shaving cream, sand, flour, or paint.
- As with letters, provide students with number tracing tools. Students can be expected to stamp and then trace the letters or they can be provided with pre-stamped numbers. Number tracing printables are also available free online.

Knowledge of time and money is essential to daily living (Browder, 2001). The intervention strategies below can assist students to learn about these key aspects of functional mathematics.

- Provide explicit instruction about time concepts (e.g., 60 seconds in a minute). Then provide students with applied opportunities to tell time during the school day. For example, identify the time students arrive at school, go to lunch, and leave for home Encourage students to attend to the lunchroom clock to determine when it is time to return to the classroom.
- Expose students to the different kinds of money (e.g., coins and paper). Provide students with applied opportunities to use money. For example, set up a token economy system where students can earn money as a result of good behavior in the classroom. Require students to add the amount of money they earned in a day or week. Students also should be required to accurately spend their money on priced items from the classroom store.

GENERAL FUNCTIONAL SKILLS

General functional skills refer to those basic adaptive skills that form the foundation for acquiring all specific functional academic skills (e.g., functional reading, writing, and math). These adaptive skills are important to success in everyday life. Examples include sorting by color at the preschool level and using commonplace resources (e.g., telephone books) at the school level.

General functional adaptive skills at the pre-academic level include the ability to sort colors, to recognize shapes, and to accurately represent the human figure. The intervention strategies below can be used to assist students to learn general functioning skills so they can experience further success.

- Expose students to primary colors (i.e., red, blue, and yellow) and label them. Allow students to mix primary paint colors to make new colors. Post colors and their names in the classroom.
- Post shapes and their names in the classroom.
- Allow students to have repeated experiences with objects of different shapes. Require students to repeatedly name the shapes and discuss how they differ.

- Discuss drawings and photographs of people in books.
- Demonstrate drawing people from scratch. As new features (e.g., eyes, nose, mouth) are added, discuss features of the human figure.

General functional adaptive skills at the academic level include the ability to use resources such as a telephone book and the Internet. General functioning skills at school may vary by students' interests and assignments. The intervention strategies below can assist students to learn general functioning skills.

- Provide applied opportunities to use resources that students will be expected to use when they are engaged in the community. For example, allow students to use the phone book to locate the address of one of the grocery stores the class plans to visit.
- Using a phone book, require students to locate specific business selected for legitimate reasons (e.g., There is no water. Thus locate a plumber).
- Allow controlled exposure to the Internet. Provide students with applied and meaningful reasons to use the Internet. For example, require students to locate the address of a local store using the Internet.

CASE STUDY

Madison, a four-year-old female, receives special education services in an inclusive pre-kindergarten classroom setting at an elementary school. Madison's parents provided her medical and educational history. She is an only child and resides with both parents. When Madison was age 1 year, her parents noticed she was not reaching developmental milestones. For example, she had difficulty sitting up, crawling, or grasping objects. Her parents referred Madison for assessment by a developmental specialist. Madison underwent Magnetic Resonance Imaging of the brain to determine if any brain damage was evident. Additionally, several genetic screenings were conducted to determine if there were any genetic abnormalities that could explain her delay. After a comprehensive genetic and neurological assessment, she was diagnosed with unspecified developmental delay and began receiving services through Early Steps, an early intervention program through the local hospital. In addition, Madison began receiving occupational and physical therapy once per week, and, when she was 2 years old, weekly speech/language therapy was added.

Madison currently receives speech/language, occupational, and physical therapies through her elementary school's special education services. Madison also receives medical care from a team that includes an early intervention specialist, geneticist, and pediatric cardiologist. Madison was diagnosed with Atrial Septal Defect, a congenital heart defect, at the age of 2. Open-heart surgery between ages of 5 and 6 has been recommended.

Madison's father is a special education teacher and her mother is a guidance counselor. Madison enjoys gymnastics and other physical activities but has difficulty participating because she struggles with simple tasks involving reading signs and counting. She is currently enrolled in a tumbling class for preschool aged children and enjoys swimming lessons.

Madison's parents provided results from the Battelle Developmental Inventory (BDI), which was completed by her elementary school psychologist and included in a Pre-Kindergarten Evaluation Report. Additionally, Madison's mother completed the ABAS-II Parent/Primary Caregiver Form for ages 0–5 and Madison's teacher completed the ABAS-II Teacher/Daycare Provider Form for ages 2–5. The purposes of these assessments were to describe Madison's level of adaptive behavior and skills, to establish a baseline against which to measure future development, and to acquire information to assist her parents and teachers in establishing needed interventions at home and school.

On the BDI, the speech/language measure yielded a total age equivalent of 21 months, while motor development and cognitive development were in the 18–22 month range. Madison's highest scores were in personal-social development and adaptive behavior development, which were in the 29–30 month range. Based on this evaluation data, it was recommended that Madison receive Pre-Kindergarten exceptional student education services. Speech/language and occupational/physical therapy evaluations were also recommended.

To gain further perspective on Madison's functional development, the ABAS-II was used. Scores from the Teacher/Daycare and the Parent/Primary Caregiver forms are found in Table 6.1. Madison's General Adaptive Composite scores of 65 on the Teacher/Daycare Provider Form and the 62 on the Parent/Primary Caregiver Form indicate her overall adaptive behavior at school and home generally is consistent and in the extremely low range. Moreover, the ABAS-II scores indicate that her functional pre-academics adaptive skills are far below average. Madison's scaled scores of 3 on both teacher and parent forms for the Functional Pre-Academic adaptive skill area are within the extremely low range, as are other adaptive skill areas included in the Conceptual composite (i.e., Communication, and Self-Direction). Additionally, Madison scored within the extremely low range in the Practical composite, which includes adaptive skill areas such as School Living, Community Use, Health and Safety, and Self-Care. Her highest scores fell within the Social composite (Leisure and Social adaptive skill areas), with her performance falling within the 5th percentile on the Teacher/Daycare Provide form and 9th percentile on the Parent/Primary Caregiver Form in this composite, which is consistent with findings on the BDI.

Information provided by Madison's mother and teacher indicates she displays some pre-requisite skills that will assist her in acquiring the functional pre-academic adaptive skills needed to participate in her daily routine. For example, she always is able to identify most of the letters of the alphabet, point to pictures in a book, name six or more colors, name at least two numbers, and hold a crayon or pencil when using paper. Madison is sometimes able to state her name when asked, count three or more objects, copy lines or shapes when imitating simple drawings, and identify four or more shapes. Madison is unable to print letters and

TABLE 6.1 Results of the ABAS-II (Parent/Primary Caregiver Ages 0–5, and Teacher/Daycare Ages 2–5) for Madison, Age 4.

Teacher/Daycare provider form Composites and Adaptive skill areas	Adaptive Skill Area Scaled Score	Composite Standard Score	Composite Percentile Rank	Composite Score Classification
General Adaptive Composite (GAC)		65	1	Extremely low
Conceptual Composite		62	1	Extremely low
• Communication	4			
• Functional pre-Academics	3			
• Self-direction	5			
Social Composite		76	5	Borderline
• Leisure	5			
• Social	7			
Practical Composite		66	1	Extremely low
• School living	6			
• Health and Safety	4			
• Self-care	5			
Motor adaptive skill area	5			

Parent/Primary caregiver form Composites and Adaptive skill areas	Adaptive Skill Area Scaled Score	Composite Standard Score	Composite Percentile Rank	Composite Score Classification
General Adaptive Composite		62	1	Extremely low
Conceptual Composite		59	0.3	Extremely low
• Communication	4			
• Functional pre-academics	3			
• Self-Direction	5			
Social Composite		80	9	Below average
• Leisure	7			
• Social	7			
Practical Composite		62	1	Extremely low
• Community use	3			
• Home living	6			
• Health and Safety	4			
• Self-care	4			
Motor adaptive skill area	7			

Note: Composites (Conceptual, Social, and Practical) and the General Adaptive Composite (GAC) have standard scores with a mean of 100 and standard deviation of 15. Adaptive skill areas (Communication, Functional Academics, etc.) have scaled scores with a mean of 10 and standard deviation of 3. Motor scores are included in calculating the GAC, but not other composites.

numbers, count from 1 to 20, recite songs or rhymes, read her name or identifying signs, state days of the week in order, write numbers, and count groups of objects.

Improvements in Madison's functional pre-academics adaptive skills would enable her to benefit more from her learning environments. For example, although reading instruction has not begun due to her developmental age, her ability to identify letters and numbers now will improve her ability to later learn basic reading and mathematics skills in a regular classroom setting. Thus, the intervention team recommended she work with holding pencils and crayons to enable her to print or draw more proficiently. Instruction is most effective when it is embedded within the natural setting and various training environments are used (Slaton et al., 1994; Browder, 2001). Thus, her parents and teachers will work to improve her letter and number identification skills by working with manipulative letters, numbers, and other objects at home and school. The counting of objects and recognizing signs and placards should be embedded within Madison's daily routines at home and school. For example, while driving, her parents can point out signs, including their color and shape, and read what they says. When reading to Madison, her parents also engage her in conversation, ask questions about what they are reading, and ask her to identify pictures – qualities that will assist Madison in developing communication skills and learning to attend to a story. Language and communication are strongly interconnected. Thus, interventions directed to improve deficient communication adaptive skills also will benefit the development of her functional pre-academic adaptive skills.

REFERENCES

Ault, M. J., Wolery, M., Doyle, P. M., & Gast, D. L. (1989). Review of comparative studies in instruction of students with moderate and severe handicaps. *Exceptional Children, 55*, 346–356.

Browder, D. M. (1987). *Assessment of Individuals with Severe Handicaps.* Baltimore: Paul H. Brookes Publishing.

Browder, D. M. (2001). *Curriculum and Assessment for Students with Moderate and Severe Disabilities.* New York: Guilford Press.

Browder, D. M., Ahlgrim-Dezell, L. A., Flowers, C., Karvonen, M., Spooner, F., & Algozzine, R. (2002). *Description of the Alternate Assessments for Students with Disabilities.* Paper presented at the meeting of the American Educational Research Association, New Orleans, LA.

Browder, D. M. & Cooper-Duffy, K. (2003). Evidence based practices for students with severe disabilities and the requirement for accountability in "No Child Left Behind." *The Journal of Special Education, 37*(3), 157–163.

Brown, L., Nisbet, J. Ford. A., Sweet, M., Shiraga, B., York, J., & Loomis, R. (1983). The critical need for nonschool instruction in educational programs for severely handicapped students. *The Journal of The Association for Persons with Severe Handicaps, 8*(3), 71–77.

Campbell, P. C., Campbell, C. R., & Brady, M. P. (1998). Team Environmental Assistant Mapping System: A method for selecting curriculum goals for students with disabilities. *Education and Training in Mental Retardation and Developmental Disabilities, 33*, 264–272.

Clark, G. M. (1994). Is a functional curriculum approach compatible with an inclusive education model? *Teaching Exceptional Children, 26*(2), 36–39.

Clark, G. M. & Kolstoe, O. P. (1990). *Career Development and Transition Education or Adolescents with Disabilities.* Boston: Allyn & Bacon.

Cronin, M. E. & Patton, J. R. (1993). *Life Skills Instruction for All Students with Special Needs.* Austin, TX: Pro-Ed.

Downing, J. E. & Perino, D. M. (1992). Functional versus standardized assessment in procedures: Implications for educational programming. *Mental Retardation, 30,* 289–295.

Ethridge, E. A. & King, J. R. (2006). Calendar math in pre-school and primary classrooms: Questioning the curriculum. *Early Childhood Educational Journal*, 32, 291–296.

Ferguson, D. L. & Baumgart, D. (1991). Partial participation revisited. *Journal of the Association for Persons with Severe Handicaps, 16,* 218–227.

Gast, D. L. & Schuster, J. W. (1993). Severe handicaps. In A. E. Blackhurst, & W. H. Berdine (Eds.), *An Introduction to Special Education*, 3rd edn., Boston: Little, Brown & Company.

Giangreco, M. F., Cloninger, C. J., Dennis, R. E., & Edelman, S. W. (1993). National expert validation of COACH: Congruence with exemplary practices and suggestions for improvement. *Journal of the Association for Persons with Severe Handicaps, 18,* 109–120.

Giangreco, M. F., Cloninger, C. J., & Iverson, V. S. (1998). *Choosing Outcomes and Accommodations for Children,* 2nd edn., Baltimore: Paul H. Brookes.

Graham, S., Struck, M., Santoro, J., & Berninger, V. W. (2006). Dimensions of good and poor handwriting legibility in first and second graders: Motor programs, visual-spatial arrangement, and letter formation parameter setting. *Developmental Neuropsychology, 29,* 43–60.

Hagner, D., Helm, D. T., & Butterworth, J. (1996). "This is your meeting": A qualitative study of person-centered planning. *Mental Retardation, 34,* 159–171.

Heller, K. W. (2001). Adaptations and instruction in science and social studies. In J. L. Bigge, S. J. Best, & K. W. Heller (Eds.), *Teaching Individuals with Physical, Health, or Multiple Disabilities,* 4th edn., Upper Saddle River, NJ: Merrill.

Jackson, L., Ryndak, D. L., & Billingsley, F. (2000). Useful practices in inclusive education: A preliminary view of what experts in moderate to severe disabilities are saying. *Journal of the Association for Persons with Severe Handicaps, 25*(3), 129–141.

Jorgenson-Smith, T. & Lewis, S. (2004). Meeting the challenge: Innovation in one state's rehabilitation system's approach to transition. *Journal of Visual Impairment and Blindness, 98,* 212–227.

Katsiyannis, A., Conderman, G., & Franks, D. J. (1995). State practices on inclusion: A national review. *Remedial and Special Education, 16,* 279–287.

Kaufman, A. S. & Kaufman, N. D. (1994). *The Functional Academic Skills Test.* Circle Pines, MN: American Guidance Services.

Kennedy, C. H. & Haring, T. G. (1993). Teaching choice making during social interactions to students with profound multiple disabilities. *Journal of Applied Behavior Analysis, 26,* 63–76.

Kennedy, C. H., Shukla, S., & Fryxell, D. (1997). Comparing the effects of educational placement on the social relationships of intermediate school students with severe disabilities. *Exceptional Children, 64,* 31–47.

Kenney, S. (2005). Nursery rhymes: Foundation for learning. *General Music Today*, 19, 28–31

McCarrier, A., Pinnel, G. S., & Fountas, I. C. (2000). *Interactive Writing: How Language and Literacy Come Together, K-2.* Portsmouth, NH: Heinemann.

Marrone, J., Hoff, D., & Helm, D. T. (1997). Person-centered planning for the millennium: We're old enough to remember when PCP was just a drug. *Journal of Vocational Rehabilitation, 8,* 285–297.

Mastropieri, M. A. & Scruggs, T. E. (2000). *The Inclusive Classroom: Strategies for Effective Instruction.* Upper Saddle River, NJ: Merrill.

Miller, J. M. & Thompson, E. M. (2005). Prevocational services: A resource for enhancing a functional academic curriculum. *Review, 37*(1), 42–48.

Miner, C. A. & Bates, P. E. (1997). The effect of a person centered planning activities on the IEP/transition planning process. *Education and Training in Mental Retardation and Developmental Disabilities, 32,* 105–112.

Nietupski, J., Hamre-Nietupski, S., Clancy, P., & Veerhusen, K. (1986). Guidelines for making simulation an effective adjunct to in vivo community instruction. *The Journal of The Association for Persons with Severe Handicaps, 11,* 12–18.

Overton, T. (1996). *Assessment in Special Education: An Applied Approach*, 2nd edn.,. Columbus, OH: Merrill.

Pinnell, G. S. & Fountas, I. C. (1998). *Word Matters: Teaching Phonics and Spelling in the Reading/ Writing Classroom*. Portsmouth, NH: Heinemann.

Ryndak, D. L. & Alper, S. (1996). *Curriculum content for students with moderate and severe disabilities in inclusive settings*. Boston: Allyn & Bacon.

Salisbury, C. L., Evans, I. M., & Palombaro, M. M. (1997). Collaborative problem solving to promote the inclusion of young children with significant disabilities in primary grades. *Exceptional Children, 63*, 195–209.

Schoen, S. & Ogden, S. (1995). Impact of time delay, observational learning, and attentional cueing on word recognition during integrated small group instruction. *Journal of Autism and Developmental Disorders, 25*, 503–519.

Slaton, D. B., Schuster, J., Collins, B., & Carnine, D. (1994). A functional approach to academics instruction. In E. Cipani, & F. Sponner (Eds.). *Curricular and Instructional Approaches for Persons with Severe Disabilities*. Needham Heights, MA: Allyn and Bacon.

Snell, M. E. & Janney, R. (2000). *Teachers' Guides to Inclusive Practices: Collaborative Teaming*. Baltimore: Paul H. Brookes.

Snell, M. E., Lewis, A. P., & Houghton, A. (1989). Acquisition and maintenance of toothbrushing skills by students with cerebral palsy and mental retardation. *Journal of the Association for Persons with Severe Handicaps, 14*, 216–226.

Thomas, S. B. & Rapport, M. J. K. (1998). The least restrictive environment: Understanding the directions of the courts. *The Journal of Special Education, 32*(2), 66–78.

Thompson, S., & Thurlow, M. (2001). 2001 *State Special Education Outcomes: A Report on State Activities at the Beginning of a New Decade*. Minneapolis: University of Minnesota, National Center on Educational Outcomes.

Thompson, S., Quenemoen, R. F., Thurlow, M. L., Ysseldyke, J. E. (2001). *Alternate Assessments for Students with Disabilities*. Thousand Oaks, CA: Corwin Press.

U.S. Department of Education (2000). *Twenty Second Annual Report to Congress on the Implementation of the Individuals with Disabilities Education Act*. Washington DC: U.S. Department of Education.

Valletutti, P., Bender, M., & Sims-Tucker, B. (1996). *A Functional Curriculum for Teaching Students with Disabilities: Functional Academics*. Austin, TX: Pro-Ed.

Wehman, P. (1996). *Life Beyond the Classroom: Transition Strategies for Young People with Disabilities*. Baltimore: Paul H. Brooks.

White, O. R. (1980). Adaptive performance objectives: Form versus function. In W. Sailor, B. Wilcox, & L. Brown (Eds.), *Methods of Instruction for Severely Handicapped Students*. Baltimore: Paul H. Brookes Publishing.

Wolery, M., Bailey, D. B., & Sugai, G. M. (1988). *Effective Teaching: Principles and Procedures of Applied Behavior Analysis with Exceptional Students*. Boston: Allyn & Bacon.

Wolery, M., Werts, M. G., Snyder, E. D., & Caldwell, N. K. (1994). Efficacy of constant time delay implemented by peer tutors in general education classrooms. *Journal of Behavioral Education, 4*, 415–436.

7

School and Home Living Adaptive Skills

Daniel E. Steere, Heather Garrison, and Joyce Burgener

Department of Special Education and Rehabilitation, East Stroudsburg University, East Stroudsburg, PA 18301-2999, U.S.A.

INTRODUCTION

This chapter addresses those adaptive skill areas that the Adaptive Behavior Assessment System-II (ABAS-II) categorizes as school and home living skills. The skills that are addressed in this section of ABAS-II, and that we discuss in this chapter, are those related to the care of one's belongings, the maintenance of the environment, and the completion of routine activities within a home environment. These adaptive skills focus primarily on the home environment; however, because a substantial amount of the development of these skills occurs within school settings, the use of these skills in school settings is also discussed. Related adaptive skill areas, such as self-care skills, are addressed in other chapters in this book. Tables 7.1–7.3 list sample adaptive skills that are assessed by ABAS-II at three age ranges (0–5, 5–21, and 16–89) and that we will address in this chapter. (Note that these tables list selected skills from the ABAS-II and are provided only to help the reader understand the types of adaptive skills that we are discussing in this chapter. Readers should refer to the ABAS-II for a complete, sequential listing of school and home living adaptive skills at the three age levels.)

Before discussing the development of school and home living skills in detail, we feel that it is essential to state that the attainment of greater independence with these skills is related directly to the amount and nature of support that people will require throughout their lives, including people with disabilities such as

TABLE 7.1 Sample school and home living skills adaptive addressed by ABAS-II for individuals from birth through age 5.

Skills related to the care of one's belongings:
- Points to the place were his/her belongings are stored in the classroom or daycare
- Hangs coat or sweater in the proper place
- Keeps toys, games, and other belongings neat and clean
- Shows respect for the property and rights of other children and teachers/daycare-providers
- Refrains from tearing or breaking toys or books in the classroom or daycare

Skills related to the maintenance of the environment:
- Shows concern when he/she spills something
- Uses light switch to turn light off and on
- Attempts to wipe up spills, even if an adult must help
- Wipes up spills at school or daycare
- Dusts or cleans furniture, whiteboard, or chalkboard when asked by teacher/daycare-provider
- Makes a contribution to keep the classroom or daycare neat and clean
- Picks up or throws away trash or paper at home

Skills related to the completion of routine activities:
- Removes cookies, chips, or other food from a box or bag
- Disposes of his/her leftover food
- Assists other people with putting away toys, games, and other items
- Assists teacher/daycare-providers with moving chairs, distributing supplies or other tasks, when asked
- Brings needed books and supplies
- Turns television on or off
- Gets own snack from cabinet or pantry
- Places dirty clothes in the proper place, for example, a hamper or clothesbasket
- Makes his or her own bed

learning, physical, behavioral, mental health, and substance abuse issues. For example, a youngster who learns to identify that the garbage is full and needs to be emptied and then can complete this task will not require assistance or support for this particular activity. Likewise, an individual who learns to put away belongings in school or at home will gain independence with this activity. In each of these cases, the individuals in question will be able to spend more of their time independently with less assistance and support. This, in turn, can create more options and choices for people with disabilities because less structured or restrictive living environments tend to allow for greater choice and self-determination for people who live within them (Howe et al., 1998; Stancliffe et al., 2000). The point that we are making is that by addressing these skills directly as early as possible in the lives of people with disabilities, educators and other practitioners are increasing the likelihood that people with disabilities will have the opportunity for greater choice, independence, and self-determination in their home living situations later in life. As O'Brien (1994) points out, a home is a place in which people typically seek to find a greater sense of choice, personalization and control of their living situation. Additionally, O'Brien (1994) states

TABLE 7.2 Sample school and home living adaptive skills addressed by ABAS-II for individuals from age 5 through 21.

Skills related to the care of one's belongings:
- Shows respect for the property and rights of other classmates and teachers
- Keeps school's supplies and notebooks neat and clean
- Keeps toys, games, and other belongings neat and clean
- Cleans his/her own desk, workspace, or locker regularly
- Folds clean clothes
- Puts things in their proper place when finished using them

Skills related to the maintenance of the environment:
- Tells teacher if repairs are needed in the classroom, for example, tells teacher if something is broken
- Wipes up spills in the classroom
- Picks up and throws away trash or paper in the classroom, school hallways, and school grounds
- Dusts or cleans furniture, whiteboard, or chalkboard when asked by teacher
- Makes a helpful contribution to keep classroom neat and clean
- Picks up and throws away trash or paper at home
- Assists in big clean-up projects at home, for example, spring cleaning or cleaning the garage

Skills related to the completion of routine activities:
- Performs daily or weekly classroom chores
- Removes tray or plate and other items from the table when finished eating in the school lunchroom
- Puts books and supplies in their proper places when finished using them
- Uses small electrical equipment in the classroom, for example, a tape player or electric pencil sharpener
- Operates electronics, for example, a television, video player, or computer in the classroom
- Places dirty clothes in the proper place, for example, a hamper or clothesbasket
- Clears the table completely after a meal
- Cleans room or living quarters regularly
- Uses a clothes dryer
- Uses a washing machine to wash clothes
- Uses a microwave oven
- Mixes and cooks fairly complex foods on a stove or oven, for example, cakes or brownies

that a true home is one in which a person has the security or safety of tenure, that is, knowing how long one may stay within that home setting. These dimensions of home that O'Brien (1994) discusses – choice, control, predictability, personalization, and security – are most likely to be attained by people who can demonstrate increased independence with the skills that we discuss in this chapter. Although these dimensions should be available to all people, our current residential service system for people with disabilities does not always allow their attainment within more restrictive residential settings. Therefore, the longitudinal development of greater independence with school and home living skills is closely tied to broader quality of life issues throughout the lifespan of people with disabilities.

An additional issue to be addressed in this chapter is that the successful demonstration of the school and home living adaptive skills described in this chapter, particularly in natural environmental situations, relies on strong self-management

TABLE 7.3 Sample school and home living adaptive skills addressed by ABAS-II for individuals from age 16 through 89.

Skills related to the care of one's belongings:
- Folds clean clothes
- Makes minor repairs to personal possessions, for example, bikes or clothes
- Puts things in their proper place when finished using them

Skills related to the maintenance of the environment:
- Wipes up spills at home
- Wipes wet or dirty shoes before entering a building
- Takes out trash when can is full
- Sweeps floor
- Cleans room or living quarters regularly
- Cleans bathroom with proper cleaning supplies
- Follows a maintenance schedule for home or car, for example, changes the oil in the care or changes the air conditioning filter

Skills related to the completion of routine activities:
- Cooks simple foods on a stove, for example, eggs or canned soup
- Makes simple meals that require no cooking, for example, sandwiches and salads
- Washes dishes either by hand or by placing them in the dishwasher
- Uses a washing machine to wash clothes
- Makes his or her own bed
- Cleans room or living quarters regularly

and generalization abilities (Steere & Burcroff, 2004). That is, individuals who are able to monitor when, how, and how well to complete tasks such as cooking, laundry, or home cleaning need less support and supervision and consequently will have greater independence. Also, because many of the skills addressed in this chapter must be done in multiple ways due to differences in equipment and materials (for example, different microwave ovens, washing machines, or other home appliances), the development of generalization skills in implementing these activities is essential for greater independence. For example, although the ability to operate one specific microwave oven may be important, the generalized ability to operate any microwave oven is a far more functional skill.

IMPORTANCE OF THE ADAPTIVE SKILL AREA

Student competence in home and school living adaptive skills is critical to independent or interdependent living, quality of life, and transition to living and learning in adulthood. The development of home living skills relate to subsequent success in the transition from school to one's own apartment or home outside of the family's home. The Individuals with Disabilities Education Improvement Act of 2004 states that students with disabilities have a right to a free and appropriate education and that an Individual Education Program (IEP) must be in place that guides the student's appropriate education. Starting at age 16, or younger if necessary, transition planning is required. A transition plan is mandated through the IEP to serve as a roadmap to adulthood. The transition process is complex and includes multiple participants and multiple domains, including home living. Transition plans must be based on student's strengths, preferences, and interests and include the domain of independent living (Steere et al., 2007).

The National Longitudinal Transition Study (NLTS), which was conducted in the 1980s, followed individuals with disabilities for 5 years. These studies concluded that daily living skills are an extremely critical instructional need for students with disabilities (Brolin & Loyd, 2004). This study was followed by the NLTS2. Data emerging from this study on personal living skills finds that more than 58% of youth with disabilities are rated more than two standard deviations below the mean and 22% are rated more than six standard deviations below the mean (Wagner et al., 2006). Behaviors that were included as personal living skills included such tasks as: personal care of self, eating and meal preparation, dressing and appropriate selection and maintenance of clothes, and domestic skills (Wagner et al., 2006). These findings should be considered within the context of literature which documents the importance of daily living skills (Cronin & Patton, 1993; Brolin & Loyd, 2004; Sitlington & Clark, 2006).

Attention to life skills for the student with disabilities should begin early and not wait until age 16, when transition planning is mandated. Szymanski (1994) advocated a "lifespan and life-space" orientation to transition. According to Szymanski (1994), transition to adulthood is a lifelong set of experiences, beginning early in childhood and continuing throughout children's lives. These longitudinal activities impact all the domains of adulthood, including both career development and independent living (Rusch & Chadsey, 1998). Transition to adulthood and independence is a process that is lifelong and begins at birth and involves all the roles that individuals play during their lifetime (Rusch & Chadsey, 1998). Szymanski (1994) suggests that one of the reasons for the lack of success in transition programs is the narrow focus and the lack of introduction of important skills during the early years of life.

Taylor et al. (2002) stated that an important key to the achievement of independence and productivity for students with disabilities was teaching independent living skills. Training in domestic skills is an important key to not only independent functioning but may also provide persons with disabilities with the opportunity to apply these skills in vocational settings as well (Taylor et al., 2002). Independent living skills include the adaptive skills addressed on the ABAS-II in the home and school living section (refer to Tables 7.1–7.3). These functional life skills are those that students need in the area of daily living. Clark et al. (1994) advocated that a functional life skills instruction approach should be a part of every school curriculum either within existing course work or as an alternative course for all students at all grade levels.

Dever (1988) developed a list of what people in the U.S.A. must be able to do to get through each day week, month, and year. Dever's (1988) taxonomy of instructional goals for individuals lists five domains, including homemaking and community life. These lists are useful for all students, including those with disabilities such as mental retardation. Included in the community living skills necessary for homemaking and community life were: keep living space neat and clean, keep clothes neat and clean, shop for foods, and prepare and serve meals. Sitlington and Clark (2006) also developed a model for outcomes for career and transition curriculum. This model contained nine domains that included among others, self-determination and independent/interdependent daily living skills.

The Life Centered Career Education Curriculum, published by the Council for Exceptional Children, acknowledges the importance of not only academic skills but also of functional skills, including daily living skills such as planning meals, buying and preparing foods, washing and drying clothing, putting away clothing, use of basic appliances, and caring for living environments (Brolin & Loyd, 2004). Laundry skills, food preparation skills, and table cleaning skills are included as important, as these skills are necessary for independence and community living (Taylor et al., 2002). Meyer and Kohl (1985) suggest that skills that are appropriate for individuals promote independence and include cleaning the kitchen and bathroom, preparing meals or snacks, and washing clothes.

Skill attainment may vary according to an individual's disability, culture, and age. It is important to note that indicators of independence vary at different age levels. According to Sitlington and Clark (2006), important behaviors for children and youth with severe cognitive or multiple disabilities include eating, bathing, taking care of personal belongings, performing simple chores, and other similar behaviors. They suggest that few individuals are ever truly independent and refer to independent and interdependent living skills at multiple ages. When deciding what skills to teach, first priority should be given to the most basic or important home and school living skills, keeping in mind the individual's environment. One question that Carothers and Taylor (2004) advocate asking is, "if the student does not learn the skill, will they be able to function as an adult?"

It is clear that the development of skills such as those discussed in this section is associated with greater adult independence for individuals with disabilities (Cronin & Patton, 1993; Taylor et al., 2002). Most students are capable of learning, to at least some degree, the basic home living and school living skills. Most school transition models advocate a quality program that takes into consideration age-appropriate, integrated, functional, and community-based instruction (Sitlington & Clark, 2006). According to Sitlington and Clark, this instruction should be increasingly functional as students get older.

As reviewed in this section, research supports the importance of home living and school living adaptive skills. These skills promote independent/interdependent living. If these home living and school living skills are not present, the student must rely on others to accomplish tasks. The attainment of these skills allows an individual a sense of pride and accomplishment. They allow for privacy and some freedom of choice. The attainment of home and school living skills is therefore integral to an increased quality of life.

ASSESSMENT OF SCHOOL AND HOME LIVING ADAPTIVE SKILLS

This text addresses the use of the ABAS-II to assess adaptive skills and to design instruction to teach these skills. In addition to the use of the ABAS-II, other forms of assessment that are particularly useful for assessing daily living skills, particularly school and home living skills, include ecological inventory, task analytic assessment, assessment of choices of the individual, and assessment of generalized abilities (Steere & Burcroff, 2004). These approaches are described briefly in this section.

ECOLOGICAL INVENTORY

Since its initial description in the late 1970s, the ecological inventory approach has been demonstrated to be one of the most direct and useful approaches to assessing functional skills (Brown et al., 1979). This assessment strategy focuses on identifying functional activities in four domains or broad categories of daily life (domestic, community, leisure, and vocational). The need for and the ability to complete functional activities related to these four domains are assessed in relation to current and likely future environments. It should be reiterated that a domain is a category of activity (adaptive skill), while an environment is a place in which specific activities take place. Therefore, it is typical for people to engage in activities in the domestic (e.g., cooking, doing laundry), leisure (e.g., watching TV, playing games), and even vocational (e.g., doing homework, preparing for work) domains within their homes. This strategy has stood the test of time because it is practical, results in the identification of functional skills, and can focus on the unique or individual context of a specific person's life. The ecological inventory approach is particularly useful in the area of home living skills, as the assessor can focus on the specific home in which an individual currently lives and then assess needed adaptive or functional skills within sub-environments or smaller locations within and around the home (e.g., kitchen, bathroom, living room, bedroom, yard). As indicated above, this allows for a high degree of individualization, as not all home living environments require the same skills. For example, one home may not have an automatic dishwasher, so washing dishes by hand may be more important. Naturally, future living situations should also be considered, which may lead to the identification of additional needed skills. Table 7.4 shows a section of an ecological inventory for home living skills.

TASK ANALYTIC ASSESSMENT

Once specific activities are identified as important for success in home living, more detailed task analytic assessment allows for a more in-depth analysis of skill development or deficits. Pancsofar (1986) described a task analytic assessment approach in which natural cues (stimuli) are identified for each step

TABLE 7.4 Section of ecological inventory of home living skills.

Individual: Angela

Domain: Domestic

Environment: Home

Sub-environment: Kitchen

Activities:

- cooking stovetop dish (e.g., soup)
- cooking simple microwave oven snack or meal
- getting a drink from the refrigerator
- putting away groceries
- washing dishes by hand
- rinsing and stacking dishes in the dishwasher
- counting out silverware and napkins to set the table

Sub-environment: Bedroom

Activities:

- making the bed
- getting dressed
- folding and putting away laundry

Sub-environment: Bathroom

Activities:

- brushing teeth
- washing face
- taking a shower

Domain: Leisure

Environment: Home

Sub-environment: Living room

Activities:

- turning on TV and changing channels to watch TV
- using CD player to listen to music
- using DVD player to watch movies

Sub-environment: Kitchen

Activities:

- sharing a snack or cup of coffee with a visitor
- cooking brownies for fun
- calling a friend on the telephone

in a task analysis. The assessor then assesses the person's reactions to each natural cue in the task sequence. If the person can complete the step in response to the natural cue with no assistance, then the assessor simply notes this. If the individual cannot respond correctly to the natural cue for a particular step, then the assessor completes the step in question in order to make the next natural cue available. This approach allows the assessor to pinpoint where difficulties lie within the completion of a functional skill. This approach also is based on the premise that independence in the completion of home living skills increases as one can respond to the natural cues or stimuli within the environment. Table 7.5 shows a brief task analysis in the form recommended by Pancsofar (1986).

TABLE 7.5 Task analysis of heating soup in a microwave oven for task analytic assessment.

Cue	Step of the Task
1. Packaged soup container	Open top of soup container
2. Top is open	Fill container with water
3. Container is full	Open microwave oven door
4. Door is open	Place soup container in oven
5. Soup container is in oven	Close door of microwave oven
6. Door is closed	Set time for heating
7. Time is set or selected	Push start
8. Microwave starts	Wait for signal for completion
9. Microwave signal	Open door to microwave oven
10. Door is open	Remove heated soup and stir

ASSESSMENT OF CHOICES

As noted by Steere and Burcroff (2004), much of what takes place in a home environment reflects personal choice. For example, people typically choose what to prepare for meals, what to watch on television, or how to spend their leisure time. Assessment of individual preferences can help to identify motivators for learning school and home living skills. For example, knowledge of eating preferences can help teachers to plan cooking instruction that focuses on a preferred meal or snack. The assessment of choices can be completed through home, daycare, or classroom observations, or through interviews with people with disabilities and/or their families. We strongly suggest that a profile of choices be developed and maintained in order to communicate to caregivers and teachers about the preferences of people with disabilities, particularly those with poor communication abilities.

ASSESSMENT OF GENERALIZED ABILITIES

As indicated above, many of the school and home living skills discussed in this chapter may be performed in a variety of ways. A perusal of Tables 7.1 through 7.3 or of the completed listing of adaptive skills in this category within the ABAS-II will reveal a number of skills that are done in varied ways. For example, one of the ABAS-II items in the 0–5 age range is "Uses wall switch to turn lights on and off …" This skill may require the use of a wide variety of light switches, depending on the specific daycare or home environment. Likewise, the use of different microwave ovens, stoves, and household appliances requires generalization of skills. The use of the general-case approach is particularly helpful in assessing and then teaching generalized skills (Horner et al., 1982; Steere, 1997). This approach is described in greater detail later in this chapter.

INTERVENTION METHODS FOR SCHOOL AND HOME LIVING SKILLS ACQUISITION

After using the ABAS-II to assess an individual's current levels of functioning as baseline data, the knowledge gained can then be used to plan effective interventions to enhance the individual's skills. As discussed earlier in this chapter, many of the functional school and home living adaptive skills identified in this chapter must be learned in multiple ways in order for the individual to complete the skill as independently as possible. Consequently, direct and systematic efforts to assist individuals in acquiring and generalizing skills are essential. This section will explore research-based interventions designed to teach and monitor the acquisition and generalization of new skills.

INTERVENTION FACTORS

When first considering interventions to teach new adaptive skills, there are several factors that teachers, parents, supervisors, and other care-providers must consider incorporating into the instructional planning process. Self-determination, generalization, prompting, level of support, home reinforcement, and self-management are discussed below in order to establish a foundational knowledge before intervention planning can begin.

Self-determination: Self-determination, or the ability to make choices and decisions, is a powerful factor in motivating behavior change, particularly the learning of new skills. The learner's personal choices must be an essential component when implementing any intervention strategy. An environment, whether home or school, that allows individuals to actively express their personal preferences will enhance their ability to learn and generalize new skills with less support. Maximum consideration must be given to the individual's preferred interests, styles, habits, and methods of completing tasks.

Generalization: Generalization, or the ability to transfer learned skills to new settings, materials, or contexts, may not occur automatically for individuals with developmental disabilities or other difficulties (Stokes & Baer, 1977; Steere et al., 1989; Taylor et al., 2002). Skills must be taught in a variety of ways that consider the natural environments in which an individual will need to perform the skill.

Prompting: Individuals with developmental and other disabilities may need varying levels of prompts, or cues, to assist them in beginning or completing an activity. Prompts can include:

- Gestural (e.g., pointing)
- Verbal (e.g., verbal request)
- Modeling (e.g., demonstration)
- Pictorial (e.g., card with picture or word)
- Partial physical (e.g., light tap on hand)
- Full physical (e.g., placing a student's hand).

The least intrusive prompt should be used that will ensure the individual's response. The nature of the skill to be learned, and the environments in which it occurs, may also provide natural prompts that should be incorporated into the intervention to increase the individual's independence in utilizing newly acquired skills. Specific prompting interventions to teach school and home living skills will be addressed later in this section.

Level of support: Level of support refers to the intensity or duration of the assistance provided when completing a task. Individuals with disabilities may need varying levels of support to learn and generalize new school and home living skills. The necessary level of support must be considered when planning interventions.

Reinforcing skills at home: Interventions used to teach adaptive skills at school can also be reinforced at home, regardless of the age of the learner. When activities are also practiced in the home, generalization is promoted due to the learner having increased experiences in different settings (Carothers & Taylor, 2004; Westling & Fox, 2004). Additionally, siblings, parents, and neighborhood peers can participate, or act as tutors, in the learning process. It is essential to respect the individual's and family's preferences and routines for completing home living skills.

Self-management: Self-management, or self-monitoring, is demonstrated by an individual's ability to independently begin and complete each step of a task or skill without reliance on another person. Since increased independence is a goal of many intervention methods, self-management is an essential element in any intervention.

INTERVENTION METHODS

There are many teaching interventions that can be used to effectively teach the skills identified in the ABAS-II, including those related to school and home living adaptive skills. It is important to select interventions that reflect the needs of the learner and the environment in which the skill will be performed. This consideration can result in the use of a very simple approach or a complex combination of interventions that creates the optimal learning situation for the individual. Several methods will be presented with research-based examples of how they can be utilized or combined to teach specific school and home adaptive skill areas.

Using General-Case Instruction to Teach School and Home Living Skills

The general-case instruction approach has been demonstrated to be an effective approach for assisting people with disabilities to learn a variety of functional skills (Day & Horner, 1986; Horner et al., 1986; Horner & Albin, 1988; Chadsey-Rusch et al., 1993; Steere, 1997). In using the general-case approach, a teacher selects representative examples of an activity to use during instruction. These representative examples reflect the range of situations to which the learner will be expected to generalize. Building on earlier work (Becker et al., 1975; Engelmann & Carnine, 1982), Horner et al. (1982) developed six steps for the implementation of the general-case approach. These six steps (adapted from Horner et al., 1982) are described below, using an example skill that is addressed by the school and home living section of ABAS-II.

Step 1 – Define the Range of Situations to Which the Learner Must Generalize: After identifying a skill to teach, the first step recommended by Horner et al. (1982) is to define what they refer to as the *instructional universe.* The instructional universe is defined by two dimensions, the scope of the activity and the range of locations in which it will be used. For example, let us assume that a 10 year old student with mental retardation has been assessed using the ABAS-II, and it has been noted that she cannot wipe up spills (item # 3 on the Teacher Form for ages 5–21 and item # 2 on the Parent Form for this age group). The school support team, in consultation with the family, identified this as an important adaptive skill for the student to learn. The instructional universe in this case could be defined as the ability to obtain a paper towel, napkin, or sponge and completely wipe up small and large spills within any school or home setting. This instructional universe describes the parameter of the activity that is being taught and indicates that the learner should be able to successfully clean up any such spill. Note that there is considerable variation in the task in terms of the size of the spill, location of paper towels/napkins/sponges, and the location and nature of the spilled liquid or material.

Step 2 – Define the Variation in the Activity: Once the instructional universe has been specified, the instructor documents the variations the learner may encounter. For example, the instructor or other care-provider in this situation would analyze and record the types and size of spills that are likely to occur in school or at home (large or small spills of beverages or foods), the location of the spills (e.g., in the cafeteria or kitchen), and the range of different approaches for cleaning them up (with sponges, wash cloths, paper towels, paper napkins, etc.). In addition, the instructor or other care-provider would collaborate with the family to analyze and document the types of spills and approaches for cleaning them that are likely to happen in the home. The student's family may indicate that spills include spilled glasses of milk, spilled food at dinner time, or spilled juice in the kitchen, and they may indicate the family typically uses paper towels and/or a sponge to clean up these messes (see Steere, 1997 for a more detailed description of how to document the variation in a task such as this).

Step 3 – Select Teaching Examples and Examples for Assessing Generalization: Once the variation in the instructional universe has been analyzed and documented, representative examples of the activity are selected for use in instruction. It is essential that these examples represent the full range of situations the individual may encounter. The key is to select the *minimum* number of examples that reflect the *maximum* variation in the activity from the instructional universe. Continuing with our example, the instructor or other care-provider may decide, after analyzing the variation in wiping up spills, that the following critical examples should be targeted for instruction:

- A spilled glass of milk in the school cafeteria cleaned up with paper napkins
- Spilled crumbs from a snack in the school classroom cleaned up with a sponge
- Spilled salt in the cafeteria to be cleaned up with a wet cloth towel
- Spilled juice in the kitchen at home, cleaned up with paper towels.

In addition to selecting teaching examples, the instructor or other care-provider should select a second set of examples, called probes, which will be used to assess for generalization once the teaching examples have been mastered. For example, the instructor could select the following probe examples:

- A spill of pudding in the school cafeteria to be wiped up with a cloth napkin
- A spill of sugar in the classroom, to be cleaned up with a paper napkin
- A spill of gravy on the dinner table at home, to be cleaned up with a sponge

It should be noted here, although the mastery of multiple, representative examples of an activity in instruction may take longer than the mastery of a single example, in the long run, this approach is more efficient, as the individual will be able to handle new situations without re-teaching (Horner & Albin, 1988).

Step 4 – Sequence the Teaching Examples: Once the teaching examples have been selected, Horner et al. (1982) suggest they be introduced simultaneously (if possible) so that important differences in situations can be pointed out to the learner. This approach is superior to teaching each example to mastery in a sequential manner. The instructor or other care-provider in our example would therefore teach this skill by creating spills of glasses of beverages in the cafeteria to be cleaned up with paper napkins and snack spills in the classroom to be cleaned up with a sponge. Differences in the size and nature of these spills would be highlighted for the learner. At the same time, the instructor or other care-provider would request that the family begin to teach the student how to clean up juice spills in her own kitchen using paper towels.

Step 5 – Teach the Skill Using the Teaching Examples: This step is essentially the instructional step, and the instructor or other care-provider would use prompting hierarchies, shaping, chaining, and reinforcement strategies to teach the learner to complete the selected teaching examples as quickly as possible.

Step 6 – Assess for Generalization: The final step of the general-case instruction approach is to assess the individual's ability to successfully complete the probe or generalization examples that were selected in step # 3. The assessment should occur after the individual has mastered all of the teaching examples. Because the probes are unfamiliar examples from the instructional universe, they provide an excellent assessment measure for the success of efforts to promote generalization of the activity.

Using Task Analysis to Teach School and Home Living Skills

Task analysis is an effective intervention method that breaks down a task, such as folding clothes or washing dishes, into sequential steps. When these steps are used to evaluate an individual's ability to complete a task, it is called a task analytic assessment (as mentioned earlier). A task analysis must consider the environment in which the task will occur and the materials to be used when completing it. A task analysis can be created by completing a task exactly as it will be done during instruction and noting each sequential step. Teachers, parents, supervisors, and other care-providers often use task analysis when teaching a new skill and it is often combined with other approaches:

- Smith et al. (1999) created a task analysis for teaching table cleaning skills to secondary students with moderate/severe disabilities that additionally indicated whether steps were to be learned through observation or direct instruction.
- Fiscus et al. (2002) developed three separate task analyses to teach elementary students with moderate to severe cognitive disabilities to make chocolate milk, cheese and crackers, and waffles and syrup.
- Taylor et al. (2002) utilized task analyses for washing and drying clothes to teach these skills to high school students with moderate mental disabilities.

Using Functional Routines and Scheduling to Teach School and Home Living Adaptive Skills

Functional routines and scheduling are similar interventions to task analyses although they additionally consider the relevant behaviors that can act as natural cues in the environment such as placing dirty clothes in a hamper after taking a shower or getting a snack from the pantry when hungry. Routines and schedules allow individuals to learn the steps to independently complete school and home living skills. Routines and schedules provide great opportunities to incorporate an individual's preferences into the activities and tasks that are to be taught. Mesibov et al. (2002) suggested using a schedule for several purposes including easing transitions between activities, performing a series of tasks independently, following sequenced activities, and taking charge of leisure time:

- Pierce and Schriebman (1994) used a schedule containing pictures of each step of a task analysis to teach children classified as autistic and moderately to severely retarded to self-manage their daily living skills. Tasks included setting the table, making the bed, getting a drink, getting dressed, and doing laundry.
- Hall et al. (1995) used picture schedules to increase the ability of children with developmental disabilities (including autism and Fragile X) to increase their independence in integrated school settings. Prompts from classroom aides were decreased as students were encouraged to

independently rely on their picture schedules to complete activities such as getting materials ready for class.

- Anderson et al. (1997) used a picture schedule to teach adults with mental retardation in a group home to manage their evening activities. Residents could place photos of activities in a photo album to choose their activities.

Using the System of Least Prompts to Teach School and Home Living Adaptive Skills

The System of Least Prompts (SLP), sometimes called least-to-most prompting, provides students with, "A hierarchy of prompts that moves progressively from having a minimal influence to having a maximum, controlling influence (the controlling stimulus). The intention is to provide a prompt on each trial with only the minimum intensity necessary to get the behavior to occur" (Westling & Fox, 2004, p. 163). The SLP often accompanies a time delay to determine if an individual will respond to the prompt before a more intense prompt is supplied. The SLP allows students to be as independent as possible when completing a school or home living task.

- Smith et al. (1999) used the SLP and verbal praise to teach table cleaning skills to secondary students with moderate/severe disabilities in the kitchen area of the classroom. They began with modeling the activity and then relied on an increasingly direct series of verbal prompts and partial physical prompts if the student did not respond. They utilized different types of buckets, tables, and cloths to increase generalizability.
- Fiscus et al. (2002) used the SLP to teach elementary students with moderate to severe cognitive disabilities to make snacks in the kitchen area of the classroom. They used a combination of modeling and verbal prompts and time delays. They also included instructive feedback into the prompting to reinforce students' correct attempts at making their snacks.
- Taylor et al. (2002) used the SLP to teach clothes washing and drying skills to high school students with moderate mental disabilities in a family living classroom. Prompts included presenting the item to the student (e.g., a basket of clothes) and verbal and modeling prompts. A time delay was also incorporated. Additionally, they incorporated incidental learning of laundry sight words (e.g., fabric, rinse, cycle). An example of a least prompting sequence for the task of using a clothes dryer is shown in Table 7.6.

Using Videotaping to Teach School and Home Living Skills

Videotaped modeling is a useful strategy, particularly if teachers do not have access to the naturally occurring environment or if access causes behavioral concerns. Another student or the teacher can be videotaped completing the task that is to be taught. Videotape copies can be used at home to reinforce the skills taught at school or videotapes can be made using the home setting. For example, Haring et al. (1987) used videotapes to teach children with autism to make purchases and provide social responses in a school cafeteria and generalize them to community settings.

TABLE 7.6 Using system of least prompts within a task analysis and a 5 second time delay.

Natural prompt occurs For this example: a dryer buzzes when the cycle is finished	• Individual opens dryer door and moves to next step in task analysis		
• 5 second delay	• If not, teacher provides verbal prompt (e.g., "The dryer just buzzed.")	• Individual opens dryer door and moves to next step in task analysis	
	• 5 second delay	• If not, teacher provides partial physical prompt (e.g., tap on hand)	• Individual opens dryer door and moves to next step in task analysis
		• 5 second delay	• If not, teacher models how to open dryer door

Note: Table created by Heather Garrison

ABAS-II GUIDELINES FOR PROGRAM PLANNING AND MONITORING

The ABAS-II describes five steps when planning interventions for individuals, as described below (Harrison & Oakland, 2003). These steps are reviewed briefly here:

Step 1: Identify the skill levels needed for an individual's current environment or the environment into which the individual is moving

- As suggested by the ecological inventory strategy, it is important to identify skills that people with disabilities need both now and in future likely environments. This includes an analysis of the importance of home living skills and the anticipated levels of support that might be needed.

Step 2: Identify current areas of strengths and weaknesses relative to environmental requirements

- Comprehensive assessment data, including the ABAS-II, should be used to create profiles of individuals with disabilities that document their strengths and needs in relation of optimal living environments. These profiles should also document support systems that allow individuals to function with greater independence.

Step 3: Identify and prioritize intervention objectives based on discrepancies between environmental needs and personal attainment

- The development of profiles of strengths and needs leads to the clarification of objectives to guide the instructional process. Again, skills that are needed for success in current and future living situations should be the priority.

TABLE 7.7 Results of the ABAS-II (Parent Form for ages 5–21 and Teacher Form for ages 5–21) for Luisa, age 12 years.

	Parent Form			Teacher Form		
Composite/Adaptive Skill Area	Adaptive Skill Area Scaled Score	Composite Standard Score	Composite Percentile Rank	Adaptive Skill Area Scaled Score	Composite Standard Score	Composite Percentile Rank
Conceptual Composite		55	0.1		61	0.5
• Communication	2			3		
• Functional academics	1			1		
• Self-direction	3			4		
Social Composite		59	0.3		68	2
• Leisure	4			3		
• Social	4			4		
Practical Composite		45	<0.1		53	0.1
• Community use	3			2		
• Home living	1			–		
• School living	–			1		
• Health and safety	2			2		
• Self-care	3			3		
General Adaptive Composite		54	0.1		54	0.1

Note: Composite scores (Conceptual, Social, and Practical) and the General Adaptive Composite (GAC) standard scores have a mean of 100 and standard deviation of 15. Adaptive skill areas (Communication, Functional Academics, etc.) scaled scores have a mean of 10 and standard deviation of 3. Table created by Patti Harrison.

Step 4: Implement interventions to achieve specific objectives

- This step utilizes evidenced-based instructional strategies, such as those discussed in this chapter.

Step 5: Monitor the implementation and effectiveness of the interventions

- Monitoring of the impact of interventions is necessary to pinpoint needed changes in instruction and to document the reduction of needed supports.

CASE STUDY

Luisa is a 12 year old girl who has been identified as having moderate mental retardation. Her profile indicates that she generally requires limited to extensive supports in most areas of adaptive skill. Table 7.7 summarizes her scores on the ABAS-II for both the Teacher and Parent forms for ages 5–21. The Teacher

Form was completed by Luisa's current teacher and the Parent Form was completed by her mother and father.

Luisa lives in a comfortable ranch style home in a residential neighborhood. She lives with her parents, both of whom work, and her younger sister, who is eight years old. Luisa's parents are both committed to helping her learn functional skills and they communicate regularly with Luisa's teachers to ensure that they are working on the same skills at home and at school. Luisa's parents report that she requires a great deal of verbal and other prompts to complete most daily activities, although she is becoming more independent with certain routine activities. Luisa's parents are hopeful that, some day, she will be able to work in the community with support and perhaps live in a supported living situation.

Luisa attends her neighborhood intermediate school, where she is in a classroom operated by a local education agency that provides services to individuals with moderate to severe disabilities within the local region. Her curriculum consists of functional academic skills (reading a simple shopping list, using a calculator to add prices), domestic skills such as simple meal preparation and washing dishes, and communication and social interaction skills. Her teacher reports that, as is the case at home, Luisa requires substantial prompting to initiate most activities, and she requires assistance in completing the steps of more complex activities.

A review of her ABAS-II assessment indicates that there are a number of adaptive skill areas in which Luisa requires substantial prompting and is therefore unable to complete independently. Luisa's ABAS-II scores show that her ability levels are significantly impaired across the composite and adaptive skill areas, including the home and school living skills areas. These scores in the home and school living adaptive skills areas indicate a need for her to learn tasks related to the maintenance of her environment, organization of her belongings, and interactions with others both at home and at school. The need for prompting across these adaptive skill areas is consistent between school and home. It is noted that Luisa made progress with similar types of tasks that were performed on a daily basis in both settings.

In addition to the ABAS-II, Luisa was assessed using task analytic assessment for specific school and home living tasks (e.g., wiping off tables, rinsing dishes and putting them in a dishwasher, using a microwave oven to heat a container of soup, etc.). These task analytic assessments showed that Luisa requires prompting for some steps of most activities but does not require prompting for all steps. In other words, she is able to independently respond to the natural cues for certain steps but not for others. This indicates that systematic prompting sequences are needed to draw her attention to natural cues within complex activities and to systematically fade the intensity of the needed assistance.

An additional issue that has been noted at both school and at home is that Luisa does not generalize her skills easily to the use of new materials. For example, she needs to be taught tasks such as wiping off tables within both the school and home, as she does not transfer learning from one setting to another.

TABLE 7.8 Luisa's priority home and school living needs.

Priority School Living Skills	Priority Home Living Skills
While in the classroom or lunchroom, Luisa will respect other's property by requesting materials without grabbing.	Luisa will respect her sister's property by requesting materials without grabbing.
Luisa will dust and clean specified areas of her classroom (e.g., chalkboard, desktop, table tops).	Luisa will clear and wash the kitchen table after a meal.
Luisa will wipe up spills in the classroom or lunchroom.	Luisa will wipe up spills at home.
Luisa will place dirty trays, plates, forks, and other items in correct disposal bins in the school lunchroom.	Luisa will put her clean laundry away in the correct dresser drawers.
Luisa will organize her backpack and desk area in the classroom.	Luisa will keep her bedroom clean by putting her toys and books in the correct location when she is finished with them.

The close communication between the school and home is a positive aspect in this regard and should help ensure that Luisa is exposed to relevant variations in home and school living activities.

Luisa's educational team, in collaboration with her parents, identified several priority skills to be included in her IEP, as identified by the ABAS-II and task analytic assessment. These skills were chosen because of their importance within her current school and home settings and in future independent living settings that she may attain in her adulthood. The home and school living adaptive skill areas identified as priorities for Louisa are shown in Table 7.8. Suggestions for interventions to address Luisa's priority need areas are provided in Table 7.9.

SUMMARY

This chapter has described the importance of home and school living adaptive skills, as assessed by ABAS-II. As described in this chapter, these skills are essential for greater independence and choice in adult living and are therefore associated with improved quality of life for people with disabilities. Home and school living skills must be taught directly and longitudinally, starting early in a child's life and with an eye toward the transition to adult life. In addition, systematic efforts must be made to ensure that skills generalize from one setting to another, and that instruction is individualized to meet the needs of each individual. Finally, it is important to remember that these skills must be considered within the context of other adaptive skill development areas that are equally important.

TABLE 7.9 Intervention suggestions for Luisa's priority home and school living needs.

Luisa's Priority Areas	Suggested Intervention Strategies
Requesting materials without grabbing, in school and at home.	• Use of videotaping to demonstrate appropriate and inappropriate behavior when Luisa wants something • Use of SLP to elicit appropriate requesting behavior • Read children's books about sharing
Perform simple clean-up activities in the classroom and at home, including wiping up spills, cleaning surfaces, etc.	• Task analyses of simple cleaning activities • General-case analysis of clean-up activities to ensure the use of a representative range of cleaning materials and procedures • Schedule regular clean-up routines for Luisa in the classroom and at home
Maintain her environment, personal spaces, and belongings, at school and at home, including backpack, desk, bedroom, toys, laundry, books, lunchroom items, etc.	• Picture card task analysis to help Luisa follow consistent steps in organizational activities • Use of SLP to assist Luisa in following the picture task analysis • Use of a chart where Luisa can place a sticker next to the picture of an activity to indicate when she has completed it

REFERENCES

Anderson, M. D., Sherman, J. A, Sheldon, J. B., & McAdam, D. (1997). Picture activity schedules and engagement of adults with mental retardation in a group home. *Research in Developmental Disabilities*, *18*, 231–250.

Becker, W., Engelmann, S., & Thomas, D. (1975). *Teaching 2: Cognitive Learning and Instruction*. Chicago: Science Research Associates.

Brolin, D. E. & Loyd, R. (2004). *Career Development and Transition Services: A Functional Life Skills Approach*, 4th edn., Upper Saddle River, NJ: Pearson: Merrill Prentice Hall.

Brown, L., Branston-McClean, M., Baumgart, D., Vincent, L., Falvey, M., & Schroeder, J. (1979). Using the characteristics of current and subsequent least restrictive environments in the development of curricular content for severely handicapped students. *AAESPH Review*, *4*, 407–434.

Carothers, D. E. & Taylor, R. L. (2004). How teachers and parents can work together to teach daily living skills to children with autism. *Focus on Autism and Other Developmental Disabilities*, *19*(2), 102–104.

Chadsey-Rusch, J., Drasgow, E., Reinoehl, B., Halle, J., & Collet-Klingenberg, L. (1993). Using general-case instruction to teach spontaneous and generalized requests for assistance to learners with severe disabilities. *Journal of the Association for Persons with Severe Handicaps*, *18*, 177–187.

Clark, G., Field, S., Patton, J., Brolin, D., & Sitlington, P. (1994). *Life Skills Instruction: A Necessary Component for all Students with Disabilities: A Position Statement of the Division on Career Development and Transition*. Arlington, VA: Council for Exceptional Children, Division on Career Development and Transition.

Cronin, M. & Patton, J. (1993). *Life Skills Instruction for all Students with Special Needs: A Practical Guide for Integrating Real-Life Content into the Curriculum*. Austin, TX: Pro-Ed.

Day, M. & Horner, R. H. (1986). Response variation and the generalization of a dressing skill: Comparison of single instance and general-case instruction. *Applied Research in Mental Retardation*, *7*, 189–202.

Dever, R. (1988). *Community Living Skills: A Taxonomy*. Washington, DC: American Association on Mental Retardation (AAMR).

Engelmann, S. & Carnine, D. (1982). *Theory of Instruction: Principles and Applications*. New York: Irvington.

Fiscus, R. S., Schuster, J. W., Morse, T. E., & Collins, B. C. (2002). Teaching elementary students with cognitive disabilities food preparation skills while embedding instructive feedback in the prompt and consequent event. *Education and Training in Mental Retardation and Developmental Disabilities, 37*(1), 55–69.

Hall, L. J., McClannahan, L. E., & Krantz, P. J. (1995). Prompting independence in integrated classrooms by teaching aides to use activity schedules and decreased prompts. *Education and Training in Mental Retardation and Developmental Disabilities, 30*, 208–217.

Haring, T. G., Kennedy, C. H., Adams, M. J., & Pitts-Conway, V. (1987). Teaching generalization of purchasing skills across community settings to autistic youth using videotaped modeling. *Journal of Applied Behavioral Analysis, 20*, 89–96.

Harrison, P. & Oakland, T. (2003). *ABAS-II: The Adaptive Behavior Assessment System II Manual*, 2nd edn., San Antonio, TX: Harcourt Assessment, Inc.

Horner, R. H. & Albin, R. (1988). Research on general-case procedures for learners with severe disabilities. *Education and Treatment of Children, 11*, 375–388.

Horner, R. H., Sprague, J., & Wilcox, B. (1982). General case programming for community activities. In B. Wilcox, & G. T. Bellamy (Eds.), *Design of High School Programs for Severely Handicapped Students*, pp. 61–98. Baltimore, MD: Paul H. Brookes.

Horner, R. H., Williams, J., & Stevely, J. (1986). Acquisition and maintenance of generalized telephone use by persons with moderate and severe mental retardation. *Research in Developmental Disabilities, 8*, 229–247.

Howe, J., Horner, R., & Newton, S. (1998). Comparison of supported living and traditional residential services in the state of Oregon. *Mental Retardation, 36*, 1–11.

Mesibov, G. G., Browder, D. M., & Kirkland, C. (2002). Using individualized schedules as a component of positive behavioral support for students with developmental disabilities. *Journal of Positive Behavior Interventions, 4*(2), 73–79.

Meyer, D. & Kohl, F. L. (1985). Teaching domestic living skills to severely handicapped students in the natural environment. *Teaching Exceptional Children, 18*, 38–45.

O'Brien, J. (1994). Down stairs that are never your own: Supporting people with mental retardation in their own homes. *Mental Retardation, 32*, 1–6.

Pancsofar, E. (1986). Assessing work behavior. In F. R. Rusch (Ed.), *Supported Employment Issues and Strategies*, pp. 93–102. Baltimore, MD: Paul H. Brookes.

Pierce, K. L. & Schriebman, L. (1994). Teaching daily living skills to children with autism in unsupervised settings through pictorial self-management. *Journal of Applied Behavior Analysis, 27*, 471–481.

Rusch, F. R. & Chadsey, J. G. (1998). *Beyond High School: Transition from School to Work*. Belmont, CA: Wadsworth Publishing Company.

Sitlington, P. L. & Clark, G. M. (2006). *Transition Education and Services for Students with Disabilities*, 4th edn., Boston, MD: Pearson: Allyn Bacon.

Smith, R. L., Collins, B. C., Schuster, J. W., & Kleinert, H. (1999). Teaching table clearing skills to secondary students with moderate/severe disabilities: Facilitating observational learning during instructional downtime. *Education and Training in Mental Retardation and Developmental Disabilities, 34*(3), 342–353.

Stancliffe, R., Abery, B., & Smith, J. (2000). Personal control and the ecology of community living settings: Beyond living-unit size and type. *American Journal on Mental Retardation, 105*, 431–454.

Steere, D. (1997). *Increasing Variety in Adult Life: A General-Case Approach (Innovations, Issue # 10)*. Washington, DC: American Association on Mental Retardation (AAMR).

Steere, D. & Burcroff, T. (2004). Living at home: Skills for independence. In P. Wehman, & J. Kregel (Eds.), *Functional Curriculum for Elementary, Middle, and Secondary Age Students with Special Needs*, 2nd edn., pp. 293–316. Austin, TX: Pro-Ed.

Steere, D. E., Pancsofar, E. L., Powell, T. H., & Butterworth, J. (1989). Enhancing instruction through general case programming. *Teaching Exceptional Children, 22*(1), 22–24.

Steere, D., Rose, E., & Cavaiuolo, D. (2007). *Growing Up: Transition to Adult Life for Students with Disabilities.* Boston: Allyn & Bacon.

Stokes, T. & Baer, D. (1977). An implicit technology of generalization. *Journal of Applied Behavior Analysis, 10*, 349–367.

Szymanski, E. (1994). Transition: Life span and life space considerations for empowerment. *Exceptional Children, 60*, 402–410.

Taylor, P., Collins, B. C., Schuster, J. W., & Kleinert, H. (2002). Teaching laundry skills to high school students with disabilities: Generalization of targeted skills and nontargeted information. *Education and Training in Mental Retardation and Developmental Disabilities, 37*(20), 172–183.

Wagner, M., Newman, L., Cameto, R., & Levine, P. (2006). The academic achievement and functional performance of youth with disabilities. A Report from the *National Longitudinal Transition Study-2 (NLTS2)*, NCSER 2006-3000. Menlo Park, CA: SRI International.

Westling, D. L. & Fox, L. (2004). *Teaching Students with Severe Disabilities*, 3rd edn., Upper Saddle River, NJ: Merrill.

8

HEALTH AND SAFETY ADAPTIVE SKILL AREA[1]

MARTIN AGRAN*, FRED SPOONER*, AND TRACIE-LYNN ZAKAS**

*Department of Special Education, University of Wyoming, Laramie, WY 82071, U.S.A.

**Department of Special Education and Child Development, University of North Carolina at Charlotte, Charlotte, NC 28223-0001, U.S.A.

IMPORTANCE OF HEALTH AND SAFETY

One's health and personal safety constitute some of our most basic needs (Maslow, 1954). Universally, after physiological needs are met (e.g., breathing, food, water), we seek safety and security throughout the various dimensions of our lives (e.g., health, body, family), irrespective of our age. We endeavor to promote a healthy and safe lifestyle while removing or minimizing all health or safety risks (Agran et al., 1994). We attend increasingly to nutrition and the nutritional integrity of the foods we consume. We learn to identify risks at home, school, work, and the community and how to avoid or respond to them. We learn to avoid potentially hazardous situations (e.g., picking up strangers, using an electric shaver while taking a bath). We learn about the unhealthy and deleterious effects of unsafe sex and substance use. Although fidelity to healthy and safe practices varies across individuals and circumstances, information about how to lead healthy and safe lives is available to all who are interested and able to

[1] The terms *student* or *children* are used in this chapter. The content of this chapter is applicable to a broad range of ages and to those for whom there are concerns about their health and safety. Thus, readers are encouraged to consider this broader perspective when reading this chapter.

access and retain it. A significant percentage of our population is committed to practices that will ensure healthy and safe lives.

The goal to prepare individuals, including those with disabilities and other challenges, to become independent and competent and to participate fully across community settings requires their learning a repertoire of health and safety skills that enable them to identify potential physical, physiological, and social risks and to know how to avoid or respond to them. Allowing them to transition from school to more mature lifestyles, including their engagement in work, the community, and in other less protected and adult settings without knowing these health and safety skills is foolhardy, unsound, and highly risky. However, the promotion of safety skills largely has been ignored as a curricular domain for students with significant cognitive disabilities (Agran et al., 1994; Gast et al., 1994; Juracek, 1994; Agran, 2004).

Many individuals with disabilities, particularly those with more significant cognitive limitations, acquire minimal knowledge of how to respond to potentially risky situations and, as a result, are victimized at levels equal to or greater than those in the general population (Agran, 2004). Nevertheless, instruction in safety skills delivered to many students with disabilities is very limited (Agran, 2004).

All home, work, and community setting pose inherent risks and can be dangerous for individuals unable to identify and respond appropriately to risk stimuli. Indeed, accidents remain the leading cause of death for children without disabilities (Haller, 1970; Peterson, 1984). Most people can identify unsafe stimuli automatically and thus generally either attend to these stimuli or take them seriously. Unfortunately, we also often assume that individuals with disabilities know how best to respond to risks and hazards. This assumption often is unfounded and can be hazardous to their health and safety.

The purpose of this chapter is to advocate for and describe a health and safety curriculum for people with significant disabilities. Issues discussed include home and community living, work, fire prevention, crime prevention, HIV/AIDS prevention, substance use, and health care. Additionally, the value of the Adaptive Behavior Assessment System-II (ABAS-II), including the health and safety adaptive skill area, is discussed. A case study illustrates the application of the educational recommendations presented in this chapter.

An examination of the components and applications of science for students with significant cognitive disabilities led Spooner et al. (2006) to conclude that *personal health* and *safety* and *avoiding injury* are functional skills that can be taught within the context of science. The National Science Education Standards (National Research Council, 1996) identified seven teaching standards for the effective pedagogy and learning of science content: science as inquiry, life science, physical science, earth and space science, science and technology, science in personal and social perspectives, and history and nature of science. Acquiring knowledge of science may be seen as less important than acquiring basic skills in reading, math, and writing. In brief, although there are been little research in teaching science skills to students and persons with significant cognitive disabilities,

11 published accounts on teaching science-related skills have been located in the literature (Courtade et al., in press). Most of these studies have examined the teaching of safety skills (e.g., Spooner et al., 1989; Gast et al., 1992; Winterling et al., 1992; Collins et al., 1993; Collins & Griffen, 1996).

ABAS-II MEASUREMENT IN HEALTH AND SAFETY

The ABAS-II offers a comprehensive, norm-referenced evaluation of individuals from birth through 89 years. This assessment is used to diagnose and classify, identify strengths and weaknesses in adaptive skills, and identify service and planning needs. Target behaviors for school-aged children and adults are assessed in the following 10 adaptive skill areas: communication, community use, functional academics, school/home living, health and safety, leisure, self-care, self-direction, social, and work (and motor skills for young children). These skills are grouped into one of three composites: conceptual, social, and practical. The health and safety adaptive skill area is categorized in a practical composite. In addition, a summary score, the General Adaptive Composite, is provided.

Each of the ABAS-II items is rated 0 (is not able to display the behavior), 1 (is able yet never displays the behavior when needed), 2 (sometimes displays the behavior when needed), or 3 (always or almost always displays the behavior when needed). Respondents record when their answer was a guess.

There are between 16 and 24 health and safety items on each of the five ABAS-II forms: Parent/Primary Caregiver Form (ages birth–5), Teacher/Daycare Provider Form (ages 2–5), Parent Form (ages 5–21), Teacher Form (ages 5–21), and Adult Form (ages 16–89). The health and safety items include behaviors associated with managing medications, hot and dangerous items, electrical outlets, scissors and sharp items, breakable objects, minor injuries and illnesses, and basic nutrition. Automobile and traffic safety, work/vocational safety, and environmental safety also are addressed.

After the respondent completes the ABAS-II, the items are scored, compared to scores obtained from the person's peer group, and transformed into standard scores. The test data can help identify target areas of need for students. Information provided through the use of the ABAS-II can be useful in developing specific goals and objectives for individual education programs, identifying detailed and explicit curriculum and interventional methods for persons with adaptive skills deficits, and monitoring change.

VALUE OF HEALTH AND SAFETY FOR GENERAL FUNCTIONING

PREVALENCE AND EPIDEMIOLOGY

Although data on accidents, victimization, or injury for persons with disabilities are limited, the available reported data suggest that individuals with disabilities sustain injuries at relatively high levels. For example, youth with disabilities comprise 2% of the population yet sustain 17% of school-related injuries (Ramirez et al., 2004). Although 17% of the population has some disability, members of this group are responsible for 47% of the medical expenditures, four times more than the non-disabled population (Rice & Trupin, 1996). Students with disabilities have a higher risk for nonfatal injuries (Xiang et al., 2005). The risk is higher for students with multiple or physical disabilities than for children with other disabilities (Ramirez et al., 2004). Preschool children with disabilities have a significantly higher risk to sustain injuries, with boys having double the number of injuries (Dunne et al., 1993).

Additional prevalence figures also suggest higher levels of involvement for people with disabilities. For example, in a sample of 11,000 individuals served by 800 vocational rehabilitation facilities, more than 4,000 injuries were reported (Agran & Madison, 1995). Research in 108 rehabilitation facilities found approximately 30% of the consumers to be HIV-positive (Jaskulski & Mason, 1992). Approximately 70% of abused children were found to have disabilities (Chotiner & Lehr, 1976). At least 90% of children with developmental disabilities reportedly have been sexually exploited (Muccigrosso, 1991), with 73% of women with disabilities reportedly have been victims of violence (Stimpson & Best, 1991). Thus, these data suggest that individuals with disabilities are injured or victimized at levels comparable to and often that exceed the general population.

PREDISPOSING PERSONS WITH DISABILITIES TO INJURY

Persons with disabilities may be predisposed to sustaining injuries because of their cognitive, physical, or sensory limitations. Even with accessible school facilities, cognitive and motor skill limitations may create problems for students with disabilities in school and community settings (Ramirez et al., 2004). Such characteristics as "... poor judgment; lack of awareness of danger; impulsiveness and restlessness; inability or difficulties in communicating; low pain threshold; abnormal muscle functioning causing difficulties in chewing, swallowing, standing, walking; and impaired vision and/or hearing" (Bryan et al., 1978, p. 8) may predispose individuals with disabilities to injury. For example, students with physical or sensory impairments (i.e., blindness) have an increased potential for injury (Ramirez et al., 2004).

HEALTH AND SAFETY CURRICULUM

Ironically, efforts to prepare children, youth, and adults to lead as full a life as possible, including their community participation, may result to a greater likelihood that an accident or other risks may occur. Participation in these settings allows individuals with disabilities to have more normalized and valued life experiences.

However, in turn, their participation may expose them to numerous risks present in these environments, some they are unaware of and others to which they may not know how to respond. Failure to learn safety skills may leave individuals vulnerable to injury, may limit their competence, and further promote their dependence on caregivers or service providers (Agran, 2004).

Critical health and safety skill areas include the following domains: home and community living, work, fire and crime prevention, HIV/AIDS prevention, substance use, and self-medication and health care (Agran et al., 1994). A brief discussion of each follows.

HOME AND COMMUNITY LIVING

Accidents occur frequently at home and in the community. One person in 11 has incurred an injury at home that requires medical attention or results in one half day or more of restricted activity (National Safety Council, 1988). One percent of the population suffers serious burn injuries each year (Tarnowski et al., 1987). Figure 8.1 presents selected safety skills areas identified by a sample of parents (Collins et al., 1992). These include: safe tool/appliance use, pedestrian and mobility skills, interacting with animals, recognizing poisons, and knowledge of electrical problems, to name a few (see Figure 8.1).

Many persons with disabilities, especially those with cognitive limitations, exhibit difficulty when transferring skills learned in one setting to other new settings. Thus, when possible, attempts to teach important skills should be conducted in the natural settings in which these skills later will be performed. However, the use of simulations is warranted when instruction in natural settings may not be feasible and to prevent them from being subjected to unnecessary risks. For example, an instructor may pretend that s/he has swallowed poison so that s/he can see how the student responds. Simulations allow for the use of frequent trials in contrast to the limited number of instructional trials that may be feasible in community settings. The use of simulations permits individuals to practice a variety of safety skills that otherwise would expose them to great danger or harm. See Chapter 5 for a more complete discussion of issues associated with preparing persons to function well in community settings.

Additionally, home and community safety skills need to be taught in the context of a natural routine (e.g., crossing a street during a shopping trip), not at an arbitrary time and place convenient for the instructor (Gast et al., 1994). Practicing safety skills in a routine allows the individual to learn what to do if an accident may occur (e.g., liquid spills on floor during a work task). Also, to minimize risk, instructional materials may need to be modified (e.g., use larger drill bits rather than small, sharp bits). These adaptations allow for instruction that would otherwise be too difficult to conduct. Safety skills, like other discrete behaviors, needs to be systematically shaped and reinforced (see Teaching Health and Safety Skills later in this chapter).

Home safety

Kitchen
Bathroom
General home areas

Community safety

Yards/playgrounds
Responding to strange animals
Bicycle use
Community mobility

Fire safety

First aid
Responding to strangers
Sex education

FIGURE 8.1 Parent identified safety skills areas.

WORK SAFETY

Virtually every work environment can potentially be dangerous (Agran & Martella, 1994). A sample of employers rated safe work behavior and safety awareness as most important for the job survival of all employees (Mueller et al., 1989). Individuals with disabilities tend to sustain injuries due to work accidents at levels comparable to, perhaps even higher than, workers without disabilities (Martella & Agran, 1994). Despite these data on the high level of work injuries sustained by persons with disabilities, few secondary-level special education personnel provide ongoing work safety skills instruction to their students (Agran et al., 1998).

Work injuries are caused by behavioral and/or environmental factors. Behavioral causes refer to the inappropriate or unsafe actions of employees or their lack of an appropriate response to an injury-causing situation (e.g., using wrong tool, not wearing goggles). Environmental causes include physical stimuli at a job site that may cause an injury (e.g., exposed electrical wiring, spilled food on floor). Not surprisingly, behavioral causes occur at a significantly higher level than environmental causes (Agran & Madison, 1995). The most frequently reported cause was general carelessness, followed by improper positioning, failure to adhere to safety procedures, and not wearing protective equipment. The most frequently reported environmental causes were objects on floor, congestion, and wet floors. What is compelling about these data is that most of these accidents are preventable since they are caused by the inappropriate actions of the employees.

Work safety skills include both generic and job-specific skills. For example, lifting boxes appropriately, attending to the work task, and not engaging in horseplay while working are necessary for all jobs. In addition, many jobs may present specific risks. A job safety analysis should be performed to identify these risks. The safety analysis includes two components. First, list the response sequence for the work task and the related environmental cues for each of these responses. Second, list all potential hazards present in the work environment to which the employee may be exposed when performing the response sequence. With this information, employees can be taught to respond appropriately to the work hazards as they complete their work tasks. Further, this process allows safety instruction to be nested into ongoing work training and performance reviews. This allows the student to have a better idea of the contexts in which an accident may happen, not as an event that occurs independently of the work routine.

Instruction in work safety involves two major components: identifying safety hazards and determining how to respond to them. In particular, a problem-solving strategy is suggested as an effective way to teach safety skills (Martella & Agran, 1994).

Specifically, individuals are taught to ask and respond to the following questions:

- How would an accident happen?
- When would an accident be prevented?
- Who would you talk to if one occurred?
- What would you do or say?

  or:
- What is dangerous (in a given environment)?
- Why is it unsafe?
- What can I do to make it safe?

Initially, students are taught to state that a problem exists (e.g., need to step over extension cord while working) and identify one or more solutions (e.g., ask co-worker to remove or cover extension cord). Following this, they are instructed to direct themselves to perform the planned response.

FIRE SAFETY

Each year home fires lead to many deaths and property destruction. The survival of individuals with disabilities during a fire may depend on their ability to learn and perform the following fire safety skills: exiting from a home if a fire has started, extinguishing a small fire if this is possible, and preventing the occurrence of the fire. Specifically, individuals need to know how to respond appropriately to nighttime emergencies (most fire emergencies occur in the night), how to respond to cooking fires (a large percentage of fires occur in the kitchen and many can be extinguished), and how to use smoking materials appropriately (appropriate lighting and disposal of cigarettes and ashes; Juracek, 1994). The infrequent occurrence of fires increases the difficulty teaching and assessing fire safety skills by preventing persons from practicing fire safety skills in vivo. Thus, learning and assessing these skills must rely extensively on simulations. Teachers, parents, supervisors, and other care providers must create situations to assess and teach mastery of these skills (Agran, 2004).

All fire safety skills require persons to follow a specified sequence. In teaching these sequences, Juracek (1994) recommends the use of direct instruction, providing a rationale, repeated practice, modeling, feedback, and self-evaluation. Training should take place in the individual's home, and training probes should be scheduled in the home at various times (especially in the nighttime). To accomplish this, a coordinated home-school/agency program involving parents, teachers, supervisors, and other stakeholders may need to be developed.

Preventive safety skills (e.g., those that help ensure a fire does not start in the first place) are critical and need to be acquired. These include the need to learn to use appliances appropriately; to store flammable objects safely; discourage cigarette use and, if used, their being extinguished properly; monitor lit candles or fires in fireplaces, and use space heaters consistent with manufacturers' recommendations (Agran, 2004). The importance of acquiring these skills cannot be overemphasized.

CRIME PREVENTION

Precise figures on the number of persons with disabilities who have been criminally or sexually abused are not available. However, the available data suggest that people with disabilities appear to be particularly vulnerable (Stimpson & Best, 1991; Sobsey, 1994; Lumley & Miltenberger, 1997). Individuals with disabilities, particularly women, are more likely to be victimized than individuals without disabilities (Sobsey, 1994). Crime prevention needs to be recognized as an essential safety skills area.

Individuals with disabilities can reduce the likelihood of their being victimized by acquiring skills in the following areas: decision making, assertiveness training, sex education, personal rights and safety, social and communication skills, property management, and responding to crimes (Sobsey, 1994). A brief discussion of each follows.

Decision making: Similar to the problem-solving procedure discussed under Work Safety, individuals should be taught to ask four questions when faced with a potentially abusive situation. First, is (self or other) _____ faced with a problem? Second, what is _______'s problem? Third, what is the best thing for _______ to do in this situation? Fourth, why is this the best choice for _______? These skills need to be acquired.

Assertiveness: Individuals need to learn to be assertive, to express their preferences, and to protect their rights (e.g., control of one's own money, freedom from unwanted interventions or medications, freedom from coercion and abuse). For example, children should learn to respond appropriately to teasing, thus possibly defusing potentially explosive situations and presenting themselves as being less vulnerable (Sobsey, 1994).

Sex education: The incidence of sexual abuse or sexual assaults may be reduced by the individual's knowledge of sexuality and sexual relationships. Ignorance about sexuality appears to be a major factor increasing an individual's risk for abuse (Muccigrosso, 1991). Thus, the use of a comprehensive and accurate sex education curriculum is essential. The skill areas individuals should know include birth control, sexually transmitted diseases, hetero- and homosexual behavior, responsibility for sexual behavior, preventing abuse, hygiene, responding to harassment, and choice making pertaining to sexual behavior (Sobsey, 1994).

Personal safety: Although the issue of teaching self-defense skills to persons with disabilities is somewhat controversial (e.g., opponents believe it will further jeopardize individuals), there is a growing opinion that these skills should be taught to persons with disabilities (Pava et al., 1991). Such instruction will enable individuals to determine if, when, and how to fight back if attacked. The presence of these skills may increase the individual's self-esteem and overcome feelings associated with learned helplessness (Sobsey, 1994).

Social and communication skills: People who are isolated because of social or communication deficits are more often victims of crime. Conversely, individuals who have active friendships and community relationships are less likely to be victimized (Sobsey, 1994). Attention should be directed toward teaching students to establish friendships, date, and develop leisure and recreational skills that provide opportunities for social interactions.

Property management: People with disabilities typically are not provided instruction in protecting personal possessions, including money. Students need to be informed that they have the right to possess and secure personal property and money. Such skills as home security (e.g., how to safely secure doors and windows), securing valuables, discouraging others from taking their possessions, using checks and credit cards, and hiding money are routinely performed by parents or caregivers, yet infrequently taught to students. Acquiring these skills is essential.

Responding to crimes: Students need to learn how and to whom to report crimes if they or others are victimized. If later warranted, they need to learn how to provide testimony and how to respond to questions from court officials. The reporting of crimes is crucial if justice is to be served.

Crime prevention skills can be acquired using the same instructional procedures as those used to promote other safety skills. Students generally need to be taught to identify potentially dangerous or abusive situations, how to respond to them if they occur (e.g., by screaming or walking away), and to report them. Most instruction will involve simulation training using individual and small group instruction, discussion, role-plays, modeling, repeated practice, and the use of pictures and audiovisual instructional materials.

HIV/AIDS PREVENTION

Health concern: Individuals with disabilities may be at higher risk of becoming infected with HIV because of inadequate sex education and HIV prevention training, ignorance about safe sex practices, engagement in high-risk sexual behavior, and vulnerability to sexual abuse (Mason & Jaskulski, 1994). Although prevalence figures remain uncertain, the number of persons with disabilities who are infected may be appreciable. The need to include HIV prevention training in a sex education program is critical to ensure the safety of people with disabilities.

AIDS prevention involves many skills (see Mason & Jaskulski, 1994; Scotti et al., 1997, for more detailed information). At the minimum, individuals need to know that AIDS is a very serious disease that can result in death; it is transmitted via unsafe sexual activity or sharing intravenous needles; and it can be prevented through safe sex practices, abstinence, and not sharing needles or syringes.

Individual or group instruction is recommended, and repeated practice of target skills should be provided as appropriate. For example, individuals can practice unrolling condoms several times during an instructional session. Also, individuals may discuss ways to appropriately refuse sexual advances or drug or alcohol use. Role-plays are strongly encouraged and, if possible, target skills should be practiced in natural environments in the community (e.g., in a car or one a busy street).

SUBSTANCE USE

Although prevalence figures regarding alcohol and drug use vary across disability groups, students with disabilities may be consuming substances at appreciable levels (Morgan, 1994). Adults with mental retardation and developmental disabilities increasingly are living in integrated community settings. Thus, we can assume that they are more likely to be exposed to and encouraged to use street drugs and other elicit substance, leading to higher levels of abuse for them (Christian & Poling, 1997).

Prevention curricula focus on promoting a diverse set of skills. Major skills areas include stress reduction, assertiveness training, problem solving, decision making, and communication. The curriculum should emphasize substance use is illegal and harmful. In addition, persons need to learn strategies to resist peer pressure, that drugs will not solve their problems, and there are better ways to obtain attention and make friends. Recommended instructional procedures include role-play, behavioral rehearsal, peer tutoring, cooperative learning experiences, and verbal instruction.

Such learning requires students to be actively engaged in instructional activities (e.g., role playing) rather than to be passive (e.g., responding to worksheets, Morgan, 1994). Also, a motivation system should be used in which students receive points or other reinforcers for acquiring and performing desired target behaviors and completing homework assignments. Ultimately, as with the other safety skill areas discussed in this chapter, students need to learn decision-making skills – to determine what is in their best interests and how to regulate their own behavior. Prevention programs must present students with sufficient information and experiences so that they can conclude unequivocally that the risks of substance use far outweigh its benefits.

SELF-MEDICATION AND HEALTH CARE

Individuals with special health care needs can be taught to have a critical role in the administration and monitoring of their own health care. For example, individuals can be taught to assist in varying degrees when tube feeding, tracheotomy suctioning, and catheterization, among a number of procedures (Lehr & Macurdy, 1994). At the minimum, they should learn to perform appropriate toileting, hand washing, and oral and nasal hygiene. Ideally, individuals with health care needs should be taught to assume full responsibility for their own health care. The decision to teach self-administration of health care procedures needs to be made carefully by the individual's planning team, including parents when legally warranted, and with the approval of a physician. For example, individuals with disabilities may be taught to assume responsibility for their medication regimens. Providing people with opportunities to be responsible for their own health and well being is important and is deserving of emphasis.

CONDUCTING ECOLOGICAL ASSESSMENTS

Ideally, people should acquire all the safety skills they may need. However, this may not be feasible. Thus, skill development may need to be prioritized. The following procedure may be useful to efforts to identify, select, and prioritize skills (Gast et al., 1994). First, identify the environments at home and in the community in which the person currently or will participate with help from teachers, parents, supervisors, and others. Next, list the types of accidents that may occur as well as the likelihood of occurrence in each of these environments needs. Last, consider the severity of a potential injury needs. A cut from a kitchen knife during food preparation is more likely to occur than a burn caused by a house fire. Nevertheless, the latter is far more serious than the former. Consequently, both the likelihood of an injury occurring as well as its seriousness or severity of consequences needs to be considered.

Second, prioritize the teaching of skills that will prevent immediate danger (e.g., using a power tool/appliance, crossing the street). Risks that have less immediate or delayed effect (e.g., HIV/AIDS, recognizing hypothermia) remain important to acquire. However, this emphasis may be delayed in favor of an emphasis on the more immediate dangers that should be addressed first. If time and resources permit, emphasize the acquisition of preventive safety skills for both immediate and future dangers and risks.

TEACHING HEALTH AND SAFETY SKILLS

Literature on some commercially available products developed to help persons acquire safety skills is reviewed below. Issues pertaining to human development and sexuality, doctors and dentists, sign recognition and traffic safety, and responses to emergencies are highlighted.

Research and other forms of scholarship that address the practical aspects of teaching and acquiring health and safety skills to persons with significant cognitive disabilities are meager. Persons with disabilities are likely to require some training to acquire functional life skills. Sadly, much of the instruction is incidental and unsupported by empirical research.

Human development and sexuality: The importance of addressing human development and sexuality increases as people mature physically. This topic can be attended to both conceptually and in a more functional context. Few people with disabilities or other challenges are given the instruction necessary to manage all aspects of their development through puberty and into adulthood (Rodgers & Lipscombe, 2005).

First, identify the areas that need to be acquired and thus to be taught. For example, Wolfe and Blanchett (2003) published an evaluation guide for teaching sex education to students with disabilities. This tool is used to assist educators and local education agencies in evaluating and selecting curricula that teaches human development, health and hygiene, sexuality, reproduction, self-protection, self-advocacy, and relationships.

Once the focus is narrowed to include a person's most critical needs, a conceptual curriculum regarding human development and sexuality can be taught using a structured and systematic approach. Several publishers have generated content-based textbooks for middle and high school aged students that address human development, life cycle, sexuality, and safety within the context of sexuality (American Guidance Service, 1999, 2001, 2007). While these texts address and access grade appropriate general education curriculum, the volume of text is reduced and vocabulary is simplified and presented in a straightforward approach to increase comprehension.

For persons with significant cognitive disabilities, the text can be adapted by further reducing the text, vocabulary, and the number of concepts presented. The text can be redrafted to create short passages. Formatting these passages in the same system as a social story (Gray, 2000) and adding pictures and picture symbols to represent the text may increase the student's ability to access and engage in the text.

When addressing relationships and intimacy from a more functional approach, the program *Circles I: Intimacy and Relationships* (Champagne & Walker-Hirsch,

1993) uses visual and spatial approaches to address appropriate human contact, physical distance, and proximity. Due to the concrete presentation of otherwise abstract concepts, students with moderate to significant cognitive disabilities may be able to perceive and absorb socio/sexual theories. The program was developed for non-readers and students requiring specific instruction in functional skills.

Medical self-advocacy: Self-advocacy is a topic that always is at the forefront of special education. Since the 1980s, self-determination increasingly has been in the spotlight as an important area of skill and knowledge development for persons with disabilities (Algozzine et al., 2001; Wood et al., 2005). Because of their limited self-care abilities and medical vulnerability, persons with disabilities were 56% more likely to require hospitalization than a person without a disability (Walsh et al., 1997). Teaching persons with cognitive limitations to report medical information correctly and completely should be considered (Brechin & Swain, 1988).

Adapted textbooks address functional curriculum while offering practical and empowering information to students with disabilities. Units in *Every Day Life Skills* (American Guidance Service, 2001) address healthy lifestyles, including prevention of injuries and illness, scheduling medical and dental appointments, safe and appropriate consumption of medications, and emotional health and self-advocacy.

When working with individuals with reading and intellectual limitations, instructors may need to identify the most imperative information from adapted texts and redraft it using commercially based software that will match pictures and picture symbols to the simplified text. The volume of text and vocabulary level is likely to need to be reduced.

Drug abuse prevention: While most individuals with disabilities or other challenges may not have access to harmful or dangerous substances (e.g., alcohol, recreational drugs, and tobacco products), some will – especially those living in community settings (Christian & Poling, 1997). Thus, drug and substance abuse prevention should be taught to students with cognitive disabilities.

Several commercially published textbooks address functional and academic curricula while offering content that emphasizes prevention and healthy living skills to persons with disabilities. Specific unites in the Life Skills series (American Guidance Service, 1999, 2001, 2007) address safe use of medicines, tobacco and alcohol use and abuse, illegal drug abuse, and chemical and drug dependency. Local and state curriculum guides also address substance abuse and prevention issues.

The Drug Abuse Resistance Education (DARE, http://www.dare.com/home/default.asp) is one of this country's most popular programs, reportedly located in 75% of school districts nationally. A survey of the organizational structure and function of the DARE. program identified several program strengths, including a well-defined organizational focus, uniform training and rapid dissemination, program monitoring, and fidelity of implementation (Merrill et al., 2006).

Unstable funding and a need to update the curricula based on current research evidence are cited as two program weaknesses. The program attempts to promote the skills students from kindergarten to grade 12 presumably need to avoid involvement in drugs, gangs, and violence. For students with disabilities, knowledge provided through the curriculum may be grasped following some adaptations and modifications to the printed and spoken lessons that are provided by local law enforcement.

Sign recognition and traffic safety: In recent years, as our academic expectations increase for students with significant cognitive disabilities (No Child Left Behind Act, 2001), concerns arise for their safety in their homes and the community. Sign recognition is a functional safety skill that can be acquired by many persons through the use of time delay and constant prompting methodologies (Ault et al., 1988; Tekin-Iftar, 2003).

Several commercially prepared curricula assist educators in teaching sign recognition. The competency-based approach, *Life Centered Career Education* (Brolin, 1997), offers structured reading and writing activities for students. Basic sign recognition is addressed briefly followed with a more extensive section on traffic safety.

Survival Signs Curriculum: One program (Haugen, 1998) teaches 80 indoor and outdoor signs through many activities. While sign identification is trained, the promotion of a deeper understanding and comprehension of each sign is the primary focus.

For students with more significant cognitive disabilities, Edmark (Austin & Boeckmann, 2002) provides a supplement sight word recognition program: *Functional Word Series: Signs Around You*. The program teaches 100 words that can be found on signs in communities. Like all Edmark programs, verbal ability is not required to learn to read. A student must have a basic indicating response, such as answering by vocalizing, pointing, nodding, or eye gazing. Worksheets are provided to supplement and support the newly introduced words and signs.

Responding to an emergency: Emergencies arise, thus underscoring the importance of persons knowing how to respond to emergency situations. Persons with cognitive impairments will need repeated trials and simulation to acquire these skills. Attempts to systematically instruct students in prevention and response constitute some of the most proactive ways to prevent risks (Coleman & Apts, 1991). Preparing persons to respond to emergencies also should have the desired effect of reducing their anxiety, should an emergency arise (Peterson, 1984).

The acquisition of community survival and resource skills has been shown to be important for persons with disabilities or other challenges to function effectively and safely in community settings. Telephone use has been identified as one of the 10 most important survival skills (Martin et al., 1982). Three important telephone functions make telephone training an important survival skill (Snell & Browder, 1987): to solicit emergency assistance, to establish and maintain social contacts, and to save time and money when shopping by phone.

Two adolescents with severe disabilities were trained to complete a 17-step task analysis as part of a training package consisting of total task presentation and a four-level prompting procedure to place phone calls from a public setting (e.g., shopping mall) with generalization to untrained settings of a movie theater and a convenience store (Test et al., 1990). Three adults with cognitive disabilities were trained to use modified telephone books to respond correctly to 18 emergency scenes by calling one of three emergency numbers (Test et al., 1990). Three students with moderate intellectual disabilities were trained to communicate an emergency by calling 911 (Spooner et al., 1989). In a practical demonstration for teachers, steps to promote a person's ability to communicate an emergency, including a task analysis for calling 911, were highlighted (Stem & Test, 1989).

Textbooks that address functional and academic curriculum while offering practical information to students with disabilities are available. Units in *Every Day Life Skills* (American Guidance Service, 2001) and *Life Skills Health* (American Guidance Service, 1999, 2007) address safe lifestyles, reducing risks of injury, first aid for injuries, and preventing violence. Local and state curriculum guides that address home safety and risk prevention are available.

CASE STUDY USING THE ABAS-II

Josh, a 15 year old boy, attends the ninth grade at a large urban high school. He is receiving the majority of his instruction in a self-contained classroom for students with severe autism and significant cognitive disabilities and is integrated in a number of general education classes. Results from a prior evaluation lead to the diagnoses of autism and mental retardation. Recent scores affirm these diagnoses. For example, in reference to mental retardation, his previous Full Scale IQ was 42 on a standardized measure of intelligence and his previous General Adaptive Composite on the ABAS-II Parent Form was 47, with significant limitations in social, communication, and daily living skills.

Josh uses picture symbols and pointing as his main method of communication. While he does present some repetitive vocalizations, most of this is echolalia that appears to not serve a functional communication purpose. He says "hello" and "goodbye" and also responds to the words, "yes" and "no."

Josh recognizes and writes his first name. He reads approximately 25–30 preprimer and primer sight words. He counts objects to 10. He sorts objects by two attributes. He seemingly understands the function of money, although he does not identify or count it.

Josh has specific behavioral challenges that are likely to stem from his lack of communication. He often hugs adults and students who enter his classroom. He often exhibits self-stimulating behaviors such as flapping his arms and rocking. These behaviors become more pronounced when he comes into contact with a stranger, suggesting that he may feel scared or nervous.

Josh takes medication daily to address a mild seizure disorder and inattentive behaviors and medication nightly to address sleeplessness. He is mildly allergic to strawberries and may break out in a rash if he eats them.

Josh lives in a group home with other children with similar disabilities. He has his own bedroom and shares a bathroom. This placement was made based on the intensity of his behaviors and his sleeplessness. He visits his family on the weekends during which time he shares a room with his typically developing one year older brother.

Table 8.1 provides the current ABAS II scores from both teacher and parent ratings. The scores are very consistent. Josh's General Adaptive Composite

TABLE 8.1 Results of the ABAS-II (Teacher Form for ages 5–21 and Parent Form for Ages 5–21) for Josh, Age 15 Years

	Adaptive Skill Area Scaled Score	Composite Standard Score	Composite Percentile Rank	Composite Score Classification
Teacher Form Composites and Adaptive Skill Areas				
General Adaptive Composite (GAC)		41	<0.1	Extremely low
Conceptual Composite		50	<0.1	Extremely low
• Communication	1			
• Functional academics	1			
• Self-direction	1			
Social Composite		55	<0.1	Extremely low
• Leisure	1			
• Social	1			
Practical Composite		47	<0.1	Extremely low
• Community use	1			
• School living	2			
• Health and safety	1			
• Self-care	1			
Parent Form Composites and Adaptive Skill Areas				
GAC		42	<0.1	Extremely low
Conceptual Composite		53	<0.1	Extremely low
• Communication	1			
• Functional academics	3			
• Self-direction	1			
Social Composite		55	<0.1	Extremely low
• Leisure	1			
• Social	1			
Practical Composite		40	<0.1	Extremely low
• Community use	1			
• Home living	1			
• Health and safety	1			
• Self-care	1			

Note: Composites (Conceptualization, Social, and Practical) and the General Adaptive Composite (GAC) have standard scores with a mean of 100 and standard deviation of 15. Adaptive skill areas (communication, functional academics, etc.) have scaled scores with a mean of 10 and standard deviation of 3.

TABLE 8.2 Planning Matrix for Teaching Health and Safety Skills for Josh, Age 15 Years

Skill	Josh's present level of performance	Goal	Activities	Lessons embedded in the academic curriculum
Appropriate meeting and greeting classroom visitors	Can say hello, but often hugs adults and students inappropriately	Josh will approach classroom visitor in an appropriate manner	Circles	*Math* – measurement, Graphing to self-monitor behaviors
			Social stories	*Reading* – Use a combination of picture symbols and text
Accurately reporting to health care providers	Josh is compliant in the physician's office, but will not interact with the physician or his/her nurses	Josh will give a brief description of his overall physical health	Picture symbols to indicate overall well being	*Literacy*
			Choice board to indicate areas of discomfort or pain	*Writing* – Complete a chart using picture symbols to indicate his overall physical feelings
Participate in a school-wide drug prevention program	Josh does not know the difference between a "good" drug and a "bad" drug	Josh will discriminate between a necessary prescribed drug and an illicit drug	Participate in the school-wide DARE program, using materials that have been adapted with reduced text and the inclusion of picture symbols	*Literacy* – Combine picture symbols with simplified text
			Sort pictures of good and bad drugs	*Math/science*
Recognize common signs in the community	Josh can find the STOP sign. He can discriminate between the Men's and Women's bathroom	Josh will identify 10 critical signs and related words in his community environment	Edmark Functional Reading Program.	*Literacy* – Sight word recognition skills
			Survival signs curriculum	*Social studies* – Sign recognition skills
Responding to a fire	Josh does respond to a fire alarm by covering his ears and wailing. He does not readily leave the building	Josh will independently vacate the school or home when he hears the fire alarm	Social stories	*Literacy* – Use a combination of picture symbols and text to address appropriate ways to cope with a fire warning

and behaviors summarized in the three adaptive composites and 10 adaptive skill areas are in the lowest percentile compared to others the same age. At both school and home, Josh requires adult assistance to comply with the most basic safety tasks. For example, he needs assistance when crossing the street and following safety rules and regulations at school and community sites. He is unable to respond appropriately to emergency situations. He would be unable to successfully access 911.

Josh requires adult supervision and assistance for medical maintenance. Although he is compliant when taking medications, he is unable to manage this process without direction and support. When participating in daily grooming activities, Josh needs help to complete basic tasks including bathing and dressing appropriately in light of the weather.

Table 8.2 provides a planning matrix that displays information about five important skills, Josh's present level of performance, goals, activities, and lessons embedded in an academic curriculum. Specific tasks are suggested to link functional health and safety skills to academic exercises. These skills can generalize throughout the school, home, and community environments.

CONCLUSION

Individuals with disabilities need to know how to identify potential risks and hazards and to perform safety skills appropriate to them. The skills described in this chapter represent a sample of those needed by individuals to lead safe and independent lives. The research literature suggests that many individuals with disabilities can acquire a repertoire of safety skills when such skills are taught systematically and through the use of sound instructional practices. Their sustained importance at home, school, work, and community should continue through their lifetime.

REFERENCES

Agran, M. (2004). Health and safety. In P. Wehman & J. Kregel (Eds.), *Functional Curriculum*, pp. 357–383. Austin, TX: Pro-Ed.

Agran, M. & Madison, D. (1995). Prevalence of injuries among supported employees. *Journal of Vocational Rehabilitation*, *5*, 5–13.

Agran, M. & Martella, R. C. (1994). Safety skills on the job. In M. Agran, N. E. Marchand-Martella, & R. C. Martella (Eds.), *Promoting Health and Safety: Skills for Independent Living*, pp. 121–134. Baltimore: Paul H. Brookes.

Agran, M., Marchand-Martella, N. E., & Martella, R. C. (Eds.) (1994). *Promoting Health and Safety: Skills for Independent Living*. Baltimore: Paul H. Brookes.

Agran, M., Swaner, J., & Snow, K. C. (1998). Work safety skills: A neglected curricular area. *Career Development for Exceptional Individuals*, *21*, 33–44.

Algozzine, B., Browder, D., Karvonen, M., Test, D. W., & Wood, W. M. (2001). Effects of interventions to promote self-determination to individuals with disabilities. *Review of Educational Research*, *71*, 219–276.

American Guidance Service (1999). *Life Skills Health.* Circle Pines, MN: American Guidance Service.

American Guidance Service (2001). *Everyday Life Skills.* Circle Pines, MN: American Guidance Service.

American Guidance Service (2007). *Life Skills Health.* Shoreview, MN: Pearson-AGS Globe.

Ault, M. J., Gast, D. L., & Wolery, M. (1988). Comparison of progressive and constant time-delay in teaching community-sign word reading. *American Journal on Mental Retardation, 93,* 44–56.

Austin, P. & Boeckmann, K. (2002). *Edmark functional word series: Signs around you.* Austin, TX: Pro-Ed.

Brechin, A. & Swain, J. (1988). Professional/client relationships: Creating a "working alliance" with people with learning difficulties. *Disability, Handicap and Society, 3,* 213–226.

Brolin, D. E. (1997). *Life Centered Career Education: A Competency Based Approach.* Reston, VA: The Council for Exceptional Children.

Bryan, E., Warden, M. G., Berg, B., & Hauck, G. R. (1978). Medical consideration for multiple handicapped children in the public schools. *Journal of School Health, 48,* 84–89.

Champagne, M. P., & Walker-Hirsch, L. (1993). *Circles I: Intimacy and Relationships.* Santa Barbara, CA: James Stanfield Publishing Company.

Chotiner, N. & Lehr, W. (1976). *Child Abuse and Developmental Disabilities: A report from the New England Regional Conference.* Boston: New England Developmental Disabilities Communication Center.

Christian, L. & Poling, A. (1997). Drug abuse in persons with mental retardation: A review. *American Journal on Mental Retardation, 102,* 126–136.

Coleman, M. & Apts, S. (1991). Home-alone risk factors. *TEACHING Exceptional Children, 23*(3), 36–39.

Collins, B. C. & Griffen, A. K. (1996). Teaching students with moderate disabilities to make safe responses to product warning labels. *Education and Treatment of Children, 19,* 30–45.

Collins, B. C., Wolery, M., & Gast, D. L. (1992). A national survey of safety concerns for students with special needs. *Journal of Developmental and Physical Disabilities, 4,* 263–276.

Collins, B. C., Stinson, D. M., & Land, L. (1993). *A Comparison of In Vivo and Simulation Prior to In Vivo Instruction in Teaching Generalized Safety Skills. Education and Training in Mental Retardation, 28,* 128–142.

Courtade, G., Spooner, F., & Browder, D. M. (2007). Review of studies with students with significant cognitive disabilities which link to science standards. *Research and Practice for Persons with Severe Disabilities, 32,* 43–49.

Dunne, R. G., Asher, K. N., & Rivara, F. P. (1993). Injuries in young people with developmental disabilities: A comparative investigation from the 1988 National Health Interview Survey. *Mental Retardation, 31,* 83–88.

Gast, D. L., Winterling, V., Wolery, M., & Farmer, J. A. (1992). Teaching first-aid skills to students with moderate handicaps in small group instruction. *Education and Treatment of Children, 15,* 101–124.

Gast, D. L., Wellons, J., & Collins, B. (1994). Home and community safety skills. In M. Agran, N. E. Marchand-Martella, & R. C. Martella (Eds.), *Promoting Health and Safety: Skills for Independent Living,* pp. 11–32. Baltimore: Paul H. Brookes.

Gray, C. A. (2000). *Writing Social Stories with Carol Gray.* Arlington, TX: Future Horizons.

Haller, J. A. (1970). Problems in children's trauma. *Journal of Trauma, 10,* 269–271.

Haugen, J. (1998). *Survival Signs Curriculum.* San Antonio, TX: PCI Educational Publishing.

Jaskulski, T. & Mason, C. (1992). AIDS policies and education: What are vocational and residential rehabilitation providers doing? *American Rehabilitation, 19*(3), 12–19.

Juracek, D. B. (1994). Fire safety skills. In M. Agran, N. E. Marchand-Martella, & R. C. Martella (Eds.), *Promoting Health and Safety: Skills for Independent Living,* pp. 103–119. Baltimore: Paul H. Brookes.

Lehr, D. H. & Macurdy, S. (1994). Meeting special health care needs of students. In M. Agran, N. E. Marchand-Martella, & R. C. Martella (Eds.), *Promoting Health and Safety: Skills for Independent Living,* pp. 71–84. Baltimore: Paul H. Brookes.

Lumley, V. A. & Miltenberger, R. G. (1997). Sexual abuse prevention for persons with mental retardation. *American Journal on Mental Retardation, 101*, 459–472.

Martella, R. C. & Agran, M. (1994). Safety skills on the job. In M. Agran, N. E. Marchand-Martella, & R. C. Martella (Eds.), *Promoting Health and Safety: Skills for Independent Living*, pp. 121–134. Baltimore: Paul H. Brookes.

Martin, J. E., Rusch, F. R., & Heal, L. W. (1982). Teaching community survival skills to mentally retarded adults: A review and analysis. *Journal of Special Education, 16*, 243–268.

Maslow, A. (1954). *Motivation and Personality*. New York: Harper & Row.

Mason, C. Y. & Jaskulski, T. (1994). HIV/AIDS prevention and education. In M. Agran, N. E. Marchand-Martella, & R. C. Martella (Eds.), *Promoting Health and Safety: Skills for Independent Living*, pp. 161–191. Baltimore: Paul H. Brookes.

Merrill, J. C., Pinsky, I., Killeya-Jones, L. A., Sloboda, Z., & Dilascio, T (2006). Substance abuse prevention infrastructure: A survey study of the organizational structure and function of the DARE program. *Substance Abuse Treatment, Prevention, and Policy, 1*(25), Retrieved June 12, 2007, from http://www.substanceabusepolicy.com/articles/browse.asp?date=9-2006.

Morgan, D. P. (1994). Preventing substance use. In M. Agran, N. E. Marchand-Martella, & R. C. Martella (Eds.), *Promoting Health and Safety: Skills for Independent Living*, pp. 135–159. Baltimore: Paul H. Brookes.

Muccigrosso, L. (1991). Sexual abuse prevention strategies and programs for persons with developmental disabilities. *Journal of Sexuality and Disability, 9*, 261–272.

Mueller, H. H., Wilgosh, L., & Dennis, S. (1989). Employment survival skills for entry-level occupations. *Canadian Journal of Rehabilitation, 2*, 203–221.

National Research Council (1996). *National Science Education Standards*. Washington, DC: National Academy Press.

National Safety Council (1988). *Accident Facts*. Chicago: National Safety Council.

No Child Left Behind Act (2001), Pub. L. No. 107–110, 115 Stat. 1425 (2002).

Pava, W. S., Bateman, P., Appleton, M. K., & Glasscock, J. (1991). Self-defense training for visually impaired women. *Journal of Visual Impairment and Blindness, 85*, 397–401.

Peterson, L. (1984). Teaching home safety and survival skills to latch-key children: A comparison of two manuals and methods. *Journal of Applied Behavior Analysis, 17*, 279–293.

Ramirez, M., Peek-Asa, C., & Kraus, J. F. (2004). Disability and risk of school related injury. *Injury Prevention, 10*, 21–26.

Rice, M. W. & Trupin, L. (1996). Medical expenditures for people with disabilities. *Disability Statistical Abstracts, 12*, 1–4.

Rodgers, J. & Lipscombe, J. (2005). The nature and extent of help given to women with intellectual disabilities to manage menstruation. *Journal of Intellectual and Developmental Disability, 30*, 45–52.

Scotti, J. R., Nangle, D. W., Masia, C. L., Ellis, J. T., Vjcich, K. J., Giacoletti, A. M., et al. (1997). Providing an AIDS education and skills training program to persons with mild developmental disabilities. *Education and Training in Mental Retardation and Developmental Disabilities, 32*, 113–128.

Sobsey, D. (1994). Crime prevention and personal safety. In M. Agran, N. E. Marchand-Martella, & R. C. Martella (Eds.), *Promoting Health and Safety: Skills for Independent Living*, pp. 193–213. Baltimore: Paul H. Brookes.

Snell, M. E. & Browder, D. M. (1987). Domestic and community skills. In M. E. Snell (Ed.), *Systematic Instruction of Persons with Severe Handicaps*, 3rd edn., pp. 390–434. Columbus, OH: Merrill.

Spooner, F., Stem, B., & Test, D. W. (1989). Teaching first aid skills to adolescents who are moderately mentally handicapped. *Education and Training in Mental Retardation, 24*, 341–351.

Spooner, F., Di Biase, W., & Courtade-Little, G. (2006). Science standards and functional skills: Finding the links. In D. M. Browder & F. Spooner (Eds.), *Teaching Language Arts, Math, and Science to Students with Significant Cognitive Disabilities*, pp. 229–243. Baltimore: Paul H. Brookes.

Stem, B. & Test, D. W. (1989). Teaching first aid skills in the classroom. *TEACHING Exceptional Children, 22*(1), 10–12.

Stimpson, L. & Best, M. C. (1991). *Courage Above All: Sexual Assault against People with Disabilities.* Toronto, Ontario, Canada: DisAbled Women's Network.

Tarnowski, K. J., Rasnake, L. K., & Drabman, R. S. (1987). Behavioral assessment and treatment of pediatric burn injuries: A review. *Behavior Therapy, 18*, 417–441.

Tekin-Iftar, E. (2003). Effectiveness of peer delivered simultaneous prompting on teaching community signs to students with developmental disabilities. *Education and Training in Mental Retardation and Developmental Disabilities, 38*, 77–94.

Test, D. W., Spooner, F., Keul, P. K., & Grossi, T. (1990). Teaching adolescents with severe handicaps to use the public telephone. *Behavior Modification, 14*, 157–171.

Walsh, K. K., Kastner, T., & Criscione, T. (1997). Characteristics of hospitalizations for people with developmental disabilities: Utilization, costs, and the impact of care coordination. *American Journal on Mental Retardation, 101*, 505–520.

Winterling, V., Gast, D. L., Wolery, M., & Farmer, J. A. (1992). Teaching safety skills to high school students with moderate disabilities. *Journal of Applied Behavior Analysis, 25*, 217–227.

Wolfe, P. B. & Blanchett, W. J. (2003). Sex education for students with disabilities: An evaluation guide. *TEACHING Exceptional Children, 36*(1), 46–51.

Wood, W. M., Fowler, C. H., Uphold, N., & Test, D. W. (2005). A review of self-determination interventions with individuals with severe disabilities. *Research and Practice for Persons with Severe Disabilities, 30*, 121–146.

Xiang, H., Stallones, L., Chen, G., Hostetler, S. G., & Kelleher, K. (2005). Nonfatal injuries among U.S. children with disabling conditions. *American Journal of Public Health, 95*, 1970–1975.

9

The Use of Leisure Time

ROBERT BELAND

Department of Tourism, Recreation and Sport Management, University of Florida, Gainesville, FL 32611, U.S.A.

INTRODUCTION AND DESCRIPTION OF LEISURE SKILL AREA

An understanding of the philosophy of therapeutic recreation promotes an understanding of the meaning and value of leisure and recreation to persons with intellectual and emotional disabilities. Professionals engaged in therapeutic recreation have been serving persons with disabilities for more than 100 years. For example, Florence Nightingale recognized the value of recreation for hospitalized soldiers and advocated for the use of games, sports and animals to aid in recovery from illness and injury. Although therapeutic recreation provides recreational and leisure services to special populations, it is used in direct therapeutic interventions and can help improve basic functioning in all persons.

The meaning of leisure and recreation has shifted from the historic belief that recreation was meant to restore individuals so that they could return to work refreshed to the belief that recreation and leisure are worthy goals in themselves. Many people are defining themselves less in terms of their careers and vocations and more in terms of their leisure roles – club members, tennis players, golfers, music lovers, sport spectators (fans), and fitness center devotees. A list of all known recreation and leisure activities in the world would be endless. Mancala, a counting game, is the most popular game throughout the world yet is hardly known in the U.S.A.

Persons can be considered engaged in leisure activities when they are interested and competent in non-work-related activities they select. The formation of a leisure lifestyle is critical to the quality of one's life. The following twelve principles address leisure adaptive behavior:

1. Understand leisure as a concept that encompasses both discretionary time and individual choice.
2. Recognize that a fuller use of discretionary time is likely to enhance the quality of life in many areas of a person's life.
3. Appreciate the wide diversity of leisure choices and lifestyles.
4. Understand the potential of leisure for both developing and responding to one's individual lifestyle.
5. Recognize that appreciation of leisure experiences will be enhanced through direct exploration and participation.
6. Acquire knowledge and skills related to understanding and identifying the wealth of leisure opportunities and resources that exist in one's community, state, and nation.
7. Develop competency in using both short and long-term planning to ensure more effective use of one's leisure time.
8. Identify and evaluate personal interests and abilities to determine participation in leisure time activities.
9. Evaluate choices and performance as related to various benefits derived from participating in specific leisure experiences.
10. Develop specific skills necessary for participation in a wide variety of leisure time activities.
11. Understand the contributions that leisure provides for self-expression as well as physical and intellectual development.
12. Develop interests and problem-solving skills that will facilitate independent pursuits of leisure in the home, school, and community.

THE ADAPTIVE BEHAVIOR ASSESSMENT SYSTEM-II

The Adaptive Behavior Assessment System-II (ABAS-II; Harrison & Oakland, 2003) provides a comprehensive assessment of the degree to which individuals independently displays functional skills in everyday living. The ABAS-II provides standard scores for three adaptive composites (e.g., conceptual, social, and practical) as well as 10 more specific adaptive skills: communication, functional academic, home and school living, leisure, self-care, self-direction, social, and either motor (for infants and young children) or work (for those engaged in sustained work). These scores are summarized to provide a General Adaptive Composite (GAC). The ABAS-II norms extend from birth through 89, thus providing a norm-referenced assessment of almost all persons.

The ABAS-II provides five forms: a Parent/Primary Caregiver Form for ages 0–5, a Parent Form for ages 5–21, a Teacher/Daycare Provider Form for ages 2–5, a Teacher Form for ages 5–21, and an Adult Form for ages 16–89.

The ABAS-II's internal consistency, test-retest reliability, and alternate form reliabilities are very high. In addition, considerable evidence supports the test's factor structure, concurrent validity, and clinical utility.

An evaluation of the ABAS-II (Meikamp & Suppa, 2005) reported in the authoritative Buros' *Sixteenth Mental Measurement Yearbook* follows:

> Data from the analyses of internal consistency, test-retest reliability, interrater reliability, and cross-form consistency are provided along with standard errors of measurement. The reliability coefficients for the GAC [General Adaptive Composite] averaged from .97 to .99 across the six standardization sample whereas the adaptive domains ranged from .91 to .98 and the skill areas were typically in the .90s, ranging from .80 to .97.... The reliability data reflect an overall high degree of internal consistency for the skill areas, adaptive domains, and GAC scaled scores and suggest the ABAS-II is reliable for assessing individuals with different levels of functioning and with different clinical diagnoses.

The review concludes with the following summary:

> The ABAS-II offers a system for assessing adaptive behavior skills based on current construct definitions for individuals from 0 to 89 in a variety of settings. It shows high convergent validity with the Vineland Adaptive Behavior Scale – Classroom Edition, another comprehensive adaptive behavior scale. However, the ABAS-II yields not only comprehensive score (General Adaptive Score) but also scores on the three American Association on Mental Retardation (AAMR) domains and the 10 DSM-TR skills. It allows guessing about a skill level and employs direct questioning instead of an indirect interview process. A supplemental analysis can be performed to identify areas of strength and weaknesses. Helpful guidelines are provided for the use of the ABAS-II within a comprehensive assessment. Detailed and well-organized research results support a high level of reliability throughout the system and present substantial validity evidence. The ability to use direct questioning of multiple respondents in multiple settings and adult self-ratings to yield assessments of adaptive behavior within the context of the AAMR domains and the DSM-TR definitions, as well as the comparison studies with other tests and diagnoses other than MR makes the ABAS-II an asset in a comprehensive assessment in a variety of clinical settings.

THE USE OF THE ABAS-II TO ASSESS LEISURE ACTIVITIES

Leisure adaptive skill activities are assessed in each of the five ABAS-II forms. The numbers of items that are included in each of the five forms follow: 22 on the Parent/Primary Caregiver Form for ages 0–5, 22 on the Parent Form for ages 5–21, 23 on the Teacher/Daycare Provider Form for ages 2–5, 17 on the Teacher Form for ages 5–21, and 23 on the Adult Form for ages 16–89.

Examples of items are provided below:

On the Parent/Primary Caregiver Form for ages 0–5: plays simple games like "peek-a-boo" or rolls a ball to others; attends fun activities at another's home.

On the Parent Form for ages 5–21: waits for his/her turn in games and other fun activities; has a hobby or creative activity that requires making or building something.

On the Teacher/Daycare Provider Form for ages 2–5: chooses a game or toy during playtime; joins a group of children in games or on the playground when encouraged by an adult.

On the Teacher Form for ages 5–21: participates with others in a game or other activity without needing encouragement; remembers the game or activity a classmate likes and offers to participate.

On the Adult Form: decides alone to participate with others playing a game or other group activity; participates in an organized program for a sport or hobby.

Examples of specific leisure skills assessed by the items include the following:

- Waits for turn in games
- Selects television programs or videotapes to keep up with an area of interest
- Follows the rules in games
- Looks at pictures or reads books or magazines
- Invites others to join him/her in playing games
- Plays with toys, games or other fun items with other people
- Attends fun community activities with others
- Plans ahead for play or fun activities on free days.
- Participates in a specific fun activity on a routine basis
- Plays alone with toys, games or other fun activities
- Invites others for a fun activity
- Tries a new activity to learn about something new
- Has a hobby or creative activity
- Reserves tickets in advance for activities

In summary, persons should be able to decide, plan, and initiate leisure and fun activities that include social, cognitive, and physical components by themselves or with others.

IMPORTANCE OF LEISURE ADAPTIVE SKILL AREA

During the 1990s, policy makers used the term *quality of life* to delineate a philosophy that guided services designed to meet the needs of persons with disabilities provided by the health care industry, education, and social service organizations. For example, during this time, federal laws were passed to ensure that residents in long-term care facilities would have a better quality of life. Health care agencies were mandated to solve problems in treatment settings and to develop better ways of providing services.

The importance of developing a meaningful leisure lifestyle leading to improvements in one's quality of life is well established (Hill et al., 1984;

Dattilo & Schleien, 1994; Schleien et al., 1996; Newman, 2004; Mactavish et al., 2005). Those with disabilities have more free time than most adults. For example, an unemployed adult with a disability and not in school has about 100 hours of available free time during the week while an average adult has about 60 hours of available free time during the week. How persons utilize their free time is critical to the overall quality of their lives.

Participation in leisure activities may be thwarted by various barriers, including attitudinal, environmental, architectural, financial, physical, and social barriers (Smith et al., 2001). In addition, persons with disabilities may need to deal with intrinsic barriers, including lack of knowledge and current deficits in leisure skills (Smith et al., 2001). However, when given the opportunity for inclusion in community recreation programs, persons with disabilities are more likely to be accepted by the public (Anderson et al., 1997).

The American Association on Intellectual and Developmental Disabilities (AAIDD, 2007) has identified leisure as one of 10 important adaptive skills. According to the AAIDD, "People with mental retardation have the right to pursue self-determined recreation activities and to experience a leisure-oriented lifestyle. Some people with mental retardation may need supports and services to assist in developing independence skills that support their leisure and recreation. AAMR calls for active consideration by local, state, national, and international organizations in recognizing that leisure and recreation are fundamental attributes of a healthy lifestyle and are associated with a high quality of life for people with mental retardation" (AAMR, 1993, p. 1).

LEISURE ABILITY MODEL

FUNCTIONAL INTERVENTION

The development of a meaningful leisure lifestyle may be difficult for some persons with disabilities. The Leisure Ability Model (Peterson & Stumbo, 2000) has been used successfully to ensure the delivery of leisure services to persons with disabilities. Within this model, one first focuses on functional interventions. The therapeutic recreation specialist uses leisure and recreation intervention activities to promote functional rehabilitation goals. For example, if the goal of rehabilitation is to improve impulse control, then the therapeutic recreation specialist may plan recreation activities that teach or train a client to be more patient. These activities include those that require a player to wait his/her turn, to make crafts that must dry after painting or heating in a kiln, and to be involved in a team sport that includes waiting one's turn to play or participate.

The promotion of a client's fine motor skills constitutes a somewhat common rehabilitation goal. Playing musical instruments and table games as well as engagement in arts and crafts involve manual dexterity and thus can promote fine motor skills. The goal to improve one's cardiovascular fitness level may lead to the client's involvement in a personal and/or nutrition exercise program or a dance and movement activity. The positive impact of exercise on body weight, blood pressure levels and resting heart rate for adults with developmental disabilities has been established (Carter et al., 2004).

LEISURE EDUCATION

The second program feature of the Leisure Ability Model focuses on leisure education. The importance of leisure education for persons with developmental disabilities has been documented. For example, leisure education can help adolescents with mental retardation transition to adult life (Bedini et al., 1993; Hoge et al., 1999). In Hoge's program, leisure coaches were employed to assist the clients with leisure planning and decision making, identifying community leisure resources, serving as an advocate with the local community recreation departments, and working with families to promote and sustain leisure activities of the client.

Programs designed to promote leisure education for people with disabilities typically includes one or more of the following three components (Peterson & Stumbo, 2000): leisure awareness, leisure skills promotion, and self-determination. Leisure awareness programs are intended to promote an awareness of the self, leisure activity, and personal resources. Leisure skills promotion programs involve leisure activity skills, community and social and communication skill development. Programs designed to promote self-determination involve decision making, leisure planning and independent leisure initiation.

For example, Dattilo and Guerin (2001) describe in detail a leisure education for a case study of an adult with mental retardation. Henderson (1994) advocates teaching leisure decision making to adolescents with mental retardation. She also emphasized the importance of understanding value systems as they relate to persons with mental retardation and for recreation professionals to be aware of bias they, the clients, or society may have toward specific leisure activities. Bullock and Mahon (1997) provide a detailed overview of the various techniques used in leisure education for persons with disabilities.

RECREATION PARTICIPATION

The third program feature focuses on recreation participation. Therapeutic recreation specialists help ensure opportunities exist for a client to be able to participate in recreation and leisure activities for enjoyment. These specialists may assist the client in identifying community or other recreation programs that are of interest, accessible, affordable, and appropriate. The involvement of the client and his or her family in these activities will help ensure their success. Bullock and Mahon (1997) provide leisure programming information for persons with mental retardation.

Successful involvement in community-based recreation and sport programs can have a significant effect on the quality of lives of persons with disabilities.

Society reveres professional athletes. Thus, persons with a disability who have quality sport experience are able to identify with what they see on television and in the news. Consequently, they may help develop an athletic identity (Zabriskie et al., 2005). A family's interaction in leisure activities benefits the family member with a disability as well as other family members (Mactavish & Schleien, 2000).

ADDITIONAL OBSERVATION, DIRECT ASSESSMENT, AND OTHER TECHNIQUES TO ASSESS LEISURE ADAPTIVE SKILL AREA

Various curricula to help promote leisure. In addition, tests and other evaluation methods to assess leisure are available. These methods are summarized below.

CURRICULUM TO PROMOTE LEISURE EDUCATION

Joswiak (1975) made the first major contribution to developing practical leisure education curricula for persons with disabilities. In his first book he provided detailed learning activities in various aspects of leisure. In 1989, he updated his earlier work.

Dattilo (1999) developed a leisure education model that has been used successfully with special populations, including persons with mental retardation. The model delineates seven areas: appreciating leisure, being aware of self in leisure, being self-determined in leisure, interacting socially in leisure, using resources facilitating leisure, making decisions about leisure, and acquiring recreation activity skills.

The School–Community Leisure Link (Bullock et al., 1992), designed to be used by therapeutic recreation specialists, includes instructional units on leisure awareness, leisure resources, leisure communication skills, independent decision making, leisure planning, and activity skill instruction. The curriculum includes program components for school, community, and family use. The therapeutic recreation specialist teaches leisure education classes, provides students with leisure education materials, trains teachers in leisure education, provides resource information, conducts workshops, consults on developing individualized education plans, and coordinates with other related services.

The Transition through Recreation and Integration for Life (i.e., Project TRAIL) curriculum (Dattilo & Hoge, 1995) is designed to facilitate the transition of young persons with mental retardation from schools to community participation. Curricular goals include gathering information about students' leisure patterns, implementing leisure education curriculum, and determining the effects of leisure education services on youth and their families. Project TRAIL includes five curricular components: (a) leisure education to facilitate choice making and independent recreation participation; (b) leisure coaching, whereby participants receive consultation, support, and assistance while participating in an integrated community recreation program; (c) family/friend support, whereby family and friends attend workshops to encourage youths' independent leisure functioning; (d) follow-up services designed to maintain participation in community recreation programs; and (e) independent community leisure participation.

The Lifelong Leisure Skills and Lifestyles for Persons with Developmental Disabilities program (Schleien et al., 1995) is designed to provide practical strategies to promote lifelong participation in leisure activities by individuals with developmental disabilities. Six curricular components taught by specialists in leisure education include: (a) the desired philosophy toward leisure education; (b) appropriate selection of leisure activities for instruction; (c) instruction for skill acquisition, including guidelines for teaching students with significant disabilities; (d) instruction for preference and generalization; (e) inclusive community leisure services; and (f) home involvement in leisure education.

TESTS AND OTHER EVALUATION METHODS

Various assessment devices are used to assess leisure competence. Task analysis may be a useful tool for assessing leisure skills and developing behavioral goals. When using task analysis, the therapeutic recreation specialist breaks down an activity into small behavioral units. The following exemplifies the use of task analysis applied to a leisure activity.

A Task Analysis of Catching a Ball (Wehman and Schleien, 1988, pp. 150–151):

1. Place mitt on non-dominant hand
2. Bend mitted arm at elbow, forming a 90 degree angle with body, forearm parallel to the ground
3. Rotate wrist so that palm of mitted hand is facing upward
4. Open mitt by extending fingers
5. Follow flight of ball through air
6. Position palm of mitt directly in path of approaching ball
7. When ball makes contact with mitt, move dominant arm sideways at shoulder, bringing arm toward ball
8. Bend elbow of dominant arm until dominant hand makes contact with ball in mitt
9. Bend elbow, moving arms inward to chest, catching ball

The Home Leisure Activities Survey (Wuerch & Voeltz, 1982) provides a practical approach to assessment. The interviewer obtains information from parents about the types of toys and play equipment found in the house as well as their opinion about their child's favorite activities.

Leisurescope Plus is a commercially available method that describes a client's interest in the following 10 leisure categories: games, sports, nature, collection, crafts, art and music, entertainment, helping others/volunteerism, social affiliation, and adventure. The client's motivations for participation in activities also are assessed. The book, *Assessment Tools for Recreational Therapy and Related Fields* (Burlingame & Blaschko, 2002) includes the Leisurescope Plus and other several practical and useful assessment measures.

INTERVENTION METHODS TO PROMOTE AND ACCOMMODATE DEFICIENCIES IN LEISURE SKILLS

The ABAS-II highlights various leisure adaptive skills important to creating a well-balanced lifestyle. The following 16 interventions reflect leisure adaptive skills assessed by the ABAS-II and exemplify how behaviors assessed by the ABAS-II may be linked to interventions that promote needed skills.

Intervention designed to promote waiting for one's turn in games and following the rules in games: This intervention addresses adaptive leisure skills associated with waiting for turn in games and following the rules in games. The ability to follow rules also prepares one to wait one's turn. To learn the rules of an activity, one must have the cognitive skills to comprehend rules generally as well as those specific to an activity. One also must be able to read the rules, if written. A staff person can read the rules to those who cannot read and work to ensure that the person understands the rules. Some persons may require extended periods of time to learn the rules and procedures. The use of a written or verbal test may be used to evaluate mastery of this skill.

Suggested activity: Initiate a board game based on the client's mental development (e.g., Shoots and Ladders for those who are younger and Parcheesi for those who are older). Explain the rules to the players and emphasize the various situations when a player may lose his/her turn. Determine which player goes first and in which direction the turns will go. Monitor and evaluate how well the client takes turns.

Interventions designed to promote the selection of television programs or videotapes that maintain one's areas of interest: This intervention addresses adaptive leisure skills related to selecting television programs or videotapes that maintain one's areas of interest. First determine one's areas of interests. One of several leisure activity interest inventories (e.g., the Home Leisure Activities Survey) may be used to help the person discover some potential interests.

Many people use a TV guide to identify desired programs. Its use requires a person either to be literate or to rely on others to read or explain the TV listings. Some TV guides list upcoming programs according to categories as well as by daily and weekly programming. Their use requires clients to be able to identify dates, times, channels. Persons also may need to be able to operate a VCR or DVD player as well as rent/return DVD/tapes or borrow them from a public or school library.

Suggested activity: Provide a client with a TV guide that lists programming options for the next week. Ask the client to indicate those TV programs he/she watched during the past week which were personally interesting. Working together, highlights those in which the client expresses a personal interest. Attempt to determine why the programs were of personal interest in an effort to help identify other programs that feature similar topics.

Intervention designed to promote listening to music for fun and relaxation: This intervention addresses skills related to listening to music for fun and relaxation. The first step, to determine the types of music in which a person is interested, can be done in various ways. The person could identity their interests after listening to music on the radio, TV, tapes/CDs, and web sites. The person must be able to operate a radio, TV, tape recorder, or CD player to perform these activities independently. If this is not possible, provide assistance. Persons who want to develop or further hone their interests in music can be advised to enroll in a music appreciation class.

Suggested activity: The first step may be for the client and therapeutic recreation specialist to listen to the different types of music on the radio. The specialist will allow the client to listen to at least 3–5 songs on various stations (e.g., country, rock, pop, jazz, rap, gospel or classical) and assess the client's interest in the various songs. The specialist may stop listening to any station if the client expresses a strong negative reaction to the music. Once this is done, the specialist will point out to the client the types of music the client preferred and show the client the channels on which they can be located on the radio. The specialist may arrange a trip to a music store to see if the client would like to purchase some CDs or tapes. Then the client should schedule a 1-hour period during the week during which he/she listens to a tape/CD of a favorite artist or genre. Ask the client to report his/her reactions to the music. Later, ask the client if he/she remains interested in the music they selected and if there was an interest in a particular artist or group.

Interventions designed to promote looking at pictures or reading books or magazines: This intervention addresses adaptive leisure skills associated with looking at pictures or reading books or magazines. A person's visual and auditory acuity should be suitable. Additionally, success in this activity is related in part to an understanding of the person's language and reading development. First, determine the person's interests and then select books consistent with his or her interests. For those who are unable to read, select books that are well illustrated. Also consider obtaining books on tape. For those who are able to read, select books at or possibly a level below the person's reading grade level. Books may be obtained from bookstores, school, or public libraries or from family members and friends. The American Printing House for the Blind (www.aph.org) also provides various print resources on tape or CDs. Consider establishing a daily or weekly routine that involves story telling or reading. Engage the person in a discussion of the reading content to promote comprehension.

Suggested activity: Arrange a visit to the local library with the client. Obtain a library card, if needed. Orient the client to that section of the library that has books consistent with his/her interests and listening comprehension or reading level. Check out three books in which he/she is interested and read at least one during the following week. Discuss the books' content with the client. Determine other topics that may be of interest to the client and obtain books on them during your next library visit.

Interventions designed to promote engagement in fun activities: This intervention addresses adaptive leisure skills associated with inviting others to join in playing games, deciding to participate with others playing a game or other group activity, inviting others home for a fun activity, and organizing a game or other fun activity for a group. All people need friends and acquaintances. This need requires one to acquire the ability to make and maintain friends. Some persons may need help to acquire these skills. Others have these skills yet need to practice them.

Friendships typically emerge between people in their natural environments (e.g., neighborhood, school, work, and other community settings) in part because people are likely to have shared experiences and interests in these similar settings. Once established, emerging friendships can be promoted through phone calls, in-person visits, letters, cards, and e-mail.

Persons need to prepare for a game or activity by having the necessary equipment and deciding if food or beverages will be served. Persons also may need to learn the etiquette of accepting offers from invited friends or family who offer to bring games, equipment, or snacks. Persons also may need to learn how to provide the correct directions to his or her residence, how to greet guests appropriately when they arrive, and make arrangements for their coats or other personal comfort. The person also must know the proper etiquette for ending the activity, including asking guests for assistance in cleaning or rearrange the room, if needed.

Suggested activity: Arrange for the client to make a list of people to invite to a card game, one that the client already knows how to play. The number invited should be consistent with the nature of the game. The client will invite them in a timely manner and keep a record of their responses. The client will prepare his/her home for guests by cleaning if necessary, obtaining the needed equipment, and preparing snacks. Upon their arrival, the client will welcome each guest by name and make them comfortable. The game should start and end at a reasonable time. The use of a card game that involves money and betting is not advised. Serve snacks when appropriate. The client should walk each guest to the door, ensure they do not leave anything behind, thank each guest for coming, and suggest a desire to be with him or her again. The use of role-play is needed for those clients learning the behaviors described above.

Interventions designed to promote attending fun activities at another's home: This intervention addresses adaptive leisure skills associated with attending fun activities at another's home. The person first must determine if an invitation has been made and then to respond appropriately and in a timely fashion. If needed, the person should obtain directions to the location and the most suitable method of transportation. If public transportation will be used, the person must be mindful of schedules for their return. The person also should determine the appropriate dress for the occasion and if he/she is allowed to bring a guest.

Suggested activity: First role-play this activity, if needed. Arrange for a staff member to pretend to invite the client to his/her home. Evaluate the client on his/her response to the invitation, including politeness, whether the client understands the specific features of the invitation, how to get to the address, and the appropriate dress. Then have the client dress for the occasion. The client may need advice as to whether he/she should bring a gift, including food or beverage.

Interventions designed to promote telling others when he/she needs free time to relax alone: This intervention addresses adaptive leisure skills associated with telling others when he/she needs free time to relax alone. A person's preference for extroverted or introverted styles may impact their desire to be with others or one's self. Those who are extroverted derive primary energy from others and thus generally prefer to be with others. In contrast, those who are introverted derive primary energy from internal sources and thus generally prefer to be alone. In life, despite our preferences for extroverted or introverted styles, all people need some time with others and some time alone.

Striking a balance between declining an invitation in order to have some time by oneself versus wanting time for oneself yet needing to accept another's invitation often is delicate. The person must recognize the value of having time alone, the need to wind down and relax, and that politely declining an invitation to do something with others is both important and does not mean subsequent invitations will stop. On the other hand, knowing when to forego one's personal desires and accept an invitation is a mark of maturity. One's personal choice to relax does not need to be justified to others.

Suggested activity: Arrange for a client to designate a suitable time during the week to relax by oneself. The client may think about what activities will enhance relaxation, including listening to music, watching TV, taking a bubble bath, or daydreaming. This activity is likely to be especially important for persons who prefer extroverted styles.

Interventions designed to promote fun community activities with others: This intervention addresses adaptive leisure skills associated with attending fun community activities with others. The person should identify friends and/or family members possibly interested in going to a movie or concert. The person should invite others to attend such events. The person must determine special transportation needs and ensure he/she has sufficient funds to purchase tickets for the event.

Suggested activity: Arrange for a client to select a movie he/she would like to see and determine a time that is best for most friends and family members to join him/her. The client should inform these friends or family members about the movie details, including the theater and the time the movie begins. The client will check the bus schedules or arrange for other transportation.

Interventions designed to promote planning ahead for play or fun activities: This intervention addresses adaptive leisure skills associated with planning ahead for play or fun activities on free days as well as planning ahead for leisure activities during breaks or vacations. All persons need to learn time management, including the need to effectively plan for free time and weekends. Issues impacting the management of one's free time should consider one's leisure time goals and interests, the financial resources related to their expressed interests, their amount of free time, whether others have considerable influence in scheduling the person's activities, transportation needs, and whether the community has the leisure resources.

Suggested activity: Arrange for the client to complete a time diary for a typical week. The client may record important daily activities in a diary or on tape recorder. The client and professional specialist should review his/her activities to determine if activities should be added or removed from a typical week. Examine whether periods of time devoted to free time or engagement in meaningful activities are sufficient. Encourage the client to propose changes, if needed. Once implemented, monitor their success and possible need for change.

Interventions designed to promote initiating games or selecting TV programs preferred by friends or family: This intervention addresses adaptive leisure skills associated with initiating games or selecting TV programs that also are preferred by friends or family. Personal maturity requires one to look beyond one's own needs and consider those of others. Persons should be able to evaluate and understand the needs, feelings, and behavior of friends, family, and co-workers. A person often learns something about his/her own leisure interests and behavior by focusing on those of others. This constitutes a lifelong learning activity.

Suggested activity: Arrange for the client to select a friend or family member with whom to do a *leisure self collage*. The goal of this activity is for the client to understand another person's leisure interests and pursuits and for the client to share his/her personal leisure interests. Prepare for this activity by having the client obtain various magazines (which later can be discarded), two poster boards about 24 × 36 inches, and tape. Each person selects, cuts, and tapes on the poster boards those pictures that represent that person's leisure interests. The client and friend will take turns explaining their choices. Each person should comment further as to whether they believe their leisure needs are being met.

Interventions designed to promote routine participation in a specific fun activity: This intervention addresses adaptive leisure skills associated with participating in a specific fun activity on a routine basis. A person first must determine those activities that are most preferred, beneficial to his/her overall welfare, can be performed on a regular basis, and are feasible in light of personal and community resources. A person also should understand changes to this preferred list are permissible, even desired. A person who encountered impediments to attempts to establish a routine needs to seek ways to overcome the obstacles or select other activities.

Suggested activity: Arrange for the client to select one or more exercises to incorporate in a daily routine. Let us assume a client has decided to walk one mile each day. The client should record on a calendar the time each day that he/she will walk this distance. The client should place a gold star or similar token of recognition on that day after completing each walk. The client also could establish a reward upon attaining 20 or 25 stars.

Interventions designed to promote playing alone: This intervention addresses adaptive leisure skills associated with playing alone. This activity is important during early child development and throughout one's life. Personal maturity requires people to perform activities independently and often alone. Again, a person should select an activity that could be done without others. Examples include reading, doing crossword or other puzzles, arts and crafts, listening to music, and exercising.

Suggested activity: Arrange for the client to select a puzzle appropriate for his/her mental age and interests. The client should set a reasonable goal of completing the puzzle and schedule some time each day to work on it. After completed it, the puzzle can be fixed to remain permanent or a picture taken of the finished work.

Interventions designed to promote trying a new activity: This intervention addresses adaptive leisure skills associated with trying a new activity. A person should fully investigate a new activity before engaging in it. For example, a person may want to learn to play golf because he/she enjoyed miniature golf. However, the person may be unaware of the financial cost, time commitment, and distances to a golf course. A new activity should be selected only if it can be attained realistically and sustained for some period of time. Before selecting the new activity, observe others performing it, and ask those who perform it for information on the resources needed to acquire and sustain it. The person should attempt the new activity before making a commitment to acquire needed skills.

Suggested activity: Let us assume for the client decided to try to learn tennis. The client first should observe others playing, ask them for information on the resources needed to acquire and sustain it, and identify others who may teach them tennis skills. The client should borrow a tennis racket and balls and play a few rounds before deciding whether to purchase or rent a tennis racquet. Visit the library for books and videos on tennis instruction. Tennis lessons should be arranged and their costs build into one's budget.

Interventions designed to promote maintaining a hobby or creative activity: This intervention addresses adaptive leisure skills associated with maintaining a hobby or creative activity that requires making or building something. Persons benefit by exposure to various hobbies and crafts through personally observing others perform them, especially family members or close neighbors, as well as through TV, magazines, and videos. Industrial arts and art teachers also can be valued resources.

Suggested activity: Arrange activities that expose a client to various hobbies and other creative activities. Note how their physical and mental aptitudes may impact these activities. After a client selects a hobby, make a field trip to a hobby and craft shop and to local arts and crafts fairs. Attempt to establish a nurturing relationship from someone skilled in the preferred hobby or craft toward the client. Encourage the client to develop a hobby corner in his/her home.

Interventions designed to promote reserving tickets in advance of desired activities: This intervention addresses adaptive leisure skills associated with reserving tickets in advance of desired activities (e.g., sports events, plays, and performances by musical groups). The selection should be an event in which the person is interested.

The local newspaper may be a source of information regarding ticket sales. The person should be aware of whether the tickets need to be purchased by phone, on line, or in person as well as the various payment methods (e.g., cash, check and credit card), including sales tax, processing fee, and seat location.

Suggested activity: Let us assume the client has selected a country music concert to attend. Arrange for the client to acquire information about the source of the tickets, their price relative to seating arrangements, and other relevant purchase-related issues, including whether the client has sufficient funds. Prepare the client for the possibility that the concern may be sold out or the choice of seating may be limited. Assist the client in making sure the correct tickets are received. Advise the client to keep the tickets in a safe place and to mark the concert day on the calendar. Advise the client to keep the stub after entering the concert, especially in case of possible conflict.

Interventions designed to promote deciding independently to join an organized group or participate in an organized recreation or hobby program: This intervention addresses adaptive leisure skill associated with deciding independently to join an organized group or participate in an organized recreation or hobby program. One should identify the various organized clubs, sports, music, and dance programs in the community that may be consistent with one's interests and membership opportunities. After narrowing the list, a person should visit as many desired organizations as possible to observe them in action. Persons who are interested in registering with a group should talk with current members and obtain descriptive literature as well as an application. Discuss the rights and responsibilities of membership. For example, membership may require persons to commit to a particular schedule, buy a uniform or special equipment, display a needed skill, and/or travel to compete or perform. The person should complete the forms and apply for membership only after understanding these and other program-related issues.

Suggested activity: Let us assume a client wants to play in an adult softball league. The client may need to go to a recreation center to meet those responsible for the league and obtain registration information. Discuss age and physical requirements or other conditions that may impact participation. Once registered and the fee paid, the client may need to purchase a uniform and glove. The client may be advised first to borrow a glove in case the client assumes a position that requires a special glove. The client also should obtain the schedule for practices and games and determine exactly where they are played with the understanding that the games will be played in different locales. The client should know the policy governing practice and games when raining. The client should attempt to locate one or more persons within his/her neighborhood with whom to drive to practices and games.

CASE STUDY

Scott, an 18 year old male with mild mental retardation, lives in a group home. He recently graduated from high school. His parents live in the same community and see him on Sunday afternoons and special family events or holidays. He never has been employed. Although he recently joined Best Buddies, his experiences were not ideal because the college student assigned to him did very few things with him during the fall term and has not contacted him this spring. Scott typically remains in his room listening to his IPOD. He likes country and western music. He sometimes watches TV in the family room. However, he has encountered problems with other clients in the group home who are more aggressive about their choice of TV shows. His group home care provider informed him about a leisure counseling program at the community recreation center. Scott decided to seek some help when he realized he was unhappy with his personal lifestyles.

He met with the therapeutic recreation specialist who first talked with Scott about his daily routine and his background, including this education, leisure activities, family, and friends. The therapeutic recreation specialist arranged for Scott's high school special education teacher to complete the ABAS-II Teacher Form (Ages 5–21) and for Scott's parents to complete the ABAS–II Parent Form (Ages 5–21) (Table 9.1).

Scott's General Adaptive Composite, a general estimate of his adaptive behavior and skills, is at the 1st percentile based on reports from both his teacher and parents. His adaptive behaviors associated with his practical adaptive behavior generally are at the 7th percentile at home and were at the 1st percentile at school. His adaptive behaviors associated with his conceptual adaptive skills generally are at the 2nd percentile at home and were at the 1st percentile at school. His adaptive behaviors associated with his social skills generally are at the 1st percentile at home and school.

His adaptive skills range somewhat broadly, from those that are within the average range (e.g., self-care) to those that are deficient (e.g., leisure and social skills). Given the importance of leisure and social skills to Scott's current and future lifestyle, he, his parents, and group home supervisor decided efforts are needed to promote them. They also saw considerable overlap between his leisure and social skill needs.

The therapeutic recreation specialist met with Scott, his parents, and group home manager to develop a leisure plan consistent with Scott's interests and that would address his major deficits. They decided to work on specific skills on which Scott scored low: to promote participating in a club, sports team or organized activity; attempting a new activity to learn about something new; and acquiring a hobby or creative activity that requires making or building something.

SCOTT'S INTERVENTION PLAN

Goal One: to promote participation in a club, sports team or organized activity, even when arranged by a teacher or parent. Scott has an interest in basketball. The therapeutic recreation specialist pointed out that the city recreation department has a basketball league that includes mostly people with mental retardation. The teams usually play one another within the city and sometimes

TABLE 9.1 Results of the ABAS-II (Parent Form for Ages 5–21, and Teacher Form for Ages 5–21) for Scott, Age 18 Years 1 Month

	Parent Form			Teacher Form		
	Adaptive Skill Area Scaled Score	Composite Standard Score	Composite Percentile Rank	Adaptive Skill Area Scaled Score	Composite Standard Score	Composite Percentile Rank
Conceptual Composite		69	2		59	1
• Communication	5			4		
• Functional academics	4			2		
• Self-direction	4			2		
Social Composite		61	1	60	60	1
• Leisure	2			2		
• Social	2			2		
Practical Composite		78	7	67	67	1
• Community use	6			3		
• Home living	4			–		
• School living	–			3		
• Health and safety	4			6		
• Self-care	9			10		
General Adaptive Composite		66	1		60	1

Note: Composite scores (Conceptualization, Social, and Practical) and the General Adaptive Composite have a mean of 100 and standard deviation of 15. Adaptive skill areas (e.g. communication, functional academics) have a mean of 10 and standard deviation of 3.

go to a nearby city to play teams in a similar league. Scott agrees to try it out. He understood that, if he joins the team, he will be committed to one practice during the week and playing at least one weekend game. Scott seems especially interested when he learns that he has to wear the team uniform. Scott also agrees to practice dribbling the basketball and shooting baskets at his group home; it has a basketball hoop.

Goal Two: Engage in a new activity to learn about something new. Scott agreed to try out one new activity each month. At the beginning of the month, he agreed to think about and discusses some things he may want to try with the group home advisor and parents. Then he, with the help of others, will spend time researching that area by either looking for that activity in the newspaper, calling someone on the phone about that activity, looking on the Internet for that activity, or in other ways. Basic information is needed on the address of the business or agency, telephone, hours of operation, costs, and equipment associated with the activity. He and his parents will develop a budget for the activity. He may need to map the bus route to and from the activity if necessary and practice using it. He will engage in the new activity after making needed preparations. After engaging in this first activity he will be expected to make a verbal report about his experience to identify if he would like to continue the activity.

Goal Three: to acquire a hobby or creative activity that requires making or building something. Scott understands how having a hobby or creative activity that requires making or building something may be beneficial. As expected, he was unsure how to begin this process. His manual skills are good. Thus, the therapeutic recreation specialist suggested that he may want to make some arts and crafts items that he either can use for his own personal welfare or give as gifts to family and/or friends. Scott liked that idea.

With assistance, he located an arts and craft store within walking distance of his home that sells supplies, has various equipment, and offers classes. Scott agreed to start by attending a class.

In summary, this plan was designed to address three critical areas associated with Scott's needs to develop leisure and social skills: to participate in a club, sports team or organized activity; to attempt a new activity to learn about something new; and to acquire a hobby or creative activity that requires making or building something. Scott is likely to improve his adaptive skills and behavior, especially his leisure lifestyle, if he is able to continue his engagement in any one or all of these three skill development activities.

REFERENCES

The American Association on Intellectual and Developmental Disabilities (AAIDD) (2007). *Fact Sheet: Leisure*. Washington, DC: AAIDD.

American Association on Mental Retardation (AAMR) (1993). *AAMR Leisure and Recreation Division Newsletter*. Volume V, No. 2, Leisure as an adaptive skill area, p. 2–4. Washington, DC: AAMR.

Anderson, L., Schleien, S. J., McAvoy, L., Lais, G., & Seligmann, D. (1997). Creating positive change through an integrated outdoor adventure program. *Therapeutic Recreation Journal, 31*(4), 214–229.

Bedini, L., Bullock, C., & Driscoll, L. (1993). The effects of leisure education on factors contributing to the successful transition of students with mental retardation from school to adult life. *Therapeutic Recreation Journal, 27*(2), 70–82.

Bullock, C. & Mahon, M. (1997). *Introduction to Recreation Services for People with Disabilities.* Champaign, IL: Sagamore Publishing.

Bullock, C., Morris, L., Mahon, M., & Jones, B. (1992). *School-Community Leisure Link: Leisure Education Program Curriculum guide.* Chapel Hill, NC: The Center for Recreation and Disability Studies.

Burlingame, J. & Blaschko, T. (2002). *Assessment Tools for Recreational Therapy and Related Fields*, 3rd edn. Enumclaw, WA: Idyll Arbor.

Carter, M., McCown, K., Forest, S., Martin, J., Wacker, R., Gaede, D., & Fernandez, T. (2004). Exercise and fitness for adults with developmental disabilities: Case report of a group intervention. *Therapeutic Recreation Journal, 38*(1), 72–84.

Dattilo, J. (1999). *Leisure Education Program Planning: A Systematic Approach.* State College, PA: Venture Publishing.

Dattilo, J. & Guerin, N (2001). In Austin, D & Crawford, M. (Ed.), *Therapeutic Recreation – An Introduction*, 3rd edn., pp. 130–156. Boston: Allyn & Bacon.

Dattilo, J. & Hoge, G. (1995). *Project TRAIL: Transition Through Recreation and Integration for Life.* Athens, GA: University of Georgia.

Dattilo, J. & Schleien, S. J. (1994). Understanding the provision of leisure services for persons with mental retardation. *Mental Retardation, 32*(1), 53–59.

Henderson, K. A. (1994). An interpretive analysis of the teaching of decision-making in leisure to adolescents with mental retardation. *Therapeutic Recreation Journal, 28*(3), 133–146.

Hill, B. K., Rotegard, L. L. & Bruininks, R. H. (1984). The quality of life of mentally retarded people in residential care. *Social Work, 29*, 275–281.

Hodges, J. (2003). Applying knowledge of motivational goals to programming for persons with mental retardation. *Therapeutic Recreation Journal, 37*(4), 326–329.

Hoge, G., Dattilo, J., & Williams, R. (1999). Effects of leisure education on perceived freedom in leisure with mental retardation. *Therapeutic Recreation Journal, 33*(4), 320–332.

Joswiak, K. (1975). *Leisure Counseling Program Materials for the Developmentally Disabled.* Washington, DC: Hawkins & Associates.

Joswiak, K. (1989). *Leisure Education: Program Materials for Persons with Developmental Disabilities.* State College, PA: Venture.

Mactavish, J., Lutfiyya, Z., Iwasaki, Y., MacKay, K., Mahon, M., Rodrigue, M., Manwaring, R., & Betteridge, D. (2005). Thanks for asking me … Individuals with intellectual disability on life quality and the leisure connection. *Abstracts from the 2005 Leisure Research Symposium*, San Antonio, TX. Arlington, VA: National Parks and Recreation Association.

Mactavish, J. & Schleien, S. (2000). Exploring family recreation activities in families that include children with developmental disabilities. *Therapeutic Recreation Journal, 34*(2), 132–153.

Meikamp, J. & Suppa, C. (2005). *Adaptive Behavior Assessment System*, 2nd edn., The sixteenth mental measurement yearbook. Lincoln, NB: Buros Institute of Mental Measurement.

Newman, J. (2004). The influence of participation in outdoor adventure programs for persons with cognitive disabilities. *American Journal of Recreation Therapy, 3*(1), 42–46.

Peterson, C. & Stumbo, N. (2000). *Therapeutic Recreation Program Design: Principles and Procedures.* Boston: Allyn and Bacon.

Schleien, S., Germ, P., & McAvoy, L. (1996). Inclusive community leisure services: Recommended professional practices and barriers encountered. *Therapeutic Recreation Journal, 30*(4), 260–273.

Schleien, S., Meyer, L., Heyne, L., & Biel Brandt, B. (1995). *Lifelong Leisure Skills and Lifestyles for Persons with Developmental Disabilities.* Baltimore: Paul H. Brookes.

Smith, R., Austin, D., & Kennedy, D. (2001). *Inclusive and Special Recreation – Opportunities for Persons with Disabilities*, 4th edn. Boston: McGraw Hill.

Voeltz, L. M. & Wuerch, B. B. (1981). A comprehensive approach to leisure education and leisure counseling for the severely handicapped person. *Therapeutic Recreation Journal*, *15*(4), 24–35.

Wehman, P. (Ed.) (1979). *Recreation Programming for Developmentally Disabled Persons.* Baltimore: University Park Press.

Wehman, P. & and Schleien, S. (1988). *Leisure Programs for Handicapped Persons*. Austin, TX: Pro-Ed, Inc.

Wuerch, B. B. & Voeltz, L. M. (1982). *Longitudinal Leisure Skills for Severely Handicapped Learners.* Baltimore, MD: Paul H. Brookes Publishing Co.

Zabriskie, R., Lundberg, N., & Groff, D. (2005). Quality of life and identity: The benefits of a community-based therapeutic recreation and adaptive sports program. *Therapeutic Recreation Journal*, *39*(3), 176–191.

10

Promoting Self-care Skills

Monica A. Wallace and Marisa W. Shubert

Psychology Department, Middle Tennessee State University, Murfreesboro, TN 37132, U.S.A.

INTRODUCTION

Adequate self-care skills are paramount in supporting basic daily functioning, community participation, appropriate and valued social roles, and access to experiences that elevate and sustain one's quality of life. The overall goal of obtaining self-care skills extends beyond maintaining basic life functions and securing independence. A focus on personal development, personal aspirations, and empowerment have replaced the individual deficit view that once served as the central paradigm guiding assessment and intervention for persons with disabilities (Thompson et al., 2002).

DEFINITION AND DESCRIPTION OF SELF-CARE SKILLS

Self-care skills are behaviors that individuals use to engage in personal care activities such as eating, dressing, toileting, grooming, and maintaining good hygiene (Langone & Burton, 1987). Self-care skills related to eating may include basic behaviors such as swallowing or chewing, or more socially based behaviors such as ordering in a fast-food restaurant. Self-care skills related to dressing may include skills such as zipping, buttoning, and determining appropriate clothing for the social situation or weather. Self-care skills related to toileting may include communicating the need for toileting and lowering clothing. Self-care skills related to grooming and maintaining good hygiene may include brushing teeth and changing clothes on a regular basis.

The importance of various self-care skills is determined by both individual needs and environmental context (American Association of Mental Retardation [AAMR], 2002). Two individuals may have the same ultimate goal (e.g., dress appropriately for work). However, depending upon their individual strengths, deficits, and situational demands, they may differ in the self-care skills needed to reach this goal. For one person, appropriate selection of wardrobe may be the target behavior while for another individual independent dressing may be the goal. Expectations for self-care skills also change with age and vary depending on the cultural context (AAMR, 2002). Most teachers and parents would likely view an absence of independent toileting skills in a 4-year-old with less concern than these same deficits in a 7-year-old.

ASSESSMENT OF SELF-CARE ADAPTIVE SKILLS ON THE ADAPTIVE BEHAVIOR ASSESSMENT SYSTEM-II (ABAS-II)

Information from the ABAS-II may help support the diagnosis and classification of such disabilities as mental retardation and developmental delay and may help identify individual patterns of strengths and weaknesses in individuals with other disorders or with various learning and behavior problems. In instances where eligibility criteria for classification or diagnosis do not require adaptive behavior assessment (e.g., learning disability, emotional disturbance), information from the ABAS-II also can be used to develop an individual profile of strengths and weaknesses and can contribute to intervention planning (Harrison & Oakland, 2003).

The ABAS-II provides normative scores for 10 adaptive skill areas, three adaptive composites (i.e., Conceptual, Practical, Social) and the General Adaptive Composite (GAC). This allows for the comparison of scores with same-age individuals and with other measures that are scored on the same metric (Harrison & Oakland, 2003).

Self-care adaptive skills are assessed on the ABAS-II across age ranges (0–89 years) and across forms (i.e., teacher/day care provider, parent/primary caregiver, teacher form, parent form, adult completed by an observer or self-report). The teacher form for ages 5–21 contains 19 items that target self-care skills. All other forms at the various age levels have 24 or 25 items that target self-care skills. The categories of self-care adaptive skills assessed on the ABAS-II are consistent with the definition of self-care skills provided by Langone and Burton (1987) and include items related to eating (e.g., drinks liquids without spilling), dressing (e.g., puts shoes on correct feet), toileting (e.g., sits on toilet or potty seat without being held), grooming (e.g., cleans underneath fingernails), and maintaining proper hygiene (e.g., washes hands with soap). Ratings in the Self-Care adaptive skill area, along with ratings in Community Use, Home

Living and Health and Safety adaptive skill areas, contribute to the Practical composite score on the ABAS-II. The Practical composite score combines with the Social and Conceptual composite scores to form the GAC (Harrison & Oakland, 2003).

Knowledge of the developmental relevance of adaptive skills is important when assessing adaptive skills (AAMR, 2002). Items on the ABAS-II were selected in part through a comprehensive review of research on developmental skills across age groups and settings. The acquisition of adaptive skills varies with age. These age group differences are reflected on the ABAS-II. The higher the raw score in each of the adaptive skill areas, the higher the age equivalent (Harrison & Oakland, 2003).

Differing environmental demands at school and home are represented on the ABAS-II by the presence of certain items on one or more forms or by putting parallel versions of items on each form. The items "washes his/her own hair" and "combines hot and cold water for shower or bath" appear on the parent form but not on the teacher form, whereas the parent form item, "uses restroom at home without help" parallels the teacher form item "uses the school restroom alone". Differing environmental demands and adult expectations also can be assessed by providing the ABAS-II forms to multiple informants so that different individuals can rate the child's performance on the same behaviors. For example, if a child's parents are divorced and custody is shared, a better description of the child's behavior may be obtained if both the mother and the father complete ABAS-II forms. Both parent and teacher forms routinely should be administered for preschool and school-age children. The adult form should be administered to family members, supervisor, caregivers, etc. and, when possible, as a self-report to the client. This contributes to multifaceted information gathering, a necessity for sound assessment and crucial when identifying supports and strengths for intervention planning (Sattler, 2001).

THE IMPORTANCE OF SELF-CARE SKILLS FOR GENERAL FUNCTIONING

Self-care skills form the core of daily independent functioning, facilitate access to various life experiences and social acceptance, and support the maintenance of a socially acceptable appearance. The ability to take care of one's own basic needs related to feeding, dressing, toileting, grooming, and maintaining hygiene is essential for a safe and healthy independent or interdependent existence (Depalma & Wheeler, 1991; Langone & Burton, 1987; AAMR, 2002). Self-care skills also provide the building blocks for additional interventions, particularly for persons with developmental disabilities (e.g., autism, developmental delay, mental retardation) who would benefit from inclusive educational environments (Benner, 1992; Lowenthal, 1996). Mastery of self-care skills such as independent toileting or feeding may be prerequisites for participation in childcare, preschool, day treatment, summer camp programs, or in any other number of experiences that typically developing persons easily access (Lowenthal, 1996).

Individually determined and culturally appropriate self-care behaviors constitute keystone behaviors (Barnett et al., 1996), that is, behaviors that can enhance functioning and support continued development. Without the acquisition of certain basic self-care skills, persons may not be afforded the opportunity to develop more advanced skills.

Consider how a 4-year-old child with autism and adequate eating self-care skills has access to the curricular benefits of eating routines in an inclusive preschool classroom. In contrast, the child without adequate eating skills may receive meals and snacks in locations isolated from peers. The isolated child may not benefit from the opportunity to develop additional adaptive (e.g., pouring juice from a child-sized pitcher), language (e.g., conversation with teachers and peers that can support vocabulary development), motor (e.g., awareness of others and personal space at the table), cognitive (e.g., counting out 5 goldfish crackers), and social (e.g., turn taking) skills that are integrated into the daily community eating routines.

CONDITIONS THAT IMPACT DEVELOPMENT AND PERFORMANCE OF SELF-CARE SKILLS

The development of self-care skills is often contingent upon motor skills, self-control, social understanding, and cognitive skills. For example, learning to button a shirt requires adequate fine motor skills. Social understanding is needed to comprehend unspoken social rules (e.g., wearing one's shirt unbuttoned may be acceptable at home and unacceptable while shopping). Cognitive skills such as sequencing and memory are needed to put a sweater on after you put on a shirt. Certain skills may be easier or harder to develop, perform, and maintain depending on an individual's pattern of strengths and weaknesses in each of these areas.

Demonstration of self-care skills also can be contingent on attitudinal and motivational factors. For some persons, lack of self-care skills may be related to a performance deficit ("will not do") rather than an acquisition deficit ("can not do") (Gresham, 2002). A child with a behavior disorder might demonstrate oppositional behaviors and be described as not regularly performing certain self-care skills on the ABAS-II by teachers and parents. Yet, in a structured assessment situation, a child may be determined to have knowledge and prerequisite behaviors to perform the skill. Thus, the conditions that impact performance in a "will not do the action" (i.e., a possible performance deficit) as compared to a "can not do the action" (i.e., a possible skill deficit) situation have implications for assessment and intervention planning. The ABAS-II allows one to determine whether deficits are either a skill or performance deficit as illustrated by the expanded scoring criteria included in the manual and on the protocol forms. Scoring criteria distinguish between a skill deficit (i.e., not being able to demonstrate a behavior: score = 0), and a performance deficit (i.e., never or almost never performing the behavior, or rarely performing the behavior unless prompted: score = 1).

The heterogeneity of strengths and deficits among persons with various disabilities, and even among those with similar disabilities, creates a plethora of conditions that impact development, performance, and maintenance of self-care skills. A child with cerebral palsy who has limited movement with his or her dominant hand and average intellectual skills faces a different set of challenges when learning to put on shoes than does a child with adequate motor skills but cognitive limitations that impact his or her ability to match shoes to the correct feet. A study of children with Fragile X syndrome found them to have fewer delays in adaptive skills associated with self-care skills than those that require higher cognitive and representational abilities (Bailey, Hatton & Skinner, 1998). A study of children with emotional disturbance found their communication and daily living skills to be average and their socialization skills to be below average (Sparrow & Cicchetti, 1987).

Teaching children with autism to brush their teeth who become fixated with the sound, feel, or look of water may require more steps (e.g., turn off the water after wetting the tooth brush) than needed for teaching similar skills to other children with autism who do not share the same fascination. Additionally, performance of self-care skills typically involves the acceptance of sensory stimuli (e.g., texture of foods, feel of sitting on the toilet seat, feel of various fabrics against the skin, sound of water running in the shower) which may pose problems for some children with autism (Depalma & Wheeler, 1991). A child who has fine motor difficulties and average intelligence may resist the use of some adaptive closures (e.g., large-size buttons) when he or she understands that different closures make him stand out from peers. Cognitive deficits may impact the number of learning trials needed to master a skill and, once learned, may impact the maintenance and generalization of a skill to different environments (Langone & Burton, 1987). The amount of effort required to demonstrate a skill may impact the likelihood of that skill being demonstrated (Horner & Day, 1991).

ADDITIONAL ASSESSMENT TECHNIQUES

No one measure of adaptive behavior captures the complete range of behaviors in a specific adaptive domain or is a perfect match with the particular skills needed for an individual to succeed in a specific environment (AAMR, 2002). An assessment of adaptive behavior and skills should determine whether deficits may be due to limited interest, opportunities, environmental expectations and social opportunities, and/or limited by health or intellectual abilities (AAMR, 2002). Observations and interviews can be structured to directly assess these issues. Components of functional assessments (e.g., observing a person in his or her normal environments) can be invaluable to assessment and support planning. Situational variables that will either impede or support self-care skill development can be identified, and clarification about expectations of parents and teachers also can occur. Observations also provide for a more ecologically valid assessment because the person is observed in the context of relevant, live, and changing situations (Benner, 1992). Observation can help determine the skills an individual will need to participate fully in a particular environment and can identify supports that would allow functioning in a more inclusive environment (Cone, 1987).

An analysis of individual scores on the ABAS-II self-care items can serve as a guide to additional assessment and intervention planning through the use of task analysis (Langone & Burton, 1987). Task analysis is a sequential and hierarchical listing of steps needed to complete a task (Kazdin, 1994). DePalma and Wheeler (1991) provided an example of steps in a task analysis for combing hair:

1. Pick up and hold comb with dominant hand.
2. Comb hair on top of the head, comb hair front to back, for a specified number of time (e.g., two times).
3. On each side of the head, comb right side top to bottom three times, then left side two times.
4. Comb the back of the head top to bottom two times.
5. Put comb back in proper place (p. 5).

Task analysis can pinpoint where the breakdown in skill performance is occurring. As noted earlier, an inability to perform a skill may be related to a lack of motor skill (e.g., being able to hold the comb), cognitive ability (e.g., having difficulty remembering to comb both front and back of the head), social skills (e.g., not seeing messy hair as inappropriate when in public), motivation (e.g., thinking the effort it takes to hold the comb is not worth the result) or any combination thereof.

INTERVENTIONS TO PROMOTE SELF-CARE SKILLS

Irrespective of the intervention being used to promote self-care skills, several basic principles should guide intervention planning. First, select the actual or similar environments in which the developing self-care skill will be used because such environments provide the best learning setting with respect to the acquisition, transfer, performance, and maintenance of skills (Langone & Burton, 1987; Gresham, 2002). The development and continued use of skills through naturally occurring routines and cues may help compensate for deficits in memory and problem solving skills (Meyer & Kohl, 1985; DePalma & Wheeler, 1991; AAMR, 2002). Motivation to demonstrate a particular self-care skill also may be higher if instruction occurs within the person's daily environment because the acquisition of the skill is directly linked to the need for the skill (Gresham, 2002). However, use of simulated environments that provide: (a) exemplars that are representative of the variation in natural settings, (b) multiple practice opportunities, (c) skill practice across varied contexts, and (d) natural consequences have been effective in teaching needed skills (Horner et al., 1986). See the chapter on community use skills for additional discussion of these issues.

Second, intervention also should focus on an individual's goals and needs. Two persons who received the same standard score on self-care skills are likely to have different goals and needs and thus require different intervention plans. Identification of the expectations and supports within an individual's environment helps determine these individual needs. Within-person characteristics (e.g., preferred learning modality and time of day when response to instruction is higher) also should be considered (DePalma & Wheeler, 1991).

Third, progress monitoring and decision making should be built into the intervention plan (Upah & Tilly, 2002). This process establishes a continuous feedback loop that links assessment and intervention. Data must be collected and summarized to evaluate and validate the success of an intervention and to make changes when the intervention is not working. Decision rules that describe what to do when certain data patterns emerge should be established in advance and used to guide the intervention process. Upah and Tilly (2002) present a detailed account of how a decision-making plan and progress monitoring should be incorporated into intervention planning.

SPECIFIC INTERVENTIONS THAT CAN BE USED TO PROMOTE SELF-CARE SKILLS

Interventions to promote adaptive skills can be as simple as informal parent education sessions where developmental expectations are clarified and/or parents are taught simple adaptive strategies to use with their children. Entry into day care, preschool, or school also may increase adaptive skills as a new environment presents new expectations and new supports (Harrison & Boan, 2004).

Many interventions reported to improve self-care skills utilize operant methodology and include such techniques as task analysis, prompting, increasing learning opportunities, and chaining. These methods are discussed below. Also, reinforcement may support the development of self-care skills while differential reinforcement may help eliminate behaviors that may prevent self-care skill development or performance. Kazdin (1994) offers comprehensive definitions for these and other behavioral techniques. Various adaptive technologies also can support the development of self-care skills (Bigge et al., 2001) and may be useful in combination with behavioral techniques.

Task analysis: Task analysis has been discussed as an assessment technique, but it can also be an integral part of promoting self-care skills. When utilizing task analysis, assessment can be linked directly to intervention. Task analysis can be used to identify exactly where a breakdown in skill performance occurs. Then an intervention can be planned to target the specific deficiency. For example, when working with a person to implement the steps listed by Depalma and Wheeler (1991) for combing hair (mentioned previously), you may observe that a person has difficulty maintaining a grasp on the comb. Additional smaller steps could be added to the task analysis to support learning to hold on to the comb. Another individual may easily maintains a grasp on the comb yet have difficulty understanding the concepts of front and back of the head. For this individual, a different type of intervention is needed to help learn these directional concepts. Perhaps picture steps rather than verbal steps may be most effective (DePalma & Wheeler, 1991).

Prompting: A prompt consists of verbal statements, gestures, guided assistance, modeling, or any other interventions that help individuals demonstrate a response (Kazdin, 1994). Modeling and manual guidance have been used to teach toileting skills (Langone & Burton, 1987) and support the development of self-care skills in children with autism (DePalma & Wheeler, 1991). Prompts may be especially useful at the beginning of an instructional program (Kazdin, 1994) and should be removed as soon as feasible (DePalma & Wheeler, 1991). Attention should be paid to an individual's response to a prompt because, for some individuals, intrusive cues such as touching may create anxiety or they may mistakenly interpret the prompt as part of the skill being learned (DePalma & Wheeler, 1991).

Horner and Keilitz (1975) used a multiple baseline across participants design to demonstrate that task analysis in combination with systematic instruction and reinforcement improved toothbrushing behaviors in four adolescents with mental retardation. The training setting was a room with a single sink and mirror. If participants performed the target step in the task analysis with no help, then reinforcement was provided and the next step in the task analysis was initiated. However, if the target step was not performed, the level of assistance increased (i.e., from no help to verbal instructions to demonstration and verbal instruction to physical guidance and instruction) until the step was performed and then social reinforcement and tokens were provided. As participants acquired successive skills, training was faded. Participants took between 18 and 30 sessions to achieve the training criterion of all steps performed correctly in two of three consecutive sessions. Toothbrushing behavior also improved in a replication group where the same procedures were applied in the bathroom of the residential setting and used only social reinforcement (Horner & Keilitz, 1975).

Increasing learning opportunities: Behaviors and routines related to self-care skills may occur infrequently (e.g., opportunities to eat or fasten clothing). However, it is possible to structure routines that increase the frequency of needed self-care skills so that additional natural contexts are provided. Simulated environments that replicate equipment, materials, and the setting in naturally occurring environments also can increase learning opportunities (Mechling & Cronin, 2006).

One strategy used to promote self-feeding behaviors in individuals with mental retardation entailed offering miniature meals in order to offer multiple opportunities to practice appropriate self-feeding behaviors (Azrin & Armstrong, 1973). This was accomplished by dividing the regular meals into smaller servings and eating hourly rather than only at typically scheduled meal times. This allowed for more daily teaching sessions and facilitated recall of previously taught skills.

Overcorrection may be used to promote rapid toilet training (Foxx & Azrin, 1973). Overcorrection involves correcting the consequences of an undesirable behavior (Kazdin, 1994) such as cleaning up a mess. The first step in the rapid method of toilet training is to increase children's liquid intake to prompt more frequent need of toileting, thus increasing learning opportunities. Extensive training time (4–8 hours each day) and high ratio of adults to children (1 adult for no more than 2 children) are required. Results may be seen in one to five days. Subsequent steps involve seating the child on the toilet followed by time off of the toilet and providing reinforcement for avoiding toileting accidents. If accidents do occur, the child is reprimanded and overcorrection may be used cautiously, if quick training is required. During the overcorrection phase, the child is made to wash out clothing, and wipe up any mess made (Foxx & Azrin, 1973).

Computer-based simulation also may be used to increase the number of learning opportunities. Mechling and Cronin (2006) used computer-based simulation to teach three high school students with moderate or severe intellectual disabilities to order food in a fast-food restaurant using an augmentative, alternative communication device. Generalization of the skills to restaurants in the community was achieved and performance was accurate during maintenance probes.

Taking advantage of naturally occurring routines throughout the day where the targeted skill may be used is another way to increase opportunities for learning. A child can engage in dressing behaviors when dressing in the morning or undressing in the evening as well as when putting on a coat to go out to the playground, when putting on a smock for a painting activity (DePalma & Wheeler, 1991), or putting on dress-up clothes for pretend play.

Chaining: Backwards chaining, or completion of the last step in a task analysis first, was reported to be the most common technique used in teaching dressing (Langone & Burton, 1987). All prior steps in the chain would be completed by the instructor with the trainee completing the very last step and then receiving reinforcement. On subsequent trials, steps are added one by one in reverse order until all steps are completed independently.

Both forward (e.g., unbutton pants first) and backward chaining (e.g., sit on toilet first) have been successful in teaching toileting skills. Individual strengths and difficulties as well as available situational supports impact which type of chaining is selected for use. For an individual with inadequate dressing skills, backward chaining may provide more immediate success in that completion of the last step is not contingent on dressing skills (Langone & Burton, 1987). For an individual who also has been working on improving dressing skills, forward chaining when also teaching toileting skills would provide another opportunity to practice these skills in an authentic environment.

Reinforcement: Reinforcement increases the frequency of a response (Kazdin, 1994). Tokens provided contingent upon the demonstration of appropriate grooming skills during morning checks improved the quality of grooming skills in individuals with moderate retardation living in a group home (Doleys et al., 1981). An acceptable rate of eating was shaped in persons with retardation by providing edible and social reinforcements contingent upon increasing the pauses between bites (Favell et al., 1980).

By definition, reinforcement could be used to promote a variety of self-care skills, particularly in situations where there is a performance deficit rather than skill acquisition deficit. For example, a behavior contract could be designed to promote a child's independent dressing. The contract could state that the child could earn something desirable for each item of clothing he put on before a set amount of time expires.

Differential reinforcement (e.g., differential reinforcement of alternative targeted behavior, differential reinforcement of incompatible behaviors, differential reinforcement of lower rates of behavior) can be used to reduce competing behaviors (Gresham, 2002) that are blocking performance of appropriate self-care skills. Differential reinforcement, a positive reductive technique that uses no aversive conditions, should be considered the first resort when trying to decrease problem behaviors (Baer et al., 2002). For example, differential reinforcement of lower rates of behavior could be used to reduce self-stimulatory behaviors of a child with autism that interfere with instruction intended to develop independent eating skills.

USE OF ASSISTIVE TECHNOLOGIES

Assistive technologies as described by Bigge et al. (2001) can provide environmental modifications that contribute to the development, performance, and maintenance of self-care skills. For tasks that require two hands, object stabilization strategies (e.g., clamping, taping, using Velcro, or suction cups) can support grasp and manipulation. These tools can make self-care activities (e.g., holding and drinking from a cup) easier. The height of surfaces such as a table can be manipulated to support sitting or provide elbow support. A U-shaped table can provide additional support. With this additional support, individuals with disabilities may be better able to feed themselves and reach for materials, including brushes or combs that are placed on the counter. Angling surfaces or slant boards that come in different angles also may support independent functioning of certain activities. Physical boundaries can be created to help objects stay within reach rather than accidentally pushed out of the way. Handles on items can be enlarged by wrapping tape or another object around them. Some everyday items such as keys, eating utensils, combs, and toothbrushes are available for purchase with large handles, grips, or attachments that support the use of fine motor skills. Electronic aids to daily living can support the use of electric appliances used in personal care or other activities. An electronic aid provides programmed and/or spontaneous control of electrical appliances, such as electric toothbrushes, thus reducing the amount of arm movement required for brushing.

SAMPLE CASE STUDY USING THE ABAS-II

Psychological Report

Name: Marianne Franklin
Date of Birth: 5-27-1997
Grade: 2nd grade

Parents: John and Jennifer Franklin
Date of Report: 10-26-2004
Age: 7 years, 5 months

SOURCES OF INFORMATION

Adaptive Behavior Assessment System-Second Edition (ABAS-II), Parent Form and Teacher Form
Stanford Binet Intelligence Scales, 5th Edition (SB-V)
School Records
Developmental interview with mother, Jennifer Franklin
Interview with teacher, Susan Smith

REASON FOR REFERRAL

Marianne Franklin, a 7-year-old female, was referred for testing by her parents who are concerned about her refusing to complete her chores around the house and her refusing to take care of her clothes and personal appearance. Marianne's parents recently divorced and each has seen an increase in problem behaviors from Marianne at home. However, Marianne's teachers report that she generally is compliant and cooperative at school. Marianne's parents requested the current psychological evaluation in order to discern whether Marianne's behavior at home is due to her individual situation or to normal development. Both Mr. and Mrs. Franklin are interested in evaluating Marianne's cognitive functioning and adaptive behavior in relation to her peers and in obtaining assistance in developing interventions that may help to improve Marianne's current behaviors.

BACKGROUND INFORMATION

Mrs. Franklin reported no prenatal, perinatal, or postnatal complications associated with her pregnancy with Marianne. Marianne is an only child. Marianne has had no medical problems to date. Mrs. Franklin stated that Marianne is extremely active and enjoys people and playing outdoors. Marianne never has been very concerned with her personal appearance and constantly has to be reminded to comb her hair, take a bath, brush her teeth, and change her clothes. Mrs. Franklin reported that, when she was still married and stayed at home with Marianne as a baby and toddler, Marianne was well behaved and rarely disobeyed house rules or parental instructions.

Since the divorce, Mrs. Franklin has been working full-time outside of the house. Marianne now alternates days and weekends with her parents. According to Mrs. Franklin, her divorce was amicable and the entire family has adjusted to their new schedule. However, Mrs. Franklin reported that both she and her ex-husband have noticed recently that Marianne is less willing to perform household chores and is more confrontational toward them. The examiner confirmed this information in a follow-up telephone conversation with Mr. Franklin.

Marianne's teacher, Mrs. Smith, reported that Marianne is well behaved and compliant at school. Mrs. Smith indicated that Marianne has formed friendships with her classmates and is particularly fond of activities such as recess and physical education. Mrs. Smith reported that Marianne's academic performance is average and typical of students her age. Marianne' s clothes are sometimes buttoned incorrectly and her hair not thoroughly brushed. Mrs. Smith also observed that Marianne has trouble tying her shoes and putting on her coat.

A review of Marianne's school records indicated that Marianne earned satisfactory grades in kindergarten and 1st grade. Marianne's mother reported that Marianne enjoys school and has not had any significant behavior problems at school. Although she spends time at both her mother's and father's houses, Marianne still attend's the same grade school.

BEHAVIORAL OBSERVATIONS

Rapport was easily established and maintained with Mrs. Franklin during the developmental interview. Mrs. and Mr. Franklin and Mrs. Smith completed the ABAS-II Forms in the presence of the examiner and appeared to carefully consider each question. Therefore, the results of the developmental interview, ABAS-II: Parent Form and ABAS-II: Teacher Form are considered to be a valid indication of Marianne's current abilities.

The examiner also quickly established rapport with Marianne prior to administering the Stanford Binet Intelligence Scales, 5th Edition (SB-V) to her. Marianne remained attentive throughout the test administration; her level of concentration was typical for children her age. Marianne was cheerful and pleasant to work with and seemed to have a strong desire to do her best on the test. Thus, the results of the intelligence scales administration are considered to be a valid indication of Marianne's current level of intellectual functioning.

Stanford Binet Intelligence Scales, 5th Edition, test results and interpretations: The Stanford Binet Intelligence Scales – 5th Edition (SB-V) is an individually administered clinical instrument for assessing the global intellectual ability of individuals between the ages of 2 and 85 (Roid, 2003). The test measures fluid reasoning, quantitative reasoning abilities, working memory, visual-spatial processing abilities, and acquired knowledge. The SB-V reports results in a Nonverbal IQ, a Verbal IQ, and a Full Scale IQ, see Table 10.1 for a summary of Marianne's scores on the SB-V.

According to the Examiner's Manual of the SB-V, the most reliable score is the Full Scale IQ as it provides a summary of the current global level of intellectual

TABLE 10.1 Score Summary of Marianne Franklin's Performance on the SB-V

Stanford Binet Intelligence Scales, 5th Edition (SB-V) *Score Summary for Marianne Franklin, Age 7-years-5 Months*

Composite Scores	Standard Scores $M = 100, SD = 15$	Percentile Rank	Confidence Interval (95%)	Score Descriptor
Non-verbal IQ (NVIQ)	95	37	89–101	Average
Verbal IQ (VIQ)	95	37	89–101	Average
Full scale IQ (FSIQ)	94	34	90–98	Average

functioning and includes both nonverbal and verbal measures. Marianne's Full Scale IQ, 94, places her in the average range and at the 34th percentile for her age group. Thus, Marianne seemingly is capable intellectually of displaying average work for her age group and, according to her teacher, does demonstrate such abilities in school. Furthermore, this average Full Scale IQ indicates that Marianne has the intellectual ability necessary to perform in her environment and to develop and use the adaptive behaviors that are typical of her age group. A comparison between her Non-Verbal IQ and Verbal IQ also shows that Marianne's verbal and nonverbal problem solving abilities are comparable. Therefore, Marianne's failure to display normal adaptive behaviors and skills at home is not a result of her intellectual functioning. Marianne has both the verbal and nonverbal intellectual ability necessary to learn and carry out adaptive behaviors and skills.

ABAS-II results and interpretations: Adaptive behavior refers to those daily skills needed to function in one's environment, including interacting with other people and independently taking care of oneself (Harrison & Oakland, 2003, p. 3). The adaptive behaviors demonstrated by an individual depend upon both societal and cultural expectations and the individual's age and motivation. Marianne's adaptive skills were assessed using the Parent and Teacher respondent forms of the ABAS-II (Harrison & Oakland, 2003). See Table 10.2 for a complete report of Marianne's scores.

Marianne obtained standard scores of 96, 92, and 103 on the GACs on the ABAS-II forms completed by her father, mother, and teacher, respectively. These scores are considered, respectively, to be as good as or better than 39.5%, 29.7%, and 57.9% of her same age peers. Relative to individuals of comparable age, Marianne's adaptive behavior can be described as being in the average range. This is consistent with her parents' reports that Marianne is an active, social child who is capable of performing various tasks asked of her. This also is consistent with Mrs. Smith's report that Marianne performs at a level typical for children her age at her school.

TABLE 10.2 Score Summary of Marianne Franklin's Performance on the ABAS-II

ABAS-II Score Summary for Marianne Franklin, Age 7-years-5 months

Adaptive Skill Areas	Parent (Father) Scaled Scores $M = 10, SD = 3$	Parent (Mother) Scaled Scores $M = 10, SD = 3$	Teacher Scaled Scores $M = 10, SD = 3$
Communication	12	10	13
Community use	10	9	10
Functional academics	8	7	10
Home/School living	10	11	12
Health and safety	9	9	10
Leisure	9	8	10
Self-care	6	5	6
Self-direction	7	7	9
Social	11	10	13

Adaptive Composites	Standard Scores $M = 100, SD = 15$	Standard Scores $M = 100, SD = 15$	Standard Scores $M = 100, SD = 15$
Conceptual Composite	94	90	105
90% confidence interval	89–99	85–95	101–109
Social Composite	100	95	108
90% confidence interval	94–106	89–91	103–113
Practical Composite	95	94	97
90% confidence interval	89–91	88–90	92–102
GAC*	96	92	103
90% confidence interval	93–99	89–95	101–105

*General Adaptive Composite.

However, on the Parent Rating Form, Mr. and Mrs. Franklin's separate ratings of Marianne indicated that the area of self-care skills is a significant weakness for Marianne. A comparison between the self-care adaptive skill area scores and the average Practical composite score showed that the self-care adaptive skill area is a significant and unusual weakness for Marianne, compared to typical patterns of scores for other children her age. Thus, a comparison across adaptive skill area scores reveals that Marianne's ability to take care of her own personal needs, such as keeping her clothing neat and maintaining her hygiene, is not as well-developed as other adaptive skill areas that contribute to the Practical composite score, such as home/school living.

Results on the Teacher Form also indicate a weakness in self-care skills at school. Mrs. Smith reported that Marianne only sometimes ties her shoes and never keeps her hair neat during the school day. This finding is consistent with both parent and teacher reports that Marianne often appears disheveled during the day and has to be reminded to change her clothes.

An analysis of the Teacher Form results also indicated that the adaptive skill areas of Communication and School Living are strengths for Marianne. This is consistent with teacher reports that Marianne communicates well in class and follows class rules. Therefore, adults should continue to make every to communicate the importance of taking care of one's self to Marianne and help her understand how following rules at home are part of her responsibility.

SUMMARY AND RECOMMENDATIONS

Marianne, a 7-year-old 2nd grader, is experiencing difficulty maintaining her personal appearance and following the directions of her parents at home. Marianne has experienced the recent divorce of her parents and now spends time at each of their homes. Information gathered from parent and teacher interviews, school records, and the ABAS-II suggests that Marianne's self-care skills are deficient. Marianne's strengths include her ability to communicate with others, follow directions and obey school rules, and to engage in activities such as recess and physical education. Results from the Stanford Binet, used to assess Marianne's current level of intellectual functioning, indicated Marianne has average intellectual abilities and thus should be able to demonstrate typical adaptive skills. Interventions used to help Marianne develop her self-care skills should utilize her intellectual abilities and built upon her strengths in communication and her current interests in school.

Interventions

1. Marianne's parents should work with Marianne to determine reasonable self-care skills she must meet in her daily routine (e.g., tying her shoes, keeping her hair neat during the day, bathing daily). Although Marianne spends time with her mother and father separately, Marianne's parents should establish similar expectations for Marianne and work to support her demonstration of these skills across environments.
2. Marianne's parents should work with Marianne to develop a schedule of chores for which she will be responsible in each home. This schedule should be displayed prominently in each home so that it serves to prompt Marianne to complete her chores.
3. Task analysis should be used to determine if Marianne has the skills necessary to complete the self-care behaviors she performs infrequently (i.e., does she have a skill deficit or a performance deficit). According to her parents and teacher, these include fastening and straightening her clothing after using the restroom, keeping her hair neat during the day, and washing her own hair. Additional skills should be taught through modeling when Marianne may not yet know the appropriate skill to complete a task.

4. Marianne's parents and teachers should work together to increase the opportunities for Marianne to learn to dress herself and maintain her hygiene at home and at school. For example, Marianne should be reminded to brush her hair and tuck in her shirt before leaving for school, before going to lunch, after playing at recess, and before going home from school. Over time, Marianne can be expected to perform skills throughout the day without adult prompting.
5. The importance of taking care of oneself should be explained to Marianne, given her strong communication skills. When Marianne performs a self-care skill, she also should be praised verbally and complimented on her appearance (e.g., Your hair looks nice today, Marianne.) in order to help her learn the social benefits that come from good self-care skills. Activities she enjoys, such as time with friends or playing outside, also can be made contingent upon Marianne's demonstration of the skills that she can perform (e.g., You can go to recess once you tuck in your shirt.). Over time, immediate and extrinsic rewards should be lessened so that Marianne performs these skills in light of her own intrinsic rewards.
6. Marianne's increasing defiance and unwillingness to take care of herself may be related to some emotional stress she is experiencing as a result of her parents' divorce. Marianne's emotional needs and stress levels should be monitored closely. Marianne may benefit from speaking to the school counselor or school psychologist if these levels appear elevated. Furthermore, Marianne's development of self-care skills should continue to be monitored as she grows older to ensure that she is following the typical developmental course and becoming more competent in these skills as she ages.

REFERENCES

American Association on Mental Retardation (AAMR) (2002). *Mental Retardation: Definition Classification, and Systems of Supports*, 10th edn., Washington, DC: AAMR.

Azrin, N. H. & Armstrong, P. M. (1973). The "mini-meal": A method for teaching eating skills to the profoundly retarded. *Mental Retardation*, *11*(1), 9–13.

Baer, G. G., Cavalier, A. R., & Manning, M. A. (2002). Best practices in school discipline. In A. Thomas & J. Grimes (Eds.), *Best Practices in School Psychology*, 4th edn., pp. 977–992. Washington, DC: National Association of School Psychologists.

Bailey, D. B., Hatton, D. D., & Skinner, M. (1998). Early developmental trajectories of males with fragile X syndrome. *American Journal on Mental Retardation*, *103*, 29–39.

Barnett, D. W., Bauer, A. M., Erhardt, K. E., Lentz, F. E., & Stollar, S. A. (1996). Keystone targets for change: Planning for widespread positive consequences. *School Psychology Quarterly*, *11*, 95–117.

Benner, S. M. (1992). *Assessing Young Children with Special Needs: An Ecological Perspective*. New York: Longman.

Bigge, J. L., Best, S. J., & Heller, K. W. (2001). *Teaching Individuals with Physical, Health or Multiple Disabilities*, 4th edn., New Jersey: Merrill Prentice Hall.

Cone, J. D. (1987). Intervention planning using adaptive behavior instruments. *Journal of Special Education*, *21*, 127–148.

Depalma, V. & Wheeler, M. (1991). *Learning Self-Care Skills from Functional Programming for People with Autism: A Series*. Bloomington: Indiana University, Institute for the Study of Developmental Disabilities, Indiana Resource Center for Autism. (ERIC Document Reproduction Service No. ED363070).

Doleys, D. M., Stacy, D., & Knowles, S. (1981). Modification of grooming behavior in adult retarded: Token reinforcement in a community-based program. *Behavior Modification*, *5*, 119–128.

Favell, J. E., McGimsey, J. F., & Jones, M. L. (1980). Rapid eating in the retarded: Reduction by non-aversive procedures. *Behavior Modification*, *4*, 481–492.

Foxx, R. M. & Azrin, N. H. (1973). Dry pants: A rapid method of toilet training children. *Behavior Research and Therapy*, *11*, 435–442.

Gresham, F. M. (2002). Best practices in social skills training. In A. Thomas & J. Grimes (Eds.), *Best Practices in School Psychology*, 4th edn., pp. 1029–1040. Washington, DC: National Association of School Psychologists.

Harrison, P. L. & Boan, C. H. (2004). Assessment of adaptive behavior. In B. Bracken (Ed.), *The Psychoeducational Assessment of Preschool Children*, 3rd edn., pp. 124–144. New Jersey: Lawrence Erlbaum Associates.

Harrison, P. L. & Oakland, T. (2003). *Adaptive Behavior Assessment System Manual*, 2nd edn., San Antonio, TX: Harcourt Assessment, Inc.

Horner, R. H. & Day, H. M. (1991). The effects of response efficiency on functionally equivalent competing behaviors. *Journal of Applied Behavior Analysis, 24,* 719–732.

Horner, R. H., McDonnell, J. J., & Bellamy, G. T. (1986). Teaching generalized behaviors: General-case instruction in simulation and community settings. In R. H. Horner, L. H. Meyer, & H. D. Fredericks (Eds.), *Education of Learners with Severe Handicaps*, pp. 289–315. Baltimore: Brookes.

Horner, R. H. & Keilitz, I. (1975). Training mentally retarded adolescents to brush their teeth. *Journal of Applied Behavior Analysis*, *8*, 301–309.

Kazdin, A. E. (1994). *Behavior Modification in Applied Settings*, 5th edn., California: Brookes/Cole Publishing.

Langone, J. & Burton, T. A. (1987). Teaching adaptive behavior skills to moderately and severely handicapped individuals: Best practices for facilitating independent living. *Journal of Special Education*, *21*, 149–166.

Lowenthal, B. (1996). Teaching basic adaptive skills to young children with disabilities. *Early Child Development and Care*, *115*, 77–84.

Mechling, L. C. & Cronin, B. (2006). Computer-based video instruction to teach the use of augmentative and alternative communication devices for ordering at fast-food restaurants. *The Journal of Special Education*, *39*, 234–245.

Meyer, D. & Kohl, F. L. (1985). Teaching domestic living skills to severely handicapped students in the natural environment. *Teaching Exceptional Children*, *18*(1), 38–45.

Roid, Gale. (2003). *Stanford Binet Intelligence Scales Manual*, 5th edn., Itasca, IL: Riverside Publishing.

Sattler, J. M. (2001). *Assessment of Children. Cognitive Applications*, 4th edn., San Diego: Author.

Sparrow, S. S. & Cicchetti, D. V. (1987). Adaptive behavior and the psychologically disturbed child. *Journal of Special Education*, *21*, 89–100.

Thompson, J. R., Hughes, C., Schalock, R. L., Silverman, W., Tasse, M. J., Bryant, B., et al. (2002). Integrating supports in assessment and planning. *Mental Retardation*, *40*, 390–405.

Upah, K. R. F. & Tilly, W. D. III (2002). Best practices in designing, implementing, and evaluating quality interventions. In A. Thomas & J. Grimes (Eds.), *Best Practices in School Psychology*, 4th edn., pp. 483–502. Washington, DC: National Association of School Psychologists.

11

SOCIAL SKILLS

KRISTY LEE PARK*, SHELDON LOMAN** AND MELISSA A. MILLER†

*University of Louisville, Louisville, KY 40292, U.S.A.
**University of Oregon, Eugene, OR 97403-1235, U.S.A.
†University of North Carolina at Chapel Hill, Chapel Hill, NC 27599-3500, U.S.A.

INTRODUCTION

Adequate social behavior and other adaptive skills are the foundations of personal and social adjustment in life (Mathur & Rutherford, 1996). A person's adaptive behavior requires a repertoire of social skills and the ability to use these skills at the right time and place to meet the daily demands of school, work, and life. This chapter will expand on the definition by Gresham et al. (2001) who defined social skills as "... socially significant behaviors exhibited in specific situations that predict important social outcomes" (p. 331). However, most professionals and parents similarly explain social skills as discrete verbal and nonverbal behaviors that are learned by watching people around them or specifically taught to maximize social reinforcement.

Social skills and social competence often are used interchangeably to describe an individual's social functioning. However, these terms should be distinguished to promote clarity for instructional purposes. *Social skills* constitute situation-specific patterns of behavior necessary for interactions with others. *Social competence* refers to how well an individual uses social skills to produce socially acceptable responses in various social situations. For example, an individual may display critical social skills to interact with others, yet display a lack of social competence because these skills are not performed at appropriate times, with other persons, and in varied settings. Under the broader construct of social competence, social skills are the building blocks of all interactions through which people learn, play, and work (Odom et al., 1992).

Social competence plays an integral part in how well a young person transitions into adulthood and develops social functioning for community living (DuPaul et al., 1997; Gresham, 1997; Newton et al., 1994). Whether the context is home, school, work, or community, children and adults must display appropriate social skills within the rules of their culture and environment and maintain relationships that will help them to be independent (Haring & Ryndak, 1994).

Gresham (1986) incorporated contextual and cultural factors in his definition of *social validation*, or the skills deemed socially important by society. An individual's level of competence is evaluated by significant others (e.g., parents, teachers, other caretakers, and peers) based on comparisons to normative samples (e.g., through the use of rating scales) and performance on specific criteria (e.g., number of social tasks correctly performed in reference to some criterion) within different social contexts (Gresham, 1981, 1986).

Persons reading this chapter on social adaptive skills are likely to benefit from reading chapters in this book that discuss other adaptive skill areas, including leisure, communication, and community use adaptive skills. The development of these and other skills helps increase a person's independence and improve the quality of an individual's life. The purpose of this chapter is to describe the importance of social adaptive skills and their implication for general functioning, discuss factors that impact the development of social skills, provide an overview of assessment procedures, and describe how to teach social skills to address deficits in adaptive behavior. A case study is presented that exemplifies assessment procedures and intervention planning using a person-centered approach to meet the needs of individuals with deficits in adaptive behavior.

MEASUREMENT OF THE SOCIAL ADAPTIVE SKILL AREA USING THE ABAS-II

The Adaptive Behavior Assessment System-Second Edition (ABAS-II) is a comprehensive measure of 10 different but related adaptive skills areas, including the social adaptive skill area. Social adaptive skills, as measured by the ABAS-II, reference an individual's interpersonal and social competence. A key focus is on how independently and frequently the behaviors needed to interact socially and get along with others are displayed. Input from people who know the individual in various settings and contexts is needed to generate a comprehensive assessment of social function (Gresham & Elliott, 1987). The ABAS-II makes this possible by providing five rating forms that may be completed by knowledgeable respondents, including an individual's parent/primary caregiver, teacher/daycare provider, supervisor, and the individual (if his or her functional skills are judged to be adequate for providing valid responses).

Information from multiple respondents provides a more complete assessment of daily functioning skills within several environments. On the ABAS-II, the availability of the Parent/Primary Caregiver and Teacher/Daycare Provider rating forms for ages 0–5, the Parent and Teacher forms for ages 5–21 years, and the Adult Form for ages 16–89 provide life-span assessment opportunities using multiple respondents. On the ABAS-II items, respondents indicate if the individual is able to independently perform an activity and, if so, how frequently (always, sometimes, or never). Three sets of ABAS-II scores are provided for each parent, teacher, and adult form: (a) overall adaptive functioning (the General Adaptive Composite), (b) three composite scores (i.e., conceptual, social, and practical), and (c) scores for 10 specific adaptive skill areas. The social composite of the ABAS-II includes two adaptive skill areas, social and leisure skills, to determine an individual's ability to demonstrate skills needed to interact socially and get along with other people (social) and engage in leisure and recreational activities (leisure).

ABAS-II sample items for the social adaptive skill area for younger children include the following; smiles when he/she sees parent, hugs and kisses parents and others, and seeks friendships with peers. Sample items for older children include the following: keeps a stable group of friends, offers assistance to others, and complements others for good deeds or behavior.

Results are used to inform instruction and intervention decisions. For example, a student score of 0 for an item (i.e., unable to perform the skill) identifies a need for the student to develop the skill. An item score of 1 (i.e., has the ability yet does not perform the skill when needed) represents a performance deficit and thus identifies the need to promote performance of the skill. Thus, item scores of 0 and 1 are likely to suggest explicit and systematic instruction. An item score of 2 (i.e., has the ability to perform the skill and displays it some of the time when needed) suggests a need for additional opportunities to practice the skill to promote maintenance and generalization. An item score of 3 (i.e., displays the behavior always or almost always when needed) reflects that the student is performing the skill as needed.

Thus, the results from the ABAS-II enable the clinician to obtain normative comparisons between an individual's adaptive behavior and the typical adaptive behavior of same-age peers as well as to establish intervention programs that can have an important functional and adaptive impact on promoting social skill development.

IMPORTANCE OF SOCIAL SKILLS

A person's social skills impact his or her ability to play, learn, work, and participate in leisure activities throughout the lifespan. Social skills are used to gain social reinforcement and acceptance as well as avoid aversive social situations (Mathur & Rutherford, 1986). Social skills represent a set of competencies that enable people both young and old to cope with and adapt to the daily demands of the social environment. Individuals who fail to develop adequate social competencies are at risk for a number of negative outcomes including peer rejection, later manifestations of psychological disorders, dropping out of school, loneliness, criminality, and poor academic performance (Gresham et al., 2006; Parker & Asher, 1987; Walker et al., 2004). Long-term personal and social adjustment is based to a large degree on one's ability to display reciprocal and appropriate social skills, including behaviors that are acceptable to others in a range of social situations.

IMPLICATIONS FOR GENERAL FUNCTIONING

Albert Bandura's (1986) theory of social cognition asserts that the acquisition of social skills is a necessary and important process of learning. Additionally, Lev Vygotsky (1978) viewed learning as a social process that emphasizes the importance of social interactions for overall cognitive development. Positive social relationships influence intellectual, communicative, interpersonal, and emotional development (Bates, 1975; Hartup, 1978; Parker & Asher, 1987). Thus, the acquisition and development of social skills are critical for all individuals, including individuals with deficits in intellectual, academic, and emotional/behavioral functioning (Gresham & MacMillan, 1997).

Social skills have a significant impact on an individual's general functioning. Several researchers have established a direct relationship between social skills and academic functioning (Bursuch & Asher, 1986; Cartledge & Milburn, 1995; Malecki & Elliott, 2002), resiliency (Benard, 1991; Taylor, 1991), and successful employment (Greenspan & Shoultz, 1981; Hagner et al., 1992). Conversely, an inability to develop adaptive social skills has a debilitating effect on many areas of an individual's life, including low academic achievement, unsuitable interpersonal relationships, exclusion from less restrictive educational settings, limited employment opportunities, and limited abilities to integrate into community activities (Greenspan & Shoultz, 1981; Schloss & Schloss, 1985).

IMPLICATIONS FOR SCHOOL SUCCESS

"Deficits in social skills are key criteria in defining many high-incidence disabilities that hinder students' academic progress, such as specific learning disabilities, Attention Deficit/Hyperactivity disorder (ADHD), mental retardation, and emotional disturbance" (Gresham et al., 2001, p. 332). Students with these disabilities, along with comorbid behavior problems, are especially at risk of exclusion from general education settings despite being likely to benefit from the typical social interactions and modeling that occur within these classrooms (Panacek & Dunlap, 2003). Additionally, individuals with disabilities and social skill deficits are more likely to experience both social and academic failure because they may display behaviors that impede learning during teacher-directed instruction, independent study, or group learning activities

(Sugai & Lewis, 1996). Social skills instruction can proactively minimize the negative impact of problem behaviors on school success.

IMPACT ON RELATIONSHIPS

The ability to interact with peers impacts friendship development, social integration in the community, and development of supportive social networks. Individuals who lack adequate social interaction skills are at risk for rejection by peers and social isolation (Sargent, 1998). Social skills training can reduce these risks and produce important improvements for children with social skills deficits (Erwin, 1994). These improvements include higher levels of social interaction and acceptance by peers and improved problem solving ability. The promotion of social interaction skills can help overcome long-term consequences, including poor social competence, low self-concept, and social rejection. In addition, meaningful relationships, which play a large role in the quality of one's life, can be developed when individuals are taught effective social interaction skills.

IMPACT ON SUCCESSFUL EMPLOYMENT AND COMMUNITY INTEGRATION

Social skills and the absence of asocial behaviors are positively associated with successful employment (Heal et al., 1989; Heal et al., 1990). Social interactions play a critical role in employment settings. Thus, the development of social skills is essential for individuals with disabilities when they make the transition from school to work (Chadsey & Shelden, 2002). In addition, employers have indicated the importance of work-related interactions such as following directions, requesting assistance, sharing work information, and accepting criticism (Chadsey et al., 1989).

In the community, how others perceive a person's social behavior may be more important than their perceptions of the person's academic or job skills (Black & Langone, 1997). For example, individuals with intellectual disabilities who demonstrated competence in social skills generally are perceived more positively than those who lacked such skills, regardless of task-related skill level (Holmes & Fillary, 2000). The notion that competence in using social skills will lead to positive perceptions of persons with disabilities can be extended to other community settings such as postsecondary education, neighborhoods, and places of worship (Brenner & Smith, 2004).

FACTORS THAT IMPACT THE DEVELOPMENT AND PERFORMANCE OF SOCIAL SKILLS

A number of qualities can impact the acquisition of social skills. For example, the development of effective social skills requires one to be able to comprehend what others are saying and to communicate clearly to others (Kennedy & Itkonen,

1996). Communication creates the opportunity for developing social relationships and thus is fundamental to participating and interacting with others (Ferguson, 1994). Consequently, individuals with communication deficits also tend to have difficulty developing adequate social skills and maintaining friendships. Therefore, an individual's learning and communicative skills should be considered when developing social skills interventions. (Readers are encouraged to read the chapter on communication adaptive skills found elsewhere in this book.)

Various qualities in one's social environment impact the development of relevant social adaptive skills. Dynamic factors within an individual's environment help define the social skills required to be socially competent within specific settings. Each environment (e.g., home, school, community, work) may differ in their basic values and social standards. Thus, a person needs to be aware of these values and standards and be sufficiently flexible to display desired social qualities. These values and social standards, which Sargent (1998) called *cultural determinants*, dictate socially accepted norms that are enforced by members within a community.

Family dynamics, ethnicity, spoken language, and traditions are examples of cultural determinants that may characterize the social skills required in the home and other settings. The cultural determinants that define social skills to be contextually relevant within the school environment include school-wide discipline policies, behavioral expectations within various school environments (i.e., cafeteria, classrooms, gymnasium, sports activities), and the dynamics of diverse peer groups. Within community settings, the social norms within the community define the social expectations from which an individual must develop to integrate successfully. The design of social skill interventions that are contextually relevant should identify the settings for which an individual participates and the social environmental qualities, including expectations and standards within those settings.

The provision of opportunities for individuals to learn and practice social behaviors with others and from appropriate role models also impacts the development of adaptive social skills. Whereas children may lack social skills due to learning and communicative deficits, some children may not acquire needed social skills because of limited opportunities or unsuitable role models (Gresham & Elliott, 1987).

Students with disabilities who are educated in special education classrooms tend to have extensive interactions with adults and limited interactions with other students, especially typically developing peers, thus restricting their opportunities to learn social skills (Foreman et al., 2004). This lack of social opportunity and access to positive role models can be particularly deleterious on students with severe disabilities, thus depriving them from learning relevant social skills and developing friendships. Therefore, the opportunities and access that people have to learn social behaviors must be considered when outlining social skill remediation.

Finally, social interactions require a reason for people to interact with one another (Kennedy & Itkonen, 1996). The reasons a person either is willing or unwilling to engage in social interactions are important and impact social skill development. Based on basic behavioral principles, an individual will develop social skills and interact with others to the extent that the outcomes of the interactions function as a reinforcer (Skinner, 1953). Essentially, people engage in social interactions in order to obtain a particular outcome (e.g., obtain attention, have a conversation, play a game, exchange information, feel good about themselves and others). Individuals will interact as long as the outcomes are reinforcing (Kennedy & Itkonen, 1996). Thus, when designing social skill instruction, one should identify the particular consequences individuals are likely to experience and/or avoid as a result of their social interactions.

ADDITIONAL TOOLS USED TO ASSESS SOCIAL ADAPTIVE SKILLS

The assessment of social skills typically has three goals: to accurately describe the skills, to identify strengths and weaknesses, and, if needed, to outline relevant and effective social skills interventions. A number of assessment tools are available to collect information pertaining to an individual's social skill performance, including person-centered planning (Holburn & Vietze, 2002) and functional behavior assessment (O'Neill et al., 1997).

PERSON-CENTERED PLANNING

Person-centered planning involves a collaborative activity in which people from different contexts of an individual's life meet to identify specific needs, outline objectives, and design interventions to improve that individual's social and interpersonal competence (Holburn & Vietze, 2002). Typical team members include the targeted individual, parents/guardians/family members, personal friends of the targeted individual, and other support personnel. By working collaboratively, team members learn more about specific behaviors and events that cause the individual to gain or lose respect among peers and adults. The process allows the team to understand an individual's prior and current level of functioning – information that serves as a basis for taking steps to improve the independent display of needed social skills.

Multiple sources of information guide professionals in identifying deficits in social skills and functional replacement skills, thus facilitating the design of relevant and effective social skill instruction. Additionally, ongoing assessment during the implementation of the instruction is essential to monitor student progress and evaluate the effectiveness of the intervention (Horner et al., 1993).

FUNCTIONAL BEHAVIOR ASSESSMENT

Students with social skill deficits also may exhibit intense problem behaviors that require individualized functional behavior assessments and a behavior support plan. A functional behavioral assessment is a systematic process of identifying problem behaviors and the events that reliably predict the occurrence and nonoccurrence of those behaviors and maintain the behaviors over time (Carr, 1994; O'Neill et al., 1997; Sugai, et al., 2000). The information obtained through indirect and direct assessment methods guides a function-based behavior support plan that targets the setting events influencing a student's problem behavior. Setting events occur outside of the immediate context of the behavior problem (e.g., missed medications, lack of sleep), whereas antecedent events occur immediately before the behavior and the consequences and function of the behavior exhibited (e.g., escape task, obtain attention, attain desired objects).

INDIRECT AND DIRECT ASSESSMENT METHODS

The information obtained from comprehensive assessments that include both indirect and direct measures assist professionals in selecting an appropriate curriculum and designing instruction or intervention to target an individual's or group's specific needs (Sugai & Lewis, 1996).

The use of direct methods to assess social skills (e.g., those described above) is important when examining the circumstances that maintain the problem social behavior (e.g., peer/adult attention, activity escape). It also is used to access the types of social skills deficits a student displays (e.g., acquisition, fluency, maintenance, generalization) and help determine instructional strategies that are likely to be most effective with a specific student or group of students. Direct methods of assessment consist of either direct observations made of students in important contexts (i.e., school, home, and community) or assessments that are directly administered to students (e.g., Brigance Comprehensive Inventory of Basic Skills, 1977). An ecological inventory (Browder, 2001), also known as a functional assessment, is an example of a common direct assessment that assists in evaluating the environment within which specific social skills are required.

The ecological-functional assessment process utilizes observational techniques to analyze social skill demands of the natural environment and determine how an individual performs within the environment. During an ecological-functional assessment, a professional first identifies the activities (e.g., calendar, show-and-tell) within an environment (e.g., classroom, cafeteria, recreation center). Next, the professional conducts an analysis (commonly referred to as a task or discrepancy analysis) that examines the student's ability to perform the steps required for important activities. Lastly, this information is used to develop a support plan for the student. The premise of conducting an ecological-functional assessment is to allow an individual's educational team to identify the steps, natural cues, and social skills required to be successful. In addition, an individual's current level of performance of social skills within important contexts. This information will allow the team to customize instruction based on the skills that are needed by the individual student within their current home, school, work, or community environment (Slaton et al., 1994; Browder, 2001).

Indirect methods for assessing social skills include commercially developed rating tools with established psychometric properties (e.g. ABAS-II, Vineland Adaptive

Behavior Scales-II, and Social Skills Rating System), interviews, and questionnaires; behavior ratings; checklists, and archival data (i.e., records documenting the individual's past and present levels of functioning). Indirect assessments are informative tools that are easily administered. The ABAS-II is an example of an indirect, comprehensive measure that usually takes respondents (e.g., parent, teacher, supervisor) about 20 minutes to complete. The information obtained from the ABAS–II provides an analysis of strengths and weaknesses in 10 adaptive skill areas. Social skills functioning and related skills such as communication, leisure, community use, self-care, and other areas, can be used to assist educational teams in developing appropriate intervention plans.

SOCIAL SKILLS INSTRUCTION

LINKING ASSESSMENT TO INSTRUCTION

Effective social skill instruction is based on comprehensive assessments conducted by a multi-disciplinary team of professionals associated with the target individual. A social skills assessment is intended to describe a person's social skills, leading to an evaluation of strengths and weaknesses and, if needed, an intervention program. A team-based person-centered planning approach is recommended when designing meaningful and effective instruction. An individual's planning team should use the results from the completed assessments that consist of indirect (e.g., ABAS-II) and direct (e.g., ecological inventory) assessment measures to design social skills instruction to meet the needs of the individual. Based on the strengths and weaknesses identified from the assessments, the team then identifies learning objectives and outlines the contexts for teaching social skills. The objectives determined by the team form the basis from which to design meaningful and effective social skills instructional methods in relevant settings for the individual.

DESIGNING SOCIAL SKILLS INSTRUCTION

The development of appropriate social skill interventions should include natural and logical outcomes. Instruction is designed to promote the learning needs displayed by the student within the contexts social skills will be used. Similar to instruction designed for academic, vocational, or community goals, teaching social skills follows these general steps: curriculum selection, design and preparation of instruction, instructional presentation, and progress monitoring (Sugai & Lewis, 1996). The selection of meaningful skills and types of social skill deficits (e.g., acquisition or performance deficits) is essential in designing relevant instruction for the individual (Gresham & Elliott, 1987; Sugai & Lewis, 1999).

Select Appropriate Skills

Although the number of social skills is exceedingly large, they typically fall into the following categories: (a) to enhance communication (e.g., starting and maintaining a conversation), (b) to promote social inclusion (e.g., self-management, personal social behaviors), (c) to promote social interaction (e.g., turn taking, duration of social interaction), and (d) to display skills important to a specific settings, including school, work, public, and family (Caldarella & Merrell, 1997; Gresham et al., 2001; Haring & Ryndak, 1994; Sargent, 1998). For example, classroom social skills may include getting the teacher's attention, asking for assistance, answering questions by the teacher, keeping one's desk in order, or entering classrooms without disruption. Social skills at the workplace may include dressing appropriately, communicating with supervisors and co-workers, handling stress, and expressing emotions. These relevant skills are selected and taught in such a way as to help individuals generalize meaningful skills in their environment, gain social acceptance, and avoid aversive situations (Mathur & Rutherford, 1996).

Identify Task Components

After selecting appropriate skills to teach, task components needed to perform the skill are identified. Published social skills curricula are useful resources for identifying sequential ordering of task components of what to teach within broad structures of social skill areas. There are many social skill curriculum programs. Thus, professionals should evaluate the quality of curriculum programs and modify lessons to match a student's specific needs. The selection of one ideal social skills curriculum is difficult due to the varied needs and personal qualities of students (Bullock & Fitzimmons-Lovett, 1997). The best social skill program is one that is relevant to the specific needs of the individual within their important social contexts (e.g., classroom, school, work, community).

Type of Social Skill Deficit

Within each task component, distinctions are made between skills that have not been learned (i.e., an acquisition deficit) and skills that have been learned but not used routinely or consistently (i.e., a performance deficit; Gresham, 1981). Acquisition deficits can be described as either the absence of knowledge about how to perform a given social skill or difficulty in knowing which social skill is appropriate in specific situations (Gresham, 1981, 1997). Acquisition deficits also can be characterized as "can't do" problems – an inability to perform needed social behaviors. To promote skill acquisition, teachers or caregivers may model the skill, explicitly teach each skill component, and provide immediate reinforcement after every correct response.

Performance deficits can be described as the failure to perform given social skills at an acceptable level even though the individual may know how to perform the social skill. This deficit is characterized as "won't do" problems (i.e., a person knows what to do yet does not perform the desired social behavior). Teachers or caregivers may address performance deficits through instructional strategies that provide more opportunities for students to practice the social behavior, differentially reinforce appropriate social skills, and correct errors to reduce problem behaviors.

Delivering Instruction

Effective delivery of social skills instruction relies on the implementation of effective teaching strategies. Given that most children learn social behaviors incidentally through observation, teachers and caregivers may instruct by displaying the desired behaviors. For example, throughout the school day, teachers model appropriate social skills and often call attention to appropriate student behaviors as correct responses that should be followed by other students. These social learning opportunities can be targeted as teaching opportunities for students who need more explicit cues to engage in social interactions. Effective instructional practices utilize these moments to teach behaviors that support learning and interactions with others continuously during the day and concurrently with academic instruction.

Individuals with cognitive delays who also display social skill deficits typically display difficulty acquiring skills through incidental learning. Therefore, they require direct and explicit instructional procedures that focus on skill acquisition and maintenance. Procedures to promote skill acquisition include modeling, leading (coaching), and testing (behavioral rehearsal; Sugai & Lewis, 1996). Teaching social skills involves adult demonstration of the skill along with the following components: a stated rationale for learning the skill, task analysis of skill components, student rehearsal of the social skill with peers, and variations of the skill to plan for generalization (Walker et al., 2004). The following strategies for teaching social skills are discussed below: function-based interventions (Horner et al., 2000), teaching acquisition through the use of the "model-lead-test" strategy (Sugai & Lewis, 1996), and promoting generalization through general case programming and milieu teaching techniques.

Function-Based Strategies

The goal of function-based interventions is to make the problem behavior irrelevant, ineffective, and inefficient by teaching and reinforcing social behaviors that produce the same function as the problem behavior (Horner et al., 2000). Based on a hypothesis developed from a functional behavioral assessment, strategies that enable students to recognize and neutralize the antecedent of the problem behavior are used. In addition, desired social behaviors and replacement behaviors that serve the same function as the problem behavior are taught and acquired. Finally, with function-based supports, the teacher identifies procedures intended to reinforce desired behaviors and provides corrective feedback for problem behaviors.

Antecedent Strategies

Environmental arrangements or antecedent strategies involve changes to the environment that (a) help establish the occasion for social behaviors to occur more often and (b) eliminate or neutralize events that trigger problem behaviors (Cooper et al., 1987). Modifications (e.g., instructional materials, physical arrangement of classroom, choice of activities) constitute antecedent strategies introduced to enhance the occurrence of social behaviors (Ellingson et al., 2000; Luiselli & Cameron,

1998). Antecedent strategies to increase social skills include peer-mediated interventions, cuing/prompting, and cooperatives games and tasks (Koegel & Koegel, 1995; Kohler & Strain, 1999). For example, using peer-mediated interventions, the teacher arranges cooperative learning activities for peers to deliver social cues and reinforce targeted behavior.

Teaching Desired/Replacement Behavior

Social learning errors (e.g., grabbing, hitting, speaking out of turn) can be viewed as problem behaviors that serve a function for the individual (i.e., obtaining and/or avoiding particular consequences). Replacement behaviors are social behaviors that should be taught explicitly as a substitute for the problem behaviors. Problem behaviors displayed by an individual may have resulted consistently in a functional and reinforcing outcome. Thus, it is essential to select replacement behaviors that are more effective and efficient in obtaining the same consequence. For example, an adult who may have consistently grabbed others (problem behavior) to gain their attention (function) is taught to make eye contact and politely say "excuse me" (replacement behavior), thus acquiring more effective ways to gain attention of others (function). When replacement behaviors are acquired and reinforced, problem behaviors become inefficient and ineffective (Crone & Horner, 2000).

Consequence Strategies

Consequence strategies increase the effectiveness of teaching social skills by minimizing reinforcement for problem behavior and increasing reinforcement for a desired/replacement behavior (Carr, 1977; Todd et al., 1999). Consequence interventions that increase social behaviors provide positive reinforcement contingent upon the demonstration of the appropriate behavior. For example, in contingent social reinforcement, instructors socially reinforce (e.g., smile, give a thumbs up) individuals when the desired skill is performed. This method often is used in conjunction with reinforcement programs such as token reinforcement in which items or tokens are exchanged for privileges, items, or special activities. Consequence strategies to reduce problem behaviors include corrective feedback (i.e., state behavioral expectation, prompt desired behavior) and planned ignoring.

Acquisition of Social Skills: Model, Lead, Test

Social skills instruction is presented in a general direct instruction format that defines the skill, models the skill actions, guides student performance, promotes independent practice, and evaluates performance (Engelmann & Carnine, 1982; Williams & Reisberg, 2003). Using a simplified format, Sugai and Lewis (1996) describe a model-lead-test format as a basic instructional model used to teach academic and social behaviors. First, the instructor *models* the behavior so that a student sees how the skill is demonstrated. Modeling provides a form of vicarious learning that exposes the child to perform the desired social skill in an appropriate manner. Second, the instructor *leads* by arranging and facilitating opportunities for students to practice the skill. During guided practice, students have opportunities to practice skills with specific instructor feedback and correction. Role-plays provide rehearsal situations in which students become actors in a simulated situation. The student may use visual prompts or skill cards to remember skill steps, and the instructor may prompt skill use right before play activities. Third, the instructor *tests* a student's understanding by evaluating independent skill use by the student. This may include the use of a checklist, an evaluation of skill use without reminders or prompts, or observations of the student in the naturally occurring setting. When testing skill use, it is important to include a range of examples that define when and where the behavior should be displayed. In addition, to help students discriminate appropriate and inappropriate use of the behavior, non-examples illustrate situations in which the behavior should not be displayed (Sugai & Lewis, 1996).

Promoting Generalization: General Case Programming and Milieu Instruction

Many students with diminished intellectual abilities and other learning or behavior problems may not transfer skills acquired in one environment (e.g., school) to other settings (e.g., home, work, and community). Thus, the acquisition of social skills is likely to be more effective when desired social skills are taught in ways that promote skill generalization across situations, settings, and people (Haring & Ryndak, 1994; Putnam et al., 1985). Generalization focuses on maximizing skill usage, moving beyond the training setting and untrained contexts to a broader range of different settings or people (Furnham, 1988; Gresham, 1982; Sugai & Lewis, 1996). In this way, instruction builds social competence for a variety of life situations.

Two approaches used to encourage generalization procedures are general case programming and milieu teaching. Using general case programming, a teacher provides instruction across a range of common situations the student may encounter daily (Chandler et al., 1992; Horner et al., 1982). There are five critical steps to implement a general case teaching approach (Horner et al., 1982). First, instructors define the instructional universe to include all possible contexts within which the learner will perform the desired social skills after instruction (e.g., requests help with academic work tasks, opening snack items, tying shoe laces). Second, teaching and testing situations are selected to include a range of situations in which the skill will be used as well as significant exceptions (e.g., asking for help in different classrooms, hallway, or cafeteria from adults who are not busy). Third, instructors sequence teaching examples with situations that focus on discrete and easy skills as well as multiple and complex skills (e.g., asking a peer tutor or others in close proximity for help, joining conversation, interrupting others). Fourth, after identifying the teaching contexts, instructors use a variety of teaching strategies during instruction (e.g., guiding support or shaping new skills, prompting the correct response, fading adult support, and reinforcing successful attempts and responses). Finally, after sufficient exemplars across contexts and instruction in multiple settings are acquired, instructors evaluate the learner in other settings (e.g., at home and in the community). Various settings (e.g., gym, cafeteria, classrooms, office), people (e.g., classroom teacher, special education teacher, instructional assistants, office support), and activities (e.g., help with reading activity, finding materials, opening snack items) are considered when developing sufficient training exemplars across contexts, using specific procedures to select and sequence teaching examples.

Milieu teaching involves the prompting of responses in the natural context (e.g., classrooms, hallways, or playgrounds) in which the learner may use the skill. For example, during opportunities to practice asking for help, the teacher may create the need (e.g., lack of supplies, blocked access to door) or one that occurs naturally during the school day. Common teaching strategies are used to promote generalization. Homework may be provided to encourage students to perform the new skill outside of the instructional context and independently at home and in the community. The transfer of skills is promoted to out-of-school settings by having learning occur in the individual's natural environment. For example, observing how peers are displaying social skills or asking relevant others to identify situations in which the learner has shown skill assets and deficits can further transfer training. In addition, teaching occurs in the natural environment with staff and students who are likely to be present in daily routines (Sugai & Lewis, 1996). Persons significant in the learner's life also can be taught to assist the learner through prompts, corrections, or social praise that reinforce the appropriate behavior. In this way, the learner is more likely to demonstrate the behavior across environments under natural situations.

Evaluating Outcomes/Continuous Assessment of Social Skills

Ongoing assessment during the implementation of social skills instruction is essential to monitor an individual's progress and evaluate the effectiveness of instruction (Horner et al., 1993). Professionals should arrange regular opportunities to evaluate their social skills teaching practices, especially at the beginning of a social skills instructional program. The use of data to evaluate progress is key to effective social skills instruction. Performance data (e.g., direct observations, teacher reports, checklists) allow the person-centered planning team to make decisions such as whether to increase or decrease instructional support, modify instructional materials and/or strategies, or discontinue instruction.

CASE STUDY

Alexander Jones, a 9-year-old boy enrolled in a fourth grade general education classroom at a public elementary school, lives with his parents who work full-time. Alex has two older siblings, a sister in the ninth grade, and a brother in the sixth grade. Alexander has received special education services under the eligibility criteria for mental retardation since age 5. He has been referred for special education testing for a triennial review to determine if he continues to remain eligible for services.

Alex's mother and father reported that he met most of his developmental milestones early, except for those pertaining to verbal language. Alex always has had difficulty with verbal expression. He is considered very sociable and engages friends and family members through the use of signs and vocalizations that approximate words he is wants to express (e.g., "wur" for "water" and "bee" for "T.V."). Due to his difficulties with expressive language, Alex has received speech and language therapy for several years and has been taught to use sign language and picture symbols to augment his communication. His parents stated that they understand almost everything he says when his vocalizations are paired with his signing. However, most people at school and all in the community are unable to understand him. Despite the interventions used to address his difficulties with expressive language, his teachers state that they believe that Alex continues to display deficits in communication, social skills, and functional academics. Alex's parents reported that he loves playing sports, especially soccer and basketball, yet has difficulty following the rules of the games. This frustrates others who play with him. While at a recent soccer clinic, Alex frequently picked up the soccer ball with his hands and ran to engage the other players in a game of chase. These types of situations occur often, and his parents are not sure what to do.

Alex's mother completed the ABAS-II Parent Form for individuals ages 5–21. Additionally, Alex's teacher completed the ABAS-II Teacher Form for ages 5–21 to better assess his functional development in adaptive skill areas and to determine which skills are priorities for teaching in the classroom. The goal was for Alex to experience more success when interacting with others both at home and in the community.

Alex's scores from both the ABAS-II Teacher Form and the Parent form can be found in Table 11.1. Their scores suggest that he displays low functioning in communication, functional academics, social, leisure, and self-direction adaptive skill areas. Alex's problems with social skills and communication are impeding his ability to participate in school and leisure activities.

Alex's strengths on individual ABAS-II items of the social adaptive skill area suggest that he has positive relationships with adults and seeks friendships with others his age. He has some emerging skills in areas that involve waiting in line at school, sometimes saying "please" when asking for something, and sometimes showing sympathy for others when they are sad or upset. Alex's age-related weaknesses, as identified on items of the ABAS-II social adaptive skill area, include: (a) lack of friends, (b) lack of expression of feelings, (c) lack of respect for or understanding of other's personal boundaries, (d) absence of understanding rules of games and social routines, and (e) lack of sympathy or recognition of other's emotions.

Additional assessment of Alex's adaptive skills used an ecological inventory (Browder, 2001) that involved direct observations of Alex by a school psychologist in a number of domains within the day, the goal being to identify strengths, deficits, and skills in need of improvement. This information provided Alex's individual education plan (IEP) team with information on his performance compared to his peers in each environment. The results indicated that Alex displayed appropriate social skills most of the time while in structured classroom settings. However, during transition times, Alex grabbed and shoved other students to obtain desired materials. Alex also attempted to engage a student sitting next to

TABLE 11.1 Results of the ABAS-II (Teacher Form Ages 5–21 and Parent Form Ages 5–21) for Alexander, Age 9.

	Adaptive Skill Area Scaled Score	Composite Standard Score	Composite Percentile Rank	Composite Score Classification
Teacher form composites and adaptive skill areas				
General adaptive composite (GAC)		56	0.1	Extremely low
Conceptual composite		50	<.01	Extremely low
• Communication	1			
• Functional academics	1			
• Self-direction	1			
Social composite		58	0.3	Extremely low
• Leisure	2			
• Social	1			
Practical composite		72	3	Borderline
• Community use	4			
• School living	6			
• Health and safety	3			
• Self-care	6			
Parent form composites and adaptive skill areas				
GAC		64	1	Extremely low
Conceptual composite		53	0.1	Extremely low
• Communication	1			
• Functional academics	1			
• Self-direction	2			
Social composite		58	0.3	Extremely low
• Leisure	2			
• Social	1			
Practical composite		85	16	Below average
• Community use	6			
• Health and safety	7			
• Self-care	6			

Note: Composites (Conceptualization, Social, and Practical) and the GAC have standard scores with a mean of 100 and standard deviation of 15. Adaptive skill areas (Communication, Functional Academics, etc.) have scaled scores with a mean of 10 and standard deviation of 3.

him by putting his face directly in front of the other student's face. While at recess and lunch, Alex displayed difficulty waiting in line, moving out of the way of others, and following the rules during a basketball game (e.g., he took the ball and ran across the yard).

The IEP team met to discuss the results of the assessments and proposed an instructional program for Alex to address his areas of weakness. In addition, when outlining individual learning units for Alex, the staff decided to ensure that skills for each domain would be infused into his school day. The IEP team established the following three social skill objectives: (a) to gain attention and request materials from peers and adults using his words and augmented communication (i.e., signs or picture symbols), (b) to wait while standing in line for his turn, and (c) to follow the rules of games in soccer, basketball, and other playground games.

To help achieve these objectives, Alex received direct instruction from the general education teacher and the instructional assistant while in the classroom and from the special education teacher during recess and lunch. Alex's speech and language therapist provided instruction one time a week with peer models in the classroom to promote his use of words and augmented communication to request materials from peers.

In class, the classroom teacher and instructional assistant provided instruction in social skills by first instructing the entire class concerning the importance of respecting one another by maintaining one's "personal space," obtaining materials in an orderly manner, gaining attention from an adult or peer appropriately, waiting in line, and following the rules of games. Examples and non-examples of these skills were explicitly taught. Each week his teacher reviewed these skills with the students and provided rewards for those who properly displaying them. In addition, teacher built into his daily lessons opportunities for Alex to practice the skills and receive appropriate feedback on his performance. The instructional assistant collected data on Alex's daily performance relevant to his three social skills objectives.

During recess, once a week, the special education teacher taught Alex and two to three classroom peers to practice strategies to help think about other people's feelings. During the first week she used a strategy called, "thinking of me, or thinking of you." She provided scenarios in which a fictional student is not displaying appropriate behavior (e.g., running away with the ball, grabbing things from others) and asked Alex and his peers, "Is this student thinking about his friends or about himself?" She helped Alex and his peers to identify what that student should do and then practice doing the appropriate behavior.

During morning and lunch recess at least twice a week, the special education teacher taught Alex how to play games appropriately by setting up organized soccer or basketball games with no more than three peers. The special educator along with the help of the physical education teacher practiced using positive examples of the rules of the games (e.g., dribbling, passing), immediately providing Alex with positive or corrective feedback in an effort to not allow him to develop patterns of error. The peers provided models of how to play the games as well as feedback to Alex when he played appropriately by praising him and giving him "high-fives." The peers also were directed to not encourage Alex by laughing or chasing him if he ran away with the ball. During these types of situations, his teacher provided another ball for the peers to play with. His teacher used the "thinking of me or thinking of you" strategy with Alex when these problems occurred, and he was taught to apologize to his friends in order to rejoin the game.

REFERENCES

Bandura, A. (1986). *Social Foundations of Thought and Action: A Social Cognitive Theory.* Englewood Cliffs, New Jersey: Prentice Hall.

Bates, E. (1975). Peer relations and the acquisition of language. In M. Lewis & L. Rosenblum (Eds.), *Friendships and Peer Relations*, pp. 259–292. New York: Wiley.

Benard, B. (1991). *Protective Factors in the Family, School, and Community.* Portland, OR: Western Center for Drug-Free Schools and Communities.

Black, R. S. & Langone, J. (1997). Social awareness and transition to employment for adolescents with mental retardation. *Remedial and Special Education, 18*(5), 214–222.

Brenner, C. D. & Smith, J. (2004). Teaching social skills. *National Center on Secondary Education and Transition Information Brief.*

Brigance, A. H. (1977). *Brigance Diagnostic Inventory of Basic Skills.* Massachusetts: Curriculum Associates, Inc.

Browder, D. M. (2001). *Curriculum and Assessment for Students with Moderate and Severe Disabilities.* New York: Guilford Press.

Bullock, L. & Fitzimmons-Lovett, A. (1997). Meeting the needs of children and youth with challenging behaviors. *Reaching Today's Youth: The Community Circle of Caring Journal, 1*(3), 54–61.

Bursuch, W. D. & Asher, S. R. (1986). The relationship between social competence and achievement in elementary school children. *Journal of Clinical Child Psychology, 15*, 41–49.

Caldarella, P. & Merrell, K. (1997). Common dimensions of social skills of children and adolescents: A taxonomy of positive behaviors. *School Psychology Review, 26*, 264–278.

Cartledge, G. & Milburn, J. (1995). Teaching social skills to children and youth. *Innovative Approaches*, 3rd edn., Boston, MA: Allyn & Bacon.

Carr, E. G. (1994). Emerging themes in the functional analysis of problem behavior. *Journal of Applied Behavior Analysis, 27*, 393–399.

Carr, E. G. (1977). The motivation of self-injurious behavior: A review of some hypotheses. *Psychological Bulletin, 84*, 800–816.

Chadsey, J. & Shelden, D. (2002) Social life. In K. Storey, P. Bates, & D. Hunter (Eds.), *The Road Ahead*, pp. 137–155. St. Augustine, FL: Training Resource Network, Inc.

Chadsey, J., Gonzalez, P., Tines, J., & Johnson, J. (1989). Social ecology in the workplace: Contextual variables affecting social interactions of employees with and without mental retardation. *American Journal on Mental Retardation, 94*, 141–151.

Chandler, L. K., Lubeck, R. C., & Fowler, S. A. (1992). Generalization and maintenance of preschool children's social skills: A critical review and analysis. *Journal of Applied Behavior Analysis, 25*, 415–428.

Cooper, J. O., Heron, T. E., & Heward, W. L. (1987). *Applied Behavior Analysis.* Columbus, OH: Merrill Publishing.

Crone, D. A. & Horner, R. H. (2000). Contextual, conceptual, and empirical foundations of functional behavioral assessment in schools. *Exceptionality, 8*(3), 161–172.

DuPaul, G. J., McGoey, K. E., & Yugar, J. M. (1997). Mainstreaming students with behavior disorders: The use of classroom peers as facilitators of generalization. *The School Psychology Review, 26*(4), 634–50.

Ellingson, S. A., Miltenberger, R. G., Stricker, J., Galensky, T. L., & Garlinghouse, M. (2000). Functional assessment and intervention for challenging behaviors in the classroom by general educators. *Journal of Positive Behavior Interventions, 2*, 85–97.

Engelmann, S. & Carnine, D. (1982). *Theory of Instruction: Principles and Applications.* New York: Irvington Publishers.

Erwin, P. G. (1994). Effectiveness of social skills training with children: A meta-analytic study. *Counseling Psychology Quarterly 7*, 305–310.

Ferguson, D. (1994). Is communication really the point? Some thoughts on intervention and membership. *Mental Retardation, 32*(1), 7–18.

Foreman, P., Arthur-Kelly, M., Pascoe, S., & King, B. S. (2004). Evaluating the educational experiences of students with profound and multiple disabilities in inclusive and segregated classroom settings: Australian perspective. *Research and Practice for Persons with Severe Disabilities, 29*, 183–193.

Furnham, A. F. (1988). *Lay Theories: Everyday Understanding of Problems in the Social Sciences.* New York: Pergamon Press.

Greenspan, S. & Shoultz, B. (1981). Why mentally retarded adults lose their jobs: Social Competence as a factor in work adjustments. *Applied Research in Mental Retardation, 2*, 23–38.

Gresham, F. M. (1981). Social skills training with handicapped children: A review. *Review of Educational Research, 51*, 139–176.

Gresham, F. M. (1986). Conceptual issues in the assessment of social competence in children. In P. S. Strain, M. J. Guralnick, & H. M. Walker (Eds.), *Children's Social Behavior: Development, Assessment, and Modification*, pp. 143–179. New York: Academic Press.

Gresham, F. M. (1997). Social competence and students with behavior disorders: Where we've been, where we are, and where we should go. *Education & Treatment of Children, 20*(3), 233–245.

Gresham, F. M. & Elliott, S. N. (1987). The relationship between adaptive and social skills: Issues in definition and assessment. *The Journal of Special Education, 21*, 167–181.

Gresham, F. M. (1982). Social skills instruction for exceptional children. *Theory Into Practice, 21(2)*, 129.

Gresham, F. M. & MacMillan, D. L. (1997). Social competence and affective characteristics of students with mild disabilities. *Review of Educational Research*, 67(4), 377–415.

Gresham, F. M., Sugai, G., & Horner, R. H. (2001). Interpreting outcomes of social skills raining for students with high-incidence disabilities. *Exceptional Children, 6*(3), 331–344.

Gresham, F. M., Van, M. B., & Cook, C. R. (2006). Social skills training for teaching replacement behaviors: Remediating acquisition deficits in at-risk students. *Behavioral Disorders, 3*, 363–377.

Hagner, D., Rogan, P., & Murphy, S. (1992). Facilitating natural supports in the work place: Strategies for support consultants. *Journal of Rehabilitation, 58*, 29–34.

Haring, T. G. & Ryndak, D. (1994). Strategies and instructional procedures to promote social interactions and relationships. In E. C. Cipani, & F. Spooner (Eds.), *Curricular and Instructional Approaches for Persons with Severe Disabilities*, pp. 289–321. Boston: Allyn & Bacon.

Hartup, W. W. (1978). Aggression in childhood: Developmental perspectives. *American Psychologist, 29*, 336–341.

Heal, L. W., Copher, J. I., DeStefano, L., & Rusch, F. (1989). A comparison of successful and unsuccessful placements of secondary students with mental handicaps into competitive employment. *Career Development for Exceptional Individuals, 12*(2), 167–177.

Heal, L. W., Gonzalez, P., Rusch, F. R., Gopher, J., & Destephano, L. (1990). A comparison of successful and unsuccessful placements of youths with mental handicaps into competitive employment. *Exceptionality, 1*, 181–195.

Holburn, S. & Vietze, P. (2002). A better life for Hal: Five years of person-centered planning and applied behavior analysis. In S. Holburn & P. M. Vietze (Eds.), *Person-Centered Planning: Research, Practice, and Future Directions*, pp. 291–314. Baltimore: Brookes.

Holmes, J. & Fillary, R. (2000). Handling small talk at work: Challenges for workers with intellectual disabilities. *International Journal of Disability, Development and Education, 47*(3), 273–291.

Horner, R. H., Sprague, J. R., & Wilcox, B. (1982). General case programming for community activities. In B. Wilcox & G. T. Bellamy (Eds.), *Design of High School Programs for Severely Handicapped Students*, pp. 61–98. Baltimore: Paul H. Brookes.

Horner, R. H., O'Neill, R., & Flannery, B. (1993). Building effective behavior support plans from functional assessment information. In M. Snell (Ed.), *Instruction of Persons with Severe Handicaps*, 4th edn., pp. 184–214. Columbus, OH: Merrill.

Horner, R. H., Sugai, G., Todd, A. W., & Lewis-Palmer, T. (2000). Elements of behavior support plans: A technical brief. *Exceptionality*, *8*(3), 205–215.

Kennedy, C. H. & Itkonen, T. (1996). Social relationships, influential variables, and changes across the lifespan. In L. K. Koegel, R. L. Koegel, & G. Dunlap (Eds.), *Positive Behavioral Support: Including People with Difficult Behaviors in the Community*. Baltimore: Brookes.

Kincaid, D. (2005). Person-centered planning. In G. Sugai & R. H. Horner (Eds.), *Encyclopedia of Behavior Modification and Cognitive Behavior Therapy*, Vol. 3, pp. 1496–1506. Educational Applications: Sage Publishing.

Koegel, R. L. & Koegel, L. K. (1995). *Teaching Children with Autism: Strategies for Initiating Positive Interactions and Improving Learning Opportunities*. Baltimore: Brookes Publishing.

Kohler, F. W. & Strain, P. S. (1999). Maximizing peer-mediated resources within integrated pre-school classrooms. *Topics in Early Childhood Special Education*, *19*, 92–102.

Korinek, L. & Popp, P. A. (1997). Collaborative mainstream integration of social skills with academic instruction. *Preventing School Failure*, *41*(4), 148–152.

Luiselli, J. K. & Cameron, M. J. (1998). *Antecedent Control: Innovative Approaches to Behavioral Support*. Baltimore, MD: Paul H Brookes Publishing Company.

Malecki, C. K. & Elliot, S. N. (2002). Children's social behaviors as predictors of academic achievement: A longitudinal analysis. *School Psychology Quarterly*, *17*, 1–23.

Mathur, S. & Rutherford, R. (1996). Is social skills training effective for students with emotional or behavior disorders? Research issues and needs. *Behavioral Disorders*, *22*(1), 21–27.

Newton, J. S., Horner, R. H., Ard, W. R., LeBaron, N., & Sappington, G. (1994). A conceptual model for improving the social life of individuals with mental retardation. *Mental Retardation*, *32*, 393–402.

Odom, S. L., McConnell, S. R., & McEvoy, M. A. (1992). *Social Competence of Young Children with Disabilities: Issues and Strategies for Intervention*. Baltimore: Brookes.

O'Neill, R. R., Horner, R. H., Albin, R. W., Sprague, J. R., Storey, D., & Newton, J. S. (1997). *Functional Assessment and Program Development for Problem Behavior: A Practical Assessment Guide*, 2nd edn., Pacific Grove, CA: Brooks/Cole.

Panacek, L. & Dunlap, G. (2003). The social lives of children with emotional and behavioral disorders in self-contained classrooms: A descriptive analysis. *Exceptional Children*, *69*, 333–348.

Parker, J. G. & Asher, S. R. (1987). Peer acceptance and later personal adjustment: Are low-accepted children "at risk?" *Psychological Bulletin*, *102*, 357–389.

Putnam, J. W., Werder, J. K., & Schleien, S. J. (1985). Leisure and recreation services for handicapped persons. In K. C. Lakin & R. H. Bruininks (Eds.), *Strategies for Achieving Community Integration of Developmentally Disabled Citizens*, pp. 253–274. Baltimore: Paul H. Brookes Publishing Co.

Sargent, L. R. (1998). *Social Skills for School and Community: Systematic Instruction for Children and Youth with Cognitive Delays*. Colorado Springs, Colorado: CEC Publications.

Schloss, P. J. & Schloss, C. N. (1985). Contemporary issues in social skills research with mentally retarded persons. *Journal of Special Education*, *19*, 269–283.

Skinner, B. F. (1953). *Science and Human Behavior*. New York: Macmillan.

Sugai, G. & Lewis, T. J. (1996). Preferred and promising practices for social skills instruction. *Focus on Exceptional Children*, *29*(4), 11–27.

Sugai, G., Horner, R. H., Dunlap, G., Hieneman, M., Lewis, T. J., Nelson, C. M., et. al. (2000). Applying positive behavior support and functional behavioral assessment in schools. *Journal of Positive Behavior Interventions*, *2*, 131–143.

Slaton, D. B., Schuster, J., Collins, B., & Carnine, D. (1994). A functional approach to academics instruction. In E. Cipani & F. Sponner (Eds.), *Curricular and Instructional Approaches for Persons with Severe Disabilities*. Needham Heights, MA: Allyn and Bacon.

Taylor, A. R. (1991). Social competence and the early school transition: Risk and protective factors for African-American children. *Education and Urban Society*, *24*(1), 15–26.

Todd, A. W., Horner, R. H., Sugai, G., Colvin, Geoffrey. (1999). Individualizing school-wide discipline for students with chronic problem behaviors: A team approach. *Effective School Practices*, *17*(4), 72–82.

Vygotsky, L. S. (1978). *Mind in Society: The Development of Higher Psychological Processes*. Cambridge, MA: Harvard University Press.

Walker, H. M., Ramsey, E., & Gresham, F. M. (2004). *Antisocial Behavior in School: Evidence-Based Practices*, 2nd edn., Belmont, CA: Wadworth/Thomson Learning.

Williams, G. J. & Reisberg, L. (2003). Successful inclusion: teaching social skills through curriculum integration. *Intervention in School & Clinic*, *38*(4), 205–210.

12

ABAS-II AND WORK SKILLS AND ATTITUDES

KAGENDO MUTUA

Department of Special Education and Multiple Abilities, University of Alabama, Tuscaloosa, AL 35487, U.S.A.

INTRODUCTION AND DESCRIPTION OF THE WORK ADAPTIVE SKILL AREA

GENERAL DESCRIPTION OF WORK SKILLS AND ATTITUDES

The ability to work and be employed is one of the most critical markers of adulthood in the United States and many other countries. To be simultaneously marked as having a disability and unable to work often means dependency and a diminished capacity to achieve a quality of life in many spheres beyond one's work life. While for most people the ability to work is taken for granted, for many individuals with disabilities, particularly significant cognitive, physical and/or multiple disabilities, the acquisition of the skills and attitudes associated with work do not occur automatically. Systematic and coordinated instruction often is needed to facilitate the acquisition of work skills and attitudes. Young people and adults with disabilities, especially those with moderate to severe disabilities, often must be explicitly taught work skills and other personal qualities that are associated with work, including the acquisition of work-related social skills. Further, many such individuals require ongoing support to enable them to acquire the work-related skills and attitudes and to acquire and sustain continuous work.

The American Association on Mental Retardation's (AAMR, 2002) concept of mental retardation provides a broad theoretical context for understanding the importance of adaptive behavior and skills related to work skills and attitudes, qualities that can and should be assessed both quantitatively and qualitatively. The quantitative elements of work skills are those that are observable and measurable. For example, an individual's ability to perform a work task can be measured in terms of degrees of correctness, completeness, thoroughness, timeliness, and neatness. On the other hand, work-related attitudes are more qualitative in nature and often require raters to use their judgment. For example, an individual's work enthusiasm, desire to work, contentment, pride, happiness, and willingness are qualitative attributes of work behaviors that often impact one's quality of work as evidenced in the behaviors previously cited as measurable qualitatively. Therefore, work skills and attitudes are intricately interconnected and synergistic and should not be separated. Indeed some researchers see the skills and attitudes as referring to one and the same construct. For example, a definition of work skills as "behaviors and attitudes associated with positive supervisor on-the-job evaluations" illustrates this point (Martin et al., 2007, p. 3).

DESCRIPTION OF THE ABAS-II AND WORK ADAPTIVE SKILL AREA

The Adaptive Behavior Assessment System, 2nd Edition (ABAS-II) is an adaptive behavior measurement tool that includes scores for a General Adaptive Composite, the three adaptive domains (i.e., conceptual, social, and practical), and 10 specific adaptive skill areas: communication, functional academics, self-direction, leisure, social, community use, home living, health and safety, self-care, and work. The ABAS-II provides important information that can be used as part of a multi-faceted evaluation process for diagnosis; determining the presence or absence of many important adaptive skills, including those related to work skills and attitudes; determining needed services and supports; program planning and monitoring, as well as gathering important information that can be utilized in research and evaluation; and program improvement (Harrison & Oakland, 2003). The ABAS-II should be administered in its entirety to provide a comprehensive assessment across many interrelated adaptive skills.

The Work adaptive skill area provides a sampling of items related to work skills and attitudes. The Work adaptive skill area is included in the Teacher and Parent Forms for ages 5–21, and the Adult Form for ages 16–89. The Work adaptive skill area is administered if the individual has a part- or a full-time job. Professionals are encouraged to obtain ABAS-II data from two or more respondents.

All items but three are similar on the Parent, Teacher, and Adult forms. The three items that are included only in the Adult Form follow: "Finds full- or part-time jobs for himself/herself", "Follows supervisor's suggestions to improve work", and "Lives on his/her own earnings". These items are clearly more appropriate for the adult population where self-determination is expected.

Viewed collectively, the items in the work adaptive skill area can be described as comprising the environmental cluster of work skills and attitudes that focus on the demands of work. Within this cluster, specific items tap into three broad constructs that undergird the environmental cluster, namely: *general work behaviors* (e.g., Attends work regularly); *physical working conditions* (e.g., Keeps working quickly and accurately, even with loud noises or distractions); and *social interactions at the worksite* (e.g., Works quietly and does not disrupt or disturb the work of others).

The work adaptive skill area along with the nine other adaptive skill areas align with and complement the use of other tools that provide information that can assist persons transitioning to work-related activities, particularly among school-age youth with exceptional needs. For example, in addition to the three work constructs found in the ABAS-II, two additional constructs have been identified as important elements of the environmental cluster that comprise demands of work skills and attitudes, namely *physical demands* (e.g., sitting/standing for a long period, manual dexterity) and *educational demands* (e.g., educational requirements/minimum requirements, reading comprehension/ability to read and comprehend at a specified level) (Clark et al., 2000).

IMPORTANCE OF THE WORK ADAPTIVE SKILL AREA AND REVIEW OF RESEARCH

IMPLICATIONS OF THE WORK SKILL ADAPTIVE AREA FOR GENERAL FUNCTIONING

One's ability to work is a critical component of adult function. As previously stated, work comprises a critical component of an adult's identity. Those who do not work often are devalued. Although this chapter focuses on work somewhat separate from other adaptive skills, work has intricate interconnections with other adaptive skill areas, including communication, social skills, community use, health and safety, and others. For example, a lack of appropriate worksite social skills, not inability to perform the essential functions of the work, was cited as the most frequent reason for failing at that worksite by youth with disabilities (Hanley-Maxwell, 1989). Therefore when discussing adaptive behaviors related to work skills and attitudes, professionals must necessarily keep in mind the complex relations that exist between the work area of adaptive behaviors and other areas of adaptive functioning. Thus, work skills and attitudes cannot be developed adequately when they are isolated from other critical adaptive skill areas of adult function.

The interconnections between work skills and attitudes and other related adaptive skill areas should be considered when performing assessment that is focused on work skills. For example, an individual with deficits in communication or self-direction may not demonstrate good work skills and/or attitudes because of deficits in other adaptive skill areas that are important to one's skills and attitudes towards work, not because of an inability to perform the essential work functions.

CONDITIONS THAT IMPACT INDIVIDUALS' DEVELOPMENT AND PERFORMANCE IN THE WORK ADAPTIVE SKILL AREA

Within special education, research on transition from school to work has found that the type and severity of a student's disability often is associated with an individual's ability to acquire needed skills and later perform work (Rusch, 2007). The more severe the person's disability, the more likely that person is to be unable to work or to be employed. Furthermore, those with more severe disabilities display a higher incidence of inappropriate social and emotional behaviors (Snell & Brown, 2000). Consequently, many individuals with severe disabilities who work are placed in facility-based segregated settings, away from their non-disabled peers, either because they lack the work skills necessary for integrated competitive employment or necessary social skills (Stancliffe et al., 2000). Although many behaviors and work attitudes may be acquired through instruction, most may be acquired through social learning, including observing others. Individuals with disabilities who do not work, or who work in segregated settings, may experience fewer opportunities to incidentally learn, acquire, and practice social skills and attitudes necessary for the workplace. Therefore, opportunities to acquire, practice, and reinforce appropriate qualitative elements of work tend to be limited for individuals with significant disabilities who often are placed in group settings and engaged in segregated work.

Furthermore, the challenges posed by deficits resulting from particular types of disabilities (e.g., severe mental retardation, autism spectrum disorders, cerebral palsy, seizure disorders) to work skills acquisition should not be overlooked. Such challenges impact the acquisition of work skills and attitudes as well as their retention and generalization. Moreover, these populations are more susceptible than others to become reliant upon adult prompting to initiate or complete a task (Apple et al., 2005; Coyle & Cole, 2004; Wert & Neisworth, 2003) and are less likely to be independent and self-motivating in reference to work.

Persons with severe disabilities experience high unemployment rates ranging from 85% to 90% (Anthony & Blanch, 1987; Mueser et al., 2004). However, the attainment of employment rates of 60% has been shown to be possible with this same population in experimental studies (Bond et al., 1997; Drake et al., 1999). The likelihood for youth and young adults with severe disabilities to successfully achieve desirable adult outcomes, including competitive employment, increases after they learn to perform their tasks independently (Wehmeyer et al., 1998). Thus, assessment that focuses on identifying problem areas experienced by this population may help efforts to teach youth and young adults with severe disabilities alternate strategies that advance and sustain their independence at the worksite. Increasing the independence of workers with disabilities positively impacts employers' and co-workers' attitudes toward them as capable employees.

Within this context, the ABAS-II can play several pivotal roles (Harrison & Oakland, 2003). First, the ABAS-II can be used to identify aptitudes, abilities, and deficits in critical adaptive skills related to work and attitudes, including the work adaptive skill area, experienced by individuals with particular types and levels of disabilities. This information can be used for instructional program planning. Second and relatedly, the assessment can indicate the types of primary and related services and supports, including assistive technology, needed to be provided in order to improve work outcomes for those individuals. Third, the assessment can assist in monitoring progress. Fourth, assessment also can be used during research and when evaluating innovative practices for implementing instruction in work skills and attitudes for those individuals.

IMPACT ON AND ISSUES IN SPECIAL POPULATIONS

The centrality of work as a desirable adult outcome has been underscored in a number of federal education-related initiatives and legislation. Public schools are charged with the primary responsibility to prepare graduates who are well equipped with skills to work and to be productive citizens. Current public school goals focus on interventions and educational practices that lead to the achievement of valued educational outcomes for all students (Morningstar & Mutua, 2003). Research in special education conducted in the late 1970s to mid-1980s reported few graduates of special education programs attained adult outcomes. Most were unemployed or underemployed (Harris & Associates, 1986), had few contacts with non-disabled peers (Gollay et al., 1978), no intimate relationships (Gollay et al., 1978); had little to no autonomy (Baker et al., 1977; Gollay et al., 1978), participated only in passive leisure activities rather than those that increased their community presence (Gollay et al., 1978), and lived at home with parents 4–5 years after leaving school (Harris & Associates, 1986).

These findings prompted the 1990 revisions of the Individuals with Disabilities Education Act (IDEA) to mandate *transition* as a component of secondary student's Individualized Educational Plan (IEP). A requirement to prepare youth with disabilities, ages 14–21, for employment/work as a desired adult outcome was among the essential elements of a transition plan. The achievement of this outcome by many such youth required sustained and systematic instruction in work skills and attitudes.

Subsequently, the decade of the 1990s saw the emergence of federal statutes and educational reform movements pointing to a renewed commitment to improving educational outcomes and to equip all high school graduates with skills necessary for achieving success in the global marketplace. Those valued educational outcomes, of which work was central, were at the core of recent federal legislation including, Goals 2000: Educate America Act, and PL 103-239, School-to-Work Opportunities Act (1994), as well as recent educational reform initiatives, including the U.S. Secretary of Education's Commission on Achieving Necessary Skills (SCANS). While these initiatives ostensibly were directed to all students, some (Phelps & Hanley-Maxwell, 1997) questioned whether all initiatives were intended to include students with disabilities. Whether or not the clause, "all students" tacitly omitted students with disabilities, the relevance of the outcomes espoused by these reform initiatives to students with disabilities is undeniable (Morningstar & Mutua, 2002).

AGE AND GENDER ISSUES

The post-Civil Rights era of the 1970s saw the emergence of different ethos about various issues affecting Americans, including views toward disability. The normalization of persons with disabilities was emphasized, resulting in a de-institutionalization process in which many former residents of state institutions were moved to community-based programs and resided in more family-like homes in integrated neighborhoods. Work within the community also was emphasized as a valuable adult outcome that is worth pursing by all.

Although the disability community generally appears to agree that community-based competitive work exemplifies best practices in the employment of adults with disabilities, the introduction of models of integrated residential and employment services has not significantly changed how community disability agencies deliver services. For example, although the percent of persons in integrated employment increased from 17% to 30% between 1986 and 1991, the number of individuals in segregated workshops also increased substantially (McGaughey et al., 1995). These results appear to suggest that integrated employment options have merely been added to an existing service continuum rather than as a replacement for segregated, facility-based programs. Indeed, among individuals with significant disabilities who moved from institutional care to community-based programs, only 13% experienced integrated employment (Stancliffe et al., 2000). Thus, although the move to community settings increased opportunities for community-based employment, the typical adult day program has remained virtually unchanged over the decades – one that continues to be segregated, congregated (such as sheltered workshops), and with little emphasis on paid work. Consequently, today, there continues to be a chronic paucity of individualized adult services. Even when adults with disabilities receive services, programs are predominantly facility based and segregated (The Arc, 1997).

ADDITIONAL TECHNIQUES TO ASSESS THE WORK ADAPTIVE SKILL AREA

Assessment that focuses on work skills and attitudes is required during transition planning for young adults with disabilities. Likewise similar assessments are needed to undergird the Individualized Habilitation Plans for the adult population. The 1990 re-authorization of IDEA added transition planning as a required component of special education services at the secondary level. Assessment services have been a required program component. Specifically, the 1990 IDEA amendments required assessments to be unbiased given in the native language, and multiple measures used to examine behaviors in various environments. Later, the 1997 IDEA amendments placed greater emphasis on the use of informal assessments, stipulating that assessments must address the extent to which the student would be integrated into the general curriculum, classrooms, and integrated work environments. Finally, the 2004 amendments made several stipulations regarding assessments, including the need to use functional assessments and focus on the individual's strengths.

The IDEA and its amendments call for the assessments of qualities essential to transition planning. Transition planning from school to employment/work requires assessment be conducted that specifically informs and promotes these efforts. Specifically, assessments should be used to determine student needs, interests, and preferences; developing an outcome-oriented process; and promote movement to post-school/adult outcomes, of which work is an integral piece. Additionally, assessment is ongoing and continuous, has a clearly specified purpose (e.g., gathering of information for purposes of planning, instruction, or placement), is individualized, and is summarized in an understandable transition profile.

Various types of assessments are used when defining transition domains as well as current and future working environments. For example, career assessments focus on developing career maturity. Initially, assessments identify general abilities and interests while later assessments identify specific career aptitudes and attitudes needed for success. Examples of assessments tools used for determining current and future working environments through the identification of career interests include Becker Reading-Free Interest Survey, Career Development Inventory, Career Maturity Inventory, Knowledge of the World of Work Scale, Kuder Vocational Preference Record, Reading-Free Vocational Interest Inventory, Self-Directed Search, and the Wide-Range Interest and Opinion Test.

Several limitations related to career surveys, aptitude measurement, and work-sample assessments have been noted. These include the limited predictive value due to the artificiality of test situation, failure to include work cues and distractions, failure to consider job accommodations and assistive technology, failure to consider other personal qualities of individuals and their response to testing situations together with concerns that informal assessments may lack reliability over time as well as across evaluators.

On the other hand, vocational assessments focus on specific jobs in terms of identifying special aptitudes, needs, work habits and behaviors, personal and social skills, attitudes, work tolerance, work adjustment, physical abilities, and dexterity. Examples of tests of work skill and aptitude measurement include the Bennet Hand-Tool Dexterity Test, Differential Aptitude Test, Macquarrie Test for Mechanical Ability, Minnesota Spatial Relations Test, and the Purdue Pegboard Test.

Functional and ecological assessments are other forms of assessments that are used routinely with students with disabilities during transition work. Functional assessments are conducted in a student's personal surroundings and environments to determine the practical skills the student needs to survive and succeed as well as the process of learning and performance. Therefore, functional assessments are intended to provide information directly related to a student's transitional outcomes by comparing a student's present levels of performance to levels required for success.

On the other hand, ecological assessments may be functional and directly related to transition outcomes. Ecological assessments are used to assess all individual environments and relationships between environments, identify aspects that impact the student's performance, and may be used to evaluate prospective environments.

Additionally, formal assessments are used in transition. The most common ones used include adaptive behavior scales, personality tests, vocational and career aptitudes, interests, worker characteristics, and occupational skills tests. For example, the ABAS-II, AAMR Adaptive Behavior Scales, and Vineland Adaptive Behavior Scales-II are formal general adaptive behavior norm-referenced scales in which teachers and parents rate student abilities on a number of life-skill areas. The Halpern's Transition Skills Inventory is a self-report that assesses domains of personal life, jobs, education, and independent living. On the other hand, Clark and Patton's Transition Planning Inventory offers three forms to be completed by the educators, family, and students. The Social and Prevocational Information Battery is narrowly focused on the vocational and community adjustment skills of middle and high school students with mental retardation.

The 1997 IDEA amendments also emphasized the use of informal assessments. They are intended to provide authentic information about how students perform in specific environments and can be used in conjunction with accommodations. For example, a student's school records could be reviewed. School records provide a cumulative record that can provide information on prior behaviors, attitudes, and performance. Such information may be pivotal in revealing whether change has occurred and the possible impact of prior behavior on current and future behavior.

Curriculum-based assessment provides a rating of progress through a particular curriculum by using measures reflecting functional expectations, thereby yielding a valid measure of attainment and possibly progress.

Portfolio assessment is a relatively new method to assess the mastery of competencies important to successful transitions. Portfolio assessments have several advantages including the accumulation of work evidence in the various academic and performance areas, thereby being a good tool for documenting transition competencies; involving students in the evaluation process; and convincing employers that a student can do the job (e.g., videotapes of work). The main disadvantages to portfolio assessments are that they tend to be subjective and thus often lack reliability or validity and that their preparation is very time consuming and may be difficult for some students to achieve.

Transition assessment needs to be ongoing and to combine a common frame of reference with transition-specific requirements for assessment and planning that uses student and family goals to form consensus-based plans. Furthermore, transition assessment requires a comprehensive profile of needs, strengths and preferences of the student; provides data that informs planning, instructional, and curriculum decisions; and utilizes of both formal and informal methods. Additionally, transition assessment requires an interdisciplinary team process designed to promote movement to meaningful adulthood behaviors. Within this framework, the ABAS-II would indeed be an excellent formal tool to assess critical adaptive skill areas for students in transition from school to work as well as the adult population already preparing for and/or receiving supports in work-related areas.

INTERVENTION METHODS THAT PROMOTE DEVELOPMENT AND ACCOMMODATE DEFICIENCIES IN THE WORK ADAPTIVE SKILL AREA

During the past 20 years, many methods have been used and evaluated in an attempt to develop transition praxis and other models of practice that promote the attainment of positive adult outcomes in work/employment, leisure/recreation, community use, postsecondary education, and independent living. However, even after these 20 year of efforts and expenses, youth with disabilities remain in need of educational services that help them reach their desired adult outcomes (de Fur & Patton, 1999; Wehmeyer & Schwartz, 1997). For example, In Alabama, youth with disabilities, compared to their non-disabled peers, experience higher rates of unemployment and underemployment, higher dropout rates, more restricted participation in community and leisure time activities, and are more dependent on parents and others (Browning et al., 1995).

Furthermore, advocates and researchers alike are in agreement on the failure of current educational interventions to prepare youth with disabilities to assume their roles as emerging adults. Turnbull (2001), a disability advocate and scholar, long noted that, in general, educational services do not yet prepare students with disabilities to lead lives that are to others enviable. And more recently, Rusch (2007), a leading expert in school to work transition, observed that:

> ...adolescents with a disability are not the recipients of an education that promotes becoming self-determined; they are not being prepared to assume the roles that they have identified as being important to them; and they are not benefiting from the supports that they need as they go on to assume adult roles (p. 13).

Literature that reviews the impact of two decades of federally supported efforts to develop model transition demonstration programs leads to the conclusion that although advances in preparing youth with disabilities for the future adult roles have been made(Kohler, 1993), and a plethora of information on transition services now exists and has led to some improvements (Flexer et al., 2005; Rusch & Chadsey, 1998; Test et al., 2006) secondary schools still are not preparing the largest majority of them to become successful adults (Rusch, 2007). Progress not withstanding, a chasm exists between what we know about school to work transition itself and the actual preparation of youth with disabilities, the recipients of transition services, to enable them to successfully assume adult roles.

The Individuals with Disabilities Education Improvement Act of 2004 defines the term *transition services* as a coordinated set of activities for a child with a disability that:

- Is designed to be within a results-oriented process, that is focused on improving the academic and functional achievement of the child with a disability to facilitate the child's movement from school to post-school activities, including postsecondary education, vocational education, integrated employment (including supported employment); continuing and adult education, adult services, independent living, or community participation.
- Is based on the individual child's needs, taking into account the child's strengths, preferences, and interests.
- Includes instruction, related services, community experiences, the development of employment and other post-school adult living objectives, and, if appropriate, acquisition of daily living skills and functional vocational evaluation [34 CFR 300.43 (a)] [20 U.S.C. 1401(34)].

Further, IDEA 2004 requires the implementation of transition assessment to develop postsecondary goals. Specifically, IDEA 2004 states that:

> Beginning not later than the first IEP to be in effect when the child turns 16, or younger if determined appropriate by the IEP Team, and updated annually thereafter, the IEP must include:

- Appropriate measurable postsecondary goals based upon age-appropriate transition assessments related to training, education, employment and, where appropriate, independent living skills.
- The transition services (including courses of study) needed to assist the child in reaching those goals.
- Beginning not later than 1 year before the child reaches the age of majority under State law, a statement that the child has been informed of the child's rights under Part B, if any, that will transfer to the child on reaching the age of majority [34 CFR 300.320(b) and (c)] [20 U.S.C. 1414 (d)(1)(A)(i)(VIII)].

This definition of transition services, underscores four essential elements of transition. Transition is an outcome-oriented process. Good instruction should lead to positive transition outcomes for students. Transition calls for a coordinated set of activities. Instruction and transition needs are to be well organized, sequential, with sufficient repetition and practice, for learning to occur. Transition should promote movement to post-school activities. Instruction should develop the knowledge, skills, attitudes, and behaviors students need to become responsible and successful adults. Transition is based on student needs, preferences, and interests. Instruction, transition planning, and other educational activities are more likely to be successful when based on student interests.

The majority of youth with disabilities currently are not prepared adequately to achieve success as adults as evidenced in their failure to achieve desirable adult outcomes such as employment. Nevertheless, evidence from successful model high school programs that prepare youth with disabilities to reach desired adult goals offer some guidance as to the nature of educational intervention that must take place in order to lead to the kind of results envisioned under IDEA. Much of what we know today about strategies for preparing youth with disabilities to achieve desirable outcomes, specifically in the area of work, were well articulated almost a decade ago (Rusch & Chadsey, 1998), including student-focused planning, student career plans, interagency collaboration, family involvement, and providing support after departure from high school. Indeed, these strategies form the cornerstone of the definition of transition put forth by IDEA. Each of these strategies is described below.

Student-focused planning: The IDEA definition of transition states transition is based on student's needs, preferences, interests, strengths, and limitations. A purpose of special education at the secondary level is preparing students for adult functioning. Thus, the student is characterized as the center piece of planning. Achieving this goal is easier said than done.

Student-focused planning must begin with self-determination. Rusch (2007) asserted that transition programs that promote students' self-determination have been associated with improved postsecondary/adult outcomes. Student-focused planning should be implemented with the student being provided the opportunity to articulate desired post-school work/employment outcome upon graduation from school. For students with moderate and severe levels of cognitive disabilities such as severe mental retardation or autism, the question "what job would you like to have when you complete school?" must be asked often and IEPs modified as needed as the students' work exploratory experiences increase.

Students who display severe levels of cognitive disabilities acquire a significantly smaller amount of knowledge and skills, acquire them more slowly, are inclined to not remember them, and display a lower capacity for knowledge and skill acquisition than that of their typically functioning peers (Heward, 2006). Therefore, educational professionals and family members should not wait until the year prior to the student's leaving school to begin engaging the student in planning post-school options.

Student career plans: Planning that is student focused should result in student career plans that are individualized. As stated above, many students with disabilities who require transition services do not succeed when typical strategies for preparing them are utilized. Rather, individualized planning must be utilized to increase the probability for their success. To do this, the work-related goals and activities that are articulated in the student's IEP must take into account the student's interests, skills, strengths, and limitations.

The development of an individualized career plan should begin with a comprehensive assessment, one that is individualized to each student's needs. One such assessment strategy employs the person-centered job selection that utilizes non-traditional assessment exercises, including a significant time investment to know the person's individual interests and desires. When using person-centered planning, the team develops jobs that are customized to the individual's strengths, needs, interests, and preferences thereby avoiding slotting the person in pre-existing job sites based merely upon the individual's disabilities. Within person-centered planning, the process of job development utilizes support networks of families, friends, and self. Specifically, job development may utilize a job carving *in which* a job developer works in collaboration with the employer to customize the job and to brainstorm and eliminate potential barriers. Additionally, if the individual will be working part-time, then job sharing agreements are established.

Within a person-centered strategy, needed supports are identified and put into place to facilitate the individual's successful work performance. Those supports may include natural utilizing generic employer training and whenever possible and removing, or at least limiting, the stigmatizing potential that exists when professional job coaches are used to provide support at the workplace. Job coaches and natural supports do not have to supplant each other, but can be used to supplement each other whenever work circumstances demand.

Interagency collaboration: Collaboration among agencies that provide adult services rarely occurs. However, interagency collaboration, including planning and resource sharing, is critical for the success of transition plans. Although interagency collaboration during transition has improved some, the urgency for more progress was underscored when the National Council on Disability advocated for a "national initiative that focuses on coordinated actions to address system reform" to improve post-school outcomes for youth with disabilities through efforts that include federal, state, and local policymakers (National Council on Disability, 2001, p. 3).

Students with more severe disabilities (e.g., those with severe mental retardation and emotional and behavior disorders) are particularly in need of coordinated supports to access various needed services once they leave school. Not surprisingly, no one agency has been able to meet all of their needs. Therefore, during the transition period, educators should work to ensure students with disabilities are connected with outside agencies prior to leaving school.

Family involvement: Typically developing young people usually become their own guardians when they reach the age of the majority, usually age 18 or 19 in many states. However, youth with disabilities often continue to have their parents or primary caregivers serve as their guardians. Therefore, for them, the primacy of parental involvement in the process of school to work transition for young persons with disabilities is pivotal. Additionally, IDEA mandates the opportunity for parent and student involvement in the educational process, specifically designating parents as key players in the IEP process. Thus, the development of transition IEP goals should be based on a sound assessment that delineates students' strengths and limitations, needs, interests, and skills and include parental input (Johnson, 2005). Therefore, this process should consider family values (Leake & Black, 2005; Valenzuela & Martin, 2005) and match them with the demands of work when feasible.

The remainder of this section focuses on specific interventions for the work adaptive skill area. As discussed in an earlier section, the demands of work are emphasized within the environmental cluster of work skills and attitudes. The three broad constructs that underscore the environmental cluster of work skills and attitudes are *general work behaviors* (e.g., attends work regularly), *physical working conditions* (e.g., keeps working quickly and accurately, even with loud noises or distractions), and *social interactions at the worksite* (e.g., works quietly and does not disrupt or disturb the work of others). While the emphasis of this chapter is on work skills and attitudes, they are not separate from other adaptive skill areas such as communication, functional academics, self-direction, social, community use, health and safety, and self-care. Indeed deficits in those other areas are guaranteed to have consequences on an individual's function at the workplace. The reader is encouraged to consult other chapters in this book that discuss other skill areas.

Many varied forms of interventions can be utilized in the work skills area of instruction. This discussion places them in three broad categories: (a) behavioral interventions, (b) cognitive interventions, and (c) social learning interventions. Although these three forms of interventions can be discussed separately, in practice they commonly are used together. Thus, many of the interventions are not mutually exclusive (i.e., an intervention can be classified simultaneously as behavioral and social learning). Additionally, rarely is an intervention used in isolation. Rather, interventions from two or more of the three categories tend to be used together.

Behavioral approaches: These are instructional approaches or intervention strategies that have a basis in classical behaviorism, specifically operant learning theory. According to operant learning principles, behavior occurs as a function of the external environment. Therefore, a behavior occurs because of its history of positive reinforcement. An individual learns a new response by attending to the discriminative stimulus. Therefore, a behavior is learned when it has come under stimulus control.

In general, behavioral interventions are more effective with persons who display lower cognitive abilities and need more direct forms of intervention and instruction to acquire, maintain, and generalize a work skill. For example, simulations can be used to reinforce safety workplace behaviors by simulating a variety of safety-related scenarios that are of relevance to the individual's specific workplace. For example, recognition that wet floors pose a safety hazard for the individual as well as the individual's co-workers can be taught by simulating a wet floor scenario, observing what the individual does in such a situation, and then teaching the correct response. The transfer of lessons taught through simulation to actual contexts is promoted by emphasizing during simulated instruction the relevant discriminative stimuli for each safety situation that the individual must attend to in order to elicit the appropriate behavior. Discriminative stimuli that can be emphasized during such simulations may include a Wet Floor warning sign placed on a wet surface, signs of dangerous chemicals, and smoke detection/fire signals. Additionally, nonspecific questioning techniques can be used to elicit responses from the individual about what he/she would do if an incident occurred at work that posed harm to him/her or to co-workers.

Other important elements of behavioral interventions include providing clear, consistent, concise expectations and demands for work, for example, maintaining consistency in regard to expectations and demands for regular attendance, attention to tasks, and working quietly to not bother co-workers. Such consistency can be established by building work routines (e.g., using a checklist where the worker checks off tasks as they are completed) or by using a task analysis approach that breaks down a complex task into small teachable steps. Completion of such work routines can be rewarded or recognized by providing positive reinforcement and/or corrective feedback.

Differential reinforcement strategies that promote learning and skill acquisition may be used to promote positive attitudes toward work. Some examples of differential reinforcement include reinforcing nonoccurrence or absence of behavior, such as complaining behavior and other signs of negative attitudes toward work. Variations of differential reinforcement of nonoccurrence or absence of behavior (DRO) include full session DRO in which reinforcement is offered at the end of the work session. For example, say, "I like the way you worked the entire morning without complaining" or "I liked your positive attitude to work this morning – that was excellent work behavior!" Professionals could also provide reinforcement at intervals by dividing the work session into smaller time segments with behaviors reinforced at regular intervals. Yet another variation of differential reinforcement schedule is one in which the professional reinforces the individual's behavior randomly, also referred to as momentary differential reinforcement method. As an individual's attitude towards work progressively improves, a professional may choose to use a differential reinforcement technique of reinforcing lower and lower behaviors. Specifically, in this strategy differential reinforcement is less frequently provided over time. Reinforcement is provided initially at a higher frequency and as the positive attitude is fostered, reinforcement is reduced over time, thus requiring persons to work longer before being reinforced for their positive attitude.

Certain workplace behaviors and/or attitudes may be easier to improve by reinforcing incompatible behaviors. In such cases, a strategy that may be effective is to use differential reinforcement of incompatible behaviors. For example, when working with an individual who complains constantly, all instances when the individual is involved in a desirable behavior that is incompatible to complaining would be reinforced. A final differential reinforcement strategy, differential reinforcement of alternative behaviors, may be used, for instance, if the individual's attitudes toward work are exemplified by sluggishness; attending to task, an alternate behavior, could be reinforced.

Cognitive interventions: Unlike behavioral interventions that rely on others to instruct the worker, cognitive interventions shift more responsibility for learning to the supported worker. The interventions used within this approach allow workers to self-instruct, self-monitor, self-reinforce and self-correct. Cognitive interventions require workers to have the ability to recognize the pre-agreed on signal to self-monitor, self-reinforce and so on. Some specific examples of a cognitive intervention may include the following scenario: encouraging the individual to complete work assignments within required time limits by providing the individual with a time-keeping system. For individuals who can tell time, such a system may utilize a watch, clock, or a calendar that the individual uses to track progress in terms of tasks completed and time allotted to complete the entire job. As a variation to the time-keeping system, a written linear sequential break down of the job may be prepared that aligns with significant portions of the day or week depending on the time allotted to complete the task. Keep the person engaged in a task by having the individual check off the completed parts of the job. Facilitate independent functioning when the individual changes from one job-related task to another without special instructions of the supervisor by providing a general task schedule that delineates the number, order, and location of work tasks that the individual is expected to complete each day. For individuals whose job tasks change daily, such a schedule should delineate the tasks for a particular day. Match the schedule to the individual's ability (e.g., pairing pictures with a written schedule for individuals with low level reading skills, using a read-free picture schedule for non-readers, or a three dimensional object schedule to provide even more concrete visual prompts for individuals who are non-readers and/or have lower cognitive abilities).

Teach self-awareness skills to facilitate the individual's ability to become aware of himself or herself at the workplace by paying attention to how he or she may be causing or contributing to disruptions at the workplace. For example, use a self-monitoring system such as an interval timer and check off on a tally sheet whether he or she is on or off task, silent or making noise every time the interval timer signal is given. The interval timer may be a digital watch that rings on 10 or 15 minute intervals, an egg timer, or a visual signal consistently given by the supervisor or a co-worker.

Social learning interventions: Interventions within this approach rely on learning of a desired behavior in light of observing a visual model without prompting. The social learning interventions have their theoretical roots in Bandura's social learning theory that states that learning is accomplished by observing models from which an individual learns both cognitively and behaviorally. An example of an intervention based on social learning may include providing a model that neatly performs a task in order to promote task neatness. The nature of the model will depend on the specific work itself. Therefore, the model may be a live depiction of an actual task that the individual emulates. For example, if the individual works in motel or hotel, the person may observe and gradually emulate a model changing and making the beds neatly and to employer standards. Work settings in which a model of the actual behavior may not be possible to enact may use pictures of the task that the person examines and follows sequentially.

Other variations of social learning interventions include role-playing or using simulations. For example, encourage the individual to request directions for tasks whenever needed by using role-play or simulating work-related instances in which the individual may need to request assistance from a supervisor or a co-worker. Use nonspecific questioning to prompt the individual to ask for directions from the appropriate person. During role-play situations, include participants who may not be appropriate persons to ask for assistance to ensure that the individual understands that there are designated/appropriate individuals from whom to seek directions about work. For example, if the role-play involves a retail scenario, some of the characters may be customers, co-workers, a supervisor, and so forth. After presenting the situation that requires the individual to seek directions, nonspecifically prompt the individual to ask for directions. The professional may say: "Now, who should you ask for directions?" The objective is to get the individual to correctly identify the right person from whom to ask directions.

SAMPLE CASE REPORT USING ABAS-II

TJ: a 16 year old young man with multiple disabilities

Evaluation Report

Client Name: Thomas C. Jones Jr. (TJ)

Parent: Edith Jones (Mother)

Dates of Evaluation: May 15–20, 2007

Date of Birth: May 12, 1991

Age: 16 years

Sources of Information

Information for an ecological assessment

- Home and school observations
- Interviews:
  Thomas C. Jones Jr. (TJ)
  Edith Jones (Mother)
  Sarah Perkins (Special Education Teacher)
  Ann Morrow (Classroom Aide)

Adaptive Behavior Assessment System, 2nd Edition (Parent Form and Teacher Form)

REFERRAL INFORMATION

TJ is a 16 year old male, who was refereed for an evaluation to better understand his current levels of adaptive skills and determine his strengths and needs for purposes of planning transition services. TJ, who is classified as having mental retardation and other health impairments, has received special education services since age 5 years. TJ recently was placed in Ms. Perkins' classroom having just transferred from a rural school where he had not previously received any transition services. Rapport with TJ and his mother was established and maintained throughout the home visit. TJ answered questions willingly and volunteered information only when asked about work, He talked excitedly about his new "job" in school. TJ participates in a situational work assessment and work sampling in school to determine his strengths, interests, and preferences, a program that should have been initiated by age 14.

BACKGROUND INFORMATION

TJ lives with his mother in a mobile home on the outskirts of a college town. His mother, Ms. Jones, and TJ's father were divorced about three years ago. After the divorce, TJ and his mother continued living in the same town. Ms. Jones decided to move this year because a friend informed her that prospects for jobs for TJ were better here and that the local school programs may be better in providing TJ with the preparation he needs for his future. Ms. Jones hopes her son will learn how to better care for himself, hold a job, and make friends, and hopefully, even have a girlfriend. She worries about what would happen to TJ if something were to happen to her. TJ is with his father one month during the summer. After the divorce, TJ's father moved to Nebraska where he works as a supervisor in a meat processing plant. Before the divorce, TJ's mother had taken care of him exclusively and had worked infrequently in a convenience store. She believes she needs to work in order to set an example of work to TJ and to also supplement their meager income which mainly is derived from federal income assistance for TJ and child support from TJ's father.

TJ has been enrolled in special education with a classification of mental retardation and other health impairment since he entered school at the age of 5 years. Previous evaluation results for TJ consistently reported intelligence test scores in the 40–50 standard score range and significant deficits in all adaptive skills areas. At age 3, TJ was diagnosed as having mild ataxic cerebral palsy. At age 6 years, TJ was found to have a seizure disorder that presently is controlled partially by medications. His mother and teacher report an average of one seizure per month. His hearing is reported to be within normal limits.

In his previous school, TJ was enrolled in a class for students with moderate/severe disabilities, His previous teacher informed TJ's mother that TJ would likely work in a sheltered workshop and could not learn skills that could lead to the kind of adult work outcomes that his mother desired for him.

TJ currently is enrolled in his high school's transition program that focuses on preparing young people with significant disabilities for adult roles in the areas of work/employment, independent living, community participation, and leisure/recreation. In his new classroom, Ms. Perkins reported that TJ, along with his classmates, spends four hours a day Monday through Thursday in individualized work-related instructional activities. Ms. Perkins is conducting situational assessments to determine the kind of work skills TJ currently displays as well as determining his needs and preferences in terms of work and other adaptive skills. Due to the fact that TJ had neither previous work experience nor any experience in any of the other transition areas, Ms. Perkins is involving him in activities that will yield information about his strengths, needs, preferences, and interests. He is participating in leisure/recreational activities with same age peers through the Parks and Recreation Agency in the city and several other social activities planned by students from the local college.

Also, a representative from an adult agency has met with his mother to discuss respite care for TJ, as well as his transportation needs. He has been assigned a case worker from the Department of Rehabilitation Services who will oversee and coordinate his employment-related support needs.

His mother reports that TJ's behaviors and independence have improved and that she can hardly keep up with his after-school engagements. This has led to an increase in TJ's self-reliance and decrease in need for some of his mother's assistance. She hopes to be able to begin looking for a part-time job by the end of the school year. The current assessment is requested as part of his multi-faceted evaluation that will enable the IEP team to better understand his diagnosis and to plan instruction to more adequately meet his transition needs.

CURRENT EVALUATION RESULTS

Observations of TJ at home and school and interviews with TJ, his mother, teacher, and classroom aide yielded the following information.

Appearance: TJ wears clean, out-dated clothing. He often exudes a noticeable body odor, and his hair often is in disarray. TJ's forearms are covered with sores in various stages of healing. The sores are caused by TJ's picking at his arms with his nails until he draws blood. He was observed to pick at his arms in one spot until blood was evident and then he moved to a new spot. The picking behavior occurs most frequently when TJ has nothing to do. His mother reported, with much excitement, that she has noticed a significant decrease in this behavior since TJ started in his new school.

Basic motor skills: TJ walks in a lurching gait due to mild ataxic cerebral palsy. In spite of his unsteady gait, he is able to ambulate to an appropriate rate of speed and can independently sit, stand, and dance (albeit with some awkwardness). TJ has trouble running. He tends to stumble and fall as his speed increases.

Communication skills: TJ understands spoken communication. Although he can communicate verbally in simple sentences and phrases, he tends to indicate his need to eat or drink by getting a spoon and a cup from the kitchen and/or pointing. The teacher reported that she is working with him to use spoken words in school and, when he does not, he is not granted the request.

Eating: TJ has eaten pureed food and cereal since a choking incident 7 years ago. Ms. Jones reports that, after this incident, TJ refused to eat solid food. In spite of medical reports that indicate no structural abnormalities of mouth and throat, TJ makes a gagging sound when he is given any other type of food. The teacher reports that he has been asked to bring age-appropriate lunches and snacks and has been eating them with few instances of gagging.

Grooming: Although TJ is able to dress and undress himself, he has difficulty with fasteners and with distinguishing front from back of some clothing items. His mother reports that TJ does not shave although he sprouts a 3–4 inch growth of sparse facial hair. He is able to shower himself, although he needs assistance washing his hair. TJ's teacher reports inconsistent use of deodorant. TJ often looses his glasses, and he never cleans them himself. When he is not wearing his glasses, he squints at things for long periods before he can identify them. Both his mother and teacher report that TJ must be reminded often to wear his glasses or, otherwise, he just stands there unable to identify things when he is not wearing them. Additionally, his mother reports that TJ has incidents of inappropriate behaviors (e.g., crying) when he cannot locate personal items. According to this mother, this behavior occurs when TJ's glasses are missing. TJ's teacher reported no such behavior.

Recreation/leisure: Prior to his enrollment in the new school, TJ spent most of his unstructured time picking at his arms. He watched TV, and his mother reports that he enjoyed playing with the family's cats. His mother and teacher report that he now actively participates in various leisure/recreation activities, including bowling, canoeing, working out, dance classes, cooking classes, and Karaoke that are organized and/or sponsored by the Parks and Recreation Agency and a fraternity/sorority from the local college.

ADAPTIVE BEHAVIOR AND SKILLS

TJ's adaptive skills were assessed using the ABAS-II Parent Form (ages 5–21), completed by his mother, and Teacher Form (ages 5–21), completed by Ms. Perkins. The ABAS-II results are summarized in Table 12.1. His extremely low scores in all domains and adaptive skill areas confirm the conclusions of the ecological assessment and document that TJ's adaptive behavior and skills are much lower (less than the 0.1 percentile) than those of his age peers.

A review of individual ABAS-II item scores rated by TJ's mother and teacher identify a number of important strengths and needs, as summarized below:

- *Communication adaptive skill area*: TJ routinely responds to others, listens closely, follows instructions, and uses people's names and sometimes uses sentences and names objects. He seldom speaks distinctly, ends conversations appropriately, and takes turns during conversations. He is not able to state his own telephone number and address.
- *Functional academics adaptive skill area*: TJ states the days of the week and reads common signs. However, he is not able read, write, or use time, measurement, or money in his daily activities.
- *Self-direction adaptive skill area*: TJ always works on activities for at least 15 minutes and stops activities when told that time is up and sometimes

TABLE 12.1 Results of the ABAS-II (Teacher Form for Ages 5–21 and Parent Form for Ages 5–21) for TJ, Age 16 Years

	Adaptive Skill Area Scaled Score	Composite Standard Score	Composite Percentile Rank	Composite Score Classification
Teacher Form Composites and Adaptive Skill Areas				
General Adaptive Composite (GAC)		40	<0.01	Extremely low
Conceptual Composite		50	<0.01	Extremely low
• Communication	1			
• Functional academics	1			
• Self-direction	1			
Social Composite		55	<0.01	Extremely low
• Leisure	1			
• Social	1			
Practical Composite		45	<0.01	Extremely low
• Community use	1			
• School living	1			
• Health and safety	1			
• Self-care	1			
Work Adaptive Skill Area	1			
Parent Form Composites and Adaptive Skill Areas				
General Adaptive Composite (GAC)		40	<0.01	Extremely low
Conceptual Composite		49	<0.01	Extremely low
• Communication	1			
• Functional academics	1			
• Self-direction	1			
Social Composite		55	<0.01	Extremely low
• Leisure	1			
• Social	1			
Practical Composite		40	<0.01	Extremely low
• Community use	1			
• Home living	1			
• Health and safety	1			
• Self-care	1			
Work Adaptive Skill Area	1			

Note: Composites (Conceptual, Social, Practical, and the General Adaptive Composite) have standard scores with a mean of 100 and standard deviation of 15. Adaptive skill areas (Communication, Functional Academics, etc.) have scaled scores with a mean of 10 and standard deviation of 3. The work adaptive skill area scores are not included in calculating composite scores.

controls anger and feelings. However, he does not work independently, arrive on time, or work hard on tasks that are not liked.

- *Leisure adaptive skill area*: TJ plays with games and others, watches TV, and attend fun activities. TJ does not follow rules in games or invite others to join in activities.
- *Social adaptive skill area*: TJ has good relationships with adults, communicates feelings, tries to please others, and has a few friends. However, he does not demonstrate acts of courtesy (e.g., saying "thank you", apologizing) or offer assistance to other people.
- *Community use adaptive skill area*: TJ follows some basic community rules such as looking before crossing a street. However, he is not able to follow directions and walk alone to community places, find restrooms, make purchases, or order food.
- *Home/school living adaptive skill area*: TJ routinely engages in a number of household and classroom tasks, such as wiping up spills, putting things away, and sweeping the floor. He does not make his bed nor keep his living area tidy at home although he does at school. Additionally, he is not able to make meals, conduct repairs, or operate appliances and electronics.
- *Health and safety adaptive skill area*: TJ shows caution around dangerous items and follows basic safety rules. He is not able to care for his own health (e.g., taking medications, caring for cuts and scrapes) or follow important community safety standards (e.g., accepting money or rides from strangers).
- *Self-care adaptive skill area*: With some assistance, TJ engages in basic eating, dressing, and grooming, such as using a fork, dressing, and showering. However, he only sometimes brushes his teeth and keeps his hair neat; he is unable to wash his hair, care for fingernails, or get out of bed on time by himself.
- *Work adaptive skill area*: Because a major purpose of the present evaluation was to determine skills that TJ needs to transition from school to work, the ABAS-II adaptive skill area of work is an important aspect of the evaluation. TJ routinely engages in several work-related behaviors that will be of assistance in a full-time, supported work setting. TJ shows a positive attitude toward work and sometimes performs work tasks neatly. However, he never engages in several other work-related behaviors that will be important for his employment, including seeking help from supervisors, respecting property of others, completing work assignments on time, and changing from one work task to another without instruction.

RECOMMEND INTERVENTIONS FOR TRANSITION

The following recommendations for planning TJ's transition, home and school interventions, and interagency collaboration are suggested to promote

TJ's transition from a school environment to a full-time, supported work environment. The results of the ecological assessment and ABAS-II suggest a number of prioritized needs that will be important for TJ's success in a work setting and also for general daily functioning. Ms. Jones and Ms. Perkins concur that, while TJ had many areas of need, interventions should focus on the following areas where the needs are most urgent:

- Work/employment skills instruction
- Self-care, especially in the area of personal grooming involving use of deodorant, showering independently, and shaving

Specific interventions were suggested for each of the aforementioned priorities.

Work/employment skills instruction: TJ will continue with his current situational assessment activities that will yield valuable data about his work-related strengths, interests, needs and preferences. The emphasis of the interventions in this area will be on fostering choice making. From TJ's ecological assessment, he has had no previous work experience and is currently engaged in situational assessments to determine his interests and preferences in the area of work. Using both behavioral and cognitive strategies involving positive reinforcement and self-monitoring with a check sheet respectively, TJ will be taught to make choices of his preferred jobs that he experiences during the situational assessment period. Specifically, TJ will be verbally prompted to engage in and/or exhibit critical work-related behaviors such as requesting help from supervisors, respecting others' property, completing work assignments in timely manner and independently moving on to the next task. These specific behaviors will be targeted for instruction because ecological assessment as well as assessment results using ABAS-II showed significant deficits in those areas. Therefore, whenever TJ engages in these behaviors independently or with prompting, positive reinforcement will be provided. The professionals working with TJ will determine the appropriate reinforcement schedule that will be followed. During the skill acquisition phase, continuous reinforcement, that is, reinforcement of every occurrence of the behaviors could be instituted and as TJ progresses in his mastery of those skills, reinforcement could be thinned and an appropriate differential reinforcement schedule be implemented. For instance, it is expected that as TJ's skill development progresses from acquisition, fluency/proficiency, maintenance, generalization to adaptation, reinforcement will be thinned and reinforcement schedules will become more conservative (i.e., he will be expected to exhibit more of the behavior or more frequently before he can be provided with positive reinforcement) while at the same time fading the prompts. This simultaneous thinning of reinforcement and fading of prompts will coincide with the implementation of cognitive approaches that rely upon self-management.

Self-management as a cognitive intervention could involve teaching TJ strategies that will shift the responsibly of learning to himself and away from others, thereby decreasing his reliance on external agents for work performance. In this case, as TJ's skill proficiency increases, TJ will be taught how to self-instruct, self-monitor, self-reinforce and self-correct. For instance, using a check sheet,

TJ will be instructed how to keep track of the daily work tasks that completes. By creating a robust check sheet, the professionals will be able to instruct TJ how to simultaneously document task completion and number of tasks completed correctly within a time period. Additionally, the check sheet might include a column to check off on a sliding scale how much he liked that particular job or job task. As TJ moves through different job assignments during the situational assessment, the data that will be collected using the check sheet will yield important information regarding the degree of TJ's preference for a particular work/job assignment, his strengths and his areas of needs that relate to a specific job or a specific attribute of a job. Such data will be a pivotal supplement to TJ's verbal statement of work/job interests, preferences, strengths, and needs.

Self-care skills instruction: This area will be targeted for instruction given its importance and high degree of social significance. Self-care skills are central to one's employability and therefore absolutely essential for function in all areas of TJ's life. Using a collaborative approach between home, school, and adult service agencies, a variety of intervention strategies involving modeling, use of unspecific questioning, simulations, and role-playing to enact scenarios involving self-care skills will be utilized to provide TJ with multiple exemplars of appropriate self-care across many different environments and activities. A task's level of complexity and the instructional context will determine the forms of the model. Unspecific questioning will be used to spur TJ to independently come up with a response or action instead of being told what to do. For example, instead of telling TJ that he needs to comb his hair, shave, or use deodorant (or engage in any of the self-care skills that were found to be lacking), a visual model comprising a photograph of himself as well groomed could be provided to spur him to emulate the model. The professionals will determine the nature of the model that will be used for this purpose, particularly after personal grooming skills have been successfully acquired. It is recommended that a similar model be used across environments in order to facilitate generalization. A photograph of himself discreetly placed in his work folder to remind him of the work-related grooming requirements, or a photograph of himself posted on his bathroom mirror at home to remind him of the school-related grooming requirements and so on could serve as important visual model for him to spur his self-care behaviors across environments. The learning of such self-care skills will bode well for successful independent functioning at work settings, recreational/leisure setting, and at home and school. Self-care skills are critical for integration in all areas of life that it is imperative that such skills be an instructional priority for TJ.

REFERENCES

American Association on Mental Retardation (AAMR) (2002). *Mental retardation: Definition, Classification, and Systems of Support.* Washington, DC: AAMR.

Anthony, W. A., & Blanch, A. (1987). Supported employment for persons who are psychiatrically disabled: An historical and conceptual perspective. *Psychosocial Rehabilitation Journal, 11(2)*, 5–23.

Apple, A. L., Billingsley, F., & Schwartz, I. S. (2005). Effects of video modeling alone and with self-management on compliment-giving behaviors of children with high functioning ASD. *Journal of Positive Behavior Interventions, 7*, 33–46.

Baker, W. R., Seltzer, G. B., & Seltzer, M. M. (1977). *As Close as Possible: Community Resident for Adults*. Boston, MA: Little, Brown.

Bond, G. R., Drake, R. E., Mueser, K. T., & Becker, D. R. (1997). An update on supported employment for people with severe mental illness. *Psychiatric Services, 48*, 335–346.

Browning, P. L., Dunn, C., Rabren, K., & Whetstone (1995). Post-school outcomes for students with disabilities: A U.S. synopsis. *Issues in Special Education and Rehabilitation, 10*(1), 31–37.

Clark, G. M., Patton, J. R., & Moulton, L. R. (2000). Informal assessments for transition planning. Austin, TX: Pro-ed.

Coyle, C. & Cole, P. (2004). A videotaped self-modeling and self-monitoring treatment program to decrease off-task behaviour in children with autism. *Journal of Intellectual & Developmental Disability, 29*, 3–15.

deFur, S. & Patton, J. (1999). *Transition and School-Based Service: Perspectives for Enhancing the Transition Process*. Austin, TX: Pro-Ed.

Drake, R. E., McHugo, G. J., Bebout, R. R., Becker, D. R., Harris, M., Bond, G. R., & Quimby, E. (1999). A randomized clinical trial of supported employment for inner-city patients with severe mental illness. *Archives of General Psychiatry, 56*, 627–633.

Flexer, R. W., Simmons, T. J., Luft, P., & Baer R. M. (2005). *Transition Planning for Secondary Students with Disabilities*, 2nd edn., Columbus, OH: Pearson, Merrill, Prentice Hall.

Gollay, E., Freedman, R. Wyngaarden, M, & Kurtz, N. R. (1978). *Coming Back*. Cambridge, MA: Abt Associates.

Hanley-Maxwell, C. (1989). An analysis of job terminations by length of time on the job for persons with severe disabilities in supported employment. *Rehabilitation Counseling Bulletin, 33*(2), 159–162.

Harris, L. & Associates, Inc. (1986). *The ICD Survey of Disabled Americans: Bringing Disabled Americans into the Mainstream.* New York: Author.

Harrison. P. & Oakland, T. (2003). *Adaptive Behavior Assessment System II: Manual.* San Antonio, TX: Harcourt Assessment.

Heward, W. L. (2006). *Exceptional Children: An Introduction to Special Education*, 8th edn., Columbus, Ohio: Pearson Merrill Prentice Hall.

Johnson, D. R. (2005). Key provisions on transition: A comparison of IDEA 1997 and IDEA 2004. *Career Development for Exceptional Individuals, 28*, 60–63.

Kohler, P. D. (1993). Best practices in transition: Substantiated or implied? *Career Development for Exceptional Individuals, 16*(2), 107–121.

Leake, D. & Black, R. (2005). *Cultural and Linguistic Diversity: Implications for Transition Personnel.* National Center on Secondary Education and Transition, Essential Tools: October 2005. Retrieved January 12, 2006, from http://www.ncset.org/publications/essentialtools/diversity/default.asp.

Martin, J. E., Woods, L. L., & Sylvester, L. (2007). Building an employment vision: Culturally attuning vocational interests, skills, and limits. In F. R. Rusch, (Ed.), *Beyond High School: Preparing Adolescents for Tomorrow's Challenges*. Columbus, OH: Prentice Hall.

McGaughey, M., Kiernan, W., McNally, L., Gilmore, D., & Keith, G. (1995). Beyond the workshop: National trends in integrated and segregated day and employment services. *Journal of the Association for Persons with Severe Handicaps, 20*, 270–285.

Mueser, K. T., Clark, R. E., Haines, M., Drake, R. E., McHugo, G. J., Bond, G. R., Essock, S. M., Becker, D. R., Wolfe, R., & Swain, K. (2004). The Hartford study of supported employment for persons with severe mental illness. *Journal of Consulting and Clinical Psychology, 72*, 479–490.

Morningstar, M. E. & Mutua, N. K. (2003). Transition to adulthood for youth with disabilities. Chapter in F. E. Obiakor, Utley, A. C., & A. F. Ratatori *Effective Education for Learners with Exceptionalities*, pp. 373–399. Oxford, UK: Elsevier Science Ltd.

National Council on Disability (2001). *Investing in Independence: Transition Recommendations for President George W. Bush.* Washington, DC: The Council.

Phelps, L. A. & Hanley-Maxwell, C. (1997). School-to-work transition for youth with disabilities: A review of outcomes and practices. *Review of Educational Research*, *67*(2), 197–226.

Rusch, F. R. (2007). *Beyond High School: Preparing Adolescents for Tomorrow's Challenges*, 2nd edn., Columbus, OH: Prentice Hall.

Rusch, F. R. & Chadsey, J. (Eds.) (1998). *Beyond High School: Transition from School-to-Work.* Pacific Grove, CA: Brooks/Cole Publishing.

Snell, M. E. & Brown, F. (2000). *Instruction of Students with Severe Disabilities*, 5th edn., Columbus, OH: Merrill.

Stancliffe, R. J., Abery, B. H., Springborg, H., & Elkin, S. (2000). Substitute decision-making and personal control: Implications for self-determination. *Mental Retardation*, *38*(5), 407–421.

Test, D. W., Aspel, N. P., & Everson, J. E. (2006). *Transition Methods for Youth with Disabilities.* Columbus, OH: Pearson Merrill Prentice Hall.

The Arc (1997). *It's Working.* (Video).

Turnbull A. P. & Turnbull, H. R. (2001). *Families, Professionals and Exceptionality: Collaborating for Empowerment*, 4th edn., Columbus, OH: Merrill Prentice Hall.

Valenzuela, R. L. & Martin, J. E. (2005). The self-directed IEP: Bridging values of diverse cultures and secondary education. *Career Development for Exceptional Individuals*, *28*, 4–14.

Wehmeyer, M. L., Agran, M., & Hughes, C. (2000). A national survey of teachers' promotion of self-determination and student-directed learning. Journal of *Special Education*, *34*(2), 58–69.

Wehmeyer, M. L. & Schwartz, M. (1997). Self-determination and positive adult outcomes: A follow-up study of youth with mental retardation or learning disabilities. *Exceptional Children*, *63*(2), 245–255.

Wert, B. Y. & Neisworth, J. T. (2003). Effects of video self-modeling on spontaneous requesting in children with autism. *Journal of Positive Behavior Interventions*, *5*, 30–34.

13

Motor Functioning and Adaptive Behavior

SARAH A. SCHOEN AND LUCY JANE MILLER

SPD Foundation, Greenwood Village, CO 80111, U.S.A.

Adaptive behavior and motor functioning are directly linked and dependent upon each other. Adaptive behavior refers to the ability to display functional skills in daily life which occur across the lifespan and in multiple settings (Shumway-Cook & Woollacott, 2001), including in one's home, school, work, and community. Motor functioning is essential for exploring and learning about the environment. As infants and toddlers master control against gravity they learn to crawl, stand, walk, and run (Kopp & McCall, 1982; Marx, 1989; Barbosa et al., 2005) and later to accomplish the many tasks of vocational, leisure, and family life.

Initially, movement is also essential to establishing reciprocal relationships with family members as the infant learns to use his/her body to signal distress, happiness, and specific needs (Ainsworth, 1982; Bowlby, 1988; Bretherton, 1992). Later, gross and fine motor skills provide the basis of interacting and playing with peers and participating in activities at home, including learning to make a bed, putting away toys, or wiping up spills on the floor.

As a child becomes older, community participation relies on motor abilities and motor control, including inhibiting movement to remain seated during a religious service, exploring a new environment to find the restroom, or walking to a friend's house. In adulthood, motor skills become foundational for functional behaviors that contribute to working, earning a living, and engaging in other essential tasks needed for survival as well as personal pleasure.

This chapter highlights the importance of the motor domain as central to adaptive functioning. The Adaptive Behavior Assessment Scale (ABAS)-II provides a valuable tool to use in a multi-method assessment process that includes evaluating motor functioning. The ABAS II Parent/Primary Caregiver Form for children birth-age 5 years and ABAS II Teacher/Daycare Provider Form for children ages 2–5 years contain the motor adaptive skill area, in addition to adaptive skill areas of communication, community use, functional pre-academics, health and safety, home/school living, leisure, self-care, self-direction, and social.

The multiple skill areas assessed by the ABAS-II provides an assessment of motor skills as well as evaluation of the impact of motor deficits on other daily adaptive skill areas. The ABAS-II, used in conjunction with diagnostic measures of motor skills, can be used to plan important interventions for motor skills as well as intervention for adaptive skills in other areas (e.g., social, communication, community use, self-care), as illustrated by the case study at the end of this chapter.

Movement, like other developmental abilities, emerges from an interaction between the individual, the environment, and the task (Chandler, 1990; Woollacott & Shumway-Cook, 1990; Rosenbaum, 1991; Eliasson, 2005). Thus, individuals generate movements to meet the demands of a task within a specific context (Henderson, 1986). One's functional capacity is determined by how successful one is at meeting the demands of the task in the environments in which tasks are performed. In their daily life, individuals perform a wide range of functional tasks that require a great variety of movement skills. The term *skilled motor behavior* refers to one's ability to adapt movement to achieve the task goal consistently and efficiently in a range of environments.

The task attributes determine, in part, the type of movement needed for success (Gentile, 1987; Gordon, 1987; Schmidt, 1988). Similarly, the environment impacts the motor skills required to complete a task (Gentile, 1987; Patla & Shumway-Cook, 1999). For example, being able to thread a needle on a moving subway requires a completely different set of postural and fine motor skills than putting one's shoes on while sitting in a chair.

As the nervous system matures, motor abilities develop as a result of the interaction of movement, postural abilities, and sensory processing. As an early theorist of motor control (Bernstein, 1967) noted that voluntary motor control is a bi-product of purposeful interactions with the environment. Newer, more complex system theories of motor control (Kelso & Tuller, 1984; Kugler & Turvey, 1987; Thelen et al., 1987; Kamm et al., 1991; Perry, 1998;

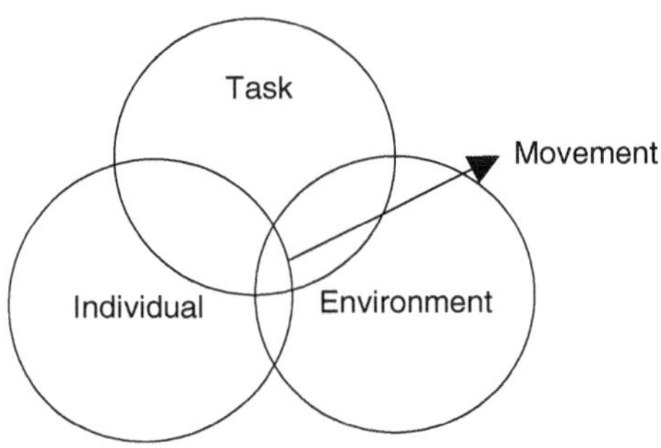

Davids et al., 2003; Wilson, 2005) elaborate on the work of Bernstein and recognize that both fine and gross motor abilities develop as a result of a complex interaction of systems within the individual and between the individual, the environment, and the task (Gordon, 1987; Horak & Shumway-Cook, 1990; Woollacott & Shumway-Cook, 1990, 1997).

Dynamic action theories of motor control (Kelso & Tuller, 1984; Kugler & Turvey, 1987; Thelen et al., 1987; Kamm et al., 1991; Perry, 1998; Davids et al., 2003; Wilson, 2005) propose that motor development results from a combination of systems within the individual, including the neuromuscular, sensory-perceptual, and musculoskeletal systems, which interact with arousal/attention, cognition/motivation, cardiovascular and respiratory efficiency, as well as nutrition and growth. Ecological theories also recognize that motor skills emerge from an interaction between the task and the environment in which tasks are performed (Woollacott & Shumway-Cook, 1990, 1997).

Interventions for children with functional skill deficits due to motor delays should consider and may be directed to all domains involved in the impairment. A skilled occupational or physical therapist assesses task performance in order to determine which system(s) is responsible for a particular functional deficit and then decides which system(s) is primarily responsible for limiting the child's skill development (Blanche, 2006).

For example, a child who is unable to get a snack from the cabinet may be unable to do so for a variety of reasons including an impairment in the musculoskeletal system that prevents him from standing on tiptoe to reach an object, an impairment in the sensory-perceptual system that results in difficulty visually discriminating the preferred snack from a distracting background, and/or an impairment in the arousal/attention system that results in difficulty focusing on the task.

Another example of the interaction of adaptive and motor function is seen in an inability to color "within the lines." Obviously this impairment also may be related a variety of problems including a musculoskeletal impairment resulting in decreased ability to grade muscle activation in the hand necessary to grasp, a sensory-perceptual impairment interfering with accurate sensory feedback from proprioceptive receptors that sense activation of muscles and joints to perform the desired movement, and/or cognitive impairment resulting in decreased motivation, reducing a child's desire to learn the task.

Motor skill acquisition is supported by developing postural control (Westcott & Burtner, 2004). Postural control refers to the ability to assume and maintain postures during static (still: e.g., sitting in a chair) and dynamic (moving: e.g., playing baseball) activities (Shumway-Cook & Woollacott, 2001). Postural control occurs in a relatively predictable sequence of progressively more challenging positions against gravity (i.e., supine, prone, sitting, and standing) (Gessell, 1928; McGraw, 1963; Campbell, 1981; Brazelton, 1984; Bly, 1991). Various components of movement are necessary to achieve motor maturity. First, stability and mobility must be integrated (Howle, 2002). The trunk, shoulders, and hips comprise the primary locations for stability and control. The upper and lower extremities are the more mobile segments of the body. Almost all movements combine well-functioning mobility with adequate stability. For example, when batting at a ball, one's feet must be stable on the ground, with back and abdominal muscles working to hold the body upright (stability); meanwhile the arms swing the bat at the ball (mobility). Similarly, when sitting in a chair doing homework, stable abdominals, back, hips, and legs, as well as shoulders must support the body so that the fingers can have automatic controlled mobility for writing.

Alignment of the body over the base of support is another important concept in motor skill development. Alignment prevents us from falling each time we engage in an activity (Zernicke & Schneider, 1993; Bradley, 2000; Gajdosik & Gajdosik, 2000). Appropriate balance is achieved when we control the position of our body as it rests over a support surface. For example, when sitting, our hips support our body weight and allow movement forward, backward, and side-to-side as needed to accomplish a task. Also, when standing, our legs and trunk provide the position of support around which we can accomplish tasks.

In addition, to perform tasks in the most efficient manner, our limbs must be able to move freely and to be independent of one another. An attempt to reach to grab or hit an object represents an early pattern of *dissociation* (e.g., the arms work independently of each other to complete a task). Early in development, when an infant swats at a toy, both hands move together in an associated pattern (bilateral reach). As the child matures, one hand can move in one direction towards a toy (unilateral reach) while the other hand does something else.

Adequate processing of sensation and sensory feedback constitutes another important construct related to developing motor skills (Thelen et al., 1993). For example, when persons pick up a cup, sensations are recorded in the muscles and joints that describe the attributes of the cup (e.g., weight, size, and position), incuding how far the cup must move to reach one's lips. Using sensory feedback, anticipatory control emerges, a mechanism by which the body remembers movements so that the individual can focus on the goal-directed outcome. This process involves a feed-forward mechanism of control (Keele & Summers, 1976; Kelso, 1976; Stelmach, 1976).

Sensory feedback refines the goal-directed outcome of movement. For example, if the paper cup were made of a heavy ceramic material, the arm/hand would automatically adjust the grasp, strength, and timing in order to successfully complete picking up and moving the cup. Simply knowing the cognitive aspect of the attributes of the cup is not adequate for successful completion of the functional task. The motor patterns are critical to accomplishing the task efficiently and safely. All functional skills are the result of this complex interaction between motor, sensory, and cognitive components of the task within an ever-changing environment (Howle, 2002).

Children with developmental delays often display motor skill problems that interfere with the acquisition of adaptive behaviors and other developmental skills, including their self-care, communication, social interaction, academic readiness, and emotional regulation. For example, in self-care, the task of brushing teeth requires the motor pattern of bringing the hand to the mouth, grasping the toothbrush with appropriate force, and rotating the forearm to orient the brush properly in the mouth. In communication, motor control problems in the lips and tongue can produce articulation errors. In social interactions, a child unable to keep up with his or her peers is likely to be at risk for making and keeping friends and may experience diminished self-esteem. Emotional issues may result from the inadequate social interactions resulting in withdrawal, anxiety, and decreased feelings of self-worth. Emotional repercussions from the child's motor problems may be significant, potentially having a considerable impact on the child's adaptive functioning. Many academic readiness skills also are dependent on fine motor abilities. Measures of preschool performance often assess fine motor skills.

Motor delays constitute the hallmark of certain developmental disorders, including Cerebral Palsy and Down syndrome, and may be a component of other conditions, including autism, fragile X syndrome, and mental retardation. Early identification of motor delays allows for timely intervention and opportunity to impact a developing central nervous system (Harris & Brady, 1986).

Various intervention frames of reference can address motor skill deficits. Commonly, neurodevelopmental treatment (NDT) and occupational therapy using a sensory integration approach (OT/SI) are utilized. NDT is used frequently for the therapeutic management and treatment of children with Cerebral Palsy. Based on the work of Karl and Berta Bobath (1984), NDT emphasizes analyzing the coordination of posture and movement and determining impairments that interfere with the acquisition of functional skills. Using NDT, the therapist chooses from strategies that address the impairments of the client (Larin, 2000). Therapists use a hands-on approach to facilitate or change aspects of the posture and movement system, promoting successful interactions with the environment (Bobath, 1959; Bobath & Bobath, 1964; Girolami et al., 2001).

Movements generated by multiple body systems include both feedback and feed-forward sensory mechanisms, conditions necessary during the early phases for learning new movements. Following repetition, motor learning transpires because an internal representation of the movement has occurred in the central nervous system, thus allowing the movement patterns to be repeated automatically (Bly, 1996; Whiteside, 1997). Referring back to the cup example, one doesn't have to concentrate about picking a cup because this movement involving the arm and hands already has been learned. The motor preparation of the arm and hand for this activity is called *anticipatory postural control.* This anticipatory postural control is a feed-forward sensory process that does not rely on sensory feedback and allows movements to be efficient (Patla & Shumway-Cook, 1999). For example, sensory feedback is necessary only if the cup is heavier, a different size or shape, or is in a different position than anticipated. Then the activity is modified by sensory feedback so that the task can be completed successfully.

An alteration in the previously prepared motor pattern follows the occurrence of an unexpected motor modification. For example, when playing tennis, the forehand

and backhand strokes need to become automatic and a part of the basic repertoire of motor patterns so that the individual can focus on strategies to refine the movements needed to direct placement of the ball on the court. The initial stage of learning results in establishing feed-forward mechanisms. However, strategies for winning the game rely on sensory feedback for specific placement.

NDT requires the active participation of the child to initiate and complete movements that are directed toward the functional goal (Schmidt, 1991). The end result of this motor intervention is the implementation of new motor skills into daily life activities in real life settings (Diamond & Schenkman, 1996).

Occupational therapy, using a sensory integration approach (OT/SI), also is widely used to address delays in motor skill development. Based on the work of A. Jean Ayres (A.J. Ayres, 1972b), sensory integration theory highlights the importance of accurate sensory processing while engaged in physical, social, and academic learning. Ayres proposed that many mental and social functions are based upon a foundation of accurate sensorimotor processing. She hypothesized that the sensory input and motor responses that occur as one moves, talks, and plays provide the foundation for more complex skills, including reading, writing, and behavioral control. Additionally, when a child's sensory processing abilities are sufficient to meet the demands of an ever-changing environment, adaptive behaviors emerge, leading to successful daily life functioning in the motor, social, emotional, and academic domains.

As defined by Ayres, sensory integration refers to "... our ability to organize sensations for use" (Ayres, 1972b). Thus, sensory integration includes making appropriate responses based on detecting, modulating, and organizing sensory information from the body and environment. The process of receiving, interpreting, and making an organized response to sensory information becomes an unconscious process that, when successful, allows purposeful responses. A well-organized, accurate flow of correctly interpreted sensations from the body contributes to the development of emotional stability and hence to social participation. In addition, it provides the prerequisites for motor skill development, including body awareness, postural control, and motor planning abilities.

Occupational therapy using a sensory integration approach emphasizes the analysis of strengths and impairments in sensory systems that interfere with the acquisition of functional skills. This approach involves the use of *clinical reasoning* (Mattingly & Fleming, 1994), that is, a problem-solving approach that allows the therapist to use various sensory strategies to address the adaptive behavior problems displayed by the client. The skillful use of sensory input, particularly in the tactile, proprioceptive, and vestibular systems, helps establish foundational abilities to feel one's body and to move and respond to gravity. Once these are established, higher level skills (e.g., adaptive behaviors and cognitive abilities) can develop (Ayres, 1972a; Bundy et al., 2002).

The seven sensory systems utilized in therapy include those that provide information from outside the body, where one's body in space, and the direction and rate of body movement (Smith Roley, 2006).

The visual sense (i.e., sight) interprets what is seen. For example, recognition of shapes, colors, letters, words, and numbers depends on the visual system. Vision frequently guides our movements, is one of three senses related to balance, and permits continually monitoring of actions resulting in safe and effective movement.

The auditory sense (i.e., hearing) relates the quality and directionality of sound. Audition allows us to turn our heads toward a car that we hear approaching. Auditory sensation permits the understanding of speech and thus is related to communication adequacy.

The gustatory sense (i.e., taste) provides information about characteristics of food (e.g., whether they are salty, spicy, sour, bitter, or sweet). This system enhances one's ability to stay alive by creating enjoyable or satisfying responses to eating.

The olfactory sense (i.e., smell) enhances the gustatory sense and is directly tied to the limbic system, resulting in memories and associations occurring when one smells something familiar.

The tactile sense (i.e., touch) provides information about the characteristics of objects in the world, specifically shape, size, and texture. Two discrete nervous system pathways for tactile information exist. One is the *light touch* system that provides a protective mechanism to warn us of danger in our surroundings. When functioning well, it engenders a feeling of safety and permits close bonding. The second system, the *discriminative* system, permits knowledge of the discrete characteristics of objects leading to proficient tool use.

The vestibular sense (i.e., sense of position and movement) provides information about movement, balance, and the relation of one's body to gravity by using its receptors located in the inner ear and pathways throughout the nervous system and body.

The proprioceptive system (i.e., sensations from the joints and muscles) provides information that contributes to our awareness of body position. Proprioception allows a person to guide his arm or leg movement without having to observe every action. Proprioception is the third sensation, along with the visual and vestibular senses, that control automatic balancing – a condition necessary for survival, including the performance of skilled tasks.

A new uniform taxonomy describing functional sensory deficits has been proposed recently and is being widely adopted (Miller et al., 2004). In the new nosology, three subtypes define the groupings of children with Sensory Processing Disorder: (1) Sensory Modulation Disorder, for example difficulty regulating sensory input, which includes sensory over-responsivity, sensory under-responsivity and sensory seeking; (2) Sensory Discrimination Disorder, – for example difficulty interpreting sensory input (*b* and a *d* may look the same, the words *cat* and *cap* may sound the same, and a *quarter* and a *nickel* may feel the same); and (3) Sensory-Based Motor Disorders – that is, difficulty organizing an efficient and effective motor response based on poor sensory processing. These sensory deficits affect motor functioning and contribute to postural disorder and/or dyspraxia.

This terminology formed the basis of two recently published diagnostic taxonomies: the Interdisciplinary Council for Developmental and Learning Disorders: Diagnostic Manual (2005) and the Diagnostic Classification: Zero to Three (Zero To Three, 2005).

A child with Sensory Processing Disorder may have delays in motor skill development similar to a child with Cerebral Palsy or Developmental Coordination Disorder. However, the etiology of motor-only and sensory-based motor disorders suggests different interventions. Remedial interventions with those who display Cerebral Palsy and Developmental Coordination Disorder focus on *motor* impairments to achieve adaptive behaviors (Henderson et al., 1992; Silver, 1988; Wilson, 2005). The likely intervention will utilize a NDT, a *hands-on* approach that activates muscles leading to the development of new patterns of movement and the successful performance of daily adaptive functioning.

However, a Sensory Processing Disorder must be treated by focusing on the *sensory* basis of the interference with the development of higher-level abilities, including adaptive behaviors. For example, a child with a strictly motor problem may have too much spasticity to coordinate the muscle co-activation necessary to fluidly catch a moving ball. However, a child with a Sensory-Based Motor Disorder who has difficulty catching a ball may have one or more disorders, including visual-spatial impairments – being unable to judge his distance from the ball, a proprioceptive impairment (e.g., poor feedback from muscles and joints) – difficulty with the anticipatory control of the limbs needed to line his body up with the trajectory of the ball, and/or an auditory filtering impairment – difficulty ignoring distracting background sounds in the environment resulting in poor ability to focus on the task of catching the ball.

Children with a Sensory Processing Disorder commonly display social and emotional difficulties. Their motor difficulties often result in their withdrawal from peers, decreased participation in many activities of daily living, and decreased self-confidence and self-esteem. The display of deficits in adaptive skills at home, in school, and in community events may become increasingly apparent with age.

Consistent with NDT, the process of occupational therapy using a sensory integration requires active participation. With therapist guidance (but not using specific hands-on techniques), the child actively generates and organizes sensory input for successful interaction with the environment (Bundy & Murray, 2002; Ayres, 2005). The therapist interacts one on one with the child in a room with specialized equipment that taps foundational sensory systems (vestibular, proprioceptive, and tactile systems) as well as the more common sensory systems. This environment is designed specifically to motivate the child and encourage his/her engagement in an activity that challenges him/her. The art of therapy is to provide the correct challenge to the child, with adequate scaffolding, so that every challenge can be completed successfully. The child's imagination may be engaged through thematic play to enhance motivation and entice the child to interact with sensory materials in a meaningful and fun manner. When therapy is successful, the child's inner drive is tapped and he/she engages spontaneously in activities.

The therapeutic alliance with the child, as well as a safe environment, facilitates the child's trust, promotes engagement, and encourages the child to accept activities that provide increasing challenges.

A casual observer of a child engaged in this type of intervention may think that the therapist and the child are "only playing." However, the activities utilize methods that stimulate all seven sensory systems to facilitate growth and development of the posture and movement systems, enhance sensory feedback to the muscles and joints, and facilitate an optimal state of arousal. The goal is to prime children for higher level and more complex tasks such as learning and adaptive behaviors. Learning occurs through the repetition of successfully interpreted sensations and responses that are organized and effective. Children's motor competency generally increases and they begin to display behaviors and the ability to participate in age-appropriate adaptive behaviors. The more talented the therapist, the more these diverse goals appear like "play."

Occupational therapy, using a sensory integration frame of reference, strives to improve gross and fine motor skills. Intervention facilitates consistent and more complex motor responses. The child is continually presented with new motor challenges that help develop needed motor skills, leading to improved self-confidence and mastery in the motor domain. Discrete skills never are practiced during intervention. Instead, the goal is to establish the foundational abilities needed for the emergence of adaptive skills, such as those assessed by the ABAS II, including community use, communication, pre-academic and functional academics, self-direction, home and school living, self-care, and social interaction.

ABAS-II CASE STUDY

Alex, a delightful 4-year, 3-month-old boy, attends preschool from 9:00 to 3:00 daily. He was diagnosed with mild Cerebral Palsy by the child developmental unit at a children's hospital and referred to the therapy center for further occupational therapy evaluation and possible intervention.

The parents raised four primary concerns at the intake interview. First, Alex displayed problems with motor skill performance. He had impaired balance and coordination when walking, running, and climbing; decreased strength and endurance; and an unwillingness to try new tasks. Alex's fine motor abilities also were of concern (e.g., he was unable to hold a crayon properly or draw a picture).

Secondly, Alex had difficulty accommodating to sensory stimuli, for example screening out background noise or visual distractions and recognizing his need to go to the bathroom. This impacted his willingness to play with other children.

Third, Alex displayed decreased awareness of tongue and mouth movements, resulting in articulation errors and drooling. Combined with his poor eye contact during verbal exchanges, he was further limited in social participation.

And fourth, Alex was emotionally labile. He had extremely poor self-regulation skills and a tendency to melt-down in public. A multi-method assessment was conducted that included standardized performance measures (e.g., the Miller Assessment for Preschoolers and the Beery Test of Visual Motor Integration), parent and teacher report scales (e.g., the Adaptive Behavior Assessment System-II, Short Sensory Profile), and clinical observations in the therapy gym. These methods provided information needed for diagnosis and intervention by identifying impairments in sensory-motor foundations, motor coordination, verbal and nonverbal skills, sensory modulation, and adaptive skill areas (communication, community use, functional pre-academics, home/school living, health and safety, leisure, self-care, self-direction, social interaction, and motor adaptive skill areas) at home, school, or other settings.

The parents expressed concerns about the impact of Alex's motor limitations on his adaptive behavior. Results of the ABAS II Parent/Primary Caregiver Form for children birth-age 5 years, completed by Alex's parents, and ABAS II Teacher/Daycare Provider Form for children ages 2–5 years, completed by Alex's preschool teacher, confirmed Alex's deficits in adaptive behavior, compared to other children his age. The ABAS-II scores are provided in Table 13.1. The General Adaptive Composites standard scores from parent and teacher forms were comparable; both were at the 1st percentile compared to other children Alex's age and classified as extremely low. Similarly, parent and teacher scores were classified as extremely low for the Conceptual and Practical composites and as borderline for the Social composite. For the specific adaptive skill areas, most scores for the parent and teacher forms were in the borderline range and consistent between parents and teacher, including consistent parent and teacher scores in the motor adaptive skill area. Scores for the social adaptive skill area were in the below average range on both parent and teacher forms. There were a few inconsistencies between parent and teacher scores for the ABAS-II adaptive skill areas. Parent scores for the self-direction and health and safety adaptive skills areas were in the below average range; in addition teacher scores for the self-direction adaptive skill area were in the extremely low range Parent scores for the self-care adaptive skill area were in the extremely low range.

The ABAS-II results identified several adaptive skill deficits that may be due to Alex's motor limitations. For example, due to delays in the gross motor development, Alex was reported on the ABAS-II forms as being unable to run without falling or to catch a ball tossed to him. Due to his fine motor delays, he is unable to independently cut with a scissor, hold a crayon properly, or color within the lines. He is unable to spontaneously draw a picture of a person.

The ABAS-II data also identified concerns about other adaptive skill areas. On the ABAS II, the following leisure and community use skills were identified as never or almost never being displayed when needed: inviting others to join in playing games, attending activities at another's home, finding a restroom in a public place, crossing a street or parking lot, and asking to go to the library or participating in an organized sport. Social skills concerns were noted related to Alex's inability to share toys willingly, to seek friendships with others, and with his tendency to become upset when a friend played with someone else.

TABLE 13.1 Results of the ABAS-II (Parent/Primary Caregiver Ages 0–5, and Teacher/Daycare Ages 2–5) for Alex, Age 4

	Adaptive Skill Area Scaled Score	Composite Standard Score	Composite Percentile Rank	Composite Score Classification
Parent/Primary Caregiver Form Composites and Adaptive Skill Areas				
General Adaptive Composite (GAC)		62	1	Extremely low
Conceptual Composite		67	1	Extremely low
• Communication	4			
• Functional pre-academics	5			
• Self-direction	6			
Social Composite		71	3	Borderline
• Leisure	4			
• Social	7			
Practical Composite		65	1	Extremely low
• Community use	5			
• Home living	5			
• Health and safety	6			
• Self-care	3			
Motor adaptive skill area	4			
Teacher/Daycare Provider Form Composites and Adaptive Skill Areas				
GAC		65	1	Extremely low
Conceptual Composite		64	1	Extremely low
• Communication	5			
• Functional pre-academics	5			
• Self-direction	3			
Social Composite		73	4	Borderline
• Leisure	4			
• Social	7			
Practical Composite		66	1	Extremely low
• School living	5			
• Health and safety	5			
• Self-care	5			
Motor adaptive skill area	4			

Note: Composites (Conceptualization, Social, and Practical) and the GAC have standard scores with a mean of 100 and standard deviation of 15. Adaptive skill areas (Communication, Functional academics, etc.) have scaled scores with a mean of 10 and standard deviation of 3. Motor scores are included in calculating the GAC, but not other composites.

Parent information obtained through the Short Sensory Profile indicated Alex's sensory over-responsivity in the tactile, auditory, visual and movement domains (with scores −3.0 standard deviations below the mean). Alex is easily overwhelmed and distressed by typical amounts of sensory stimuli commonly found in the environment (e.g., while dressing and grooming). These findings were cross-validated by scores on a number of items on the ABAS II, such as items on the self-care adaptive skills area measuring skills needed to dress oneself, sit on the toilet or potty, wipe face, wash hair, or brush teeth.

Standardized performance measures (i.e., the Miller Assessment for Preschoolers and the Beery Test of Visual Motor Integration) were consistent with results from the ABAS II. Alex obtained subtest scores 2 standard deviations below the mean on the Miller Assessment for Preschoolers, for example Foundations Index (measuring underlying neurological and sensory foundations), Coordination Index (measuring gross and fine motor skills) and Complex Tasks Index (measuring tasks requiring the integration of motor and visual abilities). Although Alex demonstrated average performance in nonverbal cognitive tasks (e.g., tasks that involved puzzles, visual matching, visual memory, and figure ground perception), deficits were noted in visual motor integration, affecting his ability to color and draw. His scores on the Beery Test of Visual Motor Integration were 1.5 standard deviations below the mean on all subtests.

Additional clinical observations in the therapy gym confirmed a diagnosis of Sensory Processing Disorder with a combination of sensory over-responsivity, postural disorder, and dyspraxia subtypes. Alex's motor planning problems were observed particularly in his interactions with gym equipment, particularly his inability to sequence multiple step tasks. The ABAS-II results cross-validated clinical information reporting that Alex had difficulty in following simple commands that included spatial concepts. Alex also had difficulty filtering relevant from irrelevant information, thus interfering with his ability to remember the steps needed for task completion. He was overwhelmed easily and needed time to relax following an activity in order to maximize his subsequent task performance. Without breaks, he quickly became emotionally upset and was unable to perform.

Alex's decreased muscle tone and postural control, muscle weakness, and low endurance contributed to his inadequate awareness of his body in space. This exacerbated his delays in gross and fine motor skill performance. His articulation errors were attributable to his poor oral awareness and faulty tongue position as well as overall muscle weakness and decreased motor control.

These evaluation results suggested impairments that appear related to Alex's presenting problems with motor coordination, emotional regulation, social interactions, and articulation. Many of his difficulties with adaptive skills are likely due to his motor incoordination and emotional lability, which often occur when a child has sensory overreactivity to unexpected sensory input. Alex's tendency to become overwhelmed and disengage in crowded settings and to avoid participation in playground and sports activities is likely to be due to his over-responsiveness to sensory input in these settings.

Difficulties with motor planning impacted many aspects of Alex's life. Alex's cognitive strengths provided many opportunities for him, but also made him acutely aware of his challenges. He became frustrated when he does not perform to his own expectations or failed to learn new activities. His emotional responses to his motor impairments were more detrimental to Alex's adaptive behavior than his specific motor deficits. His decreased willingness to attempt new tasks, to interact with peers, and to participate in school activities were causing Alex to experience programs in school. His self-esteem was plummeting.

The first stage of Alex's intervention focused on increasing his self-confidence and self-esteem and reducing the sensory over-responsivity affecting his unwillingness to engage in challenging motor activities. Alex's motivation to succeed provided a needed impetus for him to engage in challenging activities. Sensory stimuli were graded in the amount and duration of sensation he received, gradually increasing his tolerance. Movement activities first were conducted with his feet touching the floor to reduce his over-responsivity to vestibular stimulation. Hands-on facilitation maximized his posture, alignment, and control in a sitting position. A gradual increase in the amount of movement and proprioceptive inputs in the therapeutic activities provided feedback to his muscles and joints and helped regulate his sensitivity to the vestibular stimuli.

A functional component related to Alex's presenting deficits in adaptive behavior was integrated into each activity. For example, Alex would draw targets on the wall for games he played on the suspended movement equipment. This later led to his drawing a picture of a head with the therapist inserting the facial features. Alex signed all drawings as he was beginning to form the letter 'A' to acknowledge his success. To assist the teacher, Alex started to receive regular sensory breaks, (e.g., washing desks and/or drying erase board, carrying heavy books, playing with a fidget toy or using a weighted lap pad) to prevent over-stimulation in the classroom. In addition, picture schedules assisted him to sequence and execute daily classroom tasks.

Alex made important functional gains during his 4 months, three times a week occupational therapy. Post-testing included Miller Assessment for Preschoolers, the Beery Test of Visual Motor Integration, the Adaptive Behavior Assessment System-II, and the Short Sensory Profile. Scores revealed improvement in all domains. Alex's scores on the Miller Assessment for Preschoolers increased from −2 SD to normal (+1.2 SD) on the Foundations Index and to +1.5 on the Coordination Index. His scores on the Beery Test of Visual Motor Integration also increased to within normal limits (−0.5 SD). He drew a simple but discernable picture of a person. Data on the Short Sensory Profile showed a significant improvement in his sensory over-responsivity scores to within normal limits in all but one sensory domain, movement (score = −2.0SD). Thus, residual sensory over-responsivity in the movement domain remained.

Alex displayed an increased willingness to try new motor tasks and improved coordination, strength, and endurance when walking, running, or climbing. He could catch and throw a ball from a distance of 10 feet as well as bat a stationary

T-ball. He made better eye contact during verbal interactions, and his articulation improved. However, safety on the playground and his ability to maintain an optimal level of arousal remained important issues. A continued home program was suggested, including deep pressure and muscle/joint input (aka. heavy work activities) to help regulate his energy level and reduce potential for over-arousal. This type of input also will continue to enhance feedback to his skin, muscles, and joints and improve his body awareness and motor planning abilities.

Children like Alex who display strong cognitive abilities and weaknesses in the sensory motor domain and in self-regulation often need individualized occupational therapy to address the sensory and motor impairments that impact the development of age-appropriate adaptive behavior. Adaptive behavior assessments of young children should include an assessment of the motor adaptive skill area to evaluate whether underlying issues may be contributing to deficits in adaptive behavior. Clinicians must be knowledgeable regarding the contribution of motor impairments to adaptive and academic functioning. Proper integration of therapy programs in clinics and at home and in classrooms can promote social participation, self-regulation, and self-esteem. A multi-disciplinary approach is needed to promote adaptive behavior and skill performance in community and academic settings.

ASSESSMENT OF MOTOR FUNCTION

The use of multiple sources of assessment data is critical to intervention decisions (Foster & Cone, 1980; Haynes & O'Brien, 2000). Information from behavioral report-measures (Clayton et al., 2003; Achenbach & Rescorla, 2004) that is cross-validated by data from performance assessment (Baranek & Berkson, 1994) provide the most accurate predictions and have the greatest utility when planning interventions. Thus, the use of multiple evaluation tools, using multiple assessment methods and sources of information, is recommended to provide various sources of data, including direct performance assessments, clinical observations, parent and teacher reports, and caregiver interviews.

Table 13.2 exhibits sensory and motor assessments that can used with the ABAS-II in a comprehensive, multi-method assessment of motor functioning and adaptive skills (Campbell, 1981; Miller, 1982, 1988, 2006; Miller & Roid, 1994; Piper & Darrah, 1994; Dunn, 1999, 2002; Bayley, 2000; Case-Smith & Bigsby, 2000; Folio & Fewell, 2000; Ulrich, 2000; Bruininks, 2006; Parham et al., 2007). These particular tests were selected for the table because of their high frequency of use in professions that work with young children with motor coordination difficulties. Examiners must assure that the referral questions about a child match the purpose for which the assessment method or test was developed and that the psychometric characteristics of the test provide an adequate and accurate assessment of motor performance, answering the specific questions that the assessment was chosen to answer.

TABLE 13.2 Selected Sensory and Motor Assessments

Motor scales	Purpose	Type of test	Age	Domain	Reliability	Validity
Bayley, N. (2005). *Bayley Scales of Infant and Toddler Development*, 3rd edn., San Antonio, TX: Harcourt Assessment.	Assessment of developmental motor delays and assists in designing intervention.	Norm referenced	1 month to 42 months of age.	Cognition, Language Motor, Social-Emotional and Adaptive Behavior	*Internal consistency reliability Subtests*: $r = .86–.91$	Concurrent validity – with the Peabody, Preschool Language Scale, WPPSI-III and ABAS-II Discriminant validity – Discriminated between children with and without disabilities.
Case-Smith, J. & Bigsby, R. (2000). *Posture and Fine Motor Assessment for Infants (PFMAI)*, San Antonio, TX: Harcourt Assessment.	Used to assess fine motor abilities, plan intervention and track progress.	Norm and criterion referenced tool	2 to 12 months old	Postural Control, Proximal Stability/ Mobility, Fine Motor Grasping Patterns, Finger and Thumb Movements, Release and Manipulation	*Interrater reliability*: $r = .96$	Concurrent validity – with the Peabody Fine Motor Quotient, $r = .84$
Piper, M. & Darrah, J. (1994). *Alberta Infant Motor Scale (AIMS)*. NY: Elsevier.	Assessment of gross motor development	Norm referenced, performance based	2 to 18 months old	Motor performance, Weight-Bearing, Posture, and Antigravity Control	*Intrarater and interrater reliability*: $r = .97–.99$.	Scores correlated with the Bayley at 6 and 12 months ($r = .78$ and .90).
Folio, M. R. & Fewell, R. R. (2000). *Peabody Developmental*	Assessment of developmental motor skills and assists in	Diagnostic or screening tool	Birth to 5 years old	Reflexes, Balance, Locomotion, Object Manipulation, Grasping, and Visual	*Interrater reliability*: $r = .99$ *Test-retest reliability*: $ICC = .95$	Concurrent validity with other tests of motor development, including the Bayley.

(*Continued*)

TABLE 13.2 *(Continued)*

Motor scales	Purpose	Type of test	Age	Domain	Reliability	Validity
Motor Scales, 2nd edn., Los Angeles, CA: WPS.	program planning.			Motor Integration		
Henderson, S. E. & Sugden, D. A. (1992). *Movement Assessment Battery for Children*. San Antonio, TX: Harcourt Assessment.	Assessment of movement performance	Norm referenced	4 to 12 years	Manual Dexterity, Ball Skills, Static and Dynamic Balance Skills	*Interrater reliability*: $ICC \geqslant .70$ *Test-retest reliability*: $ICC \geqslant .75$	Correlated with scores on the Bruininks
Miller, L. J. & Roid, G. H. (1994). *Toddler and Infant Motor Evaluation* (*TIME*). San Antonio, TX: Harcourt Assessment.	Comprehensive assessment of quality of movement and motor abilities	Norm referenced	4 month to 3.5 years old	Mobility, Motor Organization, Stability, Functional Performance and Social/Emotional Abilities	*Interrater*: $r = .90–.99$ *Test-retest reliability*: $r = .97–.99$	Construct validity – age trends present for the functional performance test.
Miller, L. J. (1982, 1988). *Miller Assessment for*	Assessment of developmental status across	Norm referenced, screening	2.9 years to 5.8 years	Foundation Index (sensory-motor abilities)	*Interrater*: $r = .98$ *Test-Retest reliability*: 81% of group performed	Criterion Related Validity – significantly correlated to WISC, ITPA, and DDST.

Preschoolers (MAP). Los Angeles, CA: WPS.	multiple domains	tool		Coordination Index, Verbal and Nonverbal Abilities, Visuospatial/Complex Abilities	the test similarly between two trials	
Miller, L. J. (2006). *Miller Function and Participation Scales (M-FUN)*. San Antonio, TX: Harcourt Assessment.	Assessment of motor skills in the performance of functional tasks.	Norm referenced	02.6 to 07.11 years old.	Visual Motor, Fine Motor and Gross Motor	*Interrater reliability*: visual motor .91 Fine motor .93 Gross motor .91. *Test-retest reliability*: visual motor .77 fine motor .82 gross motor .77	Criterion Related Validity – significantly correlated to MAP (r = .47 to .83).
Ulrich, D. (2000). *Test of Gross Motor Development*, 2nd edn., San Antonio, TX: Harcourt Assessment.	Assessment of functional motor skills	Criterion, norm referenced screening tool	3 to 10 years old	Locomotion and Object Control	Interrater reliability (as estimated by generalizability theory) 1–4% variance between raters	Construct Validity – r = .81 to .87
Bruininks, R. & Bruininks, B. (2006). *Bruininks – Oseretsky Test of Motor Proficiency*, 2nd edn., Bloomington, MN: Pearson Assessments.	Assessment of fine and gross motor abilities	Diagnostic, norm referenced screening tool	4.5 to 14.5 years old	Running Speed and Agility, Balance, Bilateral Coordination, Strength, Upper Limb Speed and Dexterity	*Test-retest reliability – subtests*: r = .69–77 *composite scores*: r = .77–.83. *Internal consistency reliability subtests*: r = .70–.89 *composite scores*: r = .85–.93	Evidence for validity include factor analytic, correlational and clinical discrimination studies which support use as a general measure of motor abilities.

(*Continued*)

TABLE 13.2 (Continued)

Sensory scales	Purpose	Type of test	Population	Domains	Reliability	Validity
Parham, D. & Ecker, C.; Miller-Kuhaneck, H., Henry, D. & Glennon, T. (2007). *Sensory Processing Measure: Home and Classroom.* Los Angeles, CA: WPS.	Assessment of sensory processing problems in different environments	Norm referenced rating scales	5 to 11 years old	Praxis, Social Participation and Visual, Auditory, Tactile, Proprioceptive and Vestibular functioning.	*Test-retest reliability*: $r = .94–.98$	Evidence for validity include factor analytic, correlational and clinical discrimination studies.
Dunn, W. (1999). *Sensory Profile.* San Antonio, TX: Harcourt Assessment.	Assesses responses to sensory events in everyday life	Criterion referenced screening tool	Children 5 to 10 years old	Sensory Processing, Sensory Modulation, Behavioral and Emotional Responses	*Internal Consistency*: $\alpha = 0.47–0.91$	Content validity – established by expert clinicians. Discriminant validity – discriminated between children with and without disabilities.
Dunn, W. (2002). *Infant/Toddler Sensory Profile.* San Antonio, TX: Harcourt Assessment.	Assesses responses to sensory events in everyday life in very young children	Criterion referenced screening tool	Birth to 36 months	Sensory Processing, Sensory Modulation, Behavioral and Emotional Responses	*Internal Consistency*: $\alpha = 0.42–0.85$	Content validity – established by expert clinicians Discriminant validity – discriminated between children with and without disabilities.

REFERENCES

Achenbach, T. M. & Rescorla, L. A. (2004). Empirically based assessments and taxonomy: Applications to infants and toddlers. In R. DelCarmen-Wiggins, & A. Carter (Eds.), *Handbook of Infant, Toddler and Preschool Mental Health Assessment*, pp. 161–182. New York: Oxford University Press.

Ainsworth, M. D. S. (1982). Attachment: Retrospect and prospect. In C. M. Parkes, & J. Stevenson-Hinde (Eds.), *The Place of Attachment in Human Behavior*, pp. 3–30. New York, NY: Basic Books.

Ayres, A. J. (1972a). Improving academic scores through sensory integration. *Journal of Learning Disabilities*, *5*(6), 338–343.

Ayres, A. J. (1972b). *Sensory Integration and Learning Disorders*. Los Angeles: Western Psychological Services.

Ayres, A. J. (2005). What is sensory integration: An introduction to the concept. In *Sensory Integration and the Child: Understanding Hidden Sensory Challenges, 25th Anniversary Edition*, pp. 1–12. Los Angeles, California: Western Psychological Services.

Baranek, G. T. & Berkson, G. (1994). Tactile defensiveness in children with developmental disabilities: Responsiveness and habituation. *Journal of Autism and Developmental Disorders*, *24*(4), 457–471.

Barbosa, V. M., Campbell, S. K., et al. (2005). Comparison of test of infant motor performance (TIMP) item responses among children with cerebral palsy, developmental delay, and typical development. *American Journal of Occupational Therapy*, *59*(4), 446–456.

Bayley, N. (2000). *Bayley Scales of Infant Development*, 3rd edn., San Antonio, TX: Harcourt Assessments.

Bernstein, N. (1967). *The Coordination and Regulation of Movement*. London, England: Pergamon.

Blanche, E. (2006). Clinical reasoning in action: Designing intervention. In *SI: Applying Clinical Reasoning to Practice with Diverse Populations*, pp. 91–105. San Antonio, TX: Harcourt Assessments, Inc.

Bly, L. (1991). A historical and current view of the basis of NDT. *Pediatric Physical Therapy*, *3*(3), 131–135.

Bly, L. (1996). What is the role of sensation in motor learning? What is the role of feedback and feedforward? *NDT Network*, (*September/October*), 1–7.

Bobath, K. (1959). The effects of treatment by reflex inhibition and facilitation of movement in cerebral palsy. *Folia Psychiatrica, Neurological et Neurochirugical Neerlandica*, *62*(5), 448–457.

Bobath, K. & Bobath, B. (1964). The facilitation of postural reactions and movements in the treatment of cerebral palsy. *Physiotherapy*, *50*(8), 246–262.

Bowlby, J. (1988). *A Secure Base: Parent-Child Attachment and Healthy Human Development*. New York, NY: Basic Books.

Bradley, N. (2000). Motor control: Developmental aspects of motor control in skill acquisition. In S. K. Campbell, D. W. Vander Linden, & R. J. Palisano (Eds.), *Physical Therapy for Children*, 2nd edn., pp. 45–87. Philadelphia, PA: WB Saunders.

Brazelton, T. B. (1984). *Neonatal Behavioral Assessment Scale*, 2nd edn., Philadelphia: J.B. Lippincott.

Bretherton, I. (1992). The origins of attachment theory: John Bowlby and Mary Ainsworth. *Developmental Psychology*, *28*, 759–775.

Bruininks, R. H. (2006). *Bruininks-Oserstsky Test of Motor Proficiency*, 2nd edn., Circle Pines, MN: American Guidance Service.

Bundy, A. C. & Murray, E. A. (2002). Sensory integration: A. Jean Ayres' theory revisited. In A. C. Bundy, S. J. Lane, & E. A. Murray (Eds.), *Sensory integration: Theory and Practice*, 2nd edn., pp. 3–33. Philadelphia, PA: F.A. Davis Company.

Bundy, A. C., Lane, S. J., et al. (Eds.) (2002). *Sensory Integration: Theory and Practice*, 2nd edn., Philadelphia: PA: F.A. Davis Company.

Campbell, S. K. (1981). Movement assessment of infants: An evaluation. *Physical & Occupational Therapy in Pediatrics, 1*(4), 53–57.

Case-Smith, J. & Bigsby, R. (2000). *Posture and Fine Motor Assessment of Infants*. San Antonio, TX: Harcourt Assessments.

Chandler, L. (1990). Neuromotor assessment. In E. D. Gibbs, & D. M. Teti (Eds.), *Interdisciplinary Assessment of Infants*, pp. 45–61. Baltimore, MD: Paul H. Brooks.

Clayton, K., Fleming, J. M., et al. (2003). Behavioral responses to tactile stimuli in children with cerebral palsy. *Physical & Occupational Therapy in Pediatrics, 23*(1), 43–62.

Davids, K., Glazier, P., et al. (2003). Movement systems as dynamical systems: The functional role of variability and its implications for sports medicine. *Sports Medicine, 33*(4), 245–260.

Diamond, M. C. & Schenkman, M. (1996). Use of the clinical decision-making process to achieve measurable improvement in function in a patient on year post CVA. *Neurology Report, 20*(2), 72–74.

Dunn, W. (1999). *The Sensory Profile*. San Antonio, TX: Psychological Corporation.

Dunn, W. (2002). *The Infant Toddler Sensory Profile*. San Antonio, TX: Psychological Corporation.

Eliasson, A. C. (2005). Improving the use of hands in daily activities: Aspects of the treatment of children with cerebral palsy. *Physical and Occupational Therapy in Pediatrics, 25*(3), 37–60.

Folio, M. R. & Fewell, R. R. (2000). *Peabody Developmental Motor Scales*. Austin, TX: PRO-ED.

Foster, S. L. & Cone, J. D. (1980). Current issues in direct observation. *Behavioral Assessment, 2*, 313–338.

Gajdosik, C. G. & Gajdosik, R. L. (2000). Musculoskelatal development and adaptation. In S. K. Campbell (Ed.), *Physical Therapy for Children*, 2nd edn., pp. 117–140. Philadelphia, PA: WB Saunders.

Gentile, A. M. (1987). The nature of skill acquisition: Therapeutic implications for children with movement disorders. In J. Carr, R. Shepherd, & J. Gordon (Eds.), *Movement Science: Foundations for Physical Therapy in Rehabilitation*. Rockville, MD: Aspen.

Gessell, A. (1928). *Infancy and Human Growth*. New York, NY: McMillan.

Girolami, G. L., Ryan, D. F., et al. (2001). Clinical assessment of the infant. In A. L. Scherzer (Ed.), *Early Diagnosis and Interventional Therapy in Cerebral Palsy: An Interdisciplinary Age-Focused Approach*, 3rd edn., pp. 139–184. New York, NY: Marcel Dekker.

Gordon, J. (1987). Assumptions underlying physical therapy intervention: Theoretical and historical perspectives. In J. Carr, R. Shepherd, J. Gordon., et al. (Eds.), *Movement Sciences: Foundations for Physical Therapy in Rehabilitation*. Rockville, MD: Aspen.

Harris, A. H. & Brady, D. (1986). Infant Neuromotor Assessment instruments: A review. In J. K. Sweeney (Ed.), *The High Risk Neonate: Developmental Therapy Issues*. New York, NY: Academic Press.

Haynes, W. H. & O'Brien, S. N. (2000). *Principles and Practice of Behavioral Assessment*. New York: Kluwer Academic/Plenum Publishers.

Henderson, S. E. (1986). Problems in motor development: Some theoretical issues. *Advances in Special Education, 5*, 147–186.

Henderson, L., Rose, P., et al. (1992). Reaction time and movement time in children with developmental coordination disorder. *Journal of Child Psychology and Child Psychiatry, 33*, 895–905.

Henderson, S. E. & Sugden, D. A. (1992). Movement Assessment Battery for Children. San Antonio, TX: Harcourt Assessment.

Horak, F. B. & Shumway-Cook, A. (1990). *Balance: Proceedings from the APTA Forum*. Paper presented at the APTA Forum, Alexandria, VA.

Howle, J. M. (2002). Current Theoretical Foundations. In *Neuro-Developmental Treatment Approach: Theoretical Foundations and Principles of Clinical Practice*, pp. 1–79, Laguna Beach, CA Neuro-Developmental Treatment Association.

ICDL (2005). *Diagnostic Manual for Infancy and Early Childhood: Mental Health, Developmental, Regulatory-Sensory Processing and Language Disorders and Learning Challenges* (*ICDL-DMIC*). Bethesda, MD: Interdisciplinary Council on Developmental and Learning Disorders (ICDL).

Kamm, K., Thelen, E., et al. (1991). A dynamical systems approach to motor development. In J. M. Rothstein (Ed.), *Movement Science*, pp. 11–23. Alexandria, VA: APTA.

Keele, S. W. & Summers, J. J. (1976). The structure of motor programs. In G. E. Stelmach (Ed.), *Motor Control: Issues and Trends*, pp. 161–186. New York, NY: Academic Press.

Kelso, J. A. S. (1976). Two strategies for investigating action. In G. E. Stelmach (Ed.), *Motor Control: Issues and Trends*, pp. 161–186, New York, NY: Academic Press.

Kelso, J. A. S. & Tuller, B. (1984). A dynamical basis for action systems. In M. S. Gazanniga (Ed.), *Handbook of Cognitive Neuroscience*, pp. 321–356. New York, NY: Plenum.

Kopp, C. B. & McCall, R. B. (1982). Predicting later mental performance for normal, at-risk and handicapped infants. In P. B. Bates, & O. G. Brim (Eds.), *Life-Span Development and Behavior*, Vol. 4, pp. 33–61. New York: Academic.

Kugler, P. N. & Turvey, M. T. (1987). *Information, Natural Law and Self-Assembly of Rhythmic Movement*. Hillsdale, NJ: Erlbaum.

Larin, H. (2000). Motor learning: Theories and strategies for the practitioner. In S. K. Campbell, D. W. Vander Linden & R. J. Palisano (Eds.), *Physical Therapy for Children*, 2nd edn., pp. 170–197. Philadelphia, PA: WB Saunders.

Marx, J. A. (1989). Predictive value of early neuromotor assessment instruments. *Physical and Occupational Therapy in Pediatrics, 9*(4), 69–79.

Mattingly, C. & Fleming, M. H. (1994). *Clinical Reasoning: Forms of Inquiry in a Therapeutic Practice*. Philadelphia: S.A. Davis Company.

McGraw, M. (1963). *The Neuromuscular Maturation of the Human Infant*. New York, NY: Hafner.

Miller, L. J. (1982, 1988). *Miller Assessment for Preschoolers (MAP)*. San Antonio, TX: The Psychological Corporation.

Miller, L. J. (2006). *Miller Function and Participation Scales*. San Antonio, TX: Harcourt Assessments, Inc.

Miller, L. J. & Roid, G. H. (1994). *The Toddler and Infant Motor Evaluation (T.I.M.E.)*. San Antonio, TX: Therapy Skill Builders.

Miller, L. J., Cermak, S., et al. (2004). Position statement on terminology related to sensory integration dysfunction. *S.I. Focus*, 6–8.

Parham, D., Ecker, C., et al. (2007). *Sensory Processing Measure (SPM)*. Los Angeles, CA: Western Psychological Services.

Patla, A. E. & Shumway-Cook, A. (1999). Dimensions of mobility: Defining the complexity and difficulty associated with community mobility. *Journal of Aging and Physical Activity, 7*, 7–19.

Perry, S. B. (1998). Clinical implications of dynamical systems theory. *Neurology Report, 22*, 4–10.

Piper, M. C. & Darrah, J. (1994). *Alberta Infant Motor Scale (AIMS)*. Philadelphia, PA: W. B. Saunders.

Rosenbaum, D. (1991). *Human Motor Control*. New York, NY: Academic.

Schmidt, R. A. (1988). *Motor Control and Learning*, 2nd edn., Champaign, IL: Human Kinetics.

Schmidt, R. A. (1991). *Motor Learning Principles for Physical Therapy*. Paper presented at the II Step Conference, Alexandria, VA.

Shumway-Cook, A. & Woollacott, M. H. (2001). Motor control: Issues and theories. In *Motor Control: Theory and Practical Applications*, 2nd edn., pp. 1–25. Baltimore, Maryland: Lippincott Williams & Wilkins.

Silver, L. (1988). *The Misunderstood Child: A Guide for Parents of Learning Disabled Children*. New York, NY: McGraw-Hill.

Smith Roley, S. (2006). Sensory integration theory revisited. In *SI: Applying Clinical Reasoning to Practice with Diverse Populations*, pp. 1–13. San Antonio, TX: Harcourt Assessment, Inc.

Stelmach, G. E. (1976). Motor control and motor learning: The closed loop perspective. In G. E. Stelmach (Ed.), *Motor Control: Issues and Trends* pp. 93–115. New York, NY: Academic Press.

Thelen, E., Kelso, J. A. S., et al. (1987). Self organizing systems and infant motor development. *Developmental Review, 7*, 39–65.

Thelen, E., Corbella, D., et al. (1993). The transition to reaching: Mapping intentional and intrinsic dynamics. *Child Development, 64*, 1058–1098.

Ulrich, D. A. (2000). *Test of Gross Motor Development*, 2nd edn., San Antonio, TX: Harcourt Assessments, Inc.

Westcott, S. L. & Burtner, P. A. (2004). Postural control in children: Implications for pediatric practice. *Physical and Occupational Therapy in Pediatrics*, *24*(1–2), 5–55.

Whiteside, A. (1997). Clinical goals and application of NDT facilitation. *NDT Network*, (*September/October*), 1–14.

Wilson, P. H. (2005). Practitioner review: Approaches to assessment and treatment of children with DCD: An evaluative review. *Journal of Child Psychology and Psychiatry*, *46*(8), 806–823.

Woollacott, M. H. & Shumway-Cook, A. (1990). Changes in posture control across the life span: A systems approach. *Physical Therapy*, *70*, 799–807.

Woollacott, M. H. & Shumway-Cook, A. (1997). Clinical research methodology for the study of posture and balance. In J. C. Masdeu, L. Sudarsky, & L. Wolfson (Eds.), *Gait Disorders of Aging: Falls and Therapeutic Strategies*, pp. 107–121. Philadelphia, PA: Lippinocott-Raven.

Zernicke, R. F. & Schneider, K. (1993). Biomechanics and developmental neuromotor control. *Child Development*, *64*(4), 982–1004.

Zero To Three (2005). *Diagnostic Classification: 0–3-Revised*. Arlington, VA: National Center for Clinical Infant Programs.

SECTION

III

ABAS-II and Assessment Across Age Ranges

14

USING THE ABAS-II WITH INFANTS, TODDLERS, AND PRESCHOOLERS

TINA SMITH-BONAHUE

University of Florida, Gainesville, FL 32611-7047, U.S.A.

Adaptive skills comprise the most important developmental tasks accomplished during the first several years of life. Parents of infants and young children with or without disabilities wait and watch for those functional tasks – walking, communication of basic needs, independent feeding – that signal the development of independence and well-being. The importance of functional skills is reflected in the original legislation mandating services for infants and young children with and at-risk for disabilities. Federal legislation (e.g., PL 108-446, Individuals with Disabilities Education Improvement Act, IDEIA, 2004) emphasizes that assessment must be comprehensive multidisciplinary, and emphasize functional abilities. For this reason and others, understanding the adaptive skills of infants, toddlers, and preschoolers is a lynchpin of sound evaluation of young children.

The purpose of this chapter is to provide an overview of issues related to the assessment of adaptive skills using the ABAS-II with infants, toddlers, and preschoolers. The chapter begins with a general discussion of assessment within this age range, including a description of the nature of the conditions likely to result in referral for evaluation of children and special considerations for assessing very young children. Characteristics of the ABAS-II relevant to the assessment of infants and preschoolers are addressed. Finally, a case study is presented to illustrate the clinical utility of the ABAS-II with a toddler at-risk for disabilities.

OVERVIEW OF ASSESSMENT WITH INFANTS, TODDLERS, AND PRESCHOOLERS

Identifying difficulties and implementing appropriate interventions among very young children are some of the most important tasks assumed by educators, psychologists, and others responsible for the education and care of children. Beginning in 1986 with Public Law 99-457 and continuing through the most recent iteration of federal special education law, IDEIA 2004, public policy emphasizes the importance of early intervention and provides funding for the provision of services to infants and toddlers with, or at-risk for disabilities. Research continues to emphasize the crucial role of early brain development for optimizing child developmental potential.

CONDITIONS ASSOCIATED WITH DISABILITY AMONG INFANTS AND PRESCHOOLERS

Federal education law allows states to provide services both for young children with disabling conditions as well as those at-risk for later disability. This section begins with a discussion of conditions most frequently identifiable in the early years, then moves to a discussion of pre- and peri-natal conditions that increase risk for later disability.

Genetic Disorders

Genetically caused disorders comprise the most readily identifiable conditions associated with disability in early childhood. Between 65% and 70% of all pregnant women have some form of prenatal screening to identify potentially disabling conditions well before birth (Grant, 2000). Infants identified in this way are likely to be referred and monitored beginning in very early infancy.

Down Syndrome

Down Syndrome, or Trisomy 21, accounts for up to one-third of all cases of mental retardation for which the etiology is known, making it the most common cause of mental retardation that can be readily identified (Bowe, 2000). Although developmental outcomes associated with Down Syndrome vary tremendously, the disorder generally is associated with mental retardation as well as physical impairments (e.g., heart problems, vision loss, hearing loss, and hypotonia), which can interfere with adaptive skill development. Hypotonia (low muscle tone) can inhibit the development of functional motor achievements, including feeding, locomotion, and self-help skills.

Fragile X

This disorder is associated with damage to the X chromosome. Thus, it affects males and females differently and is believed to be the leading cause of mental impairment in males (Hooper & Mills, 2004). In males, Fragile X is associated with physical features (e.g., prominent jaw, large ears) as well as behavioral features that may mimic attention-deficit or autistic disorder. In females, Fragile X is associated with more subtle learning problems and generally is not identified until after school entry, if at all.

Neural Tube Defects

While not entirely genetic in origin, these defects result from the interaction of genetic and environmental risk and have been among the more common causes of disability in children (Grant, 2000). Recent advances in prevention, particularly related to folic acid intake, may result in lowered incidence for current and future generations. The nature and extent of disability depends on the location of the defect (Main & Mennuti, 1986); outcomes range from mild to severe physical and cognitive impairments. Spina bifida refers to damage to nerves, potentially affecting both afferent (to the brain) and efferent (from the brain) messages. Thorough assessment of adaptive skills is critical for educational planning for children with spina bifida in that they may be unable to monitor bodily functioning (sometimes causing incontinence) or pain.

Other Genetic Disorders

Other less common chromosomal abnormalities identified in infancy include Tay-Sachs disease, Cri du Chat syndrome, and achondroplasia (Hooper & Mills, 2004). Tay-Sachs is characterized by normal development until 6 months of age, followed by rapid deterioration of the nervous system, resulting in death by age 5. Cri du chat also is associated with severe mental retardation, with no known cure. Achondroplasia results in disproportionately short stature, some skeletal impairments, and occasional delays in developmental milestones. Although cognitive abilities for children with achondroplasia generally fall in the normal range, because of the potential for skeletal malformation, assessment of adaptive skills can be an important component of developmental monitoring to ensure appropriate intervention and accommodation.

Pre- and Peri-natal Factors

Prematurity

While medicine celebrates a steady decline in the rates of infant mortality, including deaths associated with low gestational age and birthweight, incidence of prematurity continues to rise (Alexander & Slay, 2002). Prematurity is defined as any infant born before 37 weeks gestation. With improvements in technology and medical treatment options, infants born at younger and younger ages are surviving; survival of infants born as early as 24 weeks gestation is a common occurrence. Medical intervention, particularly infertility treatments that result in multiple births, is one underlying cause of this increase (Kramer, 1998). At the same time, medical advances also have ameliorated *some* of the negative developmental outcomes associated with preterm birth. Nonetheless, a host of developmental conditions continue to be associated with preterm birth including cognitive disability, atypical gross and fine motor patterns (including incidence of cerebral palsy), attentional problems, and other behavioral and learning difficulties, all with the potential to disrupt the development of adaptive functioning.

The developmental trajectory of the premature infant is likely affected by a number of medical factors that must be considered in a thorough evaluation. Gestational age and the extent to which birthweight and head circumference are appropriate given gestational age are important considerations. Rate of post-birth growth is important in that weight gain can provide clues to the infant's overall condition. Premature infants are particularly susceptible to infection that can slow growth and potentially impact development. Intraventricular hemorrhage (IVH) is one of the more serious risks faced by preterm infants. The extent of the insult is estimated on a 1 to 4 scale, with 1 represented the least and 4 the most serious hemorrhage. While outcomes associated with IVH range from no effects to devastating effects, a study by Messinger et al. (1996) suggested that IVH is one of the most accurate predictors of long-term developmental outcome.

The first few months of life for many premature infants and their families are extremely atypical. They may spend weeks or months in the hospital and invasive procedures and medical machinery (e.g., ventilators) may be necessary, resulting in additional stress for families and significant restrictions in terms of mobility and experience for the developing baby. Because of the potential of these factors to hinder development of adaptive functioning, thorough review of medical records and interview with parents may be necessary to understand an infant's behavioral presentation.

Substance Exposure

The extent to which prenatal maternal consumption of substances affects the developing fetus depends on the properties of the substance itself as well as the timing and amount. Despite considerable attention to illegal drug abuse during pregnancy, the substances most commonly used during pregnancy include alcohol and tobacco, both of which can have deleterious effects on the developing fetus.

Alcohol

A set of clearly defined features characterizes children with Fetal Alcohol Syndrome (FAS) and can affect nearly every aspect of functioning (Streissguth & Kanter, 1997). In addition to low birth weight, microcephaly, and overall cognitive delay, deficits have been documented in motor, language, sensory, and behavioral functioning in young children with FAS. Fetal alcohol effect (FAE) is a term used to denote children who have a milder form of FAS. For young children with either FAS or FAE, adaptive skills development may be affected by cognitive, language, and motor impairments as well as poor behavioral regulation.

Tobacco

Since the late 1980s, use of tobacco during pregnancy has been implicated both in preterm birth and intrauterine growth retardation; effects of smoking on child development largely were believed to be secondary to the risks associated with intrauterine growth retardation and prematurity. Recently, however, a number of researchers have associated maternal smoking and passive smoke inhalation with delays in cognitive, academic, and social-emotional development (e.g., Day et al., 2000).

Illicit Drugs and Other Substances

In the late 1980s and early 1990s, a tremendous amount of research focused on uncovering the effects of prenatal drug use, cocaine in particular, on child developmental outcome. Early research suggested a host of short- and long-term physical and neurobehavioral effects, including serious physical malformations (e.g., Chasnoff, 1985), motor (e.g., Lester et al., 1991) and temperament differences (e.g., Edmondson & Smith, 1995; Smith, 1999). However, more recent reviews suggest that, after controlling for confounds such as alcohol and tobacco use, poverty, and so forth, no long-term effects of prenatal drug use can be found (Frank et al., 2001). Given that specific teratogenic effects have not been documented for prenatal drug use, the most relevant focus for assessment and intervention with this population are environmental variables.

DISABILITIES IDENTIFIED AMONG INFANTS, TODDLERS, AND PRESCHOOLERS

The previous section describes conditions frequently diagnosed during infancy that *may* result in disability. Because of the nature of early neurodevelopment, insults to the neurological system of infants tend to result in diffuse disability. With age, greater neurological specialization occurs. The following section describes the impairments and disabilities that may manifest prior to age 5.

Mental Retardation and Developmental Delay

Mental retardation is defined by the American Association on Mental Retardation (Luckasson et al., 2002) as subaverage intelligence as well as deficits in conceptual, social, and practical adaptive skills. The difficulty of accurately assessing IQ during the preschool years is well-established (see for example, Bagnato & Neisworth, 1994). As a result, perhaps the most frequently assigned eligibility category among preschoolers is "Developmentally Delayed (DD)." This catch-all "diagnosis" encompasses any number of underlying etiologies and behavioral and physical manifestations. The assumption underlying a DD diagnosis is that global development is "behind" that of same-age peers, but there's an expectation that the child might "catch up." In fact, this expectation is realistic in many cases. As described in the previous section, many early insults and conditions resolve over time, particularly when high quality early intervention is provided.

Motor Disabilities

Motor impairments in young children can result from any number of conditions or insults acquired pre- or peri-natally. Cerebral palsy is a term commonly used to describe a pattern of disorders of movement and posture that result from early brain trauma. Traumatic brain injuries, tumors, spina bifida, and degenerative neuromuscular disorder (e.g., Duchenne's Muscular Dystrophy) as well as genetic conditions such as Down Syndrome all are associated with motor disability (Dennis & Schlough, 2004). Because motor skills are requisite for many adaptive skills, consideration of these issues is particularly important for assessment and intervention planning.

Among young children, motor disabilities can include both disorders of movement as well as tone and posture. Among movement disorders, spasticity, characterized by stiffness of affected areas, is most common. Varying degrees of inability to voluntarily move all or part of the body is sometimes referred to as dyskinesia. Dyskinesia includes atypical movement patterns such as uncontrolled writhing, jerky movements, changes in muscle tone, and tremors.

Another important consideration for motor skills, particularly among very young children and those with significant neuromuscular disabilities is muscle tone. Some children may experience abnormally "low" muscle tone and appear "floppy;" others will have abnormally "high" tone and may appear "stiff." Further, it is possible for a child to experience both low and high tone in different body parts. For example, a child with cerebral palsy may experience low tone in his trunk, resulting in difficulties with sitting and posture, as well as high tone in his extremities, resulting in limited mobility. It is also possible for a child to experience changes in tone, moving from "floppy" to "stiff" across time.

For children with disabilities affecting the motor domain, thorough assessment of corresponding adaptive skills is critical for intervention planning. Many impairments can be treated with intervention or remediated through the use of equipment and technology. Ultimately, the goal of motor interventions is to improve the functional abilities of the child; consequently, careful assessment of adaptive skills should be incorporated into the planning, monitoring, and evaluation of these interventions.

Speech and Language Disabilities

From birth, children engage in efforts to communicate with people in their worlds. These efforts culminate with the development of spoken words, generally occurring around the first birthday, with an explosion of language development typically occurring between 18 and 24 months. During the second and third year of life, children's abilities to express themselves in sentences, signaling a staggeringly complex set of neurodevelopmental accomplishments, including auditory, motor, and cognitive systems. Conditions affecting any of these systems can interfere with language development; as a result, many disabilities diagnosed among young children have the potential to affect speech and language. For example, cerebral palsy can affect oral-motor functioning, which in turn affects articulation. Further, many children, with no other apparent disorders, demonstrate delays of deficits in speech and language.

Speech disorders can involve one or more of articulation, fluency, and voice qualities. Speech disorders often coincide with language disorders, but can occur independently of other problems. To the extent that articulation, fluency, or voice quality interferes with intelligibility of speech, they have implications for the child's functional communication skills as well as socialization.

Language, on the other hand, is a much broader concept with many components. One framework for considering components of language uses the elements of form (i.e., morphology and syntax), content (i.e., semantics), and use (i.e., pragmatics) (Easterbrooks, 2004). The impact of language disorders, particularly significant ones, is much broader, with significant implications for cognitive, behavioral, and emotional development.

Behavioral Disorders

Challenging behaviors during the preschool years are not uncommon, and in fact, in many ways, represent important developmental stages. For example, temper tantrums among 2 year olds are developmentally appropriate. Further, despite the disruptive effect of tantrums, they represent important developmental accomplishments. In the overwhelming majority of cases, the problems decline with age as children develop improved emotional and behavioral regulation. In other cases, often because behavioral disorders are secondary to disability, the problems worsen with age. Therefore, a norm-referenced comparison is critical in assessing young children with challenging behaviors and the extent to which the problematic behaviors interfere with daily functioning.

A link between language problems and challenging behaviors is well-established (Kaiser et al., 2002; Wakschlag & Keenan, 2001). Other disabilities and conditions (e.g., Down syndrome, Autism Spectrum Disorder) also have been associated with challenging behaviors. Environmental factors such as parenting practices and family atmosphere have strong links to behavioral and emotional problems (Bradley et al., 2001; Shaw et al., 1998). Challenging behaviors can affect social relationships, and to the extent that the child is noncompliant with adult requests and routines, the behaviors can interfere with daily functioning.

Autism Spectrum Disorders (ASD)

Autism is a developmental disorder with no known etiology. ASD is characterized by deficiencies in socialization and communication, and restricted, repetitive, and stereotyped patterns of behavior, interests, and activities (American Psychiatric Association, 2000). Although ASD occurs co-morbidly with a large number of conditions, including mental retardation, children with ASD tend to show a distinct pattern of adaptive skills and deficits. Strengths tend to be apparent in motor domains and self-help skills, with weaknesses apparent in communication and socialization domains.

CHALLENGES UNIQUE TO THE ASSESSMENT OF YOUNG CHILDREN

As with any evaluation, the assessment process for young children is guided by the referral question. Traditionally the functions of assessment for infants, toddlers, and preschoolers have differed somewhat from the functions generally associated with the assessment of older children. In many ways, the field of preschool assessment has been "ahead of its time." Emphasis on the authenticity of assessment and the link between assessment, intervention, and functional outcomes for young children has been deemed best practice in early childhood (Bagnato, 2007). Because development of functional, adaptive skills are the most critical activities for young children, adaptive skill assessment is critical for planning, monitoring, and evaluating early interventions.

Norm-referenced instruments such as the ABAS-II are most frequently utilized, even in early childhood contexts, for diagnosis and eligibility determination. For school-aged children, referrals for assessment generally are initiated in response to the child's academic or behavioral performance in schools, with the goal of the assessment to determine whether a student qualifies for special education services. Unlike older children, young children do not necessarily participate in organized educational experiences, and the guidelines for qualifying young children for special services differ in some important ways. In 1986, PL 99-457 significantly expanded services for young children and provided a means for extending downward the categorical definitions used for school-aged children, a process widely criticized as failing to recognize important limitations with diagnostic labels for preschoolers (Snyder et al., 1994). The same law and its successors, including the current IDEIA 2004, also provided a means whereby children could be qualified under the umbrella label of "developmental delay." Federal eligibility criteria for Part C, services for infants and toddlers to age 3, is based on prevention rationale in that it allows states to provide services for infants and toddlers both with, and notably, *at-risk for* disabilities.

SERVICES PROVIDED FOR INFANTS AND PRESCHOOLERS UNDER IDEIA 2004

Infants, toddlers, and preschoolers with, and in some cases at-risk for, disabilities are covered under a wide umbrella of services. From birth until the third birthday, infants can receive services under Part C of IDEIA; beginning at age 3, children can receive services under Part B of IDEIA. These services are similar in many ways to traditional special education services available to school-aged children. A number of important differences exist as well, however.

Under Part C, infants and toddlers deemed eligible receive services outlined in an Individualized Family Service Plan, or IFSP. For preschoolers receiving services under Part B, either an IFSP or an Individualized Education Plan (IEP) can be used. Comparable to requirements for school-aged children receiving special education services, both IEPs and IFSPs are legal documents, developed following multidisciplinary assessment, and provide a blueprint for service delivery. Many of these services resemble traditional education services, including speech-language therapy and special classrooms for preschoolers with disabilities. On the other hand, particularly for infants, services may include specialized care related to general health and development, such as specialized occupational therapy services for oral-motor issues, nursing care, and parent training.

As with all services provided under IDEIA, the services are supposed to be provided in the *least restrictive environment* (LRE) possible. For young children, determining the most appropriate LRE provides particular challenges – for some infants, toddlers, and preschoolers, the LRE is the child's home while for others it may be a large child care center, a family day care home, or some other group care facility. Parts B and C of IDEIA account for this, and services may be provided by specialists in these settings.

Other differences between services for school-aged versus younger children are worthy of note as well. The role of the family receives considerably more attention in the legislation governing services under Part C and for preschoolers under Part B of IDEIA. Generally, the younger the child, the more attention is paid to the role of the family. For example, in writing IFSPs, the family's "resources, strengths, and priorities" must be taken into account. Because under Part C, the family, rather than the individual child, is the "client," a broad array of options is possible to meet the needs of the family and by extension, the child. The breadth of assessment and service options changes as children age as well. Under Part C, the child's "overall functioning" is assessed and addressed; for preschoolers under Part B, areas of functioning are restricted to those with a direct bearing on educational outcomes.

Not only are eligibility criteria different, developmental trajectories for preschoolers differ in important ways from those of school-aged populations. The development of early learning and language skills varies, both in qualitative and quantitative ways for individual children (Shepard, et al., 1998). Further, because "school" is not mandated for young children as it is for older ones, young children experience vastly different developmental contexts. The professional who hopes to understand a preschooler's abilities and challenges must invest considerable time and energy in understanding that child's daily environment in order to make sense of test performance. As an example, consider a 4-year-old girl who spends her days watching TV with an elderly grandparent while her parents work. Compared to a child who attends a high quality preschool, the first child's performance on a traditional standardized test may more accurately reflect her limited access to developmentally appropriate activities than her abilities or potential for future growth. For example, she may fail an item requiring her to draw a straight line as a result of her inexperience with crayons rather than any deficit in her fine motor or perceptual abilities. Further, an evaluation may not predict her performance after exposure to the more enriching environment a quality kindergarten can provide.

A number of guidelines to address these issues have been recommended, most notably by the Division of Early Childhood (DEC) of the Council for Exceptional Children and the National Association for the Education of Young Children. Bagnato and Neisworth (2000) offer a definition of assessment in the context of the early years that reflects recommendations for effective practice:

> Early childhood assessment is a flexible, collaborative decision-making process in which teams of parents and professionals repeatedly revise their judgments and reach consensus about the changing developmental, educational, medical, and mental health needs of young children and their families. (p. 18)

The dynamic developmental characteristics of young children as well as the psychometric properties of early childhood instruments dictate the need for flexibility in the assessment of young children. Young children, particularly young children with disabilities, tend to tire quickly and often refuse to cooperate with sedentary activities. Normal variability in preschoolers' characteristics (e.g., their temperament or behavioral styles) may significantly affect their approach to unknown examiners and unfamiliar situations, especially those who have had few caregivers other than immediate family members. Assessment efforts will yield more accurate results if the activities are developmentally appropriate and conducted within the child's natural environment (Bagnato & Neisworth, 2000).

Frequent assessment is critical because the combination of development and intervention effects can result in dramatic changes in young children's functioning. Predictive validity of early childhood instruments is notoriously poor and significantly limits the extent to which test results can be used for long range educational planning. For this reason, assessment of young children is most appropriately considered to be a process rather than an end in itself.

USE OF THE ABAS-II WITH INFANTS AND PRESCHOOLERS

The ABAS-II is a comprehensive instrument designed for use with individuals ages birth to 89. Two forms of the ABAS-II, the Parent/Primary Caregiver Form (Ages 0–5) and the Teacher/Daycare Provider Form (Ages 2–5) are relevant for the assessment of infants and preschool children. For children who are 5 years old, the clinician may choose to use either the Parent/Primary Caregiver and the Teacher/Daycare Provider Forms of the ABAS or the school age forms, Parent Form (Ages 5–21) and Teacher Form (Ages 5–21). Authors of the ABAS-II manual (Harrison & Oakland, 2003) recommend use of the Parent/Primary Caregiver and the Teacher/Daycare Provider Forms for 5 year olds who are referred for concerns about delays in functioning or for whom comparison with an earlier administration of the infant-preschool form is desired. In addition, the Parent/Primary Caregiver and the Teacher/Daycare Provider Forms are likely to be more appropriate for 5 year olds who have not yet started kindergarten.

For infants and toddlers younger than 3, requirements of Part C of the Individuals with Disabilities Education Improvement Act (IDEIA, 2004) necessitate the assessment of 5 domains of functioning (cognitive, communication, social-emotional, motor, and adaptive). The ABAS-II can be used both to fulfill the requirement for a comprehensive adaptive skills assessment and to provide the examiner with insight regarding functional skills in conjunction with a developmental evaluation.

The Parent/Primary Caregiver Form is comprised of 241 items and is designed to address the functioning of infants and young children in the home. For infants aged birth to 11 months, the following adaptive skill areas are addressed: Communication, Health and Safety, Leisure, Self-Care, Self-Direction, Social, and Motor. For toddlers and preschoolers, the Parent/Primary Caregiver Form adds the following adaptive skill areas: Community Use, Functional Pre-academics, and Home Living. All adaptive skill areas are used to compute the General Adaptive Composite (GAC) scores. In addition to the GAC, the ABAS-II provides composite scores for the following: Conceptual, Social, and Practical. The adaptive skill areas comprising each adaptive composite are outlined in Table 14.1.

TABLE 14.1 Adaptive Skill Areas Comprising Composites for the Parent/Primary Caregiver and Teacher/Daycare Provider Forms of the ABAS-II

	Adaptive Skill Areas		
	Parent/Primary Caregiver		Teacher/Daycare Provider
Composites	Birth – 11 months	1–5 years	2–5 years
Conceptual	Communication Self-direction	Communication Functional pre-academics Self-direction	Communication Functional pre-academics Self-direction
Social	Leisure Social	Leisure Social	Leisure Social
Practical	Self-care Health and safety	Self-care Home living Health and safety Community use	Self-care School living Health and safety

Note: All adaptive skill areas above are included in the GAC. The motor adaptive skill area is included in the GAC but not the other composites. Adapted from Harrison & Oakland, 2003.

A Teacher/Daycare Provider form is available for children aged 2 through 5 who spend a significant amount of time in preschool, family day care home, child care center, or other out-of-home setting. Comprised of 216 items, this form addresses many of the same adaptive skill areas addressed by the Parent/Primary Caregiver Form, and thus provides a means to compare functioning across settings. Consistent with the Parent/Primary Caregiver Form, the Teacher/Daycare Provider form provides scores for GAC as well as Conceptual, Social, and Practical composites (see Table 14.1).

SCORING THE ABAS-II

Once the ABAS-II forms have been completed by parents or other care providers of infants, toddlers, or preschoolers, the examiner can choose to enter the child's demographic information and the total scores for each adaptive skill area into the computer scoring program, or refer to the tables included in the appendix of the manual. An assessment summary that includes norm-referenced scaled scores for each adaptive skill area (mean = 10, standard deviation = 3) and composite area (mean = 100, standard deviation = 15), as well as a graphed profile of the three adaptive composites by adaptive skill area, is generated.

ABAS-II scoring provides standard scores for the GAC and the three adaptive composites. For each composite score, percentile ranks, confidence intervals, and a qualitative range of functioning (e.g., "Below Average," "Borderline," "Extremely Low," etc.) are included. The ABAS-II scoring also provides comparisons across adaptive skill areas within each composite, as well as discrepancy comparisons between composites, to enable the examiner to identify the young child's strengths and weaknesses.

Special Consideration when Assessing Infants and Toddlers Born Prematurely

In addition to standard and scale scores and percentile ranks, ABAS-II scoring allows professionals the option of determining "test age equivalents." Because of the well-documented psychometric limitations of age equivalent scores, Harrison and Oakland (2003) urge examiners to use these scores only with extreme caution and under very special circumstances. One circumstance in which examiners are frequently tempted to use test age equivalent scores is with infants and toddlers under 2 who were preterm. To help parents understand their premature infants' developmental agendas, health care professionals often encourage them to consider their children in terms of their gestational rather than chronological ages. To this end, examiners may interpret tests in terms of test age scores. Alternatively, examiners may choose to use the infant's gestational rather than chronological age for computing scaled and standard scores. The rationale for these practices is intuitive, and in many cases, has clinical utility. With appropriate medical and educational intervention, premature infants generally "catch up" with their full term peers. The overwhelming majority of children who were born preterm show no lasting ill effects (Messinger et al., 1996).

While the practice of "correcting" for prematurity may have some merit, it also has limitations related to the reality of life outside the womb. For a variety of reasons, skill development in premature infants may or may not occur in a smooth curve, at the same rate across areas, or in patterns similar to those found in healthy full-term infants. For example, while an 8-month-old infant born at 32 weeks gestation may havc thc samc gcstational agc as a 6-month-old infant, the 8 month old has had two additional post-natal months, with the opportunities and dangers that come with the extra-uterine environment. The early experiences of premature infants and term infants often differ dramatically due to circumstances such as medical complications and time spent in hospitals. Other factors, including early educational intervention and family environment can ameliorate the negative impact of early insults. Therefore, any comparison between premature infants and their gestational age-mates is fraught with potential problems and inaccuracies. For these reasons, examiners are encouraged to explain thoroughly and carefully to parents and other consumers of test data both the rationale for and the limitations of considering test age scores or use of gestational age for score computation.

PSYCHOMETRIC PROPERTIES OF THE ABAS-II FOR USE WITH INFANTS AND PRESCHOOLERS

Norm-referenced tests of infants and young children have been the subject of significant criticism, largely due to problems with the psychometric properties of traditional instruments and the utility of such instruments in meaningful diagnosis and treatment planning (for example, see Bagnato & Neisworth, 1994.) While norming many early childhood tests, the age ranges sampled are too broad to be sensitive to the rapid development and individual variability seen in very early development. In addition, norm-referenced assessments for use with young children often have too few items and thus cannot account well for change (Neisworth & Bagnato, 2000). Under such conditions, the instrument is at best insensitive to meaningful differences and at worst inaccurate.

The developers of ABAS-II took these issues into account by including relatively large standardization samples during the first years of life and an adequate number of items in each adaptive skill area. Therefore, when used as intended as a part of a thorough evaluation, the ABAS-II can provide a valid and reliable estimate of the adaptive functioning of infants and preschoolers.

Standardization Sample

Development during the first years of life varies greatly from child to child. Thus, norm-referenced scores obtained for infants should be based on samples as similar in age as possible. In norming the ABAS-II, 1350 parents/Primary Caregivers and 750 teachers/Daycare Providers were included in the standardization samples for the Parent/Primary Caregiver and Teacher/Daycare Provider forms for use with young children. Development is most rapid during the child's first year of life, Thus, for the Parent/Primary Caregiver form from birth to 11 months, the norming sample was collected in 3 month increments (e.g., birth through 3 months, 4 through 6 months, etc.), with 100 respondents at each three month increment. Development during the next few years also can change quickly, yet normally less so that during the first year of life. Thus, beginning at age 2 for both the Parent/Primary Caregiver and Teacher/Daycare Provider forms, the norming sample is divided into 6 month increments (e.g., 13 through 18 months), with 100 respondents at each six month increment. The sample was collected to be representative of gender, race-ethnicity, parent education, and geographic region. In addition, small numbers of clinical cases representing biological risk factors, language disorders, pervasive developmental disorders (including autistic disorder), and mental retardation were included in the standardization sample.

Reliability and Validity

Reliability

The ABAS-II manual reports results of 4 forms of reliability estimates for both the Parent/Primary Caregiver and Teacher/Daycare Provider forms: internal consistency, test-retest, interrater, and cross-form consistency for 5 year olds. For children 2 years of age and older, reliability estimates for both the Parent/Primary Caregiver and Teacher/Daycare Provider forms suggest the scores generally are sufficiently reliable for individual decision-making, even for individual adaptive skill areas. Internal consistency reliability estimates tended to be slightly higher for the Teacher/Daycare Provider form, with coefficients ranging from .61 to .95 among individual adaptive skill areas (scaled score mean = 10), .80 to .95 among composite scores (standard score mean = 100), and .83 to .98 for GAC (standard score mean = 100). For the same age range (i.e., 2 to 5 years) on the Parent/Primary Caregiver and Parent Forms, internal consistency coefficients ranging from .48 to .94 among individual adaptive skill areas (scaled score mean = 10), .65 to .97 among composite scores (standard score mean = 100), and .86 to .98 for GAC (standard score mean = 100).

As with most tests of very young children, reliability estimates for the Parent/Primary Caregiver Form were lower for infants and toddlers than for children 2 years and older. A number of unavoidable factors contribute to this, including floor effects and limited numbers of items due to response repertoires of very young children. For this reason, examiners administer seven ABAS-II adaptive skill areas on the Parent/Primary Caregiver form (communication, health and safety, leisure, self-care, self-direction, social, and motor) for infants in the first year of life, and should use caution always when using adaptive skill area scores. As is typical in infant assessment, standard error of measure estimates for the composite scores tends to decrease as age increases (see Table 14.2). Therefore, the use of the ABAS-II with infant assessment should be viewed in light of a

TABLE 14.2 Standard Error of Measure of Composites and GAC on Parent/Primary Caregiver Form for Children Younger than 2½ Years

	Age group						
Composite	0–3 months	4–7 months	8–11 months	1.0–1.3 year	1.4–1.7 year	1.8–1.11 year	2.0–2.5 year
Conceptual	8.22	6.87	6.00	4.24	3.67	3.97	3.00
Social	6.54	5.20	4.97	4.50	4.97	4.74	3.67
Practical	8.87	5.61	6.36	3.67	3.35	3.67	3.00
GAC	5.61	3.67	3.67	2.60	2.12	2.60	2.12

(Harrison & Oakland, 2003).

process that utilizes multiple methods and multiple sources of information over a period of time. As with all forms of assessment during the early childhood years, the younger the child, the more caution should be used in interpreting norm-referenced scores.

Evidence of test-retest reliability is provided for ages 2–3 and 4–5 for the Teacher/Daycare Provider Form. For 2 to 3 year olds, corrected coefficients were .88 for Conceptual, .85 for Social, .88 for Practical, and .90 for GAC. For 4 to 5 year olds, corrected coefficients were .90 for Conceptual, .90 for Social, .92 for Practical, and .92 for GAC. Evidence of cross-form consistency is presented for children aged 2 to 5. Pearson's product moment correlation coefficients between Teacher/Daycare Provider and Parent/Primary Caregiver forms are .69, .58, and .58 for Conceptual, Social, and Practical respectively, and .68 for GAC.

As with internal consistency and test-retest reliability estimates, inter-rater reliability estimates suggest that ABAS-II Parent/Primary Caregiver and Teacher/Daycare Provider forms are reliable at the composite level and measure the same construct across raters. Pearson's product moment correlation coefficients between 2 respondents on the Teacher/Daycare Provider forms for 2 to 5 year olds are .83, .74, and .87 for Conceptual, Social, and Practical respectively, and .83 for GAC.

Correlations between the ratings of the same respondents 5 year olds were determined using the Parent/Primary Caregiver Form (ages 0–5 years) and Parent Form (ages 5–21 years), because both can be used with 5 year old children. Correlations of composite scores suggest that either form may be used with 5 year olds. Mean ratings across composites and GAC were slightly higher for the Parent form as compared to the Parent/Primary Caregiver form. (The mean GAC for the Parent/Primary Caregiver was 102.0; for the Parent form, the GAC was 104.6).

A similar comparison between the Teacher/Daycare Provider Form and the Teacher Form for 5 year olds found moderate correlations between the scales, with correlation coefficients of .67, .70, and .75 for Conceptual, Social, and

Practical respectively, and .74 for the GAC. As with the Parent and the Parent/Primary Caregiver forms, these findings suggest that either teacher form can be used.

Validity

The manual presents an examination of discriminant validity across all ages through intercorrelation matrices; low to moderate correlations among the individual adaptive skill areas generally suggests independent constructs. At the same time, higher correlations between individual adaptive skill areas and the composites on which they load suggest that individual adaptive skill area scores contribute to the measurement of that construct. Concurrent evidence of validity is provided by correlations between similar domains on the Vineland Adaptive Behavior Scales Interview Edition (VABS-IE) and the Parent/Primary Caregiver Form, with lower correlations between dissimilar domains. The correlation between the ABAS-II Parent/Primary Caregiver Form GAC and the VABS-IE Adaptive Behavior Composite was .70. A similar comparison between the ABAS-II Teacher/Daycare Provider Form and the Vineland Adaptive Behavior Scale-Classroom Edition (VABS-CE) provides evidence that the two instruments measure similar constructs, with a correlation of .84 between the ABAS-II Teacher/Daycare Provider Form GAC and the VABS-CE Adaptive Behavior Composite.

Similarly, moderate but significant correlations were found between the Wechsler Preschool and Primary Scale of Intelligence and the ABAS-II Parent/Primary Caregiver and Teacher/Daycare Provider forms, with correlations of .61 and .54 between the WPSSI FSIQ and ABAS-II GAC on the Teacher/Daycare Provider and Parent/Primary Caregiver Forms respectively. Clinical case data suggest that the Parent/Primary Caregiver and Teacher/Daycare Provider forms provided scores that would be expected for children with the diagnoses examined. Clinical samples included individuals with the following diagnoses: Mild and Moderate Mental Retardation, Developmental Delay, Biological Risk Factors, Motor Impairments, Language Disorders, PDD-NOS, and Autistic Disorder.

CASE EXAMPLE USING THE ABAS: ALEX

REASON FOR REFERRAL

Alex Donnelly was referred for a psychological evaluation by his preschool teacher, Ms Jones, because of concerns about behavior and lack of social interaction with his peers. An interview with his parents, Mr. and Ms. Donnelly, reveals that they too are very worried about Alex's behavior and have become frustrated with the extent to which his lack of compliance with daily routines interferes with their family's day-to-day functioning. Their primary concerns include his long-term prognosis and how to manage his behavior at home.

MEDICAL HISTORY

Alex is a 3 year, 8-month-old boy with a history of seizure disorder. He had his first seizure at 26 months of age for which he was hospitalized. The following day, while still in the hospital, he had another seizure, this time involving the right side of his face, and his right arm and leg. CT scan and MRI were found to be within normal limits. However, because his EEG showed mild epileptiform activity, he was placed on medications and followed by a neurologist. While on medication, Alex has episodes of "staring spells," believed to be absence seizures, lasting between 5 and 15 seconds several times per week. However, for the most part, his seizures seem to be under control.

DEVELOPMENTAL AND FAMILY HISTORY

Alex is the second child in the Donnelly family. His older sister, Amanda, is 6 years old and, based on parent report, is doing very well in first grade. Amanda is described as very cooperative, easygoing, and easy to parent. Alex, on the other hand, is described as significantly more active, less social, and less communicative. Mr. and Ms. Donnelly report that Alex reached most of his developmental milestones on the late end of the normal range. In terms of language, he said his first words at 18 months, and put two words together at 28 months. According to his parents, he shows little interest in conversing, or even reading books with them. He was only recently toilet trained and continues to have accidents. He also continues to have considerable difficulty using a fork or spoon independently. His mother suggests that his low frustration tolerance interferes more than his actual skills. Notably, Alex's gross motor skills developed within normal limits. For example, he walked well at 11 months and was running shortly after his first birthday.

In terms of his behavior and social relationships, his parents and teacher consistently report that he is aggressive toward other children, prefers to play alone, and has difficulty communicating with peers and adults. He is described as extremely active, even for a 3 year old, both at home and at school. According to Ms. Jones, Alex has no friends at preschool and shows little interest in the activities of other children. She describes his eye contact as avoidant and reports that he tends to play in the same area (the block area) with the same toys. On a positive note, Ms. Jones reports improvements in Alex's behavior following the implementation of a behavior plan that provides 5 minutes of access to desired toys (the block area) following cooperation with classroom routines (e.g., brushing teeth after lunch).

COGNITIVE ABILITIES

On the Kaufman Assessment Battery for Children, Second Edition (KABC-II, Kaufman & Kaufman, 2004), Alex earned a Mental Processing Index of 81 and a Nonverbal Index of 87. Alex was observed to be generally cooperative when he understood the task. However, over time, he demonstrated a number of behaviors that enabled him to avoid the tasks presented. For example, he fell off his seat, climbed under the table, and turned away from the examiner.

BEHAVIOR

Ms. Jones completed the Teacher Rating Scales – Preschool Form of the Behavior Assessment System for Children, Second Edition (BASC-II, Reynolds & Kamphaus, 2004). Externalizing Problems Composite score fell in the clinically significant range, with a T Score of 71. Individual scale scores that fell in the clinically significant included Hyperactivity (T Score = 74), Aggression (T Score = 69), Inattention (T Score = 79), and Atypicality (T Score = 70). Mr. and Ms. Donnelly's ratings on the Parent – Preschool Form of the BASC-II suggested even greater concerns: Externalizing Problems Composite (T Score = 107); Hyperactivity (T Score = 79), Aggression (T Score = 85), Inattention (T Score = 69), and Atypicality (T Score = 75). Similarly, both parent and teacher ratings suggested difficulties on the adaptive scales of the BASC-II, with Ms. Jones ratings of Alex's adaptive skills indicating as slightly better development than his parents' ratings.

ADAPTIVE FUNCTIONING

The ABAS-II Parent/Primary Caregiver and Teacher/Daycare Provider forms were completed by Mr. Donnelly and Ms. Jones. The following scores were obtained in Table 14.3.

Mr. Donnelly's ratings on the ABAS-II Parent/Primary Caregiver Form suggested extremely low functioning in all areas based on the following standard scores: GAC = 59; Conceptual = 67; Social = 56; Practical = 56. All composite standard scores were in the extremely low range. Among the individual adaptive skill areas, Mr. Donnelly's ratings suggested a relative strength in motor adaptive skills, and a relative weakness in self-care adaptive skills.

Ms. Jones' ratings resulted in a GAC of 71 (borderline range) on the ABAS-II Teacher/Daycare Provider Form. Although Alex is not functioning at the level of his peers, his functioning at preschool is somewhat more advanced than at home, according to the ABAS-II scores. On the ABAS-II Teacher/Daycare Provider Form, a significant difference was found among the composite standard scores, with a borderline score on Conceptual (78), and extremely low scores on Practical (70) and Social (58). Among the individual adaptive skill areas, communication adaptive skills emerged as a relative strength based on Ms. Jones' ratings with a scaled score of 10. On the other hand, self-direction, leisure, and social adaptive skill areas emerged as relative weaknesses, each having a scaled score of 3.

Interviews with Mr. and Ms. Donnelly and Ms. Jones reveal that Alex's behavior interferes significantly with his adaptive functioning. His parents and teacher

TABLE 14.3 Parent/Primary Caregiver and Teacher/Daycare Provider Rating Summaries for Alex, Age 3 Years, 8 Months

	Parent/Primary Caregiver Form			Teacher/Daycare Provider Form		
Composite/adaptive skill area	Composite Standard Score/Skill Area Scaled Score	Composite 95% Confidence Interval	Composite Percentile Rank	Composite Standard Score/Skill Area Scaled Score	Composite 95% Confidence Interval	Composite Percentile Rank
General Adaptive Composite	59	55–63	0.3	71	67–75	3
Conceptual Composite	67	60–74	1	78	72–84	7
Communication	7			10		
Functional pre-academics	6			7		
Self-direction	3			3		
Social Composite	56	48–63	0.2	58	50–66	0.3
Leisure	3			3		
Social	3			3		
Practical Composite	56	48–63	0.2	70	62–78	2
Community use	5			NA		
Home/School living	4			6		
Health and safety	3			4		
Self-care	1			7		
Motor Adaptive Skill Area	10			8		

Note: Composite scores (Conceptualization, Social, and Practical and the GAC have a mean of 100 and standard deviation of 15. Adaptive skill areas Communication, Functional Academics, etc.) have a mean of 10 and standard deviation of 3. Motor adaptive skill scaled scores are used in calculating the GAC, but not other composites.

agree that, while Alex has the requisite skills to perform many of behaviors involved in adaptive activities (e.g., putting away books and toys, using eating utensils appropriately), his difficulties with inattention and impulsivity interfere with his performance of these tasks. Further, his difficulties with social relationships appear to be related both to his lack of interest in others (e.g., he does not appear to have special relationships with adults or children) as well as his impulsivity and hyperactivity (e.g., reflected in his inability to play simple games.)

SUMMARY OF EVALUATION RESULTS

While Alex's cognitive abilities appear to be in the low range, parent and teacher reports and scores on the ABAS-II and the BASC-II suggest that his actual functioning is less developed than would be expected given his other scores. Although his behavior at preschool is far from typical, he is more functional there than at home.

A number of hypotheses could be generated to explain the lower than average scores on measures of cognition and particularly, adaptive behavior, the most obvious of which is a developmental disability. Alex likely meets the diagnostic criteria for a number of diagnoses, including Attention Deficit, Hyperactivity Disorder, Pervasive Developmental Disorder, Not Otherwise Specified.

On the other hand, other variables may be at play as well. A diagnosis of one so young with a significant developmental disability should occur only under the most certain of circumstances. Alex's noncompliance could be compounded by his parents' inadequate parenting. Given his complex medical history, the possibility that he experiences subclinical seizure activity that impacts his behavioral presentation should be considered and addressed medically. The effects of medication on children, particularly young children, are largely a mystery. Alex's history of medication for seizure control requires careful monitoring. Finally, psychometric inadequacies associated with the assessment of very young children may attenuate the clarity of these results. The testing is somewhat narrow and thus incomplete, the results may be imprecise, and their predictive validity is limited. Given all these factors, the most appropriate diagnosis at this time, if one is needed for the purpose of providing services, is DD. This nonspecific diagnosis will enable Alex to receive services through Part B of the Individuals with Disabilities Education Act of 2004 without giving him a label that might later be disproved following considerable anguish for his family and labeling effects for him.

INTERVENTION PLANNING

Attempts to help Alex's family and teacher address his behaviors in order to improve his adaptive functioning are more important than forming a diagnosis. ABAS-II findings provide a place to start for intervention planning. The first task for intervention planning is to identify those tasks he performs at school that he does not perform at home. The family is encouraged to prioritize from among this list to identify a manageable list of behaviors for intervention, ideally 2 or 3 to start.

Goal 1. Compliance with Verbal Requests

On the Teacher/Daycare Provider form, Ms. Jones indicated that Alex's adaptive communication skills are average. For example, he follows simple commands such as "no," and that he generally follows simple directions that include prepositions such as "over and under." Similarly, in the Health and Safety area, Ms. Jones reports that Alex always follows an adults direction to "stop" when danger is present. In contrast, Mr. Donnelly's ratings indicate that Alex rarely complies with these kinds of directions.

Setting Analysis

Comparisons of communication styles used by Ms. Jones and Mr. and Ms. Donnelly with Alex reveal several key differences. Ms. Jones always makes sure that she has Alex's attention before talking to him. For example, she often says to him, "Look at my nose," gives a gentle physical prompt when needed, and then speaks to him. In contrast, the Donnelly's often ask Alex to comply with requests while they are engaged in other activities. For example, Mr. Donnelly was observed slicing vegetables and helping Amanda with her homework while attempting to get Alex to wash his hands for dinner.

Another key difference relates to the nature of Ms. Jones' communication. She explains that she makes a conscious effort to use as few words as possible, and gives multiple, short commands when she needs Alex to comply. For example, rather than saying, "Alex, it's time to go to lunch so please put your toys away, wash your hands and line up with your friends," she says, "Alex, it's lunch time. Put the blocks in the box." Once he complies, she praises him and adds, "Wash your hands," and so on. In contrast, Ms. Donnelly reveals, and interviews support, that she often talks too much, thus giving Alex too much information or too many commands. As a result, he looses focus and fails to comply with her requests.

Finally, consequences for compliance between school and home differ. Ms. Jones immediately praises compliance, often pairing the praise with a naturally occurring reward. For example, if Alex puts away his nap cot quickly, he gets extra time to play in the block area before snack. On the other hand, his parents are often so frustrated by his noncompliance and the resulting inconvenience to the family that if and when he does comply, no rewards are forthcoming. Similarly, Ms. Jones attempts always to ensure that Alex's access to desired activities is contingent on his completing required tasks.

Development of a Behavior Plan

Based on these observations, a behavior plan is developed. Mr. and Ms. Donnelly practice more effective commands and agree to monitor each others' verbal interactions with Alex. With the help of the examiner, they identify a few times per day (e.g., brushing teeth then going to bed) when they plan to practice their "new" communication skills. They also identify a reinforcer (watching a short video) that Alex can earn by complying with their requests.

Goal 2. Increasing Social Interactions

Ms. Jones' most significant referral concern related to Alex's lack of interactions with peers at preschool. Again, responses on the ABAS-II provide a place to start. On both the Parent/Primary Caregiver and Teacher/Daycare Provider forms, items related to greeting friends and familiar adults were rated as "never." Ms. Jones and the Donnellys agree to begin a social skills intervention by teaching Alex more age appropriate manners for greeting others.

Development of a Behavior Plan

Because, although Alex possesses adequate language skills, he never engages in greeting behaviors, his parents and teacher agree on a prompt to be used consistently across settings. If he responds appropriately, verbal praise will be given, followed by intermittent activity reinforcers (e.g., "You said 'hello' to your friend Cara so nicely; would you like to invite her to play in the block area with you?").

Because assessment with young children is best viewed as a process, and rarely if ever functions as an "end" in itself, this evaluation likely will serve as the baseline for subsequent evaluations. Particularly for preschoolers with or at-risk for disability, progress monitoring ensures that educational programming and intervention is effective during those critical early years when interventions can be most effective. A frequent problem in early childhood assessment is that instruments designed for infants and toddlers are based on different theoretical orientations and utilize different frameworks than instruments designed for older children. Because the age range extends from infancy well into adulthood and includes parent and teacher forms, the ABAS-II offers the potential for seamless, multisource evaluation of adaptive functioning.

REFERENCES

Alexander, G. R. & Slay, M. (2002). Prematurity at birth: Trends, racial disparities, and epidemiology. *Mental Retardation and Developmental Disabilities Research Reviews*, *8*, 215–220.

American Psychiatric Association (2000). *Diagnostic and Statistical Manual, IV – TR*. Washington, D.C.: American Psychiatric Pub, Inc.

Bagnato, S. J. (2007). *Authentic Assessment for Early Childhood Intervention: Best Practices*. New York: The Guilford Press.

Bagnato, S. J. & Neisworth, J. T. (1994). A national study of the social and treatment invalidity of intelligence testing for early intervention. *School Psychology Quarterly*, *9*, 81–102.

Bowe, F. G. (2000). *Birth to Five: Early Childhood Special Education*, 2nd edn., Boston, MA: Delmar Publishers.

Bradley, R. H., Burchinal, M. R., & Casey, P. H. (2001). Early intervention: The moderating role of the home environment. *Applied Developmental Science*, *5*(1), 2–8.

Chasnof, I. J., Burns, W. J., Schnoll, S. H., & Burns, K. A. (1985). Cocaine use in pregnancy. *The New England Journal of Medicine*, *313*, 666–669.

Day, N. L., Richardson, G. A., Goldschmidt, L. & Cornelius, M. D. (2000). Effects of prenatal tobacco exposure on preschoolers' behavior. *Journal of Developmental and Behavioral Pediatrics, 21*, 180–188.

Dennis, C. W. & Scholough, K. A. (2004). Gross motor development. In S. Hooper & W. Umansky (Eds.), *Young Children with Special Needs*, 4th edn., Upper Saddle River, NJ: Pearson/Merrill Prentice Hall.

Easterbrooks, S. (2004). Communication. In S. Hooper & W. Umansky (Eds.), *Young Children with Special Needs*, 4th edn., pp. 346–376. Upper Saddle River, NJ: Pearson/Merrill Prentice Hall.

Edmondson, R. & Smith, T. (1995) Temperament and behavior of infants prenatally exposed to cocaine. *Infant Mental Health Journal, 15*, 368–379.

Frank, D. A., Augustyn, M., Knight, W. G., Pell, T., & Zuckerman, B. (2001). Growth, development, and behavior in early childhood following prenatal cocaine exposure: A systematic review. *Journal of the American Medical Association, 285*(12), 1613.

Grant, S. (September 30, 2000): Prenatal genetic screening. *Online Journal of Issues in Nursing. 5*, 3.

Harrison, P. L. & Oakland, T. (2003). *Adaptive Behavior Assessment System.*2nd edn., PsychCorp.

Hooper, S. & Mills, C. (2004). Developmental processes and factors affecting development. In S. Hooper and W. Umansky (Eds.), *Young Children with Special Needs*, 4th edn., Upper Saddle River, NJ: Pearson/Merrill Prentice Hall.

Individuals with Disabilities Education Improvement Act (2004). PL 108-446.

Kaiser, A. P., Cai, X., Hancock, T. B., & Foster, E. M. (2002). Teacher-reported behavior problems and language delays in boys and girls enrolled in Head Start. *Behavioral Disorders, 28*(1), 23–39.

Kaufman, A. & Kaufman, N. (2004). *Kaufman Assessment Battery for Children.* 2nd edn., AGS Publishers.

Kramer, M. S. (1998). Preventing preterm birth: Are we making progress? *Prenatal and Neonatal Medicine*, 3, 10–12.

Lester, B. M., Corwin, M. J., Sepkoski, C., Seifer, R., Peuker, M., McLaughlin, S., & Golub, H. L. (1991). Neurobehavioral syndromes in cocaine-exposed newborn infants. *Child Development, 62*, 694–705.

Luckasson, R., Borthwick-Duffy, S., Buntinx, W. H. E., Coulter, D. L., Craig, E. M., Reeve, A., et al. (2002). *Mental Retardation: Definition, Classification, and Systems of Support*, 10th edn., Washington, DC: American Association on Mental Retardation.

Main, D. M. & Mennuti, M. T. (1986). Neural tube defects: issues in prenatal diagnosis and counseling. *Obstetrics and Gynecology, 67*, 1–16.

Messinger, D. S., Dolcourt, J., King, J., Bodnar, A., and Beck, D. (1996). The survival and developmental outcome of extremely low birth weight infants. *Infant Mental Health Journal, 17*, 375–385.

Reynolds, C. R. & Kamphaus, R. W. (2004). *Behavior Assessment System for Children*, 2nd edn., AGS Publishing.

Shaw, D. S., Winslow, E. B., Owens, E. B., & Hood, N. (1998). Young children's adjustment to chronic family adversity: A longitudinal study of low-income families. *Journal of the American Academy of Child and Adolescent Psychiatry, 37*(5), 545–553.

Shepard, L., Kagan, S. L., & Wurta, E. (1998). *Principles and recommendations for early childhood assessments.* (Report No. PS026296). Washington, D.C.: National Education Goals Panel (ERIC Document Reproduction Service No. ED416033).

Smith, T. (1999). Temperament and maternal attitudes toward infants prenatally exposed to cocaine and other drugs. *Infant-Toddler Intervention, 9*, 69–86.

Snyder, P., Bailey, D. B., & Auer, C. (1994). Preschool eligibility determination for children with known or suspected learning disabilities under IDEA. *Journal of Early Intervention, 18*, 380–390.

Streissguth, A. & Kanter, J. (Eds.) (1997). *The challenge of Fetal Alcohol Syndrome: Overcoming Secondary Disabilities.* Seattle: University of Washington Press.

Wakschlag, L. S. & Keenan, K. (2001). Clinical significance and correlates of disruptive behavior in environmentally at-risk preschoolers. *Journal of Clinical Child Psychology, 30*(1), 262–275.

15

USING THE ABAS-II WITH ELEMENTARY AND MIDDLE SCHOOL STUDENTS

RANDY G. FLOYD AND RENEE BERGERON

Department of Psychology, University of Memphis, Memphis, TN 38152, U.S.A.
Hawaii Department of Education, Waipahu, HI 96797, U.S.A.

The Adaptive Behavior Assessment System, Second Edition (ABAS-II), offers a number of benefits to practitioners whose clients are enrolled in elementary school or middle school. Some of these benefits include (a) the availability of a parent–caregiver rating scale and an aligned teacher rating scale, (b) their ease of administration, and (c) the close match between the ABAS-II scores and the diagnostic criteria for mental retardation (MR) from the American Psychiatric Association (APA; 2000) and from the American Association on Mental Retardation[1] (AAMR; 2002).

The purpose of this chapter is to provide an overview of additional benefits of the ABAS-II with the elementary and middle school age group. The chapter begins with an overview of the characteristics of children in elementary school years and middle school years as well as a description of disorders and other conditions of primary relevance for adaptive behavior assessment in this age range. It continues with a description of the characteristics of assessment in this age range and follows with a summary of the technical characteristics, reliability evidence, and validity evidence supporting the use and interpretation of the

[1] The AAMR adopted the name American Association on Intellectual and Developmental Disabilities in 2007.

scores from the ABAS-II Parent Form and the ABAS-II Teacher Form. The chapter concludes with a description of two case studies in which these instruments were used as part of comprehensive assessments.

DEVELOPMENTAL AND DIAGNOSTIC ISSUES

When children enter elementary school, they face new developmental challenges, including developing cooperative peer relations, rule-governed behaviors, and competencies in reading, mathematics, spelling, and written expression. With mandatory schooling, this period is the first in which all children are required to experience traditional classrooms in which they will sit at desks, complete individual assignments, and listen to extended lectures.

In home and community settings, children entering elementary school are expected to demonstrate greater independence as their self-reflective and communication skills, physical competencies, and cognitive abilities increase with age. It is no surprise that this period is one in which discrepancies are often identified between children's actual behaviors in school, home, and community settings and those behaviors expected by teachers and parents for those their age. Disorders such as attention-deficit hyperactivity disorder (ADHD), mild MR, learning disabilities, Asperger's disorder, and some anxiety disorders are often first diagnosed during this period (APA, 2000; Barkley, 2006; Morris & March, 2004).

As children exit the elementary school and enter middle school, many will have entered puberty, are able to think hypothetically and abstractly, and begin to develop a sense of personal identity and a worldview that may be different from that of their parents. These changes are met with societal expectations of increasing competence and independence from their family. As children progress through the early adolescent years, many obtain employment outside the home, and many develop close relationships with peers of the opposite sex. Faced with these expectations, many children experience challenges related to emotion regulation, such as anxiety and depressive disorders, conduct disorder, as well as eating disorders (see Wolfe & Mash, 2006).

Based on these characteristics of children in elementary and middle school, those engaged in assessment must consider special issues that need not be considered with younger children. For example, as children develop greater self-regulatory capacities, they may be better able to conceal their behaviors through avoidance of caregivers than at earlier ages. This issue is compounded by changing societal expectations that perhaps leave adults less knowledgeable of children's behaviors. As children enter middle school, most move from one classroom to another throughout the school day. Thus, when compared to elementary school children whose teachers often spend the whole school day with them, middle school teachers often spend much less time and are far less knowledgeable of each child in their multiple classes. Furthermore, as children assert and are given more independence from their parents, parents' knowledge of their children's behaviors often declines precipitously as the teenage years progress. These influences on parent and teacher ratings may undermine the accurate measurement of adaptive behaviors. Thus, ample evidence is needed to support the use of ratings of adaptive behavior with this older age group.

Based on the epidemiology of mental disorders and other conditions for this age group, those engaged in assessment activities may be called on to use adaptive behavior assessment instruments, such as the ABAS-II, with parents and teachers of children in elementary and middle school. For example, professionals working in school settings are aware that children who received special education services for a developmental delay due to documented delays in physical development, social or emotional development, cognition, motor functioning, or adaptive development must be evaluated prior to age 9 to determine if they continue to require additional assistance. If they qualify, these children must meet eligibility criteria for another condition identified by the Individuals with Disabilities Education Improvement Act (2004). As summarized by Bergeron et al. (2008), all states in the U.S.A., except one, require consideration of adaptive behavior when identifying children as eligible for special education services for MR. In addition to developmental delay and MR, some researchers have proposed that, in addition to symptom display, assessors should identify a discrepancy between IQ and adaptive domains during a diagnostic assessment for ADHD (Roizen et al., 1994). Based on these three examples of mental disorders or disability conditions, it is clear that measures of adaptive behaviors will often be sought by those assessing children in elementary and middle schools.

EVALUATION OF EVIDENCE SUPPORTING USE AND INTERPRETATION OF ABAS-II SCHOOL-AGE FORMS

Support for the use and interpretation of the ABAS-II forms designed to be used with children in elementary and middle schools is found in the following section that reviews the psychometric properties of the ABAS-II Parent Form and the Teacher Form. It will provide the reader with conclusions about how these properties bear on the use and interpretation of scores from these forms. As an introduction to this review, it may be helpful to remind readers that both the ABAS-II Parent Form and Teacher Form produce a range of scores for a total composite, the General Adaptive Composite (GAC); three additional composites, Conceptual, Social, and Practical; and nine adaptive skill areas, communication, community use, functional academics, home living or school living, health and safety, leisure, self-care, self-direction, and social. (Scores are not available for the work skill area for children ages 6–16.) Scores stemming from the GAC, the three composites, and nine adaptive skill areas will be the focus of this review.

The criteria used to evaluate the ABAS-II Parent Form and Teacher Form were based on previous comprehensive reviews of intelligence tests, adaptive behavior instruments, and behavior rating scales (e.g., Bracken, 1987; Evans & Bradley-Johnson, 1988; Hammill et al., 1992; Flanagan & Alfonso, 1995; Bracken et al., 1998; Floyd & Bose, 2003) and *Standards for Educational and Psychological Testing* (American Educational Research Association, American Psychological Association, & National Council on Measurement in Education, 1999). We are aware of a number of insightful, published reviews targeting the ABAS-II (Rust & Wallace, 2004; Burns, 2006; Meikamp & Suppa, 2006). However, this chapter focuses solely on a more narrow age range than these reviews (i.e., 6–16 years), draws upon specific and established criteria for evaluation, includes evidence presented in sources other than the ABAS-II manual, and includes some additional analysis of data presented in the ABAS-II manual.

NORMING SAMPLE

Based on evidence presented in both the ABAS manual (Harrison & Oakland, 2000) and the ABAS-II manual (Harrison & Oakland, 2003), the ABAS-II standardization process appears to be exemplary. Ratings by parents were completed for 1,470 children age 5–16 years, and ratings by teachers were completed for 1,570 children age 5–16 years. There are at least 120 children in each 1-year norm group (ages 5–13) for the Parent Form and at least 140 children in each 1-year norm group (ages 5–13) for the Teacher Form. The norm groups for ages 13–14 and 15–16 contain from 140 to 250 children. These sample sizes exceed minimal standards for age-based norm groups (Hammill et al., 1992; Flanagan & Alfonso, 1995), and these age divisions correspond fully to the norms tables presented in the appendix of the ABAS-II manual.

Demographic information for those children rated using the ABAS-II Parent Form or Teacher Form was contrasted with that of the 1999 U.S. Census in the ABAS-II manual. As part of our review, we identified discrepancies between specific sample demographic characteristics (i.e., gender, race, socioeconomic status, community size, and region) and those in the respective census that were greater than 5 percentage points (Floyd & Bose, 2003). These discrepancies indicated oversampling and undersampling that may affect the representativeness of the norms groups.

When considering age, race–ethnicity, and the highest education level of a parent, there were only four instances (from 200 cells) of disproportionate sampling. For the Teacher Form, there was undersampling of White children ages 6, 12, and 15–16 whose parents' highest education level was completion of some college or technical school. For the Parent Form, we identified no oversampling or undersampling. When considering age, sex, and the highest education level of a parent, there were only six instances (from 100 cells) of disproportionate sampling. For the Teacher Form, there was undersampling of girls age 6 and age 12 whose parents' highest education level was completion of some college or technical school, undersampling of girls age 9 whose parents' highest education level was completion of college, undersampling of boys ages 15–16 whose parents' highest education level was completion of some college or technical school, and oversampling of girls age 9 whose parents' highest education level was completion of high school. For the Parent Form, there was undersampling of boys age 9 whose parents' highest education level was completion of some college or technical school. When considering age, sex, and race–ethnicity (80 cells), there were only two instances (from 80 cells) of disproportionate sampling. For the Teacher Form, there was undersampling of African American girls at age 9 and undersampling of White boys age 12. For the Parent Form, we identified no oversampling or undersampling. Approximately 5 percent of children in the norming sample rated by parents and approximately 8 percent of children in the norming sample rated by teachers experienced some clinical condition. The most common of these conditions were the high incidence disabilities seen in school and clinics, including learning disabilities and MR. These findings indicate that the samples from which norm-based scores for the ABAS-II Parent Form and Teacher Form stemmed from representative sampling of minority groups, sexes, and those of varying levels of education and disability groups.

RELIABILITY

Internal consistency reliability and test–retest reliability values were evaluated based on previously published standards (e.g., Bracken, 1987). For the Parent Form, the median internal consistency for adaptive skill areas for ages 6–16 all exceeded the minimal standard of .80. In fact, all adaptive skill areas exceeded .90 except for health and safety and self-care. Furthermore, the only skill area and age at which the actual internal consistency coefficient was less .80 was self-care at age 9. Median values for the three composites were all greater than .95, and median value for the GAC was .98. These exceptional internal consistency estimates were replicated in clinical samples (including mostly school-age children) with ADHD, learning disabilities, and MR as well as in a mixed clinical sample. From the clinical samples ranging in size from 26 (learning disability) to 49 (ADHD), there were only one instance in which a skill area internal consistency coefficient was less than .90 (self-care with children with ADHD). In addition, when the norming sample was divided into two groups (average and below average) based on the norm-based scores from the GAC, internal consistency coefficients corrected for range restriction also exceed minimal standards.

When the same standards were applied to internal consistency reliability coefficients for the Teacher Form, the median values for adaptive skill areas for ages 6 to 16 all exceeded the minimal standard of .80. In fact, all adaptive skill areas exceeded .90 except for community use. Furthermore, no skill area and age group (i.e., ages 6 to 16) was internal consistency coefficient less than .80. Median values for the three composites were all greater than .95, and median value for the GAC was .98. Again, these exceptional internal consistency estimates were replicated in clinical samples of children with ADHD, autistic disorder, emotional disturbance, deaf or hear of hearing, learning disability, MR, physical impairment, and behavior disorder and in a mixed clinical sample. From the clinical samples ranging in size from 19 (deaf or hear of hearing) to 248 (learning disability), there were only two instances in which an internal consistency coefficient for a skill area was less than .90. The vast majority of reliability coefficients for average and below average groups were above .90, and all coefficients were above .80 except community use at age 5–6 for average and below average groups. These exceptional reliability estimates for the GAC, the composites, and the adaptive skill areas give users of the ABAS-II Parent Form and Teacher Form confidence in interpreting obtained norm-based scores and allow for interpretation of reasonably narrow 90% confidence bands (e.g., about +/−2 standard score points (or less) for the GAC and +/−4 scaled score points (or less) for adaptive skill areas.)

The test–retest reliability of the scores from the ABAS-II Parent Form and Teacher Form were examined using total samples larger than 100 that were divided into age-differentiated subsamples that included at least 30 children. For the Parent Form, children were rated twice across 5 days to 6 weeks. All test–retest reliability coefficients for skills area scores, when corrected for range restriction or expansion, were greater than .80 except for the communication skill area for ages 5–9. The Conceptual and Practical composites and the GAC exceeded the .90 standard across all age levels while the test–retest reliability of the Social composite was below .90 for age 10–12 and age 13–21.

For the Teacher Form, children were rated twice across 3 days to 3 weeks. All test–retest reliability coefficients, when corrected for range restriction or expansion, were greater than .90 for ages 5–9. However, for ages 10–12, three skill area correlations – for communication, community use, and self-direction – were less than .80, and both the Social composite and the Practical composite correlations were less than .90. A similar pattern was present for ages 13–21. Two skill area correlations – for communication and school living – were less than .80, and the Social composite correlation was less than .90. For ages 10–12 and 13–21, the other adaptive skill areas exceeded the minimal standard, and the GAC and Conceptual composite correlations were above .90.

Interrater reliability was judged to be acceptable if the median subscale coefficient was .60 or greater for ratings conducted in similar settings (e.g., school classrooms). The standard for total scores was also set at .60 (Floyd & Bose, 2003). For the Parent Form, corrected correlations were .60 or higher, except for the social skill area for children ages 5–9. For children ages 10–18, all correlations exceeded .60. For the Teacher Form, corrected correlations were .60 or higher, except for the Conceptual composite for children ages 5–9. For children ages 10–18, all correlations exceeded .60.

SCALE/ITEM CHARACTERISTICS

Based on the standard that floors on instruments measuring adaptive behaviors are acceptable if a raw score of 1 is associated with a standard score at least two standard deviations below the normative mean, all ABAS-II adaptive skill areas across the Parent Form and the Teacher Form appear to have adequate floors. Thus, the adaptive skill areas (and their resulting composites) are sensitive to very low levels of adaptive behavior displays for children in elementary and middle school. Because the ABAS-II was not developed to measure adaptive behaviors that are in excess for children (e.g., those who are gifted) and this assessment goal is not recommended by its authors, we did not evaluate the upper range of standard scores (i.e., ceilings). However, the item gradients for each skill area appear to be acceptable (Bracken et al., 1998). Thus, item gradients for each skill area include at least 3 raw score points per standard deviation of scaled scores. These findings indicate that a few differences in scores assigned to items should not have drastic effects on the standardized scores of adaptive skill areas.

VALIDITY EVIDENCE

The ABAS-II manual presents an impressive array of validity evidence based on content, internal relations, and external relations that support the most common uses of the ABAS-II Parent Form and Teacher Form. This and other validity evidence is generally presented in accord with the five classes of validity evidence outlined in *Standards* (American Educational Research Association, American Psychological Association, & National Council on Measurement in Education, 1999).

EVIDENCE BASED ON CONTENT

Items for the ABAS-II Parent Form and Teacher Form appear to have been developed and evaluated with great care. The authors reviewed a large corpus of research about developmental disabilities and functional skills when developing items. An initial item pool of 1,500 items was reviewed by experts, and items were pruned. Items were evaluated through reviews of items by focus groups and through a nationwide item tryout study. Data from these studies were subjected to a variety of statistical analyses to examine item inter-relations, item guessing rate, and item bias. Item readability and clarity of instructions were evaluated, and clinical usefulness was evaluated by raters. These steps led to the exclusion of a number of items that failed to meet expectations (e.g., leading to frequent guessing by informants). Approximately 250 items on the Parent Form and on the Teacher Form were retained for norming of the rating scales.

When compared to many other adaptive behavior scales available to practitioners, the ABAS-II is one of only a few such scales (e.g., McCarney & Arthaud, 2006) that provides skill area scores corresponding directly to the adaptive behaviors described by APA (2000) as well as the AAMR (2002). Our review of items reveals that items appear to measure the behaviors consistent with the skill area labels while the procedure for assignment of items to adaptive skill areas has not been reported explicitly. The ABAS-II Parent Form and Teacher Form produce scores representing the three composites of adaptive functioning outlined by AAMR. In fact, the addition of the composites is the primary contribution of the ABAS-II Parent Form and Teacher Form over the respective forms from the first edition of the ABAS (Harrison & Oakland, 2000). Scores representing each skill area contribute to one of the three composites. The method for assigning adaptive skill areas to composites is consistent with that from the AAMR (2002).

EVIDENCE BASED ON RESPONSES PROCESSES

The ABAS-II manual includes the suggestion that raters complete the ABAS-II rating forms in a controlled setting within a single session lasting about 20 minutes. Alternate options for administration also are discussed. The ABAS-II manual provides a series of statements guide the raters when completing the rating forms, and written directions are included on the second and third pages of the rating forms. Both forms contain simple instructions and examples illustrating how to complete individual items. Although an option for the examiner to read items and make responses for the rater is described in the ABAS-II manual, it is expected that, in most cases, the ABAS-II rating forms will be completed by raters as they read brief statements and respond by circling a number from 0 to 3. The points on this scale range from (0) *Is Not Able*, (1) *Never or Almost Never When Needed*, (2) *Sometimes When Needed*, to (3) *Always or Almost Always When Needed*. Raters are asked to check a box to the right of the numbers if they guessed in responding, and the frequency of guessing by a rater can be compared to rates of guessing from the norming sample. The ABAS-II manual indicated the items, on average, were written at a fifth grade reading level. Thus, most parents and teachers who read English at an average level are unlikely to have difficulty comprehending the ABAS-II items.

EVIDENCE BASED ON INTERNAL STRUCTURE

To support the internal structure of the instruments, the ABAS-II manual presents correlations between skills areas, composites, and the GAC. As expected, all scores were positively correlated across matrixes. Correlations among adaptive skill areas and among composites were most frequently in the moderate range (.40 to .70) while some correlations were in the high range (.70 to .90). The ABAS-II manual also provides the results of confirmatory factor analysis (CFA) in which the correlations between skill area scores were used as data. Using a model-comparison approach, a single-factor model in which a general factor representing the GAC affected all skill area scores was compared to a three-factor model in which three inter-correlated factors representing ABAS-II composites effected skill area scores.

The results presented in the manual and our own CFA conducted using the correlation matrixes presented in the ABAS-II manual for the Parent Form (p. 118) and Teacher Form (p. 119) revealed that the three-factor model (representing each composite) provided a significantly better fit to the data than the single-factor model for both the Parent Form and Teacher Form ($p < .05$). Across analyses using both ABAS-II forms, the correlations between the three factors were very strong (≥.90 for Parent Form and ≥.96 for Teacher Form). Inclusion of a second-order factor accounting for these factor inter-correlations was admissible in all revised models. This model, including the three first-order factors representing the composites as well as the second-order factor representing the GAC, provided the exact same fit statistics as the correlated three-factor model (without the second-order factor). Across the analyses, fit statistics from the CFA indicated that the correlated three-factor model and its equivalent model including the second-order general factor provides a good yet not excellent way of explaining the relations between skill area scores. Some misfit between the theoretical model and the actual skill area inter-correlations may indicate that a revised model may be important to consider. For example, across our analyses using models for both the Parent Form and the Teacher Form, results indicated a significant relation between what is unique about the functional academics skill area and what is unique about the community use skill area when variance accounted for by a general factor, the Conceptual factor, and the Practical factor were considered. Review of the item content from the Functional Academics and Community Use adaptive skill areas does indeed indicate that many items refer to shopping, interacting with store or restaurant employees, and purchasing items in restaurants and stores. Users of the ABAS-II forms with this age group may benefit from considering these shared relations between adaptive skill areas. In summary, evidence of internal relations indicates that a powerful single factor represented by the GAC accounts for the vast majority of the variance in the skill area scores. In addition, consideration of the inter-relations between subsets of skill area scores (as often represented in composites) is supported.

EVIDENCE BASED ON EXTERNAL RELATIONS

The ABAS-II manual includes results from several studies supporting the relations between its scores and those from other assessment instruments as well as the results of studies designed to determine if ABAS-II scores differentiate between children with and without identified mental disorders and other conditions. In addition, other published resources we located also provide evidence based on external relations.

The ABAS-II manual summarizes the result of several studies in which children completed an intelligence test battery and their parents completed the ABAS-II Parent Form. Consistent with previous research, scores from the Parent Form were positively yet weakly to moderately correlated with IQs from the WISC-III (Wechsler, 1991). As expected, adaptive skill areas contributing to the

Conceptual composite (e.g., communication) demonstrated the highest correlations with the WISC-III Verbal IQ and Full Scale IQ. Patterns of correlations between scores from the Parent Form and those from the WISC-IV (Wechsler, 2003) were similar, with the resulting correlations somewhat weaker. For instance, the Conceptual composite and its constituent adaptive skill areas demonstrated the highest and most consistent correlations (in the moderate range) with the WISC-IV factor indexes and the Full Scale IQ. Findings were also similar in comparison to WAIS-III scores (Wechsler, 1997).

Although the ABAS-II manual presents correlations between scores from the preschool version of the ABAS-II Parent Form and the Scales of Independent Behavior-Revised (Bruininks et al., 1996) and the BASC-2 Parent Rating Scale (Reynolds & Kamphaus, 2004), there are no correlations reported in the ABAS-II manual between the scores from the Parent Forms and other informant-based adaptive behavior instruments. However, Sparrow et al. (2005) have presented its correlations with the Vineland II Survey Form. Corrected correlations between adaptive skill areas and composites from these instruments were positive and generally moderate in magnitude. The ABAS-II GAC and the Vineland II's Adaptive Behavior Composite correlated .78, and the mean scores from these composites were almost identical.

The ABAS-II manual summarizes the result of several studies in which children completed an intelligence test battery and their parents completed the ABAS-II Teacher Form. Results were similar to those reported earlier between the ABAS-II Parent Form and the intelligence test battery scores. From a somewhat small non-clinical sample, scores from the Teacher Form were positively and moderately correlated with IQs from the WISC-III (Wechsler, 1991). In contrast to findings using the Parent Form, the Practical composite (and its constituent adaptive skill areas) demonstrated some of the highest correlations with the WISC-III Verbal IQ, Performance IQ, and Full Scale IQ. Patterns of correlations between scores from the Teacher Form and those from the WISC-IV (Wechsler, 2003) from a large non-clinical sample were similar to those from the Parent Form study. Findings were also similar using a sample of children with autism and MR who completed the SB-IV (Thorndike et al., 1986) and a mixed clinical sample who completed the WIAT (Psychological Corporation, 1992)

The ABAS-II manual reports a number of studies yielding correlations between scores from the Teacher Form and those from other adaptive behavior assessment instruments. For example, correlations between adaptive skill areas and composites from the Teacher Form and related scores from the Vineland Adaptive Behavior Scales, Classroom Edition (Sparrow et al., 1985) from a non-clinical sample were positive and moderate to high in magnitude. The GAC and the Vineland Adaptive Behavior Composite correlated .84, and the mean scores from these composites from this sample differing by only 2.5 points (with the GAC being higher). As reported by Sparrow et al. (2006) correlations between scores from the ABAS-II Teacher Form and the Vineland II Classroom Edition were typically moderate or strong in magnitude across three age groups. Corrected correlations between the

ABAS-II GAC and the Vineland II Adaptive Behavior Composite were .55, .70, and .59 for age 5–9, 10–13, and 14–19, respectively. The mean Vineland Adaptive Behavior Composite was 2.7 points higher than the ABAS-II GAC for ages 5–9, 6.7 points lower than the GAC for ages 10–13, and approximately equal with the GAC for ages 14–19.

The ABAS-II manual presents the results of several studies examining the ability of the ABAS-II Parent Form scores to discriminate between children from its norming sample and children classified as having some mental disorder or educational condition. Perhaps the most notable finding was that parents of children with ADHD generally rated their children lowest on the self-direction skill area and significantly lower than the matched sample in the adaptive skill areas communication and functional academics. Weak skills evident in the self-direction and communication skill areas led to a similarly low score for the children with ADHD in the Conceptual composite, which was significantly lower than the matched group. Parent of children with MR, on average, rated their children lowest in functional academics skill area and in the Conceptual composite as well as highest in the home living skill area and in the Social composite. In contrast to the relatively specific deficits for the children with ADHD, children with MR were rated, on average, as having significantly lower scores than the matched sample across all adaptive skill areas and composites.

For the Teacher Form, results were obtained from several samples including children with the following conditions: Down syndrome, MR (unspecified, mild MR, moderate MR), ADHD, behavior disorder, emotional disturbance, deaf and hard of hearing, physical impairment, learning disability, and autistic disorder. Similar to the results from the Parent Form, teachers of children with ADHD, on average, rated them lowest on the self-direction skill area and the Conceptual composite. These results were similar to those from a sample of children deemed eligible for special education services for a behavior disorder. Teachers of children with MR, on average, rated them lowest in the functional academics skill area and in the Conceptual composite. They had significantly lower scores across all adaptive skill areas and composites. Children with autism were rated lowest in the health and safety skill area and in the Practical composite.

EVIDENCE BASED ON CONSEQUENCES

Instrument developers increasingly need to document probable or actual outcomes of the use of assessment instruments. The ABAS-II manual provides some evidence of probable outcomes. In order to prevent errors in clinical decision making by users, the manual provides details about the manner in which ABAS-II scores should be used within a comprehensive assessment and offers a caveat against using ABAS-II score profiles in isolation to diagnose mental disorders or other conditions. In order to facilitate the treatment utility of the ABAS-II, the manual describes the manner in which the results of the ABAS-II can be use for planning and monitoring interventions. In addition, case examples are included that outline interpretation of comprehensive psychoeducational assessments including the ABAS-II forms. Despite attention paid to its intended uses, like many other rating scales for children, research is needed to provide evidence of its treatment utility (Nelson-Gray, 2003).

SUMMARY

The ABAS-II authors and their development team have made great contributions to the assessment of the adaptive behaviors of elementary and middle school children by providing a pair of rating scales that are well normed and psychometrically sound for this age group. Barring a very few discrepancies with the results from the 1999 census, ABAS-II norms appear to represent well the population of children in the U.S.A. The ABAS-II Parent Form and Teacher Form also have evidenced strong psychometric properties by meeting or exceeding many published criteria for reliability and validity. As is typical with scores from rating scales, those scores that stem from the greatest number of items (i.e., that are the most global) tended to be the most reliable. Thus, users of the ABAS-II Parent Form and Teacher form can place the greatest weight on the GAC and the three composites. Validity evidence was well developed for these instruments. ABAS-II item content was based on careful review of recent diagnostic classification systems research, and items were selected for inclusion based on both manifest and empirical criteria. Evidence based on internal structure was provided in the form of correlations between ABAS-II scores as well as CFA. Although alternate models may be possible, a model that groups skill area scores into composites, with all adaptive skill areas also contributing the GAC, seems to fit the data reasonably well. Thus, interpretations based on the composites and the GAC from the ABAS-II Parent Form and Teacher Form seem supported by evidence based on internal relations. In addition, a variety of studies presented within the ABAS-II manual and in other sources provide strong evidence of external relations. Evidence of convergent validity and discriminative validity are apparent. More evidence of discriminant validity would be useful to support the validity of the skill area and composites scores.

Overall, the authors of the ABAS-II Parent Form and Teacher Form appear to have met their design goals and produced instruments that are both easy to administer and score as well as linked to the standard diagnostic nomenclature for assessment of MR and other developmental disabilities. The original ABAS and the revised and extended ABAS-II seem to have provided a strong body of evidence supporting the reliability and validity of rating scales used to assess adaptive behaviors in children, whereas reliance on interviews to obtain such information (especially with parents) was the status quo in adaptive behavior assessment. We believe that these innovations have already begun to affect the revision and development of other adaptive behavior inventories.

CASE STUDIES

We end this chapter by presenting two case studies in which the ABAS-II was used as part of a comprehensive assessment for referral concerns like those encountered by psychologists and other assessment professionals. The first case study describes results for a child suspected of having MR, and the second case study describes results for a child with difficulties in emotion regulation and peer relations. The case studies demonstrate how the ABAS-II can be useful in identifying either pervasive deficits or specific deficits in adaptive behaviors.

CASE STUDY 1: MENTAL RETARDATION

STUDENT: Josh Bates	PARENTS: Anthony and Angelina Bates
BIRTHDATE: 3/15/1998	AGE: 8 years, 1 months
GRADE: 2	SCHOOL: Riverdale Elementary

Sources of Information

Parent Interview
Teacher Interview
Stanford–Binet Intelligence Scales, 5th Edition
Woodcock–Johnson III Tests of Achievement
Adaptive Behavior Assessment System, 2nd Edition Parent Form
Adaptive Behavior Assessment System, 2nd Edition Teacher Form

Background Information

Josh was referred for this evaluation by the Student Support Team to understand better his intellectual, academic, and adaptive functioning.

Ms. Bates described her pregnancy with Josh as difficult. She was hospitalized 24 weeks into her pregnancy due to preterm labor, and Josh was delivered at 28 weeks via Cesarean section. Josh weighed 2 pounds, 14 ounces at birth. He was also jaundiced and was treated using bilirubin lights. Josh remained hospitalized for 2 months following birth. Because of the risk factors associated with prematurity and low birth weight, Josh was enrolled in an early intervention program and received services until age 3. Ms. Bates she could not recall at which ages Josh met developmental milestones.

Despite early health concerns, Ms. Bates reported that Josh is a healthy child. She stated that his vision and hearing were recently assessed and found to be within normal limits. However, Ms. Bates reported that Josh has had difficulty "fitting in" since he began school. She said that he seems to have few friends compared to his peers and believes that he is frequently teased by classmates. Josh's current teacher, Ms. Ariaza confirmed that Josh has few friends. She described him as friendly. However, he seemingly does not know how to initiate appropriate conversations with peers.

Ms. Ariaza described Josh as irresponsible with personal and classroom belongings and added that he frequently misses instructional time because he is looking for necessary materials. She reported that Josh is performing below grade level in all academic areas and that he has difficulty comprehending new concepts, focusing on assignments, and listening to directions. Ms. Ariaza noted that Josh will try hard when receiving individual assistance and has difficulty maintaining focus when required to work independently.

Cognitive Functioning

Josh's general intellectual functioning as measured by the Stanford–Binet Intelligence Scales, 5th Edition (SB5) falls in the Mildly Delayed range and at the 1st percentile when compared to others his age. He obtained a Full Scale IQ of 65 (with 95% confidence that his true score falls between 62 and 70), which is at the 1st percentile. Josh demonstrated similar performance on nonverbal reasoning (Nonverbal IQ = 69) and verbal reasoning (Verbal IQ = 64) tasks and across measures of specific intellectual abilities.

Academic Functioning

Josh's academic functioning as measured by the Woodcock–Johnson III Tests of Achievement is consistent with his level of intellectual functioning and reflects significant weaknesses across academic areas compared to his same-age peers. His standard scores were 69 on the Basic Reading Skills cluster (2nd percentile), 61 on the Reading Comprehension cluster (<1st percentile), 68 on the Math Calculation cluster (2nd percentile), 64 on the Math Reasoning cluster (1st percentile), and 64 on the Written Expression cluster (1st percentile).

Adaptive Functioning

Adaptive behavior often is described as those everyday skills needed to function effectively in the environment and include behaviors such as communication, adaptability, and social skills. Because adaptive behavior refers to a person's typical performance of the day-to-day activities required for personal and social sufficiency, results on adaptive behavior measures reflect what a person actually does, rather than what the person is able to do. Josh's mother completed the ABAS-II Parent Form, and his teacher completed the ABAS–II Teacher Form to obtain perspectives on Josh's adaptive functioning in the home and school settings.

Ratings from Josh's mother and teacher suggest that Josh has considerable deficiencies in his general adaptive functioning in both the home and school settings when compared to others his age. Both Ms. Bates and Ms. Ariaza reported that Josh exhibits adaptive behavior deficits across composites and skill areas when compared to others his age.

	Mother		Teacher	
Composites	Standard score	Qualitative range	Standard score	Qualitative range
Conceptual	70	Extremely low	75	Borderline
Social	68	Extremely low	66	Extremely low
Practical	70	Extremely low	53	Extremely low
General Adaptive Composite	65	Extremely low	61	Extremely low

Note: Composite standard scores have a mean (average) of 100 and a standard deviation of 15.

	Mother	Teacher
Adaptive skill areas	Scaled score	Scaled score
Communication	3	4
Functional academics	5	5
Self-direction	4	5
Leisure	4	3
Social	3	3
Community use	5	4
Home/school living	3	2
Health and safety	5	2
Self-care	5	2

Note: Adaptive skill area scaled scores have a mean (average) of 10 and a standard deviation of 3.

Summary and Recommendations for Intervention

Josh's performance on the SB5 indicates that his overall intellectual functioning is Mildly Delayed compared to others his age. Consistent with his intellectual functioning, Josh demonstrates considerable weaknesses across the reading, writing, mathematics, and language usage domains when compared to his same-age peers. Across adaptive areas, Ms. Bates and Ms. Ariaza reported that Josh exhibits considerable deficiencies in adaptive functioning relative to his same-age peers in both the home and school settings. Based on this information, Josh appears to meet the eligibility criteria for mild mental retardation.

Josh's parents and teacher are encouraged to work with the school-based intervention team to develop a behavior support plan to addresses his deficits in adaptive functioning in both home and school settings. Instruction in specific adaptive skills is most useful when it occurs within the context of daily routines across home, school, and community environments. Assistance from the school-based social worker is recommended to assist the family with seeking community support and resources for Josh.

CASE STUDY 2: GRIEF, EMOTION REGULATION, AND SOCIAL SKILL DEFICITS

STUDENT: Sara Roberts	PARENT: Sean Roberts
BIRTHDATE: 12/12/1995	AGE: 11 years, 1 month
GRADE: 6	SCHOOL: Watson Elementary

Sources of Information

Parent Interview
Teacher Interview
Wechsler Intelligence Scale for Children, 4th Edition
Wechsler Individual Achievement Test, 2nd Edition
Beck Youth Inventories of Emotional and Social Impairment
Adaptive Behavior Assessment System, 2nd Edition (ABAS–II) Parent Form
Adaptive Behavior Assessment System, 2nd Edition (ABAS–II) Teacher Form

Background Information

Sara was referred by her father to understand better her emotional adjustment.

Sara was born full-term and reached all developmental milestones within normal limits. Mr. Roberts reported that, as a child, Sara was outgoing and playful and was involved in a variety of activities (e.g., soccer and ballet). He added that Sara has always been a good student. Eight months ago, Sara's mother was killed in an accident, and Mr. Roberts reported that Sara has had difficulty adjusting to the loss of her mother. For example, Sara wakes up approximately 2 to 3 times per week during the night saying that she dreamt that her father has been killed in an accident as well. Although Sara has maintained a consistent "B" average in all academic areas this school year, Mr. Roberts reported that Sara has become very withdrawn and often chooses to be alone in her room rather than play with her friends. Sara's teacher, Ms. McKinely, described Sara as a diligent and polite student. She reported that Sara seems somewhat shy and that, when given free time, Sara usually chooses to complete academic assignments rather than interact with peers.

Cognitive Functioning

Sara's overall intellectual functioning as measured by the Wechsler Intelligence Scale for Children, 4th Edition is Average compared to others her age (Full Scale IQ = 102, 55th percentile). Factor index scores were all in the average range for her age except for the Processing Speed index, which was in the high average range.

Academic Functioning

Sara's performance on the Wechsler Individual Achievement Test, 2nd Edition indicates that her academic skills are Average across domains when compared to others her age. Her standard scores were 100 on the Reading composite (50th percentile), 103 on the Math composite (58th percentile), and 97 in on the Written Language composite (42nd percentile).

Emotional Functioning

Sara completed selected measures from the Beck Youth Inventories of Emotional and Social Impairment to provide further information on her emotional functioning. Her responses suggest that she experiences feelings of anxiety at about the same frequency as other girls her age. However, she reported moderately elevated levels of depressive symptoms (Depression Inventory T = 61). Her responses to specific items indicate occasional feelings of emptiness, sadness, and loneliness; difficulty sleeping; and regret for previous actions. Sara's responses also indicate that her perceptions of her competence and worth are lower than those of her same-age peers (Self-Concept T = 42). During a follow-up interview, Sara reported that she has felt lonely since her mother's death. She added that she has little interest in engaging in play activities with peers.

Adaptive Functioning

Mr. Roberts completed the ABAS-II Parent Form, and Ms. McKinely completed the ABAS–II Teacher Form to provide information on Sara's adaptive functioning.

	Father		Teacher	
Composites	Standard score	Qualitative range	Standard score	Qualitative range
Conceptual	95	Average	103	Average
Social	68	Extremely low	78	Borderline
Practical	89	Below average	95	Average
General Adaptive Composite	85	Below average	94	Average

Note: Composite standard scores have a mean (average) of 100 and a standard deviation of 15.

Ratings from Sara's father and teacher suggest a similar pattern of adaptive behaviors. Both reported that Sara exhibits average functioning in the Conceptual composite and near average functioning in the Practical composite. Mr. Roberts indicated that his daughter has some weaknesses in the health and safety and self-care skill areas. However, ratings from Mr. Roberts and Ms. McKinely indicate that Sara's weakest area of functioning is in the Social composite. Both reported that Sara exhibits normative weaknesses in engaging in leisure activities and in exhibiting age-appropriate social skills. Specifically, their responses indicate that Sara does not participate in organized activities (e.g., clubs or sports),

	Father	Teacher
Adaptive Skill Areas	Scaled score	Scaled score
Communication	8	10
Functional Academics	10	11
Self-Direction	9	10
Leisure	5	6
Social	4	5
Community Use	9	9
Home/School Living	8	11
Health and Safety	7	9
Self-Care	7	8

Note: Adaptive skill area scaled scores have a mean (average) of 10 and a standard deviation of 3.

does not invite others to play with her, does not try new activities, and does not have a stable group of friends.

Recommendations for Intervention

Because Sara's display of social skill deficits seems to stem from grief from the loss of her mother, it is recommended that Sara receive individual and group counseling to address these issues. Specifically, Sara's sense of belonging in group settings should be encouraged by her participating in the "Good Grief" counseling group for students who have experienced the death of a family member. Sara's social skills in her school setting could be promoted by her helping some classmates who are having academic difficulty. Sara should begin participating in a community group in which she expresses interest following discussions with the school counselor. A follow-up assessment targeting Sara's adaptive and emotional functioning is recommended in 3 months.

REFERENCES

American Association on Mental Retardation (AAMR) (2002). *Mental Retardation: Definition, Classification, and Systems of Supports*, 10th edn. Washington, DC: AAMR.

American Educational Research Association, American Psychological Association, & National Council on Measurement in Education (1999). *Standards for Educational and Psychological Testing*. Washington, DC: American Educational Research Association.

American Psychiatric Association (APA) (2000). *Diagnostic and Statistical Manual of Mental Disorders*, 4th edn., text revision. Washington, DC: APA.

Barkley, R. A. (2006). *Attention Deficit Hyperactivity Disorder: A Handbook for Diagnosis and Treatment*, 3rd edn. New York: Guilford.

Bergeron, R., Floyd, R. G., & Shands, E. L. (2008). State criteria for mental retardation. *Education and Training in Developmental Disabilities*, *41*, 123–131.

Bracken, B. A. (1987). Limitations of preschool instruments and standards for minimal levels of technical adequacy. *Journal of Psychoeducational Assessment, 5*, 313–326.

Bracken, B. A., Keith, L. K., & Walker, K. C. (1998). Assessment of preschool behavior and social-emotional functioning: A review of thirteen third-party instruments. *Journal of Psychoeducational Assessment, 16*, 153–169.

Bruininks, R. H., Woodcock, R. W., Weatherman, R. F., & Hill, B. K. (1996). *Scales of Independent Behavior-Revised.* Chicago: Riverside Publishing.

Burns, M. K. (2006). [Review of the Adaptive Behavior Assessment System(r), 2nd Edition]. In R. A. Spies & B. S. Plake (Eds.), *The Sixteenth Mental Measurements Yearbook* [Electronic version]. Retrieved April 30, 2006 from the Buros Institute's *Test Reviews Online* website: http://www.unl.edu/buros.

Evans, L. D. & Bradley-Johnson, S. (1988). A review of recently developed measures of adaptive behavior. *Psychology in the Schools, 25*, 276–285.

Flanagan, D. P. & Alfonso, V. C. (1995). A critical review of the technical characteristics of new and recently revised intelligence tests for preschool children. *Journal of Psychoeducational Assessment, 13*, 66–90.

Floyd, R. G. & Bose, J. E. (2003). A critical review of rating scales assessing emotional disturbance. *Journal of Psychoeducational Assessment, 21*, 44–78.

Harrison, P. L. & Oakland, T. (2000). *Adaptive Behavior Assessment System manual.* San Antonio, TX: PsychCorp.

Harrison, P. L. & Oakland, T. (2003). *Adaptive Behavior Assessment System*, 2nd edn. *Manual.* San Antonio, TX: PsychCorp.

Hammill, D. D., Brown, L., & Bryant, B. R. (1992). *A consumer's Guide to Test in Print*, 2nd edn. Austin, TX: Pro-ed.

Individuals with Disabilities Education Improvement Act, Pub. L. 108-446 (2004).

McCarney, S. B. & Arthaud, T. J. (2006). *Adaptive Behavior Evaluation Scale, Revised Second Edition: 4–12 Years School Version technical manual.* Columbia, MO: Hawthorne Educational Press.

Meikamp, J. & Suppa, C. H. (2006). [Review of the Adaptive Behavior Assessment System(r)-Second Edition]. In R. A. Spies & B. S. Plake (Eds.), *The sixteenth mental measurements yearbook* [Electronic version]. Retrieved April 30, 2006 from the Buros Institute's *Test Reviews Online* website: http://www.unl.edu/buros.

Morris, T. L. & March, J. S. (2004). *Anxiety disorders in children and adolescents*, 2nd edn. New York: Guilford Press.

Nelson-Gray, R. O. (2003). Treatment utility of psychological assessment. *Psychological Assessment, 15*, 521–531.

Psychological Corporation (1992). *The Wechsler Individual Achievement Test.* San Antonio, TX: Psychological Corporation.

Reynolds, C. R. & Kamphaus, R. W. (2004). *Behavior Assessment System for Children*, 2nd edn. Circle Pines, MN: American Guidance Service.

Roizen, N. J., Blondis, T. A., Irwin, M., & Stein, M. (1994). Adaptive functioning in children with attention-deficit hyperactivity disorder. *Archives of Pediatric and Adolescent Medicine, 148*, 1137–1142.

Rust, J. O. & Wallace, M. A. (2004). Test review [Review of the test *Adaptive Behavior Assessment System(s)*, 2nd Edition]. *Journal of Psychoeducational Assessment, 22*, 367–373.

Sparrow, S. S., Cicchetti, D. V., & Balla, D. A. (1985). *Vineland Adaptive Behavior Scales, Classroom edition manual.* Circles Pines, MN: American Guidance Service.

Sparrow, S. S., Cicchetti, D. V., & Balla, D. A. (2005). *Vineland Adaptive Behavior Scales*, 2nd edn. *Survey forms manual.* Circles Pines, MN: American Guidance Service.

Sparrow, S. S., Cicchetti, D. V., & Balla, D. A. (2006). *Vineland Adaptive Behavior Scales*, 2nd edn. *Teacher rating form manual.* Bloomington, MN: Pearson Assessments.

Thorndike, R. L., Hagen, E. P., & Sattler, J. M. (1986). *Stanford–Binet Intelligence Scale*, 4th edn. Chicago: Riverside.

Wechsler, D. (1991). *The Wechsler Intelligence Scale for Children*, 3rd edn. San Antonio, TX: Psychological Corporation.

Wechsler, D. (1997). *Wechsler Adult Intelligence Scale*, 3rd edn. San Antonio, TX: Psychological Corporation.

Wechsler, D. (2003). *The Wechsler Intelligence Scale for Children*, 4th edn. San Antonio, TX: Psychological Corporation.

Wolfe, D. A. & Mash, E. J. (Eds.). (2006). *Behavioral and Emotional Disorders in Adolescents: Nature, Assessment, and Treatment.* New York: Guilford.

16

USING THE ABAS-II WITH ADOLESCENTS AND YOUNG ADULTS

S. CRAIG RUSH[*], MICHELLE MAJOR-SANABRIA[**] AND STEPHANIE CORCORAN[†]

[*]*School Psychology Program, University of Alabama, Tuscaloosa, AL 35487-0231, U.S.A.*
[**]*Department of Psychology, Barry University, Miami Shores, FL 33161-6695, U.S.A.*
[†]*Shelby County Public School System, Alabaster, AL 35007, U.S.A.*

The Adaptive Behavior Assessment System (ABAS-II), 2nd Edition may be used to understand the adaptive behaviors of adolescents and young adults with various problems and for various purposes. This chapter discusses adaptive behavior as it is related to adolescents and young adults, the validity of the ABAS-II with adolescents and young adults, and a psychoeducational case study that includes ABAS-II data from multiple respondents.

ADAPTIVE BEHAVIOR AND CHARACTERISTICS OF ADOLESCENTS AND YOUNG ADULTS

ADOLESCENT DEVELOPMENT AND IMPORTANCE OF ADAPTIVE BEHAVIOR

In industrial societies, adolescence occurs during the teen years (Schlegel & Barry, 1991), while young adulthood, although more loosely defined, is frequently described as occurring during the early to mid twenties. Various changes occur during adolescence and young adulthood, including changes in physiology, cognition, emotion, and behavior. Many of these changes are set in motion by the onset of puberty, but other changes are charged by environment and contextual factors, such as new learning environment and structure, social challenges, and the realization that the responsibilities of adulthood are near or have begun to arrive. As a result, adolescence and young adulthood are critical periods for identity and vocational development, and for contemplating higher education (Robin, 1998) and other future endeavors such as long-term love relationships and starting a family (Berk, 1998; Lefrancois, 1999). Such development and contemplation often take place through psychological separation from parents and other adult family members as adolescents and young adults begin the task of defining and planning their lives (Berk, 1998).

Given the new and challenging academic and social structures that children with which entering adolescence and young adulthood must contend, adaptive skills become increasingly important during this period of development. Adaptive behavior is broadly defined as "the collection of conceptual, social, and practical skills that have been learned by people in order to function in their everyday lives" (American Association of Mental Retardation (AAMR), 2002, p. 41), and, unlike cognitive ability, can increase with interventions, training, and experience (Freeman et al., 1999; Bolte & Poustka, 2002). Like cognitive ability, adaptive skills are relative to one's age. As children enter adolescence, the everyday tasks of life become different and more complex and adaptive skills must grow and change to address the tasks. The challenge of the secondary education environment becomes a particular concern as demands are increased in areas such as grasping information, indicating knowledge through classroom tests, expressing thoughts through writing, working independently, staying organized, using cognitive strategies, interacting socially, and being motivated to learn (Mercer & Mercer, 1993).

Similarly, obtaining and maintaining employment becomes more of a concern during the later stages of adolescent and young adult development than in earlier stages (Langone & Burton, 1987; Berk, 1998; Lefrancois, 1999). The transition to employment (which also can be conceptualized as synonymous with the transition to adulthood) is one of, if not, the most important and most difficult tasks of adolescence and young adulthood, and is even more so in today's age of technology and globalization in the workplace (Langone & Burton, 1987; Krieg et al., 1995; Berk, 1998; Lefrancois, 1999). Vocational-related adaptive functioning deficits may be overlooked in adolescence and only become evident as the individual leaves the structured educational environment and transitions into the more autonomous school and work environments. For adolescents and young adults with adaptive functioning concerns, teaching vocational and independent living skills is a critical target transitional goal (Langone & Burton, 1987). The *School-to-Work Opportunity Act* (1994) and the *Carl D. Perkins Vocational and Applied Technology Act* (1990) attempted to address these concerns by providing all adolescents and young adults the opportunity to complete vocational training and obtain suitable employment. Furthermore, the *Individuals with Disabilities Education Improvement Act* (IDEIA, 2004) mandates a plan for transitional services for children with disabilities, including post-secondary education or employment. Under IDEIA, Schools are required to begin planning transitional services at age 14 and commence implementation of the services by age 16. The aforementioned pieces of legislation are important because each can potentially address work-related adaptive behavior problems of adolescence and young adults with and without disabilities.

DISORDERS AND DISABILITIES AFFECTING ADAPTIVE BEHAVIOR OF ADOLESCENTS AND YOUNG ADULTS

Adolescents and young adults, both with and without various disabilities and disorders, can exhibit adaptive behavior deficits as well as maladaptive behavior problems. For example, if a teenager is emotionally "acting out," such behavior might very well interfere with daily functioning, but it does not necessarily constitute an adaptive behavior deficit (AAMR, 2002) and in some ways could even be conceptualized as being adaptive. On the other hand, if the same individual has not developed the repertoire of skills to communicate in a manner other than "acting out," then he or she might be considered to have an adaptive behavior deficit. There are a number of disorders and disabilities that affect adaptive behavior as well as cause maladaptive behavior problems for individuals, and have a relatively high onset in and particular salience to adolescence and young adulthood.

Traumatic brain injury: As adolescents and young adults are more likely to engage in risk taking behaviors (Arnett, 1992), they are at higher risk for a traumatic brain injury (TBI). Adolescents and young adults between the ages of 15 and 19 have some of the highest rates of TBI (Langlois et al., 2006). TBIs among all children have been estimated to annually result in approximately 150,000 hospitalizations, and 30,000 children becoming permanently disabled (Savage & Wolcott, 1995). Although individuals differ in how they function after a TBI, problems with one or more areas of adaptive skills (e.g., self-care, interpersonal relations, self-regulation, communication, academics, etc.) are not uncommon for such individuals, particularly in more severe cases (Savage & Wolcott, 1995; Thurman et al., 1999). Furthermore, vocational preparation also is a major concern for individuals with a TBI (Corrigan et al., 2004). As a result of the seriousness of TBI in the school-age population, the *Individuals with Disabilities Education Act* (IDEA, 1990) added TBI as a special education category, where it remains under IDEIA (2004). TBI also is covered under Section 504 of the Rehabilitation Act (1973), which mandates schools to offer reasonable accommodations to students with disabilities.

Mood disorders: Mood disorders also have a high onset among adolescents and young adults. The approximate age of onset is 13–30 for bipolar disorders

(Kronenberger & Meyer, 2001) and 11–19 for depressive disorders and depressive symptoms (Lewinsohn et al., 1988; Burke et al., 1990; Birmaher et al., 1996; Hammen and Rudolph, 1999), while the overall prevalence of mood disorders has been reported as high as 8% in adolescence and young adulthood (Kronenberger & Meyer, 2001). Moreover, approximately 15% of adolescents in North America report feeling depressed, anxious, confused, and emotionally empty (Offer et al., 1984). Mood disorders can affect adaptive skills in a number of areas such as self-care, interpersonal relations, communication, functional academics, occupational performance, self-direction, and health and safety (Sparrow & Cicchetti, 1987; APA, 2000; Kronenberger & Meyer, 2001). Under IDEIA (2004), adolescents with mood disorders often are addressed under the special education category of emotional disturbance.

Schizophrenia: Schizophrenia is a disorder with a high onset in adolescence and young adulthood and can affect adaptive skills in areas such as self-care, academics, communication, interpersonal relations, and general goal directed behavior (APA, 2000; Kronenberger & Meyer, 2001). The onset of schizophrenia is typically between late adolescence and the early part of adulthood with the mean age of onset for men in the early to mid 20s and in the latter 20s for women (APA, 2000). There is not a separate category for schizophrenia under IDEIA (2004); however, the disorder is typically addressed under the special education category of emotional disturbance.

Attention-deficit/hyperactivity disorder: Although attention-deficit/hyperactivity disorder (ADHD) is typically diagnosed during childhood, the disorder can persist and even worsen in adolescence and young adulthood (Barkley et al., 1990a; Abramowitz & O'Leary, 1991; Jaffe, 1995; Biederman, et al., 1996). The American prevalence of ADHD has been reported as being between 3% and 7% of school-age children and is characterized primarily by a consistent pattern of inattention and/or impulsivity (APA, 2000). Adolescents and young adults with ADHD are at a higher risk for psychological and or learning problems that can continue into later adulthood (Barkley, 1990, 1998; Slombowski et al., 1995; Seidman et al., 1997; Robin, 1998; APA, 2000). ADHD may be associated with a number of adaptive skill problems in areas such as interpersonal relations, functional academics, occupational performance, health and safety, and communication and can become even more pronounced with the increasing self-directed environments typical of adolescence and young adulthood (Cunningham & Siegal, 1987; Barkley et al., 1990a, b, 1992; Weiss & Hechtman, 1993; Erhardt & Hinshaw, 1994; Faraone et al., 1995; Sealander et al., 1997; Seidman et al., 1997; Robin, 1998; APA, 2000). Under IDEIA (2004), ADHD typically is addressed under the special education category of other health impaired (OHI). ADHD also is covered under Section 504 of the Rehabilitation Act (1973).

Learning disabilities: Like ADHD, learning disabilities are typically diagnosed during childhood (APA, 2000). However, adaptive functioning deficits of adolescents and young adults with learning disabilities may become increasingly evident as they enter more autonomous environments such as secondary and post-secondary education, work, and various social settings (Weller & Strawser, 1987). Learning disabilities are specifically addressed under IDEIA (2004) and are covered under section 504 of the Rehabilitation Act (1973).

Antisocial personality disorder and conduct disorder: Antisocial personality disorder is not diagnosed until late adolescence (age 18), and includes some symptoms of conduct disorder, a disorder with typical onset between middle childhood and adolescence (APA, 2000). The hallmark feature of antisocial personality disorder, as well as conduct disorder, is a lack of regard toward the feelings of others (APA). It is not uncommon for adolescents and young adults with antisocial personality disorder or conduct disorder to have adaptive skills problems in the areas of health and safety, occupational performance, daily living, self-direction, and interpersonal skills (APA). Although IDEIA (2004) does not cover egosyntonic disorders such as antisocial personality disorder and conduct disorder, both disorders rarely present alone and are often comorbid with other disorders such as mood disorders, learning disabilities, and ADHD (APA; Kronenberger & Meyer, 2001).

Substance-related disorder: The disorders, disabilities, symptoms, and behaviors that are common among adolescents and young adults can be the catalyst for alcohol and substance abuse (APA, 2000; National Institute on Drug Abuse (NIDA), 2004). There is a high prevalence of overall substance use among adolescents and young adults, with alcohol being the most commonly abused and the leading cause of injuries and fatalities during this period of development (Berk, 1998; Lefrancois, 1999; Jenkins, 2000). Initial episodes of alcohol intoxication are most likely to occur during adolescence, while the onset of alcohol dependence rises in young adulthood (APA). Chronic alcohol and/or substance abuse can cause severe cognitive, motor, and psychological problems which can affect adaptive skills in areas such as self-care, academic and occupational performance, health and safety, interpersonal relations, and communication (APA; Fishman et al., 1997; Nanda & Konnur, 2006). Substance-related disorder is not specifically covered under IDEIA (2004), but, for some adolescents, may be addressed under the special education category of Emotional Disturbance, which includes "maladaptive behaviors" as one of the defining criteria for that classification. Substance-related disorder also is covered under Section 504 of the Rehabilitation Act (1973).

Mental retardation: Although the onset of mental retardation occurs in infancy or very early childhood, it is a disorder that has lifelong consequences (APA, 2000) and therefore warrants some mention with regard to adaptive behavior in adolescence and young adulthood. Mental retardation is conceptualized as significant intellectual limitations that exist along with deficits in conceptual, social, and practical adaptive behavior areas (AAMR, 2002). As children with mental retardation move into adolescence and young adulthood, more adaptive skill deficits become apparent. Given new and varying challenges of the period of development, problems with the use of practical, social, and conceptual skills become particularly salient for adolescents and young adults with mental retardation (AAMR).

Mental retardation is addressed as a specific category under IDEIA (2004) and requires an assessment of adaptive behavior. See Chapter 18 for a complete discussion of adaptive behavior and mental retardation.

Autism: Autism also occurs in early childhood and persists life long (APA, 2000). Some individuals with autism are very high functioning, but may nevertheless have some deficits in various adaptive skills. As such, adaptive behavior can be a very critical component of academic, vocational, and social development for higher functioning adolescents and young adults with autism (Adreon & Durocher, 2007). For those children with autism who have lower abilities, adaptive behavior concerns may become even more magnified. Autism is addressed as a specific category under IDEIA (2004). See Chapter 19 for a complete discussion of autism and other pervasive developmental disorders.

ASSESSING ADAPTIVE BEHAVIOR AND VALIDITY OF THE ABAS-II WITH ADOLESCENTS AND YOUNG ADULTS

ADAPTIVE BEHAVIOR ASSESSMENT OF ADOLESCENTS AND YOUNG ADULTS

To this end, it is particularly important that adaptive behavior be assessed regularly when working with adolescents and young adults with disabilities, disorders, and other problems that contribute to deficits in adaptive functioning (Harrison, 1987, 1990; Reschly, 1990; Harrison & Boney, 2002). Adaptive measures can assist in identifying strengths and weaknesses when planning transitional recommendations (McCarver & Campbell, 1987; Carter et al., 1998) as well as serve as a sensitive tool in monitoring change (Felce et al., 1986), which are key elements to increasing adaptive skills and fostering vocational, educational, and personal success for all students with adaptive functioning concerns (Felce et al., 1986; Carter et al., 1998; Stuart & Smith, 2002; Eiseman, 2003; Kraemer et al., 2003; Katsiyannis et al., 2005).

Multiple adaptive behavior data sources should be considered to determine the most appropriate intervention plan for adolescents and young adults with adaptive behavior deficits. Furthermore, consideration should be given to the individual's particular adaptive and cognitive strengths along with addressing areas of weakness. Specific interventions for adolescents and young adults with adaptive behavior deficits might include: vocational programming, social skill training, oral communication skills training, teaching problem solving and planning skills, scaffolding learning, positive reinforcement, creating conversational opportunities, academic accommodations such as study guides, self-advocacy training, self-monitoring, and learning how to navigate various community resources.

It also is important to keep in mind that measuring the adaptive functioning of adolescents and young adults, as well as of the adaptive function of individuals in other developmental ranges, is different from measuring other psychological constructs. For example, adaptive behavior assessment is different from cognitive assessment, in that adaptive behavior assessment examines skills that are *actually* performed regularly in everyday life, not only the ability to perform a skill or complete a specific task at a point in time. Thus, adaptive behavior assessment is typically conducted with rating scales and interviews of informants that have adequate opportunity to observe an individual's adaptive skills and report about typical performance in natural settings. As mentioned previously, the construct of cognitive ability is different from adaptive behavior in that cognitive ability remains fairly stable over time, whereas adaptive functioning can improve with interventions and appropriate experiences (Freeman et al., 1999; Bolte & Poustka, 2002). Adaptive behavior assessment also is different from social-emotional assessment in that social-emotional assessment is designed to examine internalized and externalized emotional psychopathology, not necessarily the ability to perform specific day-to-day life functions need for personal and social competence.

SUITABILITY OF ABAS-II STRUCTURE TO UNDERSTANDING ADOLESCENTS AND YOUNG ADULTS

The ABAS-II provides a comprehensive, norm referenced assessment of adaptive behavior and skills. The instrument contains readily observable, developmentally appropriate, age-sensitive items that are appropriate for use with adolescents and young adults for a variety of purposes, including transitional planning and monitoring (Harrison & Oakland, 2003). Furthermore, the ABAS-II allows for multiple respondents across various settings, and therefore is well suited for comprehensive assessment of adolescents and young adults in their relevant contexts such as work, school, home, and other settings for which a respondent may be familiar. This is a particularly important feature as the degree to which an adaptive behavior measure promotes functional definitions of target behaviors determines its efficacy as a tool for developing interventions (Gresham & Elliot, 1987).

Of the five forms of the ABAS-II, three can be used with adolescents and young adults: the Parent Form (ages 5–21), Teacher Form (ages 5–21), and Adult Form (ages 16–89). For adolescents and young adults who are in the 16–21 age range and in a secondary school setting, the Parent and Teacher Forms are typically used. The Adult Form is better suited for adolescents and young adults who are 16 years of age and older and no longer in a secondary school setting; the Adult Form uses informants such as family members and supervisors and also allows a self-rating by individuals with perquisite skills needed to report their adaptive activities.

The ABAS-II contains three broad composites (Conceptual, Social, and Practical) and an overall, General Adaptive Composite (GAC). Each composite contains a number of adaptive skill areas. For the three ABAS-II forms applicable to adolescents and young adults, the Conceptual Composite contains the adaptive skill areas of communication, functional academics, and self-direction; the Social Composite contains the adaptive skill areas of leisure and social; and the Practical Composite contains the adaptive skill areas of community use, home living (school living on the Teacher Form), health and safety, and self-care. An overall composite score, the GAC, is provided.

In addition, all three of the ABAS-II forms that are applicable to adolescents and young adults contain a work adaptive skill area. Items about work-related aspects of behavior are important as they can increase the predictive validity of an adaptive behavior measure (Kamphaus, 1987) for adolescents and young adults. The work adaptive skill area, however, is optional for ages 16 and older on each form, and should only be used if the individual being assessed has ever been employed. The work adaptive skill area does not contribute to the GAC on the Parent and Teacher Form, but is included in the GAC and within the Practical Composite if used on the Adult Form.

CONTRIBUTIONS OF ABAS-II COMPOSITES

Practical composite: Each composite area of the ABAS-II makes a unique contribution to understanding the adaptive behavior of adolescents and young adults. As the practical skills required to live independently are considered to be paramount to the development of adolescents and young adults (Berk, 1998; Lefrancois, 1998), the Practical Composite is especially apt for understanding the adaptive skills of individuals within this population as it covers four specific adaptive skill areas on the school-age forms (community use, home/school living, health and safety, and self-care) and five specific adaptive skill areas (work, community use, home/school living, health and safety, and self-care) on the Adult Form, the most adaptive skill areas covered by any composite on the ABAS-II. Of these, the work adaptive skill area, which assesses adaptive skills needed to function in a work environment, is a particularly important practical adaptive skill area as vocational preparation is one of the most important aspects of adolescent and young adult development (Langone & Burton, 1987; Krieg et al., 1995; Berk, 1998; Lefrancois, 1999). The community use adaptive skill area also is important to understanding the practical adaptive skills of adolescents and young adults because individuals during this period begin to independently traverse day-to-day functions in the community such as driving and purchasing goods and services. Similarly, the home living (school living on the Teacher Form) adaptive skill area is an important component as the period of adolescence and young adulthood is marked by preparing for the responsibilities of living in an environment separate from parents or other caregivers. As adolescence and young adulthood is a period of increased risk taking behavior (Arnett, 1992), the health and safety adaptive skill area is a significant and potentially focal aspect of practical adaptive behavior during this period. Finally, given the increased concern about physical appearances during adolescence and young adulthood (Bibby & Posterski, 1992), the self-care adaptive skill area holds great significance to understanding the practical adaptive behavior of individuals during this period of development.

Social composite: The social adaptive skill area, part of the Social Composite of the ABAS-II, is important for understanding the social adaptive behavior of adolescents and young adults because social skills are a requisite for functioning in the academic, social, and work environment, as well as for becoming an independent member of the community (Gresham & Elliot, 1987). Social relationships with others during this period can affect current and future social behavior, academic performance, and vocational achievement (Bishop & Inderbitzen, 1995). Similarly, the leisure adaptive skill area, also part of the Social Composite, examines skills needed to engage in leisure activities, including activities with others (Harrison & Oakland, 2003), which is a key part of identity and self-development during adolescence and young adulthood (Hart & Yates, 1996).

Conceptual composite: Within the Conceptual Composite of the ABAS-II, the self-direction adaptive skill area is described as "[s]kills needed for independence, responsibility, and self-control ..." (Harrison & Oakland, 2003, p. 5). This description is consistent with the transitional tasks particular to adolescence and young adulthood, which involves greater self-reliance (Krieg et al., 1995). Also within the Conceptual Composite is the communication adaptive skill area. Communication skills continue to develop through adolescence, and are related to adolescent and young adults' increased ability to think and verbally articulate in an abstract manner (Berk, 1998). The Secretary of Labor's Commission on Achieving Necessary Skills (1991) included communication skills as one of the major components of the basic skills required to successfully transition from school to work. Last, the functional academics adaptive skill area of the Conceptual Composite reflects the ability to apply basic academic concepts to daily functioning. During adolescence and young adulthood, applying such concepts to higher order tasks such as monetary budgeting, applying for employment or admission to college, writing correspondence, reading important information, etc. are necessary for functioning independently at present and in the future.

VALIDITY STUDIES ON THE ABAS-II

Evidence of validity is found in a test's theory and empirical evidence (American Educational Research Association, American Psychological Association, & National Council on Measurement in Education, 1999). The validity of the ABAS-II has been examined across specific samples of adolescents and young adults as well as more generalized samples that include adolescents and young adults. The validity of the ABAS-II for use with adolescents and young adults can be found, in part, in data that examine its factor structure, intercorrelations, as well as through clinical studies.

Factor structure: Empirical evidence of a test's factor structure provides foundational information on its validity (American Educational Research

Association, American Psychological Association, & National Council on Measurement in Education, 1999). Confirmatory factor analyses with data from each form applicable to adolescents and young adults support both a three-factor model consistent with the Conceptual, Social, and Practical Composites of the ABAS-II, as well as a one-factor model. These data provide support for the measure's intended factor structure.

Intercorrelations of data: Data on intercorrelations between adaptive skill areas, composites, and the GAC provide evidence of the internal stability and thus validity of a test. One strives to build a test in which the subtests correlative higher with their intended composites than with the other composites. Furthermore, the composites should correlate modestly with the total score. The results of studies using data from the Teacher Form for ages 15 and 16 and ages 17 to 21, the Parent Form for ages 15 and 16 and ages 17 to 21, and the Adult Form for self-ratings and ratings from others for ages 16 to 21 are summarized below.

Data from the Teacher Form for ages 15 and 16 and ages 17 to 21 show intercorrelations among the adaptive skill areas that are moderate (range = .36 to .84) and generally lower than those between the adaptive skill areas and the GAC (range = .50 to .86). Data from the Parent Form for ages 15 and 16 and ages 17 to 21 also show intercorrelations among the adaptive skills areas that are moderate (range = .40 to .80) and lower than those between the adaptive skill areas and the GAC (range = .57 to .86). Similar to the data from the Teacher and Parent Forms, the Adult Form for self-ratings and ratings from others show intercorrelations among the adaptive skill areas that are moderate (range = .37 to .83) and lower than those between the adaptive skill areas and the GAC (range = .55 to .87).

Clinical studies: Evidence of the convergent and discriminant validity of ABAS-II data with adolescents and young adults is found in the instrument's ability to discriminate between individuals with and without disabilities. A number of clinical validity studies were conducted with adolescents and young adults using ABAS-II data. These results are summarized below.

Using the Teacher Form for ages 5 through 21, the profiles of 114 individuals with learning disabilities, ages 13 through 21, were compared to a matched control group. The adolescents and young adults with learning disabilities displayed significantly lower ABAS-II scores than the matched control group. Those with learning disabilities scored significantly lower on the GAC (M = 87) than the matched control group (M = 94). Mean composite scores for the sample with learning disabilities were significantly lower than those for the matched control group. Mean scores for the adaptive skill areas also were lower for those with learning disabilities. Approximately 31% of the sample with learning disabilities group had a GAC or one or more composite scores that lower than two standard deviations in contrast to 18% for the control group. Furthermore, approximately 48% of the group with learning disabilities had two or more adaptive skill area scores that were lower than two standard deviations below the mean versus approximately 36% for the control group.

Although not specifically focused on adolescents and young adults, a number of adolescents and young adults were included in other clinical studies. For example, on the Parent, Teacher, and Adult Forms across five school-age samples (ages 5 through 21) and one adult sample (ages 17 through 72), the mean GACs for individuals with mental retardation were significantly lower than those for the matched control groups. On the Teacher Form the GACs for school-age samples of individuals with physical impairments (ages 5 through 20), autistic disorder (ages 5 through 18), behavior disorders (ages 5 through 21), and emotional disturbance (ages 5 through 18) were significantly lower than those for matched control groups. On the Parent Form, the mean GAC from a sample of individuals with ADHD (ages 6 through 21) was significantly lower than those for a matched control group.

CASE STUDY

PSYCHOEDUCATIONAL REPORT

Name: Sara Smith
Age 17 years, 0 months

Sources of Information

Adaptive Behavior Assessment System, 2nd Edition (ABAS-II)

- Teacher Form for ages 5–21 (completed by Lori Morgan, Lead Special Education Teacher)
- Parent Form for ages 5–21 (completed by Ann Smith, biological mother)

Oral and Written Language Scales (OWLS)
Wechsler Adult Intelligence Scale, 3rd Edition (WAIS-III)
Wechsler Individual Achievement Test, 2nd Edition (WIAT-II)
Behavior Assessment System for Children, 2nd Edition (BASC-II)

- Teacher Rating Scale for ages 12–21 (completed by Jim Farmer, Academic Enhancement Teacher)

School Records

Reason for Referral

Sara Smith, a 17-year old. 11th grade student at Madison High School, and is receiving special education services. Sara was referred due to the need to complete a 3-year re-evaluation required for special education services. Her parents and teachers requested current assessment data to determine an appropriate intervention program.

Background Information

Sara lives at home with her parents, twin sister, and younger brother. Her parents and teachers express no concerns about her school behavior and attendance.

During the 10th grade school year, Sara received general education instruction for all core and elective classes. Sara's only special education class was for academic enhancement, which is a small group class that meets three times weekly to promote study skills. Her class grades for the 1st semester were 73 in algebra IB, 87 in U.S.A. history, 70 in English 10, 81 in coordinated studies, 73 in physical science, 92 in health, and 96 in academic enhancement. Sara received inclusion support from her special education teacher for algebra, history, English, coordinated studies, and physical science classes. Sara recently attempted the state's high school graduation exam and did not pass any portion of the exam.

Assessment Results

Intellectual abilities: Sara's intelligence was assessed with the WAIS-III, an individually administered intelligence test. Sara obtained Full Scale IQ of 64, which is descriptively classified in the extremely low range. She obtained a Verbal Scale IQ of 66 which, is descriptively classified in the extremely low range, and a Performance IQ of 70, which is descriptively classified in the borderline range.

Achievement: Sara's achievement was assessed with the WIAT-II, an individually administered assessment of achievement. She obtained a reading composite score of 69, a math composite score of 61, an oral language composite of 80, and a written expression composite of 68. Overall, Sara's achievement scores are consistent with her intellectual functioning.

Language: Sara's language skills were assessed with the OWLS, an individually administered assessment of receptive and expressive language. Sara obtained a listening comprehension score of 70 and an oral expression score of 60. Sara's language scores are consistent with her general intellectual functioning and achievement.

Social-emotional: The BASC-II rating scale was completed by Sara's academic enhancement teacher, Jim Farmer, in order to understand Sara's behaviors and emotions. The only reported area of clinical significance on this measure was in learning problems.

Adaptive behavior: Sara's adaptive behaviors were assessed using the Adaptive Behavior Assessment System, 2nd Edition (ABAS-II) Parent Form and Teacher Form. Sara's lead special education teacher, Lori Morgan, and her mother, Ann Smith, served as the respondents for the ABAS-II.

On the ABAS-II Teacher Form, Sara's General Adaptive Composite (GAC) is 77 and at the 6th percentile. There is a 90% level of confidence that Sara's true GAC is within the range of 75 to 79. Sara's GAC is descriptively classified in the Borderline range. Sara obtained a score of 55 (<1st percentile).on the Conceptual Composite, which is descriptively classified in the extremely low range. She obtained a score of 75 (5th percentile) on the Social Composite, which is descriptively classified in the borderline range. On the Practical Composite, Sara obtained a scored of 82 (12th percentile), which is descriptively classified in the below average range.

Sara obtained a GAC of 68 on the ABAS-II Parent Form and is at the 2nd percentile. There is a 90% level of confidence that Sara's true GAC is within the range of 66 to 70. Sara's GAC is descriptively classified in the extremely low range. Sara obtained a score of 55 (<1st percentile) on the Conceptual Composite, which is descriptively classified within the extremely low range. She obtained a score of 75 (5th percentile) on the Social Composite, which is descriptively classified in the borderline range. On the Practical Composite, Sara obtained a scored of 82 (12th percentile) which is descriptively classified in the below average range.

The Teacher Form data reflect a significant difference of 20 points between Sara's Conceptual Composite score (extremely low range, <1st percentile) and her Social Composite score (borderline range, 5th percentile). The difference between the Conceptual and Social Composites is considered unusual, occurring in approximately 5.8% of the standardization sample. The Teacher Form data also reflect a significant difference of 27 points between Sara's Conceptual Composite score and her Practical Composite score (below average, 12th percentile). The difference between the Conceptual and Practical Composites also is considered unusual, occurring in approximately 1.2% of the standardization sample. Thus, Sara appears to demonstrate a relative strength in the Practical Composite, compared to other composites, on the ABAS-II Teacher Form. Her lowest level of scores was for the Conceptual Composite.

The Parent Form data reflect a significant difference of 20 points between Sara's Conceptual Composite score (extremely low range, <1st percentile) and her Social Composite score (borderline range, 5th percentile). The difference between the Conceptual and Social Composites is considered unusual, occurring in approximately 3.9% of the standardization sample. The Parent Form data also reflect a significant difference of 27 points between Sara's Conceptual Composite score and her Practical Composite score (below average, 12th percentile). The difference between the Conceptual and Practical Composites also is considered unusual, occurring in approximately 2.0% of the standardization sample. Thus, Sara appears to demonstrate a relative strength in the Practical Composite, compared to other composites, on the ABAS-II Parent Form, as well as on the Teacher Form. However, her lowest level of scores was for the Conceptual Composite.

Both sets of ABAS-II ratings are consistent with Sara's intellectual, achievement, and language assessments. Sara's GAC and the three adaptive composites are consistent at home and school. Sara's conceptual-related adaptive behaviors are consistently lower than her other composites, a finding consistent with the communication and learning problems evidenced from other assessment measures. Data from both the Teacher and Parent Forms indicate that Sara's adaptive skills generally are below average range for community use, home and school living, health and safety, leisure, and self-care adaptive skills. In contrast, she displays pronounced weaknesses in communication, functional academics, self-direction, and social adaptive skills.

A side-by-side comparison of Sara's scores from the ABAS-II Parent Form and Teacher Form are presented below:

ABAS-II Results

Name: Sara Smith
Age: 17 years, 0 months

	Parent		Teacher	
Composite/Adaptive Skill Area	Standard/ Scaled Score	Percentile	Standard/ Scaled Score	Percentile
General Adaptive Composite	68	2nd	77	6th
Conceptual Composite	55	<1st	55	<1st
• Communication skill area	2		2	
• Functional academics skill area	3		1	
• Self-direction skill area	1		3	
Social Composite	75	5th	75	5th
• Leisure skill area	7		7	
• Social skill area	3		4	
Practical Composite	82	12th	82	12th
• Community use skill area	7		7	
• Home/school living skill area	7		7	
• Health and safety skill area	7		7	
• Self-care skill area	7		8	

Note: The GAC and composite scores are standard scores with mean of 100 and standard deviation of 15. The adaptive skill area scores are scaled scores with mean of 10 and standard deviation of 3.

Scores from 90 to 109 are considered in the average range for the overall GAC and the composites. Scores from 8 to 12 are considered in the average range for the adaptive skill areas.

Recommendations

Specific recommendations for Sara, her parents, and her teachers, based on ABAS-II and other assessment results, are as follows:

Communication skills: Given Sara's weak communication skills as evidenced by low scores in that area on the ABAS-II and the OWLS, therapy with the speech-language pathologist that focuses on listening comprehension and conversational skills should be considered. Likewise, teachers should continue to work on the promotion of organizational strategies to assist her in planning and making oral presentations. Increased opportunities in the classroom for conferencing, problem solving, sharing, presenting, and brainstorming can give Sara the opportunity to practice her new skills. Fostering functional classroom communication skills such as hand raising also should be beneficial to Sara's learning.

Social skills: Sara's weak social skills as indicated by scores on the ABAS-II suggest that she may not have regular interactions with friends nor seek such interaction. Sara's diminished social and communication skill deficits are likely to be linked. Thus, efforts are needed to jointly promote these skills. Sara's relatively higher adaptive skills in community use, leisure, and school/home living constitute strengths upon which to further build her social and communication skills. For example, Sara should join one or more interest activities/clubs at school, church, or in the community. Additionally, she needs explicit instruction to acquire social skills, including how to start, maintain, and end conversations. Explicit instruction may involve the use of video modeling and self-monitoring strategies. Sara's BASC-II scores suggest she is unlikely to experience emotional difficulties that could additionally impede her social skills instruction and performance.

Self-direction skills: Sara needs to prepare for post-school experiences, including work, independent living, developing self-direction skills. Sara's weak self-direction skills as indicated on the ABAS-II suggest that she may need explicit instruction to learn such as problem solving, anger management, organization, and self-monitoring. These skills will help prepare her for independent living and a work environment. Attempts to promote Sara's social and communication skills also should consider their applications to a work environment. Referral to vocational rehabilitation services, including a vocational evaluation to identify Sara's interests and aptitudes, will likely promote vocational preparation.

Functional academic skills: As indicated on the ABAS-II, Sara has deficits in her ability to use basic academic skills for day-to-day living tasks such as telling time, counting and making change, and writing notes. Such defects will negatively impact her ability to function independently. As a result, explicit instruction is needed to help her apply basic academic skills to independent living tasks along with using necessary compensatory accommodations/strategies. For example, Sara needs to tell time and/or to read a digital watch, read and/or recognize important warning signs, read a calendar and/or use an auditory calendar, and count change and/or use a portable change counter.

Monitoring progress: Sara's adaptive skills should be measured regularly in order to monitor her progress and to make needed changes to her program.

REFERENCES

Abramowitz, A. & O'Leary, S. (1991). Behavioral interventions for the classroom: Implications for students with ADHD. *School Psychology Review*, *20*, 220–234.

Adreon, D. & Durocher, S. (2007). Evaluating the college transition needs of individuals with high-functioning autism spectrum disorders. *Intervention in School and Clinic*, *42*, 271–279.

American Association of Mental Retardation (AAMR) (2002). *Mental Retardation: Definition, Classification, and Systems of Support.* Washington, DC: AAMR.

American Educational Research Association, American Psychological Association, & National Council on Measurement in Education (1999). *Standards for Educational and Psychological*

Testing. Washington, DC: American Educational Research Association, American Psychological Association, & National Council on Measurement in Education.

American Psychiatric Association (APA) (2000) *Diagnostic and Statistical Manual of Mental Disorders*, 4th edn., text rev. Washington, DC: APA.

Arnett, J. (1992). Reckless behavior in adolescence: A developmental perspective. *Developmental Review*, *12*, 339–373.

Barkley, R. A. (1990). *Attention-Deficit Hyperactivity Disorder: A Handbook for Diagnosis and Treatment.* New York: Guilford Press.

Barkley, R. A. (1998). *Attention-Deficit Hyperactivity Disorder: A handbook for Diagnosis and Treatment*, 2nd edn. New York: Guilford Press.

Barkley, R. A., DuPaul, G., & McMurray, M. (1990a). A comprehensive evaluation of attention deficit disorder with and without hyperactivity. *Journal of Consulting and Clinical Psychology*, *58*, 775–789.

Barkley, R. A., Fischer, M., Edelbrock, C., & Smallish, L. (1991b). The adolescent outcome of hyperactive children diagnosed by research criteria: III. Mother–child interactions, family conflicts, and, maternal psychopathology. *Journal of Child Psychology and Psychiatry*, *32*, 233–255.

Barkley, R. A., Grodzinsky, G., & DuPaul, G. J. (1992). Frontal lobe functions in attention deficit disorder with and without hyperactivity: A review and research report. *Journal of Abnormal Child Psychology*, *20*, 163–188.

Berk, L. (1998). *Development Through the Lifespan.* Toronto: Allyn and Bacon.

Bibby, R. & Posterski, D. (1992). *Teen Trends: A Nation in Motion.* Toranto: Stoddart.

Biederman, J., Faraone, S., Milberger, S., Curtis, S., Chen, L., Marrs, A., Ouellette, B., Moore, P., & Spencer, T. (1996). Predictors of persistence and remission of ADHD into adolescence: Results from a four-year prospective follow-up study. *Journal of the American Academy of Child and Adolescent Psychiatry*, *35*, 343–351.

Birmaher, B., Ryan, N., Williamson, D., Brent. D., Kaufman, J., Dahl, R., Perel, J., & Nelson, B. (1996). Childhood and adolescent depression: A review of the past 10 years. Part I. *Journal of the American Academy of Child and Adolescents Psychiatry*, *35*, 1427–1439.

Bishop, J. & Inderbitzen, H. (1995). Peer acceptance and friendship: An investigation of their relation to self-esteem. *Journal of Early Adolescence*, *15*, 476–489.

Bolte, S. & Poustka, F. (2002). The relation between general cognitive level and adaptive behavior domains in individuals with autism with and without comorbid mental retardation. *Child Psychiatry and Human Development*, *33*, 165–172.

Burke, K., Burke, J., Reiger, D., & Rae, D. (1990). Age of onset of selected mental disorders in five community populations. *Archives of General Psychiatry*, *47*, 511–518.

Carl D. Perkins Vocational and Applied Technology Act (1990). P.L. 99-457.

Carter, A., Volkmar, F., Sparow, S.S., Wang, J., Lord, C., Dawson, G., Fombonne, E., Loveland, K., Mesibov, G., & Schopler, E. (1998). The Vineland adaptive behavior scales: Supplementary norms for individuals with autism. *Journal of Autism and Developmental Disorders*, *28*, 287–302.

Clark, C., Prior, M., & Kinsella, G. (2002). The relationship between executive function abilities, adaptive behavior, and academic achievement in children with externalizing behavior problems. *Journal of Child Psychology and Psychiatry*, *43*, 785–796.

Corrigan, J., Whiteneck, G., & Mellick, D. (2004). Perceived needs following traumatic brain injury. *Journal of Head Trauma Rehabilitation*, *19*, 205–216.

Cunningham, C. & Siegal, L. (1987). Peer interactions of normal and attention-deficit disordered boys during free play, cooperative task, and situated classroom situations. *Journal of Abnormal Child Psychology*, *15*, 247–268.

Eiseman, L. (2003). Theories in practice; School-to-work transitions-for-youth with mild disabilities. *Exceptionality*, *11*, 89–102.

Erhardt, D. & Hinshaw, S. (1994). Initial socioeconomic impressions of attention-deficit hyperactivity disorder and comparison boys: Predictions from social behaviors and from nonverbal variables. *Journal of Consulting and Clinical Psychology*, *62*, 833–842.

Faraone, S., Chen, W., Warburton, R., Biederman, J., Milberger, S., & Tsuang, M. (1995). Genetic heterogeneity in attention-deficit hyperactivity disorder. *Journal of Abnormal Psychology, 104*, 334–345.

Felce, D., de Kock, U., Thomas, M., & Saxby, H. (1986). Change in adaptive behavior of severely and profoundly mentally handicapped adults in different residential settings. *British Journal of Psychology, 77*, 489–501.

Fishman, M., Bruner, A., & Adjer, H. (1997). Substance abuse among children and adolescents. *Pediatric Review, 18*, 394–403.

Freeman, B. J., Del'Homme, M., Gurthrie, D., & Zhang, F. (1999). Vineland adaptive behavior scale scores as a function of age and initial IQ in 210 autistic children. *Journal of Autism and Developmental Disorders, 29*, 379–384.

Gresham, F. & Elliott, S. (1987). The relationship between adaptive behavior and social skills: Issues in definition and assessment. *The Journal of Special Education, 21*, 167–181.

Hammen, C. & Rudolph, K. (1999). The context of depression in clinic-referred youth: Neglected areas of treatment. *Journal of the Academy of Child & Adolescent Psychiatry, 38*, 64.

Harrison, P. (1987). Research with adaptive behavior scales. *Journal of Special Education, 21*, 37–68.

Harrison, P. (1990). Mental retardation, adaptive behavior, and giftedness. In A. S. Kaufman (Ed.), *Assessing Adolescent and Adult Intelligence.* Boston: Allyn and Bacon.

Harrison, P. & Boney, T. (2002). Adaptive behavior assessment. In A. Thomas & J. Grimes (Eds.), *Best Practices in School Psychology*, 4th edn. Bethesda, MD: National association of School Psychologists.

Harrison P. & Oakland, T. (2003). *Adaptive Behavior Assessment System: Manual.* San Antonio: Harcourt.

Hart, D. & Yates, M. (1996). The interrelation of self and identity in adolescence: A developmental account. *Annals of Child Development, 12*, 207–242.

Individuals with Disabilities Education Act (IDEA) (2004). P.L. 101–476

Individuals with Disabilities Education Improvement Act (IDEIA) (2004). P.L. 108-446.

Jaffe, P. (1995). History and overview of adulthood ADHD. In K. G. Nadeau (Ed.), *A Comprehensive Guide to Attention Deficit Disorder in Adults*, pp. 3–17. New York: Brunner/Mazel.

Jenkins, R. (2000). Substance abuse. In R. Behrman, R. Kliegman, and H. Jenson, (Eds.), *Nelson Textbook of Pediatrics*, 16th edn. Philadelphia, PA: Saunders.

Kamphaus, R. (1987). Conceptual and psychometric issues in the assessment of adaptive behavior. *The Journal of Special Education, 21*, 27–35.

Katsiyannis, A., Zhang, D., Woodruff, N., & Dixon, A. (2005). Transition supports to students with mental retardation: An examination of data from the national longitudinal transition study 2. *Education and Training in Developmental Disabilities, 40*, 109–116.

Kraemer, B. R., McIntyre, L. L., & Blacher, J. (2003). Quality of life for young adults with mental retardation during transition. *Mental Retardation, 41*, 250–262.

Krieg, F., Brown, P., & Ballard, J. (1995). *Transition: School to Work Models for Effective Transition Planning.* Bethesda, MD: National Association of School Psychologists.

Kronenberger, W. & Meyer, R. (2001). *The Child Clinician's Handbook*, 2nd edn. Boston: Allyn and Bacon.

Langlois, J., Rutland-Brown, W., & Thomas, K. (2006). Traumatic brain injury in the United States: Emergency department visits, hospitalizations, and deaths. *Centers for Disease Control and Prevention, National Center for Inquiry Prevention and Control.*

Langone, J. & Burton, T. A. (1987). Teaching adaptive behavior skills to moderately and severely handicapped individuals: Best practices for facilitating independent living. *Journal of Special Education, 21*, 149–165.

Lefrancois, G. (1999). *The Lifespan*, 6th edn. Belmont, CA: Wadsworth.

Lewinsohn, P., Hoberman, H., & Rosenbaum, M. (1988). A prospective study of risk factors for unipolar depression. *Journal of Abnormal psychology, 97*, 218–243.

McCarver, R. B. & Campbell, V. A. (1987). Future developments in the concept and application of adaptive behavior. *The Journal of Special Education, 21*, 197–207.

Mercer, C. & Mercer, A. (1993). *Teaching Students with Learning Problems*, 4th edn. Columbus, OH: Merrill.

Nanda, S. & Konnur, N. (2006). Adolescent drug and alcohol use in the 21st century. *Psychiatric Annals*, *36*, 706–712.

National Institute on Drug Abuse (NIDA) (2004). High school and youth trends. Available at www.nida.hih.gov. Accessed June 15, 2007.

Offer, D. O., Ostrov, E., & Howard, K. (1984). *Patterns of Adolescent Self-Image*. San Francisco: Josey-Bass.

Rehabilitation Act (1973). P.L. 94-142.

Reschly, D. (1990). Best practices in adaptive behavior. In A. Thomas & J. Grimes (Eds.), *Best Practices in School Psychology II*. Washington, DC: The National Association of School Psychologists.

Robin, A. (1998). *ADHD in Adolescents: Diagnosis and Treatment*. New York: Gilford Press.

Savage, R. & Wolcott, G. (1995). Educational issues for students with brain injuries. In R. Savage & G. Wolcott (Eds.), *An Educator's Manual: What Educator's Need to Know About Students with Brain Injury*. Washington, DC: Brain Injury Association, Inc.

Schlegel, A. & Barry III, H. (1991). *Adolescence: An Anthropological Inquiry*. New York: The Free Press.

Sealander, K., Eigenberger, M., Schwiebert, V., Wycoff, H., & Ross, J. (1997). Academic underachievement and attention deficit hyperactivity disorder: Characteristics and interventions. *The Journal of the Professional Counselor*, *12*(2), *9–20*.

Secretary of Labor's Commission on Achieving Necessary Skills (1991). *What Work Requires of Schools: A SCANS Report for America 2000*. Washington, DC: Secretary of Labor's Commission on Achieving Necessary Skills.

Seidman, L., Biederman, J., Faraone, S., Weber, W., & Ouellette, C. (1997). Toward defining a neuropsychology of attention-deficit-hyperactivity disorder: Performance of children and adolescents from a large clinically referred sample. *Journal of Consulting and Clinical Psychology*, *65*(1), 150–160.

Slombowski, C., Klein, R., & Mannuzza, S. (1995). Is self-esteem an important outcome in hyperactive children? *Journal of Abnormal Child Psychology*, *23*, 303–315.

Sparrow, S. S. & Cicchetti, D. V. (1987). Adaptive behavior and the psychologically disturbed child. *The Journal of Special Education*, *21*, 89–100.

Stuart, C. H. & Smith, S. (2002). Transition planning for students with severe disabilities: Policy implications for the classroom. *Intervention in School and Clinic*, *37*(4), 234–236.

Thurman, D., Alverson, C., Dunn, K., Guerrero, J., & Sniezek, J. (1999). Traumatic brain injury in the United States: A public health perspective. *Journal of Head Trauma Rehabilitation*, *14*, 602–615.

Weiss, G. & Hechtman, L. (1993). *Hyperactive Children Grown Up: ADHD in Children, Adolescents, and Adults*, 2nd ed. New York: Guilford Press.

Weller, C. & Strawser, S. (1987). Adaptive behavior of subtypes of learning disabled individuals. *The Journal of Special Education*, *21*, 101–115.

SECTION IV

ABAS-II and Assessment for Special Populations

17

Using the ABAS-II in Promoting and Evaluating Autonomy for Adults with Cognitive Impairments

Steve Woolf,* Christine Merman Woolf**

*BEACON Services, Milford, MA 01757, U.S.A.

**Capella University, Minneapolis, MN 55402, U.S.A.

Adaptive behavior assessment plays a critical role when evaluating persons with disabilities, including adults. For example, the diagnosis of mental retardation requires subaverage intellectual functioning, usually meaning an IQ at or below 70, with concurrent deficits in adaptive functioning (American Psychiatric Association, APA, 2000). Mental retardation occurs in approximately 1% of the population (APA, 2000). Information from measures of intelligence and adaptive behavior is essential when assessing individuals with mental retardation relative to diagnosis and intervention design (Sattler, 2001).

Historically, the assessment of mental retardation did not always require the use of these two types of measures (see Chapter 1 of this Book). Before the introduction of intelligence tests, verbal reports from family members describing adaptive behavior deficits were the primary method used to diagnose mental retardation or developmental disability (Nihira, 1999). Exclusive reliance on verbal reports of adaptive behaviors when diagnosing mental retardation changed with the advent of intelligence tests in the early 1900s. Soon thereafter, the diagnosis of mental retardation began to rely solely on data obtained through intelligence tests (Brown et al., 1999).

Standardized definitions of adaptive behavior started to evolve when the American Association of Mental Deficiency (AAMD) included it in its 1959 definition of mental retardation. At that time, the AAMD revised its diagnostic criteria for individuals with disabilities to include subaverage general intelligence functioning and general adaptive behavior. The inclusion of adaptive behavior in these criteria resulted in a renewed research emphasis on adaptive behavior, including the behaviors that contribute to the construct of adaptive behavior. As a result, adaptive behavior research has been primarily conducted with participants diagnosed with mental retardation or other developmental disabilities.

Due to varied community standards, adaptive behavior was difficult to define, (Langone & Burton, 1987). Grossman (1973) was one of the first researchers to develop a standardized definition of adaptive behavior. He defined adaptive behavior as "the effectiveness and degree to which the individual meets the standard of personal independence and social responsibility expected for his and her cultural group" (Grossman, 1973, p. 11). Ten years later, Grossman (1983) provided further details by defining adaptive behavior as what people do to "take care of themselves and relate to others in daily living" (p. 42).

ADAPTIVE BEHAVIOR CONSIDERATIONS

Five important considerations govern the assessment of adaptive behavior and skills of adults with mental retardation. First, one should view adaptive behavior from a developmental perspective or trajectory in which an individual learns to acquire adaptive skills as a function of age and educational experiences (Sattler, 2002). Second, intellectual capacity influences the development of adaptive behavior. Adaptive behavior and intelligence correlate moderately, between .30 and .40 (Harrison & Oakland, 2003), suggesting the two behaviors share between 9% and 16% common variance.

Third, definitions or standards for evaluating what constitutes adaptive behavior may inadvertently neglect community standards and socioeconomic status (McMillan, 1982). A standardized definition of adaptive behavior may not account for subtle yet important differences in community, cultural, or home settings. Adaptive behavior should be evaluated, in part, based on the standards established and exhibited by one's community and culture (Sattler, 2002).

Fourth, the assessment of adaptive behavior should reflect performance on a constellation of behaviors, rather than a single behavior. Moreover, knowledge of the display of needed adaptive behavior and skills in two or more settings provides a clearer understanding of a person's strengths and weaknesses. Finally, the assessment of adaptive behavior provides information about the degree to which an individual independently negotiates and manages his/her environment. Adaptive behavior refers to the culmination of behaviors an individual should display in order to live independently in a community environment (Schalock & Braddock, 1999).

INTERVENTIONS RELATED TO ADAPTIVE BEHAVIOR

During the early 19th century, public policy and associated treatment practices for individuals with mental retardation started to change in the United States and Western Europe (Jacobson, et al., 2005). In the United States, individuals diagnosed with mental retardation typically moved to state supported institutions rather than remaining in the community (Harris et al., 2004; Klotz, 2004). These institutions maintained individuals within insular social environments in which they were cared for yet experienced restricted opportunities to integrate in typical community and vocational settings (Jackson & Veeneman-Panyan, 2002).

During the 1960s, public policy began to emphasize the inclusion of individuals with mental retardation as functional members of society (Walmsley, 2005). The inclusion movement emphasized the term *adaptive behavior* to refer to independent living skills (Langone & Burton, 1987). The term *independent living skills* more adequately describes the skills necessary for individuals with mental retardation and others to integrate into communities (American Association on Mental Retardation, 2002).

Toward the end of the 1960s and through the early 1980s, political and social movements established policies to protect and safeguard the civil rights of individuals with disabilities (Klotz, 2004; Walmsley, 2005). Educational reforms such as Public Law 94-142 required students with disabilities be offered a free appropriate education (Cooper et al., 1994). The Americans with Disabilities Act of 1990 also emphasized the desire for individuals with disabilities to live and work in community settings. This legislation resulted in critical social changes, including the closing of many large residential institutions in favor of smaller community-based residential group homes and residences for individuals with mental retardation (Owens, 2004). Thus, political reform and public policy supported individuals with disabilities living in community settings.

Starting in the 1970s, adults with disabilities increasingly worked in competitive community jobs with support (Owens, 2004). They often entered supported employment programs in which job coaches assisted clients in mastering their job responsibilities (Rusch & Braddock, 2004). Job coaches often worked side by side with the client to model and teach appropriate job skills. Job coaches also taught social and adaptive behaviors that would allow the client to function more independently within the vocational setting. For example, a job coach may teach the client how to set an alarm clock to wake up for work every morning or how to socialize with non-disabled employees during a lunch break (Jackson & Veeneman-Panyan, 2002).

Since the beginning of the 20th century, services provided to individuals with disabilities changed significantly (Brown et al., 1999). Policies of social inclusion and community integration replaced policies of social exclusion and institutionalization. Although at one time psychological testing was used mainly to diagnose, many tests have been redesigned to assess areas of personal strengths and weaknesses (Perkins-Dock, 2003). The identification of an individual's areas of personal strengths and weaknesses facilitates treatment protocols, environmental modifications, and educational plans designed to promote a higher quality of life for persons with disabilities in mainstream community settings (Klotz, 2004). The current perception of individuals diagnosed with a developmental disability emphasizes building skills leading to their successful integration into communities, including supported community employment, supported living arrangements, and inclusive educational opportunities (Perkins-Dock, 2003).

Social policy changes' that impacting individuals with disabilities extended to their living conditions (Rusch & Braddock, 2004). In the 1970s, individuals with disabilities began working with supported living coaches who taught them to live more independently in a community residence. The function of the supported living coaches is to teach such adaptive skills as cooking, cleaning, managing money, and shopping. The deinstitutionalization policies that began in the 1960s became the catalyst for a wide range of efforts to increase the independence of individuals with mental retardation. Changes in public policy and related treatment practices emphasized a more autonomous existence for them, including a focus on their acquiring needed adaptive behaviors and skills (Kennedy, 2001).

The deinstitutionalization and educational mainstreaming movements created an immediate desire for individuals with disabilities to receive the required skill training to successfully integrate into normalized environmental settings (Kennedy, 2001). Most individuals with disabilities lacked the basic social and life skills needed to independently function in community environments. Thus, many adults with mental retardation were arrested, jailed or hospitalized for aberrant behaviors, or became homeless (Anderson et al., 2005).

The deinstitutionalization and mainstream movements emphasized the acquisition of adaptive behavior skills to enable individuals with disabilities to become self-sufficient in normalized or traditional community settings. The emphasis on independent living skills for individuals with disabilities increased the relevance and importance of acquiring adaptive behavior and skills (Anderson et al., 2005). For example, high school curricula for students diagnosed with mental retardation changed their emphasis from prioritizing academic attainments to acquiring behaviors that promote independence in community settings (Jackson & Veeneman-Panyan, 2002; Anderson et al., 2005).

An effective evaluation of the adaptive behaviors and skills of persons with mental retardation often is prerequisite to achieving their successful transition into community-based residences and jobs. An analysis of adaptive functioning can indicate strengths and weaknesses within adaptive skill domains (Staddon, 2001). Assessment of adaptive behavior may facilitate the work of teachers and therapists/interventionists in their efforts to effectively program treatment plans intended to lead to community integration. An assessment of adaptive skills also assists in determining whether a person with disabilities displays the degree of independent living skills needed to work and live successfully and safely in community settings.

The passage of the 1983 Individuals with Disabilities Education Act (P.L. 98-199) introduced the need to provide transition services to promote community integration for individuals with developmental disabilities. The number of individuals with disabilities placed in competitive employment opportunities began to increase. Rusch and Braddock (2004) suggest this increase would be greater if public schools better prepared individuals with disabilities to work competitively. They recommend that students with disabilities receive continued educational support in competitive job placements upon exiting high school. This support should include the development of social and other adaptive behaviors required to function independently in community settings. They also suggest that most students with disabilities lack the prerequisite adaptive behavior and skills required to be successful in community-based employment.

Skill development, personal and practical vocational support, and long-term planning are essential to efforts that promote and sustain successful integration into community settings. However, most state and federal agencies are more likely to provide funding for segregated work programs found in sheltered workshops (Wehman & Revell, 2005). Sheltered workshops minimize opportunities for community independence by segregating individuals with disabilities and limiting social contact with non-disabled peers (Rusch & Braddock, 2004).

Increased independence is a key goal when working with individuals with mental retardation (Kennedy, 2001). Increased independence allows them to have increased access to the community and thus increased use of community resources and a quality of life. Autonomous individuals who utilize public transportation, dress and feed themselves, manage their time, and display other valued and needed adaptive skills have a higher quality of life than peers who require supports to maintain a basic standard of existence.

STANDARDIZATION OF ABAS-II ON ADULT POPULATION

The Adaptive Behavior Assessment System-II (ABAS-II; Harrison & Oakland, 2003) is used to assess the adaptive behaviors and skills through its five forms: two for younger children, two for school age children to age 21, and an adult form for ages 16 through 89. This chapter focuses only on the adult form. The adult form is completed either by one's self (if the individual displays needed cognitive abilities) or by individuals familiar with the participant's day activities. These respondents may include family members, counselors, professional care-givers, job and living coaches, work supervisors, and/or teachers (Harrison & Oakland, 2003).

TABLE 17.1 Adult Standardization Samples by Age Group.

	ABAS-II adult form	
Ages	Self-report	Rated by others
16–21	150	100
22–29	150	140
30–39	180	160
40–49	180	180
50–64	110	150
65–70	120	100
75–89	100	90
Total	990	920

The ABAS-II was normed on 1910 adults ABAS-II (Harrison & Oakland, 2003). During its norming, 990 adults completed the self-report form and 920 respondents rated other adults. The standardization samples (self-report and rated by others) were divided into seven age groups (see Table 17.1).

The ABAS-II normative samples generally are consistent with the U.S. census data. For example, samples were stratified by race/ethnicity (White, African-American, Hispanic, and other) in each of the above age ranges to be representative of U.S. population. Forty-seven percent were female. The standardization samples were stratified by education levels based on number of years of school completed. On the adult form rated by others, respondents commonly included mother (12%), wives (22%), and husbands (20%) (Harrison & Oakland, 2003).

The ABAS-II also included a proportionate number of individuals diagnosed with low prevalence disabilities, including those with an attention deficit hyperactivity disorder, Alzheimer's disease, epilepsy, learning disability, mental retardation, Parkinson's disease, stroke, brain injury, as well as those with auditory or visual impairments (Harrison & Oakland, 2003).

Internal consistency refers to the reliability of test scores derived from the statistical interrelationships of responses among item responses or scores on separate parts of a test. Evidence of internal consistency typically is expressed through a correlation coefficient. Reliability data from the seven adult age groups used to standardize the self-report forms are significant across the ten adaptive skill areas, three adaptive composites (Conceptual, Social, and Practical), and the General Adaptive Composite. Reliability data from the adult form rated by others as well as for the adult clinical groups (e.g. Alzheimer's disease, mental retardation, and neurological disorders) also is very high (Harrison & Oakland, 2003).

Specifically, reliability coefficients using the Parent/Primary Caregiver form with 27 individuals diagnosed with mild mental retardation were .97 for the General Adaptive Composite (GAC), from .92 to .94 for the three composites, and from .70 to .92 for the adaptive skill areas. Reliability coefficients for 22 individuals diagnosed with moderate mental retardation were .98 for the GAC, from .93 to .95 for the three composites, and from .79 to .93 for the adaptive skill areas. Reliability coefficients for 40 individuals rated on the Parent Form and diagnosed with mental retardation were .99 for the GAC, from .97 to .99 for the three composites, and from .94 to .97 for the adaptive skill areas. Finally, the reliability coefficients for 30 adults diagnosed with mental retardation and rated on the Adult Form by others were .99 for the GAC with and without work, .97 or .98 for the three composites, and from .91 to .97 for the adaptive skill areas (Harrison & Oakland, 2003). Also, average corrected internal consistency reliabilities for adults who completed the self-rating form and earned a GAC of 89 or less were .98 for the GAC with work, .97 for the GAC without work, .94 to .96 for the three composites, and .86 to .95 for the adaptive skill areas (Harrison & Oakland, 2003).

Studies examining a test's validity provide evidence needed to ensure the test is measuring what it is designed to measure. The test's content validity is supported in its adherence to the 10 adaptive skill areas and the three domains (Conceptual, Social, and Practical) derived from the AAMR's (2002) definition of adaptive behavior. Thus, the ABAS-II displays considerable content validity.

The diagnosis of mental retardation typically requires deficits in both intelligence and adaptive behavior. As a measure of adaptive behavior, the ABAS-II plays a critical role relative to assessing the initial and continued diagnosis of mental retardation. Based on standards established by the DSM – IV-TR (2000), one expects those with mental retardation to score two or more standard deviations below the mean on a measure of intelligence together with concurrent deficits or impairments in adaptive functioning in at least two of the ten adaptive skill areas assessed by the ABAS-II for persons above age 4. The onset of these behaviors must occur before age 18.

The following samples were studied in order to assess the validity of the ABAS-II using the Teacher Form: 21 individuals with Down syndrome, 84 individuals with mental retardation (Unspecified), 66 individuals with mild mental retardation, and 27 individuals with moderate mental retardation. The Parent Form was completed for 41 individuals with mental retardation (Unspecified), and the Adult Form– Rated by Others was completed for 30 individuals with mental retardation (unspecified). Data from each of these samples were compared with data from matched controls. In all comparisons, those diagnosed with mental retardation earned scores 2 or more standard deviations below the mean at a rate significantly higher than those in the matched control groups. These significant differences were reflected in the GAC, three domains, and nine to ten adaptive skill area standard scores (Harrison & Oakland, 2003).

The ABAS-II manual summarizes these comparisons by stating that "among the adaptive domains, individuals with mental retardation showed the greatest deficits in Conceptual and Practical. Among the nine skill areas, the samples of individuals with mental retardation performed most poorly in Functional Academics and Communication. About 65%–100% of the samples with mental retardation scored at least two SDs below the mean on Functional Academics

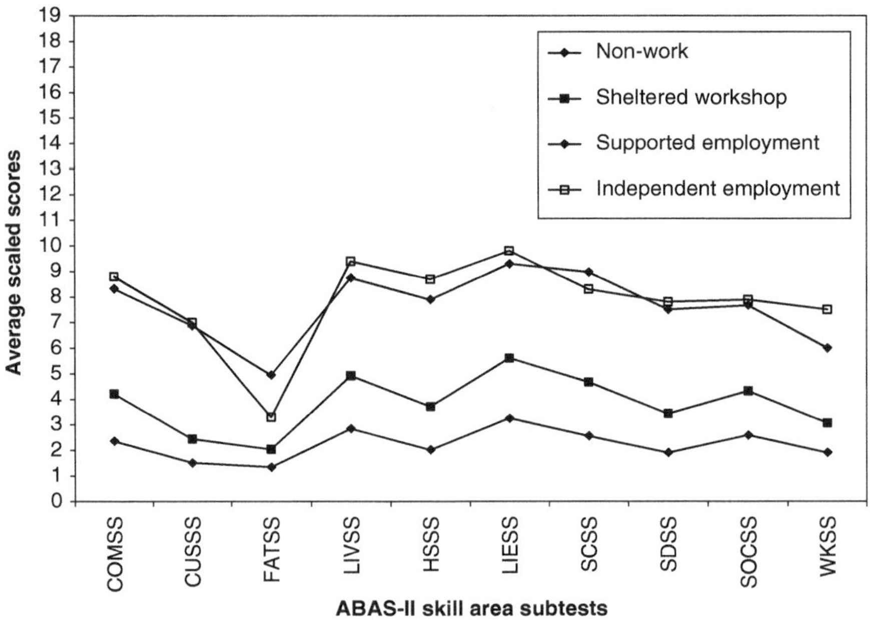

FIGURE 17.1 ABAS-II skill area profile analysis according to employment status adults with disabilities sample size = 272. COMSS: Communication scaled score; CUSSS: Community use scaled score; FATSS: Functional academic scaled score; LIVSS: Home/School living scaled score; HSSS: Health and safety scaled score; LIESS: Leisure skills scaled score; SCSS: Self-care scaled score; SDSS: Self-direction scaled score; SOCSS: Social skills scaled score; WKSS: Work scaled score. *Source*: Woolf (2006).

and Communication, while only 0%–29% of the matched control group did so" (Harrison & Oakland, 2003, p. 147).

A study by Woolf (2006) examined relationships between adaptive behavior as measured by the ABAS-II and two independent variables, vocational and community independence, for adults with mental retardation (Woolf, 2006). Vocational status had four sub-categories identified in decreasing order of independence: working independently in competitive employment, working with a job coach in competitive employment, working in a sheltered workshop for individuals with disabilities and participating in an unpaid training setting.

Among adults with mental retardation, their ABAS-II General Adaptive Composites and their degree of community and vocational independence are closely related. Persons with higher adaptive behavior also displayed higher levels of community and vocational independence. Their adaptive skills and community independence also are closely related.

The adaptive behaviors of individuals with disabilities living independently in the community and those living in restrictive community settings differed. Those living more independently displayed higher levels of adaptive behavior.

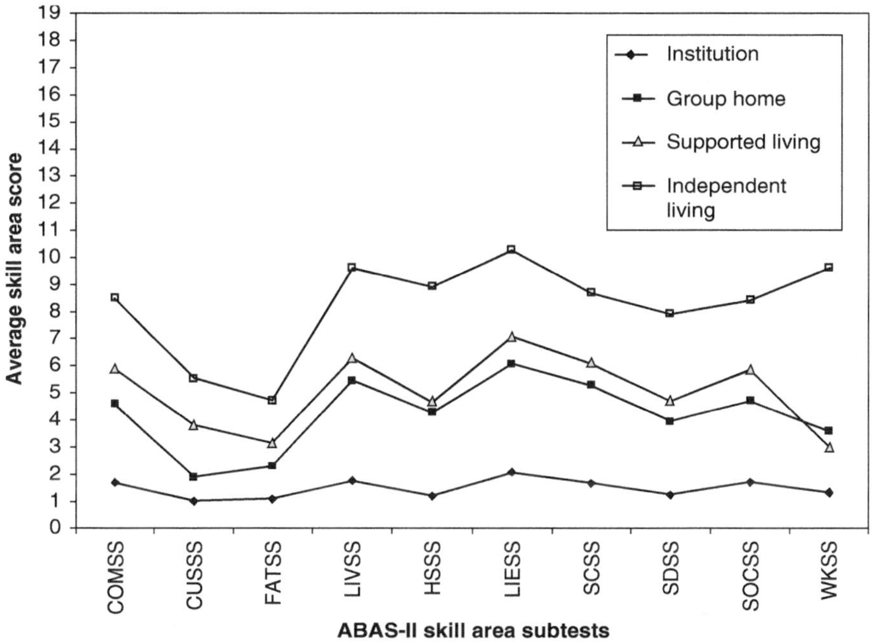

FIGURE 17.2 ABAS-II skill area profile analysis according to home living status adults with disabilities sample size = 272. COMSS: Communication scaled score; CUSSS: Community use scaled score; FATSS: Functional academic scaled score; LIVSS: Home/school living scaled score; HSSS: Health and safety scaled score; LIESS: Leisure skills scaled score; SCSS: Self-care scaled score; SDSS: Self-direction scaled score; SOCSS: Social skills scaled score; WKSS: Work scaled score. *Source*: Woolf (2006).

An analysis of ABAS-II skills indicated those associated with communication, home living, health and safety, and leisure best distinguish those who have competitive employment from those who work in unpaid settings. Differences between these two groups are smaller on skills that reflect community use, self-direction, and functional academics. Figure 17.1 visually depicts the ABAS-II profile analysis for vocational independence.

Community living status also was divided into four sub-groups, again identified in decreasing order of independence: living independently in the community (e.g., an apartment or home), living in a community supported by a living coach, living in a group home designed for disabled individuals, and living in a residential treatment setting (i.e., institutionalization).

Adults with disabilities who lived independently in community settings compared to those who resided in institutional settings displayed the largest discrepancy in areas related to work skills, self-care, leisure, health and safety, and home-living skills. The adaptive skill areas with the smallest degree of variance relative to living independently included community use and functional academics. Figure 17.2 visually depicts the adaptive skill area ABAS-II profile analysis for these variables.

EDWARD: ABAS-II CASE STUDY

Edward, a 36-year-old male, participated in a sheltered workshop designed for adults with disabilities. Edward was paid at a piecework rate for assembling pens and boxes, folding fliers, and shredding paper. He also lived in a group home designed for residents with developmental disabilities.

Edward had worked at the sheltered workshop and resided in a group home since completing high school at age 22. His WAIS-III Full-Scale IQ was 58, Verbal IQ was 61, and his Performance IQ was 58. Edward also exhibited several challenging behaviors that impeded his social and vocational development. Specifically, Edward exhibited verbal aggression towards others when asked to engage or complete a non-preferred task. For example, Edward often took long "coffee breaks" to avoid non-preferred work assignments such as placing form letters in envelopes. When a staff member requested Edward to return to his workstation, he often responded with verbal aggression towards others. Upon hearing the verbal threat, staff members typically walked away and re-approached Edward every 5 minutes to administer a verbal prompt to return to work.

During Edward's yearly support plan he reported that his long-term goal was to live in his own apartment and make more money. Ideally, Edward wanted to work in the food court at a local mall for about 30-hours per week. Edward acknowledged that he needed help from this support team to achieve this goal. The team agreed that Edward possessed the capacity to work and live independently, but required skill development relative to behavioral control and self-care skills. Based on Edward's request to live and work independently, the evaluator administered the ABAS-II and completed a functional behavior assessment (FBA).

Results from Edward's FBA indicate that Edward's verbal aggression toward others was maintained by escaping/avoiding non-preferred work activities. Edward also exhibited verbal aggression toward his group home staff to escape non-preferred self-care tasks in his group home. Behavioral background information indicated that Edward had a long-standing history of obtaining immediate escape from non-preferred activities upon exhibiting verbal aggression toward others.

The ABAS-II was administered to evaluate Edward's areas of adaptive strength and weaknesses. Specifically, the ABAS-II was used to assess his current level of adaptive independence and to target specific areas for improvement to facilitate vocational and residential independence. His service coordinator at the day workshop and the manager of his group home both completed an ABAS-II adult form. The ABAS-II scores are given in Table 17.2.

Edward and his support team set the following intermediate goals: First, Edward would work for a minimum of 10-hours per week in a competitive community job with the assistance of a job coach within 1-year of his current annual support plan date. Secondly, Edward would reside in an apartment with the assistance of a supported living coach within 1-year of this annual support plan date.

Edward and his support team set the following three short-term goals. Edward's frequency of verbal aggression toward others (in the group home and workshop) will decrease from an average of six incidents per month to zero

TABLE 17.2 ABAS-II Scores for Edward, Age 36 Years.

Adaptive skill area/ adaptive composite/ GAC	Scaled scores adult form, rated by others	
	Residential setting	Vocational setting
Adaptive skill areas		
Communication	4	3
Community use	7	7
Functional academics	7	8
Home living	4	3
Health and safety	6	7
Leisure	6	5
Self-care	4	4
Self-direction	4	4
Social	6	7
Work	6	7
Conceptual composite	72	70
90% confidence interval	69–75	67–73
Social composite	78	70
90% confidence interval	73–83	65–75
Practical composite	67	67
90% confidence interval	64–70	64–70
General Adaptive Composite	69	70
90% confidence interval	67–71	68–72

Note: Adaptive skill area scores are reported as scaled scores ($M = 10$, $SD = 3$). Composite Scores are reported as standard scores ($M = 100$, $SD = 15$).

incidents per month within 3 months. Edward will increase the percent of time intervals he spends working at his workstation from an average of 54% of intervals to 90% of intervals within 3 months. Edward will increase the frequency of independent engagement in self-care/leisure/and home safety behaviors from an average of six behaviors to 20 behaviors per day within 3 months. Independent engagement was defined as independently initiating home based adaptive skills without verbal prompts from staff.

INTERVENTIONS

A behavior contract was signed upon in which Edward agreed to stay in his work area and follow a posted breaks schedule. The contract outlined a 15-minute interval schedule. Edward checked a box on his data sheet for each 15-minute interval he remained at his workstation. The percent of intervals was recorded on Edward's work graph and adjusted for schedule breaks (work breaks, restroom breaks). The graph (Figure 17.3) also was visually posted at Edward's workstation as a self-management tool. Figure 17.3 summarizes Edward's monthly progress toward remaining at his workstation.

Based on an analysis of the ABAS-II, Edward required specific skill training to promote communication with others, self-care skills, and home-living skills. An item analysis identified four critical skill deficits relative to communication/socialization: how to look at the faces of others when speaking, how listen to others when others speak, how to nod and smile when others are speaking, and how to introduce and talk with new people. An item analysis from the ABAS-II self-care adaptive skill area indicated deficits related to cleaning fingernails, keeping hair neat, and independently brushing teeth. An item analysis of the home-living adaptive skill area indicated deficits related to folding cloths, taking the trash out, making the bed, and cleaning the bathroom.

Based on these identified deficits, a didactic skill acquisition program was set up in Edward's sheltered workshop and group home. The group home addressed skills related to independent home living (home living and self-care). The workshop completed daily training in areas related to communication. A psychologist designed sequential components to teach each skill. The teaching procedures included didactic skill instruction, modeling, roleplaying, performance feedback, and generalization into the natural setting.

RESULTS

The combination of skill training and behavioral programming appears to have assisted Edward in meeting his short-term and immediate goals of moving into an independent living setting. The combination of these interventions is thought to have increased the social reinforcement available in the environment and amount of money he earned at the sheltered workshop. Edward's acquisition rate of learning independent behaviors was maintained by natural environmental contingencies

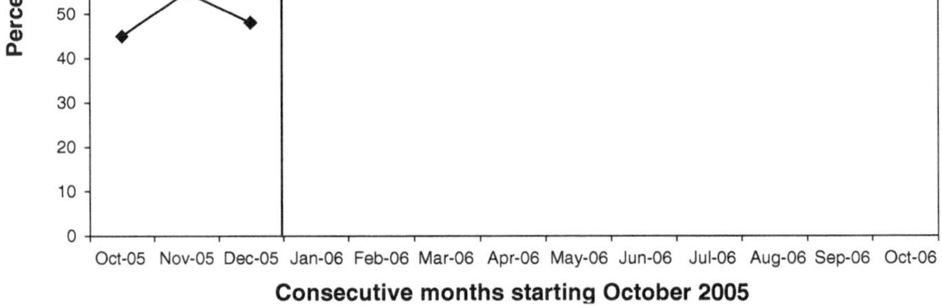

FIGURE 17.3 Percent of intervals Edward remained in work area.

(socially mediated attention and money). Figure 17.4 visually depicts the actual monetary production after interventions took place in the target settings.

Edward also required less verbal prompts to complete his home self-care program after receiving didactic instruction to correct adaptive skill weakness identified on the ABAS-II. Figure 17.5 visually depicts Edward's increasing independence relative to completing home maintenance and self-care skills.

Edward effectively met his annual goal of living independently and working competitively. The ABAS-II was effective in identifying adaptive skills essential for independent living. Currently, Edward rents an apartment in a complex designed for individuals with disabilities. He also maintains a 30-hour per week position making minimum wage as a member of the janitorial crew at a local mall.

SUMMARY

The ABAS-II is a clinically important assessment tool to assist professionals relative to the diagnosis of adult disabilities and interventions design for them. The ABAS-II can be used to identify the adaptive skill areas associated with successful vocational and residential independence for adults with disabilities. The ABAS-II also may target specific areas of adaptive skill weakness for which a skill acquisition program and task analysis may be designed for purposes of learning. Overall, the ABAS-II has shown to be a useful and effective instrument when working with, developing goals, designing interventions and evaluating adults with disabilities.

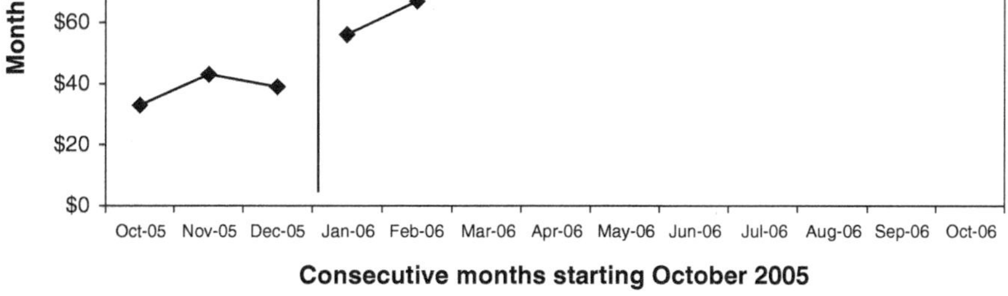

FIGURE 17.4 Edward's earned monthly dollars.

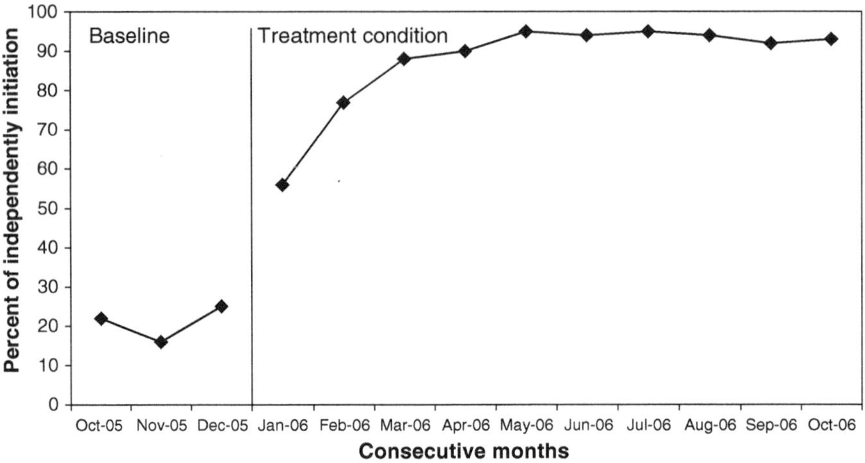

FIGURE 17.5 Percent of Edward's independently engaged life skills activities in group home.

REFERENCES

American Association on Mental Retardation (2002). *Mental Retardation: Definition, Classification, and Systems of Support* Washington, DC: AAMR.

Anderson, R., Carter, I., & Lowe, G. (2005). *Human Behavior in the Social Environment*, 5th edn., Piscataway, NJ: Aldine Transaction.

American Psychiatric Association (APA) (2000). *Diagnostic and Statistical Manual of Mental Disorders: Text Revision*, 4th edn.,Washington, DC: APA.

Brown, R., Reynolds, C., & Whitaker, J. (1999). Bias in mental testing since bias in mental testing. *School Psychology Quarterly 14*(3), 208–239.

Cooper, P., Smith, C., & Upton, G. (1994). *Emotional and Behavioral Difficulties: Theory to Practice*. London, New York: Rutledge.

Grossman, H. (Ed.) (1973). *Manual on Terminology and Classification in Mental Retardation.* Washington, DC: American Association on Mental Deficiency.

Grossman, H. (Ed.) (1983). *Manual on Terminology and Classification in Mental Retardation*, Vol. 2, Washington, DC: American Association on Mental Deficiency.

Harris, H. S., Maloney, D. C., & Rother, F. M. (2004). *Human Services: Contemporary Issues and Trends*, 3rd edn., Boston, MA: Allyn & Bacon.

Harrison, P. & Oakland, T. (2003). *Adaptive Behavior Assessment System (ABAS-II)*, 2nd edn., San Antonio, TX: The Psychological Corporation.

Jackson, L. & Veeneman-Panyan, M. (2002). *Positive Behavioral Support in the Classroom.* Baltimore, MD: Brookes Publishing.

Jacobson, J., Mulick, J., & Foxx, R. (2005). Historical approaches to developmental disabilities. In J. Jacobson, J. Mulick, & R. Foxx (Eds.), *Controversial Therapies for Developmental Disabilities: Fads, Fashion, and Science and Professional Practice*, pp. 61–84. Mahwah, New Jersey: Lawrence Earlbaum Associates.

Kennedy, C. H. (2001). Social interaction interventions for youth with severe disabilities should emphasize independence. *Mental retardation and developmental disabilities*, *7*, 122–127.

Klotz, J. (2004). Sociocultural study of intellectual disability: Moving beyond labeling and social constructionist perspectives. *British Journal of Learning Disabilities*, *38*(2), 93–104.

Langone, J. & Burton, T. (1987). Teaching adaptive behavior skills to moderately and severely handicapped individuals: Best practices facilitating independent living. *The Journal of Special Education, 21*(1), 149–165.

McMillan, D. (1982). *Mental Retardation in School and Society*. Boston, MA: Little, Brown.

Nihira, K. (1999). *Adaptive Behavior and Its Measurement: Implications for the Field of Mental Retardation*. In R. Schalock & D. Braddock (Eds.), Washington, DC: American Association on Mental Retardation.

Owens, C. (2004). The glass-walled asylum: A description of a lay residential community for the severely mentally ill. *Journal of Mental Health, 13*(3), 319–332.

Perkins-Dock, R. (2003). Test review of adaptive behavior. *Rehabilitation Counseling, 46*(3), 183–186.

Rusch, F. & Braddock, D. (2004). Adult day programs versus supported employment (1988–2002): Spending and service practices of mental retardation and developmental disabilities state agencies. *Research and Practice for Persons with Severe Disabilities, 29*(4), 237–242.

Sattler, J. (2001). *Assessment of Children: Cognitive Applications*, 4th edn., San Diego, CA: Author.

Sattler, J. (2002). *Assessment of Children: Behavioral and Clinical Applications*, 4th edn., San Diego, CA.

Schalock, R. & Braddock, D. (Eds.) (1999). *Adaptive Behavior and Its Measurement: Implications for the Field of Mental Retardation*. Washington, DC: American Association on Mental Retardation.

Staddon, J. E. R. (2001). *Adaptive Dynamics: The Theoretical Analysis of Behavior*. Cambridge, MA: MIT Press.

Walmsley, J. (2005). Institutionalization: A historical perspective. In K. Johnson (Ed.), *Deinstitutionalization and People with Intellectual Disabilities: In and Out of Institutions*, pp. 50–65. Philadelphia, PA: Jessica Kingsley Publishers.

Wehman, P. & Revell, G. (2005). Lessons learned from the provision and funding of employment services for the MR/DD population. *Journal of Disability Policy Studies 16*(2), 84–101.

Woolf, S. (2006). *Critical elements of adaptive behavior in promoting community independence for individuals diagnosed with developmental disabilities*. (Doctoral dissertation, Capella University, 2006). Dissertation Abstracts International, UMI: 3239155.

18

ABAS-II: Adaptive Behavior Assessment for Children with Intellectual and Developmental Disabilities

KATHLEEN ARMSTRONG, HEATHER CURTISS, KYLE POPKAVE, AND CAROL LILLY

Department of Pediatrics, University of South Florida, Tampa, FL 33612, U.S.A.

Adaptive behavior functioning, or an individual's ability to take care of oneself and interact with others, is intimately tied to the diagnosis and classification of intellectual and developmental disabilities (IDD) as well as planning necessary interventions and environmental supports. The purpose of this chapter is to provide an overview of characteristics of individuals with IDD, and the key role played by adaptive behavior assessment in diagnostic decision making and problem solving to support the needs of this population.

The terminology *intellectual and developmental disabilities* (IDD) will be utilized throughout this chapter to refer to such individuals, rather than the term *mental retardation* in keeping with recommendations of the American Association on Mental Retardation (AAMR), newly renamed the *American*

Association on Intellectual and Developmental Disabilities (AAIDD, 2007). However, classification systems such as the *Diagnostic and Statistical Manual of Mental Disorders*, Fourth Edition, Text Revision (DSM-IV-TR, 2000), *Individuals with Disabilities Education Improvement Act* (IDEA, 2004), and state regulations continue to use the term *mental retardation*. Legal, professional, and diagnostic issues associated with assessment of adaptive behavior functioning relative to IDD will be discussed. Recent advances in prevention and early intervention for IDD will be offered. Research on the validity and guidelines for use of the Adaptive Behavior Assessment System (ABAS-II), 2nd Edition (Harrison & Oakland, 2003) for individuals with IDD will be presented. The final section of this chapter will present a case study of a child with Fragile X syndrome in which the ABAS-II was utilized within a comprehensive assessment process to establish a diagnosis, and to identify strengths and needs for intervention planning, as well as to monitor progress.

CHARACTERISTICS OF INDIVIDUALS WITH IDD AND ADAPTIVE BEHAVIOR

Approximately 3 out of 100 people in the United States have been diagnosed with IDD, or mental retardation, defined as sub-average intellectual functioning and concurrent impairment in adaptive functioning occurring before the age of 18 (American Psychiatric Association [APA], 2000; Association for Retarded Citizens [ARC], 2001). Prevalence for males may be five times higher than for females and is also higher in lower socio-economic populations (Oakland et al., 2003). IDD is neither a medical nor a mental disorder inherent in a person but rather a disorder that has been defined by statistical concepts as well as societal influence (Barlow & Durand, 1999). Three of the most common causes of IDD are Fragile X syndrome, Down syndrome (both genetic disorders), and fetal alcohol syndrome (prenatal exposure to alcohol). Nearly 500 genetic disorders have been linked to IDD. The cause of IDD remains unknown in one-third of cases (Boyd-Wright, 2000; Zeanah, 2000). Individuals with IDD are 3 to 4 times more likely to experience co-morbid health and mental health disorders compared to the general population (Murphy et al., 1998).

The *DSM-IV-TR* (2000) text revision classifies mental retardation, or IDD, according to sub-average intellectual functioning and concurrent impairment of adaptive functioning that occur before age 18. According to the *DSM-IV-TR* text revision, adaptive functioning must be viewed within age and culturally based expectations of performance, and a classification of mental retardation must include deficits in at least two of the following areas: communication, self-care, home living, social/interpersonal skills, use of community resources, self-direction, functional academic skills, work, leisure, and health and safety.

Eighty-five percent of individuals with IDD are considered to be functioning in the mild range, meaning that their measured intelligence quotient (IQ) falls 2 to 3 standard deviations below the mean along with significant deficits in adaptive behavior functioning. Many individuals with mild IDD develop communication, self-care, and social skills commensurate with peers during the early childhood years and as a consequence may not be distinguishable until early adolescence or later when academic and social demands increase (Sattler, 2002). Adults with mild IDD are capable of social and vocational success when given appropriate education and training, although they may need more guidance when faced with serious social or economic stressors.

Approximately 10% of those with IDD are considered to be functioning in the moderate range or 3 to 4 standard deviations below the mean (APA, 2000). Individuals with moderate IDD require more intensive supports, particularly in school and in transition to work. These individuals often show delays in early development, especially delays in communication and intellectual skills, and later in academic skill acquisition. With ongoing support, they can become contributing members to their families and communities. Similar to individuals with mild IDD, they may be more vulnerable to social or economic stressors.

Those individuals considered to be functioning in the severe to profound range (5 or more standard deviations below the mean) require extensive supports and supervision across environments (ARC, 2001). They frequently are diagnosed in infancy due to significant impairments in their development, including the inability to develop early communication and motor skills (Zeanah, 2000). Vision and/or hearing deficits also are prevalent in these individuals. Genetic disorders and prenatal events such as fetal alcohol exposure or brain malformations underlie the majority of severe cases of IDD (Murphy et al., 1998). Regardless of the severity of IDD, the assessment of adaptive behavior functioning is critical to the diagnostic process and in intervention planning for individuals diagnosed with IDD (ARC, 2001; AAMR, 2002; Kamphaus & Frick, 2002; Reschly et al., 2002).

Individuals with IDD often demonstrate varying degrees of proficiencies in adaptive functioning (Harrison & Oakland, 2003). Its developmental nature is critical to the construct of adaptive functioning in that expectations for adaptive skills increase and become more complex as individuals grow older and demands of their environment increase. Delays in self-help, early interaction, and communication skills may be first noted in the early childhood years, while lags in social, academic, and vocational skills may become more apparent in later childhood and adolescence (Grossman, 1983). Further, because adaptive skills are developmental in nature, they are amenable to intervention (Harrison & Raineri, 2007). Adaptive functioning assessment takes into account the individual's current performance in multiple contexts and is a key component of a comprehensive, ongoing, problem-solving process. Interventions and supports developed as a result of this process will help to assure that individuals with IDD achieve greater independence, happier relationships, and increased inclusion in their schools and communities.

LEGAL, PROFESSIONAL, AND DIAGNOSTIC ISSUES AND ASSESSMENT OF ADAPTIVE BEHAVIOR

LEGAL, PROFESSIONAL, AND DIAGNOSTIC ISSUES

Three federal lawsuits allege the overrepresentation of African-American students in special education classes due to their performance on measures of intelligence. In *Larry P. v. Riles* (1979, 1984), the federal district court in California ruled that standardized intelligence tests are culturally biased and could not be used for placement in special education classes. An appeal filed in 1984 upheld the court's initial verdict. However, federal courts in Illinois (1980) and later Georgia (1985) ruled that intelligence tests were not biased against African-American children and that disproportionate placement in special education classes did not discriminate against them. As a result of these rulings, the sole use of intelligence tests to find children eligible for special education has been deemphasized and more emphasis has been placed upon the assessment of adaptive functioning.

Education legislation began with the Education for All Handicapped Children's Act of 1975 (PL 94-142), with a goal to ensure educational rights to all children, including those with IDD. PL 94-142 defined mental retardation within the context of limitations in intelligence and adaptive behavior. This law was amended in 1986 to include services for children ages 3–5 and early intervention for infants and toddlers with disabilities. Most recently, IDEIA (2004) entitles children from birth through age 21 to receive support and related services needed for education and learning. Further, IDEIA emphasizes the importance of adaptive behavior in both assessment of functional performance and in addressing deficits that adversely affect the child's educational performance. In 2002, up to 613,000 school-age children or about 10% of students in special education were receiving services under the category of mental retardation (26th Annual Report to Congress, U.S. Department of Education, 2004).

ASSESSMENT OF ADAPTIVE BEHAVIOR

Professionals assessing children with IDD must ensure that assessment methods are non-biased and comprehensive (Riccio et al., 1998). Best practice in assessment and evaluation utilizes a process whereby referral problems are connected to assessment methods, which are selected based upon the characteristics of the individual and focus on prevention/intervention rather than diagnosis or eligibility alone. Cultural and linguistic factors as well as physical impairments must be taken into account to guard against discrimination in assessment (Ortiz, 2002). The reported scores should reflect the strengths and needs of the individual within the context of age, culture, and environmental expectations (Reschly & Grimes, 1995, 2002) as well as acknowledge the limitations of the instrument when reporting and interpreting scores. Tools that assess adaptive behavior can be utilized within a problem-solving framework to make diagnostic and eligibility decisions as well as for intervention planning (Oakland & Matusek, 1976).

ADVANCES IN PREVENTION AND EARLY INTERVENTION FOR IDD

IDD can result from prenatal, perinatal, and postnatal factors. Mothers with known biological risk factors such as prenatal drug or alcohol abuse should be educated along with provision of adequate prenatal care (Center for Disease Control, 2001). Other known environmental risk factors, such as those associated with extreme poverty, call for ongoing parental care including counseling about nutrition, especially to assure adequate folic acid intake. Prenatal screening including the Alpha-fetoprotein Test (AFT) and the Triple Test (AFP) (human chorionic gonadotropin, and estriol), may be used to detect neural tube defects and Down syndrome before birth. Advances in molecular biology will make treatment of Fragile X syndrome more likely in the future. Significant advances have been made in newborn screening for phenylketonuria, congenital hypothyroidism, Rh disease, and Sickle Cell disease. As a result of early detection, IDD can be prevented or ameliorated in affected children (Shonkoff & Phillips, 2001; Sobesky et al., 1996).

Central to the provision of early intervention is the need for early recognition of children with developmental delays. Due to the frequency of well-care visits needed during the first 3 years of life, pediatricians are likely to be the first-contact professionals for children with developmental delays. As such, the American Academy of Pediatrics (AAP, 2006) has adopted guidelines for management of these children. Furthermore, the AAP has developed indicators for evaluating children to ensure they are receiving routine, coordinated care that is family centered.

Finally, early intervention services and school programs typically are the first line of intervention for children with developmental delays. Programs that emphasize structured developmental activities that focus on improving child–caregiver interactions as well as the development of functional skills typically are the most effective at addressing the needs of at-risk children and their families (Shonkoff & Phillips, 2001). Toward this end, a central focus of early intervention is to increase adaptive skill development so that children become increasingly independent and able to interact with others across environments.

ABAS-II: VALIDITY AND ASSESSMENT OF INDIVIDUALS WITH IDD

The ABAS-II is a norm-referenced assessment of adaptive skills that may be utilized to diagnose disabilities and disorders, to assist in intervention planning, to identify specific skill strengths and weaknesses, as well as to monitor an individual's development. The ABAS-II provides a comprehensive assessment that measures adaptive skills listed in the AAMR (2002) definition of adaptive behavior. The behaviors measured include 10 specific adaptive skill areas that fall under one of three composites (Social, Practical, and Conceptual). A General Adaptive Composite is obtained by combining all adaptive skill areas. Parents, teachers, and others who know the child well can serve as respondents to the ABAS-II for children.

EVIDENCE OF VALIDITY FOR THE ABAS-II

The *Standards for Educational and Psychological Testing* (American Educational Research Association [AERA], 1999) identify various sources of evidence that may be utilized for test validation. These include evidence based on the test's theory, content, response processes, internal structure, and other variables. As such, the standards suggest that these sources, taken together, form a unitary concept of validity which determines the degree to which the proposed interpretation of test scores is appropriate for particular purposes (AERA, 1999). Although the test developer is responsible for demonstrating evidence that the test is appropriate for its intended use, test users also are responsible for evaluating evidence of valid instrument use and its administration.

TEST CONTENT

Items from the ABAS-II fall in one of the 10 adaptive skill areas that the AAMR (2002) supports as important to successful and independent functioning. These adaptive skill areas include communication, community use, functional academics, health and safety, home or school living, leisure, self-care, self-direction, social, and work. An assessment of motor skills is included when assessing children ages 0–5. In accord with the AAMR guidelines (2002), the ABAS-II groups these 10 adaptive skill areas into three broad composites: Conceptual, Social, and Practical. To develop test items, the authors of the ABAS-II conducted a comprehensive literature search to identify categories of adaptive skills that are necessary for successful and independent functioning across multiple settings and a wide range of developmental stages (e.g., infants and young children to adults).

RESPONSE PROCESS

A respondent completing the ABAS-II must have observed the behaviors in the individual for some time and be able to understand the intent of the questions. Thus, questions must be written in a language that is understood by people of diverse backgrounds and at a low reading level. The ABAS-II was normed on a large, representative sample by age (e.g., 0–89 years), race/ethnicity (e.g., White, Black, Hispanic and Other), and five education levels of parents.

Respondents (i.e., those parents and teachers completing the ABAS-II items) use a four-point Likert-type scale when answering each item. The choices for each item are: 0 is not able (i.e., cannot perform the behavior); 1 has the ability to perform the behavior yet never or almost never does it when needed; 2 has the ability to perform the behavior and displays it sometimes when needed; and 3 has the ability to perform the behavior and always or almost always does so when needed. During standardization, participants commented on the ease of completing the items. The participants reported the items are easy to complete, the response choices are clear, and there is little need to guess (Harrison & Oakland, 2003). Further, the items are written at a 5th grade level or lower (Oakland & Lane, 2004).

Toward this end, the professional is always responsible for determining the appropriateness of administering the ABAS-II across special subgroups. Respondents must know the individual well enough to respond to the items accurately and should be motivated to complete the assessment in an accurate fashion. The directions should be explained to respondents to ensure their understanding. Finally, the ABAS-II is available in Spanish and French Canadian for use with persons for whom these are their preferred languages.

INTERNAL STRUCTURE

The internal structure of a test refers to the degree to which the relationships among test items and test components conform to the construct on which the proposed test score interpretations are based (AERA, 1999). The structure of the ABAS-II is based on the definitions of adaptive skills as set forth by the AAMR (1992, 2002) and *DSM-IV-TR* (2000) text revision. The ABAS-II incorporates the three constructs (i.e., Conceptual, Social, and Practical) identified by the AAMR (2002) as comprising adaptive behavior.

The *ABAS-II Manual* provides detailed information on internal consistency of scores obtained from items in each of the 10 adaptive skill areas, the three composites, and the General Adaptive Composite (GAC). Reliability estimates for the six standardization samples are high (e.g., typically in the .90s). The reliability coefficients of scores obtained on the adaptive skill areas and adaptive composites range from .80 to .97 and .91 to .98, respectively. The GAC reliability coefficients range from .97 to .99. Reliability coefficients are available for performance levels and for samples with different clinical diagnoses. For individuals with IDD, the reliability coefficients of scores obtained on the adaptive skill areas and adaptive composites are much higher and ranged from .91 to .97 and .96 to .98, respectively. The GAC reliability coefficient is .99 with and without the adaptive skill area of Work.

Age group differences: ABAS-II items are sensitive to age differences. Thus, older individuals are more likely to display a specific behavior than younger individuals. However, adaptive skills are dependent upon a person's general level of development. Thus, as expected, adaptive skills vary across age ranges.

Factor structure: Confirmatory factor analysis was utilized to provide further evidence of the test's validity. Using this approach, a test's factor structure is specified by the researchers prior to performing the statistical analyses (Sattler, 2002). All five forms of the ABAS-II were evaluated using goodness-of-fit measures. A one-factor model was identified as providing a good fit to the obtained data. Evidence supporting a three-factor model (i.e., Social, Practical, Conceptual) was also obtained, thus supporting the AAMR's (2002) delineation of three adaptive behavior domains.

OTHER VARIABLES

Relationships between test scores and external variables provide evidence of a test's validity (AERA, 1999). Two broad forms of the ABAS-II's validity are examined: studies conducted concurrently with the standardization of the ABAS-II to examine the relationships between scores from the ABAS-II and other measures of adaptive functioning, as well as studies that examine the validity of using the ABAS-II with groups that have different diagnoses (e.g., individuals with IDD, learning disabilities, physical impairments).

The concurrent validity of the ABAS-II is supported through studies evaluating relationships between the ABAS-II and other measures of adaptive behavior, including the Vineland Adaptive Behavior Scale-Classroom Edition (VABS-CE), the Vineland Adaptive Behavior Scale-Interview Edition (VABS-IE), the Scales of Independent Behavior-Revised (SIB-R), and the Behavior Assessment Scale for Children (BASC). A brief discussion of each study is presented and detailed information can be found in the manual (Harrison & Oakland, 2003).

ABAS-II correlations with the Vineland Adaptive Behavior Scale: Total scores from the ABAS-II Teacher/Daycare Provider Form and the VABS-CE correlate significantly (r = .75) with an ethnically diverse, non-clinical sample (N = 44) of children (ages 3 years 3 months to 5 years 11 months). Correlations between the ABAS-II composite and the VABS-CE Adaptive Behavior Composite ranged between .58 to .73. The correlation between the General Adaptive Composites from the ABAS-II Teacher Form and the VABS-CE is .84. Correlations between the ABAS-II composites and the VABS-CE Adaptive Behavior Composite range between .77 and .81 in a sample of 57 predominantly white students (90%, ages 5–12 years, mean 8½ years).

Relationships between data obtained from the ABAS-II Parent/Primary Caregiver Form and the VABS-IE were examined in a somewhat diverse sample (73% White, 7% African-American, 18% Hispanic, 2% other) of 45 children (ages 1 month to 5 years 9 months). The correlation between the total scores from the ABAS-II and the VABS-IE was substantial: .70. ABAS-II composite scores correlate with the VABS-IE Adaptive Behavior Composite scores between .61 and .74.

ABAS-II correlations with the Scales of Independent Behavior-Revised (SIB-R): Data on the ABAS-II and two forms of the SIB-R were acquired on 34 ethnically diverse children (ages 2 months to 1 year 11 months; 56% female). The SIB-R Forms (Early Development and Short Form) are brief measures of adaptive behavior functioning. In contrast, the ABAS-II provides a comprehensive measure of adaptive behavior (Harrison & Oakland, 2003). Correlations between the ABAS-II Parent/Primary Caregiver Form and the Broad Independence Score from the SIB-R: Early Development Form are low and range between −.04 and .41. The ABAS-II General Adaptive Composite and the SIB-R Broad Independence Score correlated .18. Correlations between the ABAS-II Teacher/Daycare Provider Form and the Broad Independence Scale from the SIB-R: Short Form range between .14 and .67. The correlation between scores on the ABAS-II General Adaptive Composite and the SIB-R Broad Independence Score was moderate in the teacher sample (.59). The authors of the ABAS-II suggest that these lower correlations provide general information on how a briefer tool relates to a very comprehensive assessment of adaptive behavior (Harrison & Oakland, 2003).

ABAS-II correlations with the Behavior Assessment Scale for Children (BASC): The correlation between scores on the ABAS-II and BASC Adaptive Skills was .80 among a sample of ethnically diverse preschoolers as rated on the teacher forms from both measure. As expected, negative correlations were obtained between scores on the General Adaptive Composite and the BASC Externalizing Problems, Internalizing Problems, and Behavior Symptoms Index composites (−.49, −.39, and −.66, respectively). Adaptive behavior is lower in children who display more behavior problems.

ABAS-II correlations with measures of cognitive abilities: The results from several studies provide evidence of relationships between the ABAS-II and intelligence (e.g., WISC-III, WISC-IV, WPPSI-III, SB-IV) and achievement (WIAT). These samples ranged in size from 19 to 306; some included mixed clinical samples and others were non-clinical samples and varied in their ethnic representation. The correlations between ABAS-II and intelligence generally were in the .40s and .50s and those between the ABAS-II and achievement generally were in the .60s. These correlations are consistent with previous research that suggests that adaptive behavior and cognitive abilities represent separate yet related constructs.

CLINICAL VALIDITY STUDIES

Research examining the utility of the ABAS-II with various clinical populations also informs the test's validity. Individuals who displayed various disorders or disabilities were matched by age, gender, social class, geographic region, and race/ethnicity with persons selected from the ABAS-II standardization sample (Harrison & Oakland, 2003). A within-subject design was utilized to evaluate mean score differences on ABAS-II data between the clinical and matched control groups. The clinical samples were collected from independent researchers from various clinical settings, and the diagnoses may have been based on different criteria (Harrison &

Oakland, 2003). Toward this end, the authors discourage the test user from interpreting these results as representative samples of clinical populations in general. These results are best interpreted as further evidence of validity for the use of the ABAS-II to assess adaptive skills of individuals in special groups.

Mean scores across the 9 or 10 adaptive skill areas, three composites, and the General Adaptive Composite generally were lower among the clinical samples than the matched controls. Furthermore, compared to their matched controls, a higher proportion of participants from the clinical samples had mean scores lower than 2 standard deviations on at least one or more adaptive composites or the General Adaptive Composite. Lowest skill scores typically included communication, functional pre-academics, social, and self-direction across all disability groups, age levels, and rating forms.

INDIVIDUALS IDENTIFIED WITH IDD

Ten studies were conducted to evaluate the performance of individuals with IDD on the ABAS-II. These studies included samples of preschool-age and school-age children, as well as adults.

Preschool-age samples: Table 18.1 provides an overview of the results for the preschool samples based on data from the Teacher/Daycare Provider Form and the Parent/Primary Caregiver Form. In general, the children's mean General Adaptive Composite scores were 2 or more standard deviations below the mean for all four clinical groups. In addition, all groups had a large percentage of participants (77–86%) with at least one composite score that was 2 or more standard deviations

TABLE 18.1 Results of Preschool Samples with IDD

Group	*n*	Conceptual Composite Mean (*SD*)	Social Composite Mean (*SD*)	Practical Composite Mean (*SD*)	GAC Mean (*SD*)
Teacher/Daycare Provider Form					
Sample 1 – mild IDD	31	67.3	71.1	70.5	67.1
(ages 2:6–5:10)		(12.1)	(13.1)	(16.5)	(13.4)
Sample 2 – moderate IDD	19	65.8	67.7	68.4	64.6
(ages 2:7–5:11)		(14.7)	(13.3)	(17.1)	(15.2)
Parent/Primary Caregiver Form					
Sample 3 – mild IDD	27	68.0	70.5	70.9	66.0
(ages 2:6–5:10)		(12.8)	(12.0)	(15.4)	(13.2)
Sample 4 – moderate IDD	22	62.5	68.5	67.7	62.8
(ages 2:7–5:11)		(13.0)	(18.0)	(17.8)	(16.4)

Note: Composite scores (Conceptualization, Social, and Practical) and the General Adaptive Composite (GAC) have a mean of 100 and standard deviation of 15.

below the mean. Furthermore, most participants also scored 2 or more standard deviations below the mean on the communication and functional pre-academics adaptive skill areas with the exception of children with mild IDD as assessed on the Parent/Primary Caregiver Form.

Preschool-age participants with mild IDD displayed higher skill area scores, composite scores, and General Adaptive Composite scores compared to participants with moderate IDD. Participants across all groups of individuals with mild and moderate IDD displayed somewhat lower scores on the Conceptual Composite (M = 62 to 68, SD = 12 to 15) than on the Social Composite (M = 68 to 71, SD = 12 to 18) and Practical (M = 68 to 71, SD = 15 to 18). In addition, scores from parents and primary caregivers tended to be 1 to 2 points lower than those obtained from the teachers and daycare providers. In contrast to scores obtained by preschool-age children with mild and moderate IDD, those from the matched controls were in the average range on all composites and the General Adaptive Composite (M = 97 to 103, SD = 10 to 15). All effect sizes for adaptive skill areas, composites, and General Adaptive Composite comparisons were large (Cohen's $d \geqslant .80$). Thus, practical and significant differences were observed between the clinical and matched controls pre-school samples.

School-age samples: Results from five school-age samples of persons with IDD from the Teacher and the Parent Forms are summarized in Table 18.2. In general, participants in all five clinical groups, on average, had mean General Adaptive Composite scores $\leqslant$2 standard deviations below the mean. In addition, all groups had a large percent of participants (61–96.3%) with at least 1 composite score $\leqslant$2

TABLE 18.2 Results of School-Age Samples with IDD

Group	*n*	Conceptual Composite Mean (*SD*)	Social Composite Mean (*SD*)	Practical Composite Mean (*SD*)	GAC Mean (*SD*)
Teacher Form					
Sample 1 – Down syndrome (ages 5–21)	21	57.8 (9.6)	70.4 (13.2)	56.4 (17.0)	56.1 (14.9)
Sample 2 – IDD (unspecified) (ages 5–21)	84	61.8 (11.3)	73.7 (14.3)	65.4 (16.7)	61.9 (15.1)
Sample 3 – mild IDD (ages 5–21)	66	72.1 (15.9)	81.6 (13.6)	76.5 (19.2)	72.9 (17.6)
Sample 4 – moderate IDD (ages 5–21)	27	57.6 (7.5)	72.0 (13.3)	62.6 (17.4)	59.3 (14.7)
Parent Form					
Sample 5 – IDD (unspecified) (ages 5–21)	41	64.2 (15.9)	73.9 (17.9)	65.7 (21.9)	63.7 (19.8)

Note: Composite scores (Conceptualization, Social, and Practical) and the General Adaptive Composite (GAC) have a mean of 100 and standard deviation of 15.

standard deviations below the mean. Furthermore, most participants also scored ⩾2 standard deviations below the mean on the adaptive skill areas of communication, community use, and functional pre-academics. Participants across groups generally were rated lowest on the Conceptual Composite (M = 58 to 72, SD = 7.5 to 16) and highest on the Social Composite (M = 70 to 82, SD = 13 to 14) and the Practical Composite (M = 56 to 76, SD = 17 to 19). The matched controls scored in the average range across composite scores and the General Adaptive Composite (M = 97 to 103, SD = 14 to 20).

Results of the within-subject tests indicate that mean scores between clinical samples and matched controls differ significantly ($p < .01$) across adaptive skill areas, composite scores, and the General Adaptive Composite. Most effect sizes for the adaptive skill area, composite, and General Adaptive Composite comparisons are large (Cohen's $d \geqslant .80$). The sample with mild IDD rated by the teachers has somewhat smaller yet still significant effect sizes for school living, health and safety, and social adaptive skill areas (.77, .65, and .78, respectively). Thus, differences that impact practice between the clinical and matched controls school-age samples are apparent.

Adult samples: Results from an adult sample of 30 persons with IDD – unspecified, rated by others are summarized in Table 18.3. In general, the mean General Adaptive Composite (without the work adaptive skill area), and composite scores were 2 or more standard deviations below the mean. In addition, a large percentage of participants (80%) had at least one composite score 2 or more standard deviations below the mean. Mean scores are similar for the Conceptual (M = 62, SD = 13) and Practical (M = 62, SD = 15.3) composites and higher on the Social Composite (M = 70, SD = 13). The matched control scores are in the average range across the three composite scores and the General Adaptive Composite (M = 93 to 95, SD = 14 to 17). Results of the within-subject tests indicated that mean scores between this clinical sample and matched controls differ significantly ($p < .01$) across adaptive skill areas, composite scores, and the General Adaptive Composite. Most effect sizes for the adaptive skill area, composite, and General

TABLE 18.3 Results of Adult Sample with IDD

Group	n	Conceptual Composite Mean (SD)	Social Composite Mean (SD)	Practical Composite Mean (SD)	GAC Mean (SD)
Adult Form, Rated by Others					
Sample 1 – IDD (unspecified)	30	61.5	69.7	61.7	57.8
(ages 17–72)		(12.9)	(12.7)	(15.3)	(14.1)

Note: Composite scores (Conceptualization, Social, and Practical) and the General Adaptive Composite (GAC) have a mean of 100 and standard deviation of 15.

Adaptive Composite comparisons are large (Cohen's $d \geqslant .80$). Thus, differences that impact practice between the clinical and matched controls school-age samples are apparent.

SUMMARY OF SPECIAL GROUP PERFORMANCE ON THE ABAS-II

Results from the validation samples and special group studies provide support for the validity and clinical utility of the ABAS-II. Evidence suggests that the ABAS-II differentiates clinical and non-clinical samples, including individuals with IDD. Significant differences were observed between clinical samples of individuals with IDD and matched control samples, with most participants from the clinical samples displaying adaptive behaviors at least two standard deviations below the mean on one or more the three adaptive domains or on the General Adaptive Composite. In addition, large effect sizes were obtained for the majority of analyses, thus suggesting practical significance. Clinical sample sizes were small, and no adjustments for Type I error were made. Thus, these results are best interpreted as examples and not necessarily representative of the diagnostic groups. Toward this end, the validity studies with non-clinical and clinical samples demonstrate that the ABAS-II can provide a valid assessment of adaptive behavior and skills in a wide range of populations, including individuals with IDD.

CASE STUDY OF A 5 YEAR OLD BOY WITH FRAGILE X SYNDROME

JM, a 5 year old boy with a history of global developmental delays and challenging behaviors documented since age 2 in multiple settings, presented to a multidisciplinary team at a child development clinic. JM's challenging behaviors included frequent and extended tantrums comprised of crying, hitting and biting, and falling on the floor. Other than engaging in occasional chase activities, he did not initiate play and showed little interest in playing with others. JM was pre-occupied with a few toys, generally those with wheels, which he would spin rather than roll. He sometimes stared off into space. Both mother and teacher described JM as moody and reported that he rarely smiled or laughed. JM showed little interest in dressing or toilet training and would scream when adults assisted him with those skills. The team was asked to formulate a diagnosis for JM and to recommend interventions and services to support his development.

DEVELOPMENTAL HISTORY

Reviewing a developmental history is essential to diagnostic practice and should consist of a thorough records review, including medical and family history, timing and pattern of development, as well as the presence or absence of regression, standardized test results, and other laboratory and/or genetic tests. Caregiver interviews are also utilized to fill in the gaps. Congenital or genetic syndromes often present in early infancy and with specific clinical criteria.

JM lives with his parents and two older sisters, both of whom are doing well in school. Due to lack of health insurance and frequent family moves, JM had several different health providers. Thus, there was little documentation of early medical history. At age 2, he was seen by a pediatrician who noted significant communication delays along with tantrums, poor eye contact, and an unusual fascination with the wheels on his toy truck. He was referred to the Early Intervention Program in the community and subsequently received speech and occupational therapies. At age 3, JM transitioned into the local school system's Early Exceptional Learning Program where he attended school daily in a multi-age group preschool setting. He is eligible for kindergarten in the fall, and the school system and parents are evaluating various placement decisions.

A thorough family and developmental history was conducted. His mother reported an uncomplicated pregnancy during which she received inadequate prenatal care due to lack of insurance. She reportedly did not consume alcohol or drugs during her pregnancy and did smoke one pack of cigarettes per day. JM was described as a fussy baby who was difficult to sooth and feed. His overall development seemed slower compared with his sisters. For example, he did not crawl until he was 18 months or walk until he was 20 months, and was very delayed in using words.

JM has a history of frequent ear infections for which he was treated with antibiotics and pressure-equalization tubes at age 3. JM failed several audiological evaluations due to non-compliant behavior. A recent auditory brainstem response assessment revealed intact hearing. His mother thinks he may have allergies due to frequent congestion and colds, but this has not been confirmed. No problems were reported with respect to sleeping or eating, although JM is a picky eater who shuns vegetables and prefers foods such as pizza and chicken nuggets.

Physical and neurological examinations indicated that JM was a well-developed boy with mild macrocephaly (i.e., his head circumference was above the 90th percentile) while his weight and height were in the 25th and 50th percentiles, respectively. No dysmorphic features were obvious. He had a mild heart murmur, described as a mid-systolic click, and flat feet. His joints were lax and muscle tone was on the low end of normal. His neurological exam did not reveal any focal weaknesses, and reflexes were equal throughout. His gait was immature, as he was unable to hop on one foot or walk on a line. However, he was able to run and jump off of both feet without difficulty.

STANDARDIZED TEST RESULTS

At age 32 months, JM was evaluated by the Early Intervention Program. Scores from both the Bayley Scales of Infant Development, 2nd Edition (BSID-II, Bayley, 1993) and the Pre-School Language Scale, 4th Edition (PLS-IV, Zimmerman

TABLE 18.4 Results of the BSID-II and PLS-IV for JM, Age 32 months

Composite	Composite Standard Score	Percentile
BSID-II Mental Score	55	1
BSID-II Motor	80	8
PLS-IV Total Language	53	1
PLS-IV Auditory Comprehension	59	1
PLS-IV Expressive Communication	56	1

Note: Composite scores of BSID-II and PLS-IV (Mental Score, Motor, Total Language, Auditory Comprehension, Expressive Communication) have a mean of 100 and standard deviation of 15.

TABLE 18.5 Results of the WPPSI-III for JM, Age 5

Composite	Composite Standard Score	Percentile
WPPSI-III		
Full Scale	56	1
Verbal Index	58	1
Performance Index	62	1

Note: Composite scores (Full Scale, Verbal Index, Performance Index) have a mean of 100 and standard deviation of 15.

et al., 2002) are summarized in Table 18.4. These evaluations identified developmental delays in cognitive and communication skills. Relative strengths were noted in motor skills, gross motor abilities in particular. At age 5 years, the school system's multidisciplinary team completed a standardized assessment battery that included the Wechsler Preschool and Primary Scale of Intelligence, 3rd Edition (WPPSI-III; Wechsler, 2002), the ABAS-II (Parent/Primary Caregiver and Teacher/Daycare Provider Forms) and the Gilliam Autism Rating Scale (GARS; Gilliam, 1995). These tools were selected to assist in diagnostic and classification purposes, and the ABAS-II was utilized to identify functional skills for intervention planning.

The WPPSI-III is a measure of cognitive functioning, normed for ages 2 years 6 months to 7 years 3 months. This measure utilizes six subtests that yield two composite scores (Verbal and Performance IQ), as well as a Full Scale IQ (FSIQ) On the WPPSI-III, JM obtained a Verbal IQ of 62, Performance IQ Score of 68, and a FSIQ of 62 placing him in the 1st percentile compared to same-age peers (see Table 18.5). This score falls in the *extremely low* range, indicating significant delays in cognitive development. Receptive language was a relative strength, while JM displayed most difficulty on expressive language tasks.

TABLE 18.6 Results of the ABAS-II (Parent/Primary Caregiver Form for Ages 0–5, and Teacher/Daycare Provider Form for Ages 2–5) for JM, Age 5

	Primary/Primary Caregiver Form		Teacher/Daycare Provider Form	
Composites/Adaptive Skill Areas	Standard/ Scale Score	Percentile Rank	Standard/ Scale Score	Percentile Rank
Conceptual Composite	47	<0.1	7	<0.1
• Communication	1		1	
• Functional academics	2		2	
• Self-direction	1		1	
Social Composite	48	<0.1	49	<0.1
• Leisure	1		1	
• Social	1		1	
Practical Composite	45	<0.1	49	<0.1
• Community use	1		–	
• Home living	2		–	
• School living	–		2	
• Health and safety	1		2	
• Self-care	2		1	
Motor Adaptive Skill Area	5		5	
GAC	45	<0.1	44	<0.1

Note: Composite scores (Conceptualization, Social, and Practical) and the General Adaptive Composite (GAC) have a mean of 100 and standard deviation of 15. Adaptive skill areas (Communication, Functional Academics, etc.) have a mean of 10 and standard deviation of 3. Motor adaptive skill area scores are not included in calculating composite scores but are used in calculating the GAC.

Based on parent and teacher ratings of adaptive functioning on the ABAS-II Parent/Primary Caregiver Form and Teacher/Daycare Provider Form, JM was found to be performing in the *extremely low* range on all areas of adaptive functioning. JM earned GAC scores of 45 (Parent Form) and 44 (Teacher form), which fall below the 1st percentile as compared to same-age peers (see Table 18.6). His scores were consistently low across the ABAS-II adaptive skill areas, although motor adaptive skills were a personal strength commensurate with previous evaluation results. There were no significant discrepancies between Conceptual, Social or Practical Composites.

In addition to assessing cognitive and adaptive skills, the Gilliam Autism Rating Scale (GARS; Gilliam, 1995) was administered. The GARS is a standardized assessment tool designed for screening and assessment for autistic and other severe behavior disorders. Items on this instrument are based upon the definitions of autism as adopted by the Autism Society of America (1994) and the *DSM-IV-TR* (2000) text revision. The GARS may be used to discriminate individuals with autism from other diagnostic groups including IDD.

Based upon history, clinical observation, and results of the GARS, JM demonstrated symptoms that indicated a very *likely probability* of autism. His overall Autism Index of 106 placed him at the 66th percentile compared to same-age peers. Subtest scores indicated that stereotypical behaviors were in the 37th percentile, social interactions were in the 95th percentile, and development, or at the, while communication was in the 9th percentile.

GENETIC AND LABORATORY TESTS

The severity and global nature of JM's delays coupled with specific physical findings suggesting Fragile X syndrome. There is a family history of learning problems. Thus, additional medical testing was ordered to include blood testing for lead, an EEG, and MRI. Results of these tests were normal. Chromosomal DNA analysis were also completed to rule out genetic syndromes, including Fragile X syndrome. The Fragile X syndrome study indicated an FMR-1 mutation with 220 repeats and 100% methylation. This mutation is identified in 100% of affected males (Meadows & Sherman, 1996).

RECOMMENDATIONS FOR FOLLOW-UP CARE

Fragile X syndrome and developmental delays are highly co-morbid. Therefore, children diagnosed with Fragile X syndrome are eligible for early intervention services under IDEA Part C. Early diagnosis facilitates the initiation of early intervention and family support services. Given the severity of JM's developmental delays, early intervention services were initiated somewhat later than what is supported by best practice.

The multidisciplinary team determined that JM and his family would benefit from long term case management of his health, developmental, emotional, and educational needs. Given JM's diagnosis of Fragile X syndrome and the related behavioral and functional challenges, he was at significant risk for co-morbid emotional and behavioral disorders. Due to these risks, it was imperative for JM to receive adequate health services, educational supports, as well as mental health services (McHugh, 2003).

Positive behavioral interventions were recommended for use by JM's family and teachers, with an emphasis on identifying the function of JM's maladaptive behaviors. The clinician also discussed the importance of setting developmentally appropriate goals for JM with his caretakers. Additionally, it was recommended that JM be taught new adaptive behaviors to replace the maladaptive behaviors. In order to determine which adaptive skills JM needed to be taught, the assessment results from the ABAS-II were analyzed. The ABAS-II identifies specific, developmentally relevant behaviors for children of all ages, and is useful for identifying target skills. For example, on this administration of the ABAS-II, on the item "able to sit on the toilet or potty seat without being held," JM was rated by his caregivers as *Sometimes* [able] *When Needed*. JM's rating on this item was thought to be a performance deficit and not a skill deficit. It is important to differentiate between performance and skill deficits because the intervention may differ. In JM's case, the behavior was determined to be a performance deficit, thus behavioral interventions were implemented. Components of the intervention included scheduled toileting times, reinforcement for engaging in desired behavior, and redirection for refusals. If the behavior were a skill deficit, the intervention typically would involve task analysis and specific teaching steps.

The use of adaptive assessment methods such as the ABAS-II ensures that a child's functional performance is taken into account, and is useful for planning and monitoring interventions to teach needed skills. At age 5, data from the ABAS-II identified JM's functional skills to be less developed compared with his performance on other standardized measures. The team hypothesized that specific challenging behaviors were impeding his progress and were able to target needed skills and develop interventions to improve his engagement in educational and family activities.

SUMMARY

Adaptive behavior is a critical component in the assessment and diagnosis of IDD. The ABAS-II is designed to measure adaptive skills included in the AAMR (2002) definition of adaptive behavior. The ABAS-II provides a standardized, multi-informant assessment with technical adequacy that can be utilized to identify adaptive skills from birth through adulthood. It identifies adaptive skills, and their strengths and weaknesses, and thus can aid in the design of developmentally appropriate goals and interventions. This chapter provides a case study showing how the ABAS-II can be used to establish a diagnosis of IDD and to identify adaptive skill weaknesses in need of intervention.

REFERENCES[1]

American Academy of Pediatrics (2006). Identifying infants and young children with developmental disorders in the medical home: An algorithm for developmental surveillance and screening. *Pediatrics*, 118(1), 405–420.

American Association on Mental Retardation (1992). *Definitions, Classifications, and Systems of Supports*, 9th ed., Washington, DC: AAMR.

American Association on Mental Retardation (2002). *Mental Retardation: Definitions, Classifications, and Systems of Supports*, 10th ed., Washington, DC: AAMR.

American Educational Research Association (1999). *Standards for Educational and Psychological Testing*. Washington, DC: American Educational Research Association.

[1] The name of the American Association on Mental Retardation was changed to the American Association on Intellectual and Developmental Disabilities. Retrieved March 13, 2007 from www.aamr.org/About-AA/DD/MR.

American Psychiatric Association (2000). *Diagnostic and Statistical Manual of Mental Disorders*, 4th ed., text revision. Washington, DC: APA.

Association for Retarded Citizens (2001). *Introduction to mental retardation*. Retrieved December 15, 2006, from http://thearc.org.faqs/mrqa.html.

Autism Society of America (1994). Definition of autism. *The Advocate: Newsletter of the Autism Society of America*, 26(2), 3.

Barlow, D. & Durand, V. M. (1999). *Abnormal Psychology*. Pacific Grove, CA: Brooks/Cole.

Bayley, N. (1993). *Bayley Scales of Infant Development*, 2nd ed., San Antonio, TX: Psychological Corporation.

Boyd-Wright, E. (2000). Mental retardation. In C. R. Reynolds & E. Fletcher-Janzen, eds., *Encyclopedia of Special Education*, 2nd ed., New York: Wiley.

Center for Disease Control (2001). Genetic epidemiology and the future disease prevention and public health. Retrieved January 29, 2008 from http://epirev.oxfordjournals.org

Gilliam, J. (1995). *Gilliam Autism Rating Scale*. Austin, TX: Pro-ed.

Grossman, H. J., ed. (1983). *Classification of Mental Retardation*. Washington, DC: American Association of Mental Deficiency.

Harrison, P. L. & Oakland, T. (2003). *Adaptive Behavior Assessment System*, 2nd ed., San Antonio, TX: The Psychological Corporation.

Harrison, P. L. & Raineri, G. (2007). Adaptive behavior assessment for preschool children. In B. A. Bracken & R. J. Nagle, eds., *Psychoeducational Assessment of Preschool Children*, 4th ed., Mahwah, NJ: Lawrence Erlbaum Associates.

Individuals with Disabilities Education Act Amendments of 1997 (1999). Final Regulations. *Federal Register*, 64(48).

Individuals with Disabilities Education Improvement Act (2004). Retrieved December 14, 2006 from http://edworkforce.hourse.gove/issues/108th/education/idea/conference report/confrep.htm.

Kamphaus, R. W. & Frick, P. J. (2002). *Clinical Assessment of Child and Adolescent Personality and Behavior*, 2nd ed., Boston: Allyn & Bacon.

Meadows, K.L. & Sherman, S.L. (1996). Fragile X syndrome: Examination of issues pertaining to publication-based screening. Screening, 4(4), 175–192.

McHugh, S. (2003). Fragile X Syndrome. In E. Fletcher-Janzen & C. R. Reynolds, eds., *Childhood Disorders*. Hoboken, NJ: John Wiley & Sons.

Murphy, C. C., Boyle, C., Shendel, D., et al. (1998). Epidemiology of mental retardation in children. *Mental Retardation and Developmental Disabilities Research Reviews*, 4, 6–13.

Oakland, T., & Lane, H. B. (2004). Language, reading, and readability formulas: Implications for developing and adapting tests. *International Journal of Testing*, 4, 239–252.

Oakland, T. & Matuszek, P. (1976). Using tests in nondiscriminatory assessment. In T. Oakland, ed., *Non-biased assessment of minority group children: With bias toward none* (pp. 27–34).

Oakland, T., Mpofu, E., Glasgow, K., et al. (2003). Diagnosis and administrative interventions for students with Mental Retardation in Australia, France, United States, and Zimbabwe 98 years after Binet's first intelligence test. *International Journal of Testing*, 3(1), 59–75.

Ortiz, S. (2002). Best practices in nondiscriminatory assessment. In A. Thomas & J. Grimes, eds., *Best Practices in School Psychology IV*. Bethesda, MD: NASP.

Reshley, D. J. & Grimes, J. P. (1995). Best practices in intellectual assessment. In A. Thomas & J. Grimes, eds., Best practices in School Psychology-III (pp. 763–773). Washington, DC: National Association of School Psychologists.

Reshley, D. J. & Grimes, J. P. (2002). Best practices in intellectual assessment. In A. Thomas & J. Grimes, eds., Best practices in School Psychology-IV (pp. 1337–1350). Washington, DC: National Association of School Psychologists.

Reschly, D. J., Myers, T. G., & Hartel, C. R. eds. (2002). *Disability Determination for Mental Retardation*. Washington, DC: National Academy Press.

Sattler, J. (2002). *Assessment of Children: Behavioral and Clinical Applications*. San Diego, CA: Jerome Sattler, Publisher, Inc.

Sherman, S. (1996). Epidemiology. In R. J. Hagerman & A. C. Cronister eds., *Fragile X syndrome: Diagnosis, treatment and research* (2nd ed., pp. 165–192).

Shonkoff, J. P. & Phillips, D. A. (2001). *From Neurons to Neighborhoods*. Washington, DC: National Academy of Sciences.

Sobesky, W. E., Taylor, A. K., Pennington, B. F., Bennetto, I., Porter, D., Riddle, J., & Hagerman, R. J. (1996). Molecular/clinical correlations in females with fragile X. *American Journal of Medical Genetics*, 64(2), 340–345.

Wechsler, D. (2002). *Wechsler Preschool and Primary Scale of Intelligence*, 3rd edn., San Antonio, TX: Harcourt Assessment.

Zeanah, C. H. (2000). *The Handbook of Infant Mental Health*, 2nd edn., New York: Guilford Press.

Zimmerman, I., Steiner, V., & Pond, R. (2002). *Preschool Language Scale*, 4th edn., San Antonio, TX: Harcourt Assessment.

19

Intervention Design and Diagnosis for Young Children with Autism Using the ABAS-II

STEVEN WOOLF* AND CHRISTINE MERMAN WOOLF**

*BEACON Services, Milford, MA 01757, U.S.A.
**Capella University, Minneapolis, MN 55402, U.S.A.

Parents, educators, and other professionals in the United States and elsewhere have become concerned about the rising prevalence of autism and related disorders together with services for those with an autism spectrum disorder (ASD). Kanner (1943) was the first researcher to identify the features associated with autism. He reported that this condition differed from those of other psychological disorders. Although Kanner did not define the diagnostic criteria of autism, he presented case histories of 11 children with the disorder. Some of the behavioral/psychological characteristics first identified included the following five. Children with this disorder have difficulty socializing, relating, and empathizing with others. They display delays in their expressive and receptive language; abnormal communicative patterns including echolalia and ritualistic use of language also may be present. Persons with this disorder display abnormal sensory reactions to environmental objects and events. Their rote memory tends to be relatively well developed. Finally, their gross and fine motor development generally is normal.

ASD is characterized as a developmental disability. It affects thousands of children and families nationwide (Ozonoff et al., 2005). According to the Center of Disease Control (CDC), approximately 34 of every 10,000 children between ages 3 and 10 have been diagnosed with ASD. The Autism Society of America (ASA) reports that one in 166 babies develop ASD (Ranta, 2007). ASA reports that 1.5 million Americans, including children and adults, have ASD and another 15 million Americans (e.g., family, educators, and healthcare workers) are affected by ASD.

ASD is a life-long disorder that affects persons from all socioeconomic and educational levels. Tests of medical and physical qualities, including brain imagery devices that differentiate or diagnose children with autism, do not exist. Although many theories have been postulated to explain the development of autism, there is no empirical evidence that explains the origin for an autistic disorder. Current research focuses on gene mutations during the fetus' development.

ASD is viewed on a spectrum from mild to severe. Placement on the spectrum is based on the severity of autistic symptoms exhibited by the person. A psychologist, developmental pediatrician, neurologist, or other medical professional typically makes the initial diagnosis of autism. This assessment relies upon behavioral observations, adaptive behavior measures, behavior checklists specific to autism, sensory screenings, interviews, and developmental/cognitive measures (Sattler, 2002).

CORE COMPONENTS OF ASD

Autism is one of five disorders that falls under the umbrella of Pervasive Developmental Disorders (PDD), a category of neurological disorders characterized by severe and pervasive impairment in several areas of development. The following five PDD disorders are described in the *Diagnostic and Statistical Manual of Mental Disorders* (American Psychiatric Association, 2000): Autistic Disorder, Asperger's Disorder, Childhood Disintegrative Disorder, Rett's Disorder, and PDD-Not Otherwise Specified. Autism is the most common of the PDD (Centers for Disease Control and Prevention, 2006).

The incidence of ASD is thought to be increasing, some believe at a startling rate of 10 to 17 percent per year (Ranta, 2007). ASA estimates that the prevalence of autism could reach 4 million Americans in the next decade (Ranta, 2007).

The essential features of ASD include significant impairments in social interaction and communication skills and a highly restricted area of activities and interests (American Psychiatric Association, 2000). Children diagnosed with autism exhibit a restricted range and repertoire of activities and interests together with stereotypic or self-stimulatory behaviors. They also often exhibit high levels of challenging behaviors such as screaming, hitting, and biting (Hintze & Eckert, 2001), thus, creating substantial challenges and obstacles for individuals responsible for their education and well-being (Carr & Durand, 1985). Parents experience increased stress as a result of caring for a child with ASD. Parents usually require specialized training to learn to use behavioral methods to promote their child's social and language skills and to manage challenging behaviors (Carr & Durand, 1985; Sundberg & Partington, 1998).

ESSENTIAL CHARACTERISTICS OF ASD

The primary behavioral deficit of children with autism is marked impairment in social interaction skills. Children with autistic disorder often are perceived by others as aloof, antisocial, and/or emotionally distant. These children exhibit an impaired ability to perceive and process social and emotional cues from people and the environment and appear to be non-responsive to the emotional and social behaviors of others (Preis, 2006; Scattone, D & Wilczynski, 2006). Due to these characteristic, children with autism must receive direct and often prolonged instruction on how to initiate and maintain social interactions.

Children with autism also have significant deficits in expressive language skills. Whether these deficits result from a neurological abnormality that impedes expressive language, a lack of reinforcement that results from socially engaging others, or a combination of the two is difficult to determine. Early intervention research has demonstrated that children with ASD can be taught to communicate, socialize, and adapt to novel settings (Lovaas, 1977; Ozonoff et al., 2005). Alternative communication systems, including picture exchange, sign language, and verbal behavior, can be developed through one-to-one instruction (Scattone et al., 2006). Early intervention services for children with ASD benefit the child and family as well as result in substantially reducing treatment costs when evaluated over one's lifespan (Jarbrink & Knapp, 2001).

RELEVANT RESEARCH

Research has examined the adaptive behavior of children with autism, often using the Vineland Adaptive Behavior Scale (Dirk, 2000; Kraijer, 2000). Several studies have documented adaptive behavior deficits, especially in social and communication development, in individuals with autism (Gilham et al., 2000; Paul et al., 2004). Deficits in social and communication skills are more pronounced in children with autism than in those with other PDD.

Although studies of adaptive behavior displayed by children with autism primarily have identified socialization and communication skill deficits, there has been little research on their adaptive skills using measures of adaptive behavior that assess more current concepts, including the 10 specific adaptive skill areas, such as those provided by the Adaptive Behavior Assessment System-II (ABAS-II; Harrison & Oakland, 2003) .

The ABAS-II provides a direct assessment of many of the core deficits displayed by children and youth with ASD, including but not limited to social and communication skills. The use of the ABAS-II enables service providers to identify adaptive skill strengths and weakness, thus helping professionals and parents to target specific skills for interventions.

Data from standardized tests typically are used to compare one person with a representative sample of same-age persons nationally. Standardized tests rarely provide separate norms for the clinical groups with whom tests may be used. Moreover, persons within a clinical group, including those with autism, differ considerably in their intellectual and other personal qualities, thus precluding the identification of a homogeneous population from which to draw a comparison group.

Thus, the ABAS-II does not contain separate norms for children with autism. However, children with autism were included in the standardization samples (Harrison & Oakland, 2003). Small numbers of toddlers and preschool children with autism were included in each of the standardization samples for the teacher/daycare provider and parent/primary caregiver forms. In addition, small numbers of school-age children with autism were included in the standardization samples for the teacher and parent forms. The ABAS-II manual reports the following percentages of Autistic Disorder clinical cases included in the standardization sample: 0.13 in the Teacher/Daycare Provider sample, 0.07 in the Parent/Primary Caregiver sample, 0.41 in the Teacher sample, and 0.24 in the Parent sample (Harrison & Oakland, 2003).

The ABAS-II manual also reports several clinical validity studies in which ABAS-II scores for children with autism and PDD-not otherwise specified were compared to scores of matched control groups. Data from the teacher/daycare form for 35 children with autism ages 3 years 2 months to 5 years as well as data from the parent/primary caregiver form for 34 children with autism ages 3 years 1 month to 5 years 11 months indicate that children with autism, compared to a normal control group, were significantly lower on seven of the eight ABAS-II adaptive skill areas (i.e., communication, school and home living, health and safety, leisure, self-care, social, and motor skills) as well as on the conceptual, social, and practical composites and the General Adaptive Composite (GAC). Group differences were not apparent on functional pre-academics skill on the parent/primary caregiver form. Among the 35 children with autism for whom the Teacher/Daycare Provider Form was completed, 71% had GAC scores at least two standard deviations below the mean, compared to 0% of the matched control group. Among the 34 children with autism for whom the Parent/Primary Caregiver Form was completed, again 71% of the GAC scores were at least two standard deviations below the mean, compared to 6% for the matched control group. Their deficits in communication, health and safety, leisure, and social adaptive skill areas are most apparent.

Data on 32 children with autism, ages 5–18 and assessed with the teacher form, found them to score significantly lower than matched controls on all adaptive skill areas, the three composites, and the GAC. Among this sample, 84%

had GAC scores at least two standard deviations below the mean, compared to 3% of the matched control group.

Data for 19 children with PDD-not otherwise specified assessed with the teacher/daycare provider form and 18 children with PDD-not otherwise specified assessed with the Parent/Primary Caregiver form also were significantly lower than matched controls on all adaptive skill areas, the three composites, and the GAC. Among the 19 children for whom the Teacher/Daycare Provider Form was completed 56% had GAC scores at least two standard deviations below the mean compared to 11% of the matched control group. Among the 18 children for whom the Parent/Primary Caregiver Form was completed, 50% had GAC scores at least two standard deviations below the mean compared to 0% of the matched control group.

ABAS-II data were collected upon initial treatment intake of 218 children between ages 3 to 5 (M = 3.5 years) diagnosed with autism (Woolf, Ross, & Littleton, 2008). Parents completed the parent/primary caregiver form of the ABAS-II after an early autism diagnosis. Children received ABA early home based instructional interventions between 10 and 25 hours per week. Figures 19.1 and 19.2 profile data from these children.

Their average GAC, 68, is in the extremely low range. Mean scores that reflect the sample's average conceptual (77), social (70), and practical (67) composites are in the borderline or extremely low range.

The sample's lowest average composite score, the practical composite, include the adaptive skill areas of community use, home living, health and safety, and self-care skills. In contrast, the sample of children with autism generally displayed more advanced development in the adaptive skill areas of the conceptual composite (Figure 19.1). Their functional pre-academic skills generally were

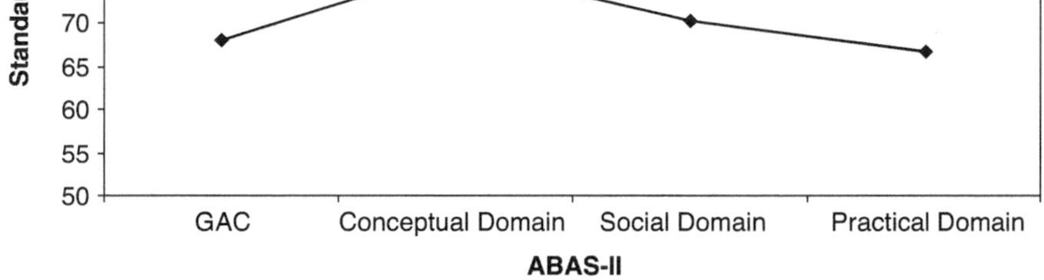

FIGURE 19.1 Average ABAS-II scores in GAC and Domain Scores Parent/Primary Caregiver Rating Form (0–5) children diagnosed with Autism ages 3 to 5, $N = 62$. *Source*: Woolf et al., 2008.

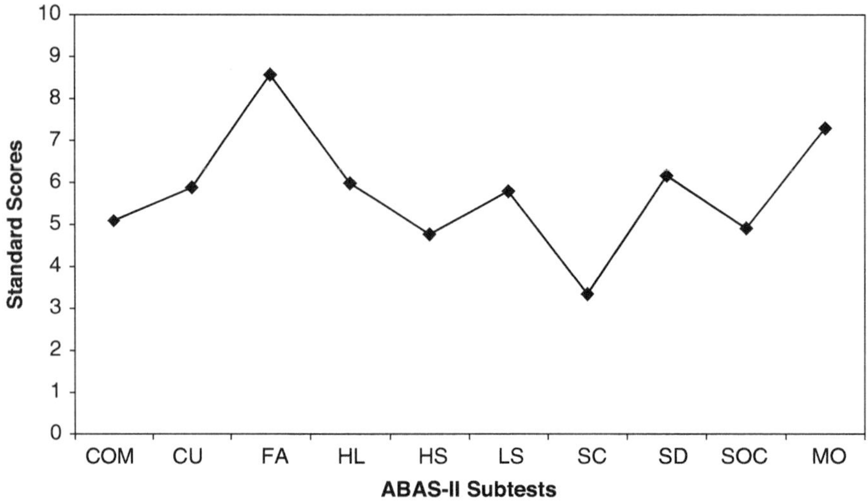

FIGURE 19.2 ABAS-II Parent/Primary Caregiver Rating Form (0–5) subtest profile analysis children diagnosed with Autism ages 3 to 5, $N = 62$. COM: Communication; CU: Community Use; FA: Functional pre-academics; HL: Home living; HS: Health and safety; LS: Leisure; SC: Self-care; SD: Self-direction; SOC: Social; MO: Motor. *Source*: Woolf et al., 2007.

highest (Figure 19.2). This finding is consistent with that reported by Harrison and Oakland (2003). The receipt of an average of 10 instructional hours per week by these children, using ABA methods, also may have contributed to these higher skill levels. The instruction may have resulted in the elevation of the functional academics adaptive skill area scores.

ABA procedures emphasize academic readiness skills typically taught at a tabletop. Academic readiness skills that constitute the focus of instruction include sitting in a chair for more than 10-seconds, waiting for an instructor prompt, and maintaining eye contact (attending) with academic materials are directly reinforced.

Young children in this study generally display a decided weakness in their self-care skills. Examples include difficulty independently feeding oneself, helping an adult with a task, wiping up spills at home, and keeping belongings neat and clean. Self-care skills typically are acquired by observing others perform the skill or are taught directly by parents. Self-care skills typically are adopted quickly by the child and thus, at later ages, require less adult prompting and assistance to perform them.

The deficit in self-care skills seen in the above sample suggest parents may be over prompting or assuming too much responsibility for the self-care of their children with autism. The ABAS-II data also indicate weaknesses in home/safety, communication and social adaptive skill areas. Thus, this profile reflects the signature deficits associated with autism: communication and socialization skills.

CASE STUDY

Thomas, a 6-year, 1-month-old male, was diagnosed with ASD at age 2 by a pediatric neurologist. Thomas exhibited communication delays and seemed apathetic and unresponsive toward parental support/affection. Thomas received early intervention services, including speech language therapy, sensory integration therapy, and floor-time instructional procedures. Unfortunately, despite 2 years of weekly therapy, Thomas did not acquire formal communication and exhibited increasing degrees of self-stimulatory and self-abusive behaviors together with person-directed aggression.

Thomas was referred for private ABA services after 2 unsuccessful years in a public school's developmental preschool program. Specifically, the school requested an individualized educational program for 25-hours per week at school and 10-hours per week at home. The private provider also was required to integrate the school and home programs to increase continuity and promote generalization across settings.

The psychologist completed an assessment that included structured observations in school and home, functional behavior assessment, the Preschool Language Skills Test, and the ABAS-II completed by parents and teachers. Results from this assessment indicated the Thomas' person-directed aggression was maintained by escaping non-preferred task demands. Specifically, Thomas had learned that adults would remove tasks requiring instructional engagement after he exhibited aggressive behaviors. Thomas also exhibited self-abusive behavior in the form of hand biting. Thomas' self-abusive behavior was maintained by escaping non-preferred task demands and socially mediated attention from adults. Thomas typically would bite his hand if attempted physical aggression toward others did not result in removal of task demands. Additionally, when task demands were not present, Thomas' hand biting behavior would result in adult intervention in the form of problem solving, "talking him down", or a verbal reprimand. Figure 19.3 represents the rate of his challenging behaviors in the classroom before intervention.

Results from Thomas's (age 6 years, 1 month) teacher and parent completed ABAS-II is shown in Table 19.1.

ABAS-II results from Thomas' parent and teacher indicate significant deficits in his general adaptive behavior, three composites, and 9 skills, with lowest skills in communication, social, and functional academics. Thomas' low functional academic skills reflect his escaping non-preferred academic tasks when exhibiting challenging behaviors. Thomas' low communication and socialization skills are common among children with autism. Collectively, these scores help confirm the need for interventions designed to help promote communication, socialization, and functional academic skills. Communication and socialization often are highly related. Therefore, interventions may address these concerns simultaneously.

Specifically, Thomas does not possess the formal communication skills to appropriately escape non-preferred tasks. The exhibition of aggressive behaviors constitutes his primary form of communication. Additionally, Thomas does not possess

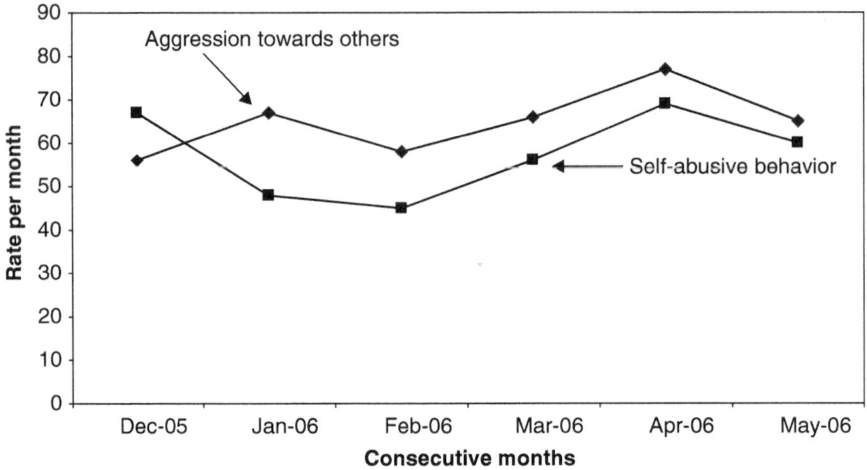

FIGURE 19.3 Thomas' monthly rate of challenging behaviors at school.

TABLE 19.1 ABAS-II Results for Thomas, Age 6 Years, 1 Month

Adaptive Skill Area/ Adaptive Composites/ GAC	Scaled Scores	
	Parent Form	Teacher Form
Adaptive Skill Areas		
Communication	3	3
Community use	4	4
Functional academics	2	2
Home living	5	4
Health and safety	6	6
Leisure	7	8
Self-care	2	5
Self-direction	3	5
Social	4	2
Conceptual Composite	59	65
90% confidence interval	55–63	61–69
Social Composite	75	75
90% confidence interval	69–81	71–79
Practical Composite	68	72
90% confidence interval	63–73	68–76
General Adaptive Composite	63	68
90% confidence interval	60–66	66–70

Note: Adaptive skill area scores are reported as scaled scores ($M = 10$, $SD = 3$). Composite scores are reported as standard scores ($M = 100$, $SD = 15$).

the academic readiness skills prerequisite to benefit from academic instruction. For example, Thomas does not sustain eye contact with his instructor, remain seated in the instructional setting, or follow one-step directions. Deficits in these academic and other readiness skills impede his ability to effectively engage academic tasks.

Thomas' previous intervention strategies utilizing sensory integration training and floor-time instructional procedures were discontinued due to their limited outcomes and in favor of an ABA instructional program designed for school and home settings.

A reinforcer assessment indicated that Thomas enjoyed squeezing rubber balls of different texture, looking through a kaleidoscope, eating raisins, and swinging in a hammock. An instructional table with chairs for Thomas and the instructor were placed in a quiet area in his classroom. On the instructional table was a visual schedule sequencing photographs of tasks to be completed. At the end of the picture sequence was a photograph of a reinforcing activity (i.e., playing with preferred toy). At the beginning of the sessions, Thomas was escorted to the table, prompted to complete a simple task (e.g., placing 5 blocks in a shape sorter), and given 5-minute access to the reinforcing activity. A hand-over-hand prompting procedure was used to insure that Thomas completed the task and gained access to the reinforcing activity.

Task demands increased systematically and reinforcement intervals decreased. Eventually, Thomas was reinforced for following one-step directions, maintaining eye contact with the instructor, and waiting with his arms folded for the instructional assignment. The hand-over-hand prompting procedures also were faded systematically to his visual schedule. Additionally, his home and school program incorporated a picture communication system (Frost & Bondy, 2002) through which Thomas gained access to preferred items by independently selecting a picture of the item to exchange for the actual item. Figure 19.4 visually depicts the effects of the intervention/treatment phase at school.

Other measures of intervention effectiveness assessed the frequency of picture exchanges, spontaneous verbalizations, prompt usage, and sustained academic engagement. Data from these measures indicated Thomas' rate of aggressive behaviors decreased significantly as his skills to communicate through the use of picture exchange increased. Additionally, Thomas eventually was moved from an individualized training setting to a traditional classroom setting. He maintained a one-to-one instructional aid that prepared his daily visual schedule and maintained his picture communication system book. At home, Thomas' parents reported a significant decrease in his challenging behaviors based on the implementation of his pictorial communication system. His parents also report Thomas' rate of self-stimulation decreased as his ability to follow simple directions increased. School personnel and parents report satisfaction with the behavioral procedures. The ABAS-II, completed 6 months after the intervention, showed significant improvements across adaptive areas.

Thomas's (age 6 years, 7 months) teacher and parent completed ABAS-II is shown in Table 19.2. These scores, compared to those from six months earlier,

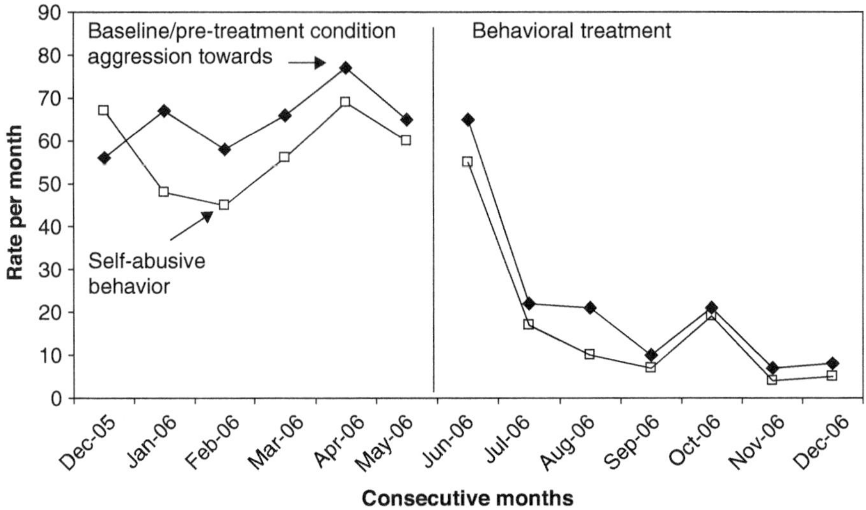

FIGURE 19.4 Thomas' monthly rate of challenging behavior at school.

TABLE 19.2 ABAS-II Results for Thomas, Age 6 years, 7 months.

Adaptive Skill Area/ Adaptive Composites/ GAC	Scaled Scores	
	Parent Form	Teacher Form
Adaptive skill areas		
Communication	6	6
Community use	6	7
Functional academics	6	7
Home living	7	5
Health and safety	6	6
Leisure	7	6
Self-care	4	5
Self-direction	4	5
Social	5	5
Conceptual Composite	75	84
90% confidence interval	71–79	80–88
Social Composite	79	78
90% confidence interval	73–85	74–82
Practical Composite	79	83
90% confidence interval	74–84	79–87
General Adaptive Composite	71	79
90% confidence interval	68–74	77–81

Note: Adaptive skill area scores are reported as scaled scores (M = 10, SD = 3). Composite scores are reported as standard scores (M = 100, SD = 15).

show considerable improvement, especially in the Conceptual Domain. Important changes occurred on Communication, Functional Academics, and Communication Skills. These data support the value of the ABAS-II in identifying skills as well as assisting in the development and evaluation of skill-based interventions.

SUMMARY

Measures used to assess adaptive behavior typically have been used to diagnose children with mental retardation. Their use in helping to understand and improve needed skills displayed by children with autism and other PDD is gaining in popularity. Data from these measures are not needed to diagnose autism and thus can be used exclusively to assist in efforts to develop, implement, and monitor interventions. Research that describes the development of adaptive skills of young children with autism is needed. The ABAS-II offers significant potential to assist in efforts to develop, implement, and monitor interventions designed to increased autonomy in the use of functional adaptive skills.

REFERENCES

American Psychiatric Association (2000). *Diagnostic and Statistical Manual of Mental Disorders: Text Revision*, 4th edn., Washington, DC: American Psychiatric Association.

Carr, E. & Durand, M. (1985). Reducing behavior problems functional communication training. *Journal of Applied Behavior Analysis*, *18*, 111–126.

Centers for Disease Control and Prevention (2006). *Autism Spectrum Disorders Fact Sheet*. Atlanta, GA: Centers for Disease Control and Prevention.

Dirk, K. (2000). Review of adaptive behavior studies in mentally retarded persons with autism/pervasive developmental disorder. *Journal of Autism and Developmental Disorders*, *30*(1), 39–49.

Frost, L. & Bondy, A. (2002). *PECS Training Manual*, 2nd edn., Newark, DE: Pyramid Educational Products.

Gilham, J., Carter, A., Volkmar, F., & Sparrow, S. (2000). Towards a developmental operational definition of autism. *Journal of Autism and Developmental Disabilities*, *30*(4), 269–278.

Harrison, P. & Oakland, T. (2003). *Adaptive Behavior Assessment System-Second Edition (ABAS-II)*, 2nd edn., San Antonio, TX: The Psychological Corporation.

Hintze, J. & Eckert, T. (2001). The use of functional assessment and analysis to reduce problem behavior of a child with autism. *Proven Practice: Prevention and Remediation Solutions for Schools*, *3*, 9–15.

Jarbrink, K. & Knapp, M. (2001). The economic impact of autism in Britain. *Autism*, *5*(1), 7–22.

Kanner, L. (1943). Autistic disturbances of affective contact. *Nervous Child*, *2*, 217–250.

Kraijer, D. (2000). Review of adaptive behavior studies and mentally retarded persons with autism/pervasive developmental disorder. *Journal of Autism and Developmental Disabilities*, *30*(1), 39–47.

Lovaas, O. I. (1977). *The autistic Child: Language Development Through Behavior Modification*. New York: Irvington Publishers: Distributed by Halsted Press.

Ozonoff, S., Goodlin-Jones, B., & Solomon, M. (2005). Evidence-based assessment of autism spectrum disorders in children and adolescents. *Journal of Clinical Child and Adolescent Psychology*, *34*(3), 523–540.

Paul, R., Miles, S., Cicchetti, D., Sparrow, S., Klin, A., Volkmar, F., et al. (2004). Adaptive behavior and autism and pervasive developmental disorder-not otherwise specified: Microanalysis of scores on the Vineland adaptive behavior scales. *Journal of Autism and Developmental Disorders, 34*(2), 223–228.

Preis, J. (2006). The effects of picture communication symbols on the verbal comprehension of commands by young children with autism. *Focus on Autism and Other Developmental Disabilities, 21*(4), 194–210.

Ranta, K. (2007). ASA in the News for CDC Study Released Retrieved February 19, 2007 from http://www.autism-society.org/site/News2?page=NewsArticle&id=9291&news_iv_ctrl=-1

Sattler, J. (2002). *Assessment of Children: Behavioral and Clinical Applications*, 4th edn., San Diego, CA.

Scattone, D., Dorothy, T., & Wilczynski, S. (2006). Increasing appropriate social interactions of children with autism spectrum disorders using social stories. *Focus on Autism and Other Developmental Disabilities, 21*(4), 211–222.

Sundberg, M. & Partington, J. (1998). *Teaching Language to Children with Autism or Other Developmental Disabilities.* Danville, CA: Behavior Analysts, Inc.

Woolf, S., Ross, R., & Littleton, R. (2008, February). Differential effects of ABA instructional intensity. Presented at the Annual Conference of the California Association of Behavior Analysis, Garden Grove, CA.

20

ASSESSMENT OF ADAPTIVE BEHAVIOR IN ADULT FORENSIC CASES: THE USE OF THE ADAPTIVE BEHAVIOR ASSESSMENT SYSTEM-II

J. GREGORY OLLEY* AND ANN W. COX**

*Center for Development and Learning, University of North Carolina at Chapel Hill, Chapel Hill, NC 27599-7255, U.S.A.

**Frank Porter Graham Child Development Center, University of North Carolina at Chapel Hill, Chapel Hill, NC 27599-8040.

The assessment of adaptive behavior has several core components that must be considered in any setting. When assessing adaptive behavior in forensic (legal or court related) settings, some special considerations must be addressed. The core strategies are as follows: the use of multiple types of information, the use of multiple informants, the examination of behavior over time, beginning with childhood, the examination of behavior in two or more environments, and the use of multiple methods to obtain information. This chapter considers each of these strategies in detail as they apply to the assessment of adaptive behavior in forensic settings. The focus is on the challenges in the assessment of adaptive behavior in the diagnosis of mental retardation (also referred to as intellectual disability) and its application in legal proceedings with emphasis on capital cases.

Throughout the history of the Unites States' legal system and its predecessors in the American Colonies and English Common Law, an individual's level of functioning has been considered in both civil and criminal proceedings. Early courts made crude distinctions between individuals who displayed what we now refer to as mental illness and those with mental retardation or intellectual disability (Wickham, 2002, 2006). Individuals with such disabilities and children and youth have been recognized as special classes who are less culpable for criminal acts and whose rights under the law can be limited.

In earlier periods, before the development of intelligence tests, the diagnosis of mental retardation was based on deficits in everyday performance (see Oakland and Harrison, Chapter 1 for additional details on the history of mental retardation). In other words, adaptive behavior historically has been a key aspect of the diagnosis of mental retardation in all circumstances, including legal matters. In 1961 the American Association on Mental Deficiency (now American Association on Intellectual and Developmental Disabilities or AAIDD) changed its definition of mental retardation to add a formal requirement of deficit in adaptive behavior, defining mental retardation as, "... subaverage general intellectual functioning which originates during the developmental period and is associated with impairment in adaptive behavior" (Heber, 1961, p. 3).

Recent legislation and court decisions have spelled out many specific examples and clarifications of the legal status of individuals with developmental disabilities (Landau, 2007). A valid assessment of adaptive behavior is important in several legal matters, such as the need for a guardian, competency to retain custody of a child, eligibility for services or entitlement programs (e.g., Medicaid, Social Security benefits, special education services), competency to execute a will or a contract, and most recently, eligibility for the death penalty.

DEFINITIONS OF MENTAL RETARDATION/ INTELLECTUAL DISABILITY

The most widely recognized and authoritative sources on the definition and diagnosis of mental retardation make little reference to the application of these standards in forensic settings. However, best practices in forensic work are based on current standards. Knowledge of current standards is essential for experts working with the courts (Bonnie & Gustafson, 2007).

Several recent authoritative publications can be used to guide legal proceedings in the diagnosis of mental retardation. Virtually all recent definitions of mental retardation or intellectual disability contain the three elements in the 1961 American Association on Mental Deficiency (AAMD) definition (Heber, 1961): significant impairment in intelligence, significant impairment in adaptive behavior, and origin of the disability during the developmental period. The 2002 *Atkins v. Virginia* U.S. Supreme Court ruling that prohibited the execution of individuals with mental retardation noted these three components and left to the states the responsibility of determining their procedures to establish mental retardation in capital cases. Prominent attorneys and professional organizations have recommended procedures to implement *Atkins* at the state level (Ellis, 2003; Bonnie, 2004; American Bar Association, 2006; Bonnie & Gustafson, 2007). However, many details remain controversial (Duvall & Morris, 2006; Olley et al., 2006).

Although the existing standards for the diagnosis of mental retardation have much in common, the application of these standards to forensic settings is challenging. The most widely accepted current standard in the United States is that of the American Association on Mental Retardation (AAMR) (1992, 2002). The 1992 definition was current at the time of the *Atkins* decision. However, the 2002 AAMR/AAIDD definition now is widely accepted. One of the differences between the two standards concerns the definition of adaptive behavior and deficits in adaptive behavior. The 1992 AAMR definition required evidence of significant deficits in 2 or more of the following 10 adaptive skills: Communication, Community Use, Functional Academics, Home Living, Health and Safety, Leisure, Self-Care, Self-Direction, Social, and Work. The 2002 standard identified three broad adaptive domains (i.e., Conceptual, Social, and Practical) and specified that significant impairment in at least 1 of the 3 areas is required for a diagnosis of mental retardation. When using a standardized measure of these three domains, such as the ABAS-II, an overall (total) score also can be used (AAMR, 2002).

The American Psychiatric Association's *Diagnostic and Statistical Manual of Mental Disorders* (DSM) (2000) is the other most widely cited authority on the definition of mental retardation. The DSM definition of mental retardation retained the AAMR's 1992 standard of impairment in 2 of 10 adaptive skill areas, and, unlike the AAMR, it maintained an older classification system that identified degrees of impairment, using the terms *mild*, *moderate, severe*, and *profound* mental retardation. Although the AAMR/AAIDD has dropped these terms in favor of a system that classifies the level of supports that the individual needs, the older labels often are used in court to note that there are degrees of severity of this condition. Most people with mental retardation fall into the mild category with IQs between 55 and 70. Most individuals with mental retardation who commit criminal acts display mild mental retardation (Greenspan & Switzky, 2006). The DSM states that, "Impairments in adaptive functioning, rather than a low IQ, are usually the presenting symptoms in individuals with Mental Retardation" (DSM, 2000, p. 42).

Following the AAMR and DSM standards, several valuable books to clarify the concepts, definitions, research basis, and clinical applications of these definitions (Jacobson & Mulick, 1996; Switzky & Greenspan, 2006; Jacobson et al., 2007). The National Research Council (2002) has established standards for the diagnosis of mental retardation for eligibility for Social Security benefits. These well-respected sources address the assessment of adaptive behavior yet offer little for applications in forensic settings. Thus, our challenge is to apply these established assessment procedures and ethical standards (American Psychological Association, 2002; American Academy of Psychiatry and the Law, 2005; Committee on the Revision of the Specialty Guidelines for Forensic Psychology, 2006) to the specific questions posed by the court.

The challenges of the *Atkins* decision and related legislative and judicial decisions seem to have raised more questions than answers (Olley et al., 2006). However, several recent publications by attorneys, psychologists, and educators have pointed toward a growing consensus in some areas, including the assessment of adaptive behavior and skills. The remainder of this chapter reviews the issues in the assessment of adaptive behavior with emphasis on *Atkins* cases and the use of the Adaptive Behavior Assessment System.

CHALLENGES IN ADAPTIVE BEHAVIOR ASSESSMENT IN *ATKINS* CASES

Although deficits in adaptive behavior have been the basis for diagnosis of mental retardation for as long as this disorder has been recognized, the development of scientifically sound intelligence tests about 100 years ago shifted attention from adaptive behavior to intelligence as the key requirement in diagnosis. As noted earlier, it was not until 1961 that the organization then known as AAMD introduced adaptive behavior deficits as a formal criterion for the diagnosis of mental retardation (Heber, 1961). Bonnie and Gustafson (2007) argued that the science of measurement of intelligence is more precise than the science of measurement of adaptive behavior. Therefore, the examiner must be very thorough and draw relevant information from many sources in order to arrive at a valid conclusion. Even with this effort, Bonnie and Gustafson (2007) asserted that clinical judgment plays a greater role in assessing adaptive behavior than intelligence.

Schalock and Luckasson (2005) have provided a thorough guide to clinical judgment in the diagnosis of mental retardation. They emphasized that clinical judgment is more than an impression. Clinical judgment in the diagnosis of mental retardation requires a clinician to have experience with the diagnostic process and the population of people with mental retardation and to consider scientific evidence applicable to this population. The following considerations should be included in the assessment of adaptive behavior for the diagnosis of mental retardation in criminal cases.

THE NATURE OF ADAPTIVE BEHAVIOR

Many disagreements in court derive from different views of the nature of adaptive behavior. The 2002 AAMR definition stated: "Adaptive behavior is the collection of conceptual, social, and practical skills that have been learned by people in order to function in their everyday lives" (p. 73). As this definition has been applied to *Atkins* hearings, writers have found it necessary to emphasize some aspects of adaptive behavior for clarity. For example, adaptive behavior assessment describes an individual's actual functional performance and is not used to speculate as to a person's potential. In other words, a person's adaptive behavior is what a person has done rather than what he or she may have done or could have done if raised in more ideal conditions (Schalock, 1999; Stevens & Price, 2006; Bonnie & Gustafson, 2007; Schalock et al., 2007).

As an example of this issue, some have argued in court that the observed deficits in adaptive behavior are simply a result of poor motivation. Thus, if the person had tried harder (e.g., in school), he or she would not have shown these deficits. The recently published AAIDD *User's Guide* (Schalock et al., 2007) described "several reasons for limitations in adaptive behavior [which] may include not knowing how to perform the skills (acquisition deficit), not knowing when to use learned skills (performance deficit), or other motivational factors that affect the expression of skills (performance deficit). When an individual has limited intellectual capacity, both acquisition and performance deficits may be attributed to the disability" (p. 13). Thus, poor motivation is better used as an argument *for* the diagnosis of mental retardation than as an argument against it.

This clarification of the nature of adaptive behavior is very important in *Atkins* hearings because, when all of the evidence for deficits in adaptive behavior is presented, the defense may argue that the evidence supports a diagnosis of mental retardation while the prosecution may argue that the same evidence supports a different diagnosis. That is, evidence of impaired adaptive behavior may reflect a comorbid condition or be interpreted as evidence for another diagnosis (e.g., conduct disorder, antisocial personality disorder) or simply as laziness or lack of motivation, not as evidence for mental retardation. In fact, mental retardation can co-exist with these and other diagnoses; they are not mutually exclusive (Fletcher et al., 2007).

The AAMR (2002) and other definitions make no mention of the cause of the adaptive deficit. If the deficit exists with impairment in intelligence that originated in childhood and adolescence, the diagnosis of mental retardation is made regardless of the presumed cause of the impairments.

This 2002 definition also makes an important distinction between problem behavior and deficits in adaptive behavior. Diagnoses such as conduct disorder are indicated by problem behavior rather than deficits in adaptive behavior. "Adaptive behavior is considered to be conceptually different from maladaptive or problem behavior ... Therefore, behaviors that interfere with a person's daily activities, or with the activities of those around him or her, should be considered problem behavior rather than the absence of adaptive behavior" (AAMR, 2002, p. 79). This distinction also is emphasized in the AAIDD's *User's Guide* (Schalock et al., 2007).

Several writers have clarified that adaptive behavior refers to behaviors typically expected in one's community (National Research Council, 2002; Brodsky & Galloway, 2003; Stevens & Price, 2006; Bonnie & Gustafson, 2007; Schalock et al., 2007). Thus, examples of isolated behavior are not useful in determining what is typical. The prosecution in many *Atkins* hearings has introduced the facts of the crime to demonstrate that the sophistication and planning of the crime rule out mental retardation. To the extent that the defendant's behavior related to the crime is representative of his or her community performance since childhood and adolescence, it is relevant. If the crime required sophisticated thinking and behavior, the remainder of the defendant's life also should illustrate high levels of adaptive behavior in order to rule out mental retardation. Several recent articles have argued against the relevance of the facts of the crime for assessment of adaptive behavior (Everington & Olley, in press; Greenspan & Switzky, 2006; Stevens & Price, 2006).

The evidence for adaptive behavior strengths or deficits must illustrate typical community functioning. The emphasis on community functioning also addresses the controversial issue of assessing the defendant's current functioning in jail or prison. Experts in this area have pointed out that the restrictive and structured environment of incarceration makes it impossible to assess typical adaptive behavior (Everington & Olley, in press; Greenspan & Switzky, 2006; Patton & Keyes, 2006; Stevens & Price, 2006; Bonnie & Gustafson, 2007). Thus, reports from corrections officers or other observations of current functioning in prison are not valid indicators of level of adaptive behavior.

THE ISSUE OF RETROSPECTIVE ASSESSMENT

Mental health experts often are called upon to testify regarding the retrospective assessment of the mental state of the defendant at the time of a crime or other significant event (Simon & Shuman, 2002). Although such testimony is more commonly about mental illness, the challenge is similar in the diagnosis of mental retardation. That is, the expert is asked to review all available evidence and to render an expert opinion about the defendant's mental state at an earlier time. As an example of the retrospective assessment of adaptive behavior, experts commonly are asked to assess earlier functioning and render an opinion in cases of disputed wills. That is, the expert is asked to determine retrospectively whether the person who made the will was competent to do so at the time. The issues raised in cases of disputed wills are similar to those described in this chapter to assess adaptive behavior in *Atkins* cases.

In such cases, all available types and sources of adaptive functioning should be examined. When using informant information, the validity of the expert's conclusion relies heavily upon the memories of the individuals who provide the information. In *Atkins* cases, informants may be asked to remember the defendant's adaptive functioning from one to more than 20 years ago. Several writers have pointed to this problem of reliance on memory as an indication that available clinical procedures (e.g., interviews and adaptive behavior scales, such as the ABAS-II) are of questionable validity for this purpose (Greenspan & Switzky, 2006; Stevens & Price, 2006; Bonnie & Gustafson, 2007). Although this criticism is an important caution, it should not rule out the use of such procedures. It is important to bear in mind that psychologists and psychiatrists include, as part of their assessment, methods that are not validated for the specific question being asked. For example, psychologists use standardized personality tests and projective tests to assist in decision-making on a wide range of topics (e.g., child custody decisions in divorces, competence to regain custody of a child from a social service agency). Yet these tests may lack empirical evidence for these specific purposes. The question is not whether the test or interview procedure is valid for this purpose. The question is whether the totality of the available information is sufficient for the expert to make a well-founded and ethical clinical judgment about the question at hand. Thus, the focus should be on the proper use of all available assessment methods and sources of information. With the best available information in hand, the expert can exercise clinical judgment to reach a conclusion.

RELIANCE ON MULTIPLE SOURCES

Many writers on this topic have emphasized that no single source of information or test score should be the sole source of information to determine whether a significant impairment in adaptive behavior exists (Everington & Keyes, 1999; National Research Council, 2002; Greenspan & Switzky, 2006; Patton & Keyes, 2006; Stevens & Price, 2006; Bonnie & Gustafson, 2007; Olley, 2007; Schalock et al., 2007; Everington & Olley, in press). Olley (2007) noted that possible sources of adaptive behavior information in *Atkins* cases could include interviews with the defendant; interviews with family, friends, former neighbors, teachers, and employers; and archival information, such as school and other juvenile records. As indicated earlier, corrections officers do not have the necessary information about community functioning to be a valid source (Patton & Keyes, 2006; Stevens & Price, 2006; Bonnie & Gustafson, 2007; Olley, 2007; Everington & Olley, in press).

By using multiple sources of information and thoroughly understanding the nature of mental retardation, the expert can reach a conclusion that has consensual validity. Ideally, many sources of information are congruent and lead to a single conclusion. In *Atkins* hearings and other forensic cases, a perfect congruence of all sources of information is unlikely, yet the expert who relies on multiple sources is better equipped to use his or her judgment to draw a valid conclusion.

USE OF THE *ADAPTIVE BEHAVIOR ASSESSMENT SYSTEM IN ATKINS* CASES

The administration of standardized scales, such as the *Adaptive Behavior Assessment System* (ABAS-II) (Harrison & Oakland, 2003), is one of the most widely used and accepted methods for the assessment of adaptive behavior. Since Heber introduced adaptive behavior as a component of the AAMD definition in 1961, more than 200 formal and informal instruments have been developed to assess adaptive behavior. There are marked differences among them in content and in psychometric properties (Spreat, 1999). Given this great variability among instruments, it is essential to choose an adaptive behavior scale with strong psychometric properties.

ATTRIBUTES OF THE ABAS-II

Although the ABAS-II should not be the only source of adaptive behavior information, it has several advantages that address the challenges to adaptive behavior assessment. First, the ABAS-II is a standardized measure with strong psychometric properties. Several recent writers have pointed to the psychometric strengths of the ABAS and ABAS-II (National Research Council, 2002; Stevens & Price, 2006; Borthwick-Duffy, 2007).

Second, clinical validity studies that compared the mean scores for people with mental retardation with match controls demonstrated that the ABAS-II can provide a valid assessment of adaptive skills for individuals with mental retardation. The results are provided in the ABAS-II manual for the Parent Form, Teacher Form, and Adult, Rated by Others Form (Harrison & Oakland, 2003). The authors (Harrison & Oakland, 2003) concluded that these data "indicate that all samples of individuals with mental retardation scored significantly lower on the ABAS-II than the matched control groups and demonstrated deficits in skill areas, adaptive domains, and overall adaptive functioning ..." (p. 147).

Finally, the standardized administration and scoring based on a well-standardized norm group has obvious advantages over the use of unstructured or semi-structured interviews. The ABAS-II provides scaled scores for the 10 adaptive skill areas that define adaptive functioning in the 1992 AAMR definition as well as composite scores for the three adaptive domains (i.e., Conceptual, Social, and Practical) in the 2002 definition. The General Adaptive Composite provides an overall standardized score. These scores provide information that is needed to measure adaptive behavior in most states that have statutes or court precedents that guide procedures in *Atkins* hearings.

The standardized wording and instructions for administration provide protection against bias in the administration and interpretation of the instrument. In forensic settings concerning people with mental retardation or low intelligence, several cautions should be emphasized in ABAS-II administration.

INFORMANT SELECTION

The scale should be completed only by informants who have known the defendant well, preferably during childhood and adolescence. The person administering the scale should spend some time getting acquainted with the informant before deciding whether this person can provide suitable information. For example, the examiner should establish the nature of the relationship between the defendant and the informant. Are they related? How long they have known each other? In what capacity have they known each other (e.g., relative, friend, neighbor, former teacher, employer, coach, scout leader)? Some informants may have known the defendant's functioning well in one setting and be able to provide useful anecdotes, yet not know enough to complete all sections of the ABAS-II. If the focus of adaptive behavior is work, the informant may be a former employer or co-worker. He or she may provide useful information by completing only the Work adaptive skill area. If the focus of adaptive behavior is school, the informant may be one or more educators with whom the ABAS-II's Teacher Form would be used. If the focus of adaptive behavior is home, the informant may be a parent, siblings, other relative, or close neighbor. Use the Parent Form when assessing persons younger than 22 and the Adult Form when assessing persons 22 and older.

Before administering the ABAS-II, discuss with the informant the importance of providing complete, honest, unbiased information. The expert must testify under oath that he or she believes that the obtained information will contribute to a valid conclusion. The ABAS-II will not provide a useful contribution to the legal process if the examiner believes that the information is biased.

TIME FRAME FOR SCORING

As noted earlier, the administration of the ABAS-II used in forensic settings usually focuses the assessment of adaptive functioning at some time in the past. This procedure has been criticized (Greenspan & Switzky, 2006; Stevens & Price, 2006; Bonnie & Gustafson, 2007) because the ABAS-II and other adaptive behavior scales were standardized by asking informants about current functioning or functioning in the recent past. Although all adaptive behavior testing relies on accurate memory, reliance on memory from the distant past is a departure from the standardized procedure. Nevertheless, information obtained in this way can contribute to a valid conclusion.

State laws and policies help define the age at which mental retardation should be determined and the qualities that constitute mental retardation. Although uniform national laws and policy on these two issues would be helpful, they do not exist. Thus, an examiner's first task is to determine the standards that apply to the definition of mental retardation in the state in which he or she is practicing.

The examiner must make every effort to establish with the informant the time frame in which the items apply. The informant must express confidence that he or she remembers the defendant's activities at that time. To accomplish this, the examiner must ask careful questions to establish the most recent time at which the informant knew the defendant well. For example, if the informant is the defendant's mother, inquire whether she knew the defendant's activities well at the time of the crime. If this is the case, the items on the ABAS-II may be answered with reference to the defendant's community functioning at the time immediately before the crime.

If the informant has a clear memory of the defendant's functioning at this time, the examiner should emphasize that all items on the ABAS-II are in reference to functioning on that date. Accuracy of information is increased to the extent that the informant has a clear memory of events during this time period and answers consistently with regard to functioning at this period. Data from the ABAS-II would be considered less accurate if the informant cannot remember events clearly and consistently during a specified period in the defendant's life. Although such an informant may be able to offer important anecdotes or examples of effective or impaired functioning at different ages, this information would not produce useful ABAS-II standard scores.

If the examiner determines that the informant has the required information and can report consistently with regard to functioning at a certain date, that date should be considered the date of the defendant's functioning and may be recorded as "Today's Date" on the ABAS-II rating form or other suitable location. Scoring should be carried out using that date in order to compare the defendant with the standardization sample of the same age. For example, if the defendant who is incarcerated is age 28, and informants report adaptive functioning at age 22, then age of 22 should be considered his or her chronological age, and norms based on this age group should be used to derive ABAS-II scores.

Before administering the ABAS-II, review with the informant the general purpose of the assessment and the scoring criteria. The informant must know whether the defendant was not able to perform the behavior (i.e., exhibited a skill deficit), able yet never or almost never performed it when needed (i.e., exhibited a performance deficit), sometimes performed it when needed, or always or almost always performed it when needed. These four response options are used with all ABAS-II items.

Thus, the results of the ABAS-II should accurately indicate the extent of the defendant's independence to perform the behavior without help, the frequency of the adaptive behavior (i.e., how often it is displayed), whether the behavior is used in appropriate circumstances – when it is needed, and the extent to which the performance is typical and not an isolated instance.

CONDUCTING THE INTERVIEW IN PERSON

Although the scale may be administered over the telephone or by having the informant read and complete the items, it is preferable to administer the scale in person in a setting in which the informant is comfortable, such as his or her own home. First, discuss the purposes of the interview, the scoring criteria, and the need for accurate information. Continue by asking the respondent to describe the defendant's behavior at home, school, or work at a particular age. This discussion may provide a general understanding of the defendant's adaptive skills and behaviors at that time. The examiner should continue by reading the items aloud while the informant answers the questions assisted by knowing the four response options stated above. Providing these options on a separate card or providing another ABAS-II rating form also may clarify the items and the scoring criteria.

This approach provides some assurance that the informant understands each item and does not fall into a response bias (e.g., giving the same answer to nearly every item). Items should be read as they appear, and they may be repeated to assure understanding. If the informant does not understand the wording, it is permissible to paraphrase the item. However, it is essential not to change the meaning of the item or to include wording that suggests an answer. Clarification is helpful, but coaching in any form is not permissible.

Clarification may be needed if the informant provides information that is incongruent with other information pertaining to the defendant's history. In such a case, the clarification should be a reminder of the four-option scoring criteria, not a suggestion of how to reply. Clarification also may be needed if the informant answers *yes* or *no* to a question. In response to a *yes* response, the examiner may ask, "Did you mean always (3) or sometimes (2)?" In response to a *no* response, the examiner may ask, "Do you mean that he was not able to do it (0) or that he could do it and never or rarely did when needed? (1)." This distinction may be difficult for some informants. Nevertheless, an examiner can assure more accurate answers by clarifying without guiding responses.

These steps are necessary precautions when using the ABAS-II retrospectively because they help to protect against bias and assure accurate reporting to the extent that it is possible when relying on memory of earlier events. An examiner is likely to obtain valid information by selecting and interviewing several informants using the safeguards described above. However, locating suitable informants may be difficult.

ADMINISTERING THE ABAS-II TO THE DEFENDANT

The ABAS-II is the only contemporary scale of adaptive behavior that offers the option of administering the items directly to the defendant and scoring with the use of separate self-response adult norms. Thus, although its use may be considered when the defendant displays suitable intellectual ability, including memory, this and other scales of adaptive behavior should not be used when either is diminished.

Defendants on death row or those awaiting trial for capital crimes have an incentive either to exaggerate their deficits to avoid execution or to exaggerate their accomplishments to save face or achieve a "cloak of competence" to avoid the stigma of mental retardation (Edgerton, 1967, 2001; Greenspan & Switzky, 2006; Schalock et al., 2007). Instead of using the ABAS-II in a standard fashion, examiners may elect to use its questions to guide their interview of the defendant with regard to his or her functioning when not incarcerated. Such an interview may provide information about the defendant's ability to understand the questions and his or her tendency either to exaggerate accomplishments or to malinger in order to appear to have mental retardation. However, one may be able to gather only limited valid information from a defendant regarding his own community functioning. Cautions regarding interviewing the defendant are discussed in the next section.

OTHER SOURCES OF INFORMATION

A score on the ABAS-II or other measure of adaptive behavior serves as one piece of information that can be added to information from other sources to contribute to a valid conclusion regarding typical adaptive functioning. Other sources may include the defendant, family members, neighbors, friends, former employers, and teachers as well as archival information. Each source will be examined in terms of its suitability for providing useful information about the defendant's adaptive behavior.

INTERVIEW THE DEFENDANT

An examiner may elect to conduct an interview of the defendant with or without following questions from the ABAS. Under the best of circumstances, interviews of people with mental retardation can easily lead to incorrect conclusions due to the way that questions are presented (Finlay & Lyons, 2001). An interview may reveal information pertinent to the defendant's current mental health. Many defendants may be able to provide some history regarding their education, work, or friends that can be externally validated. However, the interview of the defendant should not be the centerpiece of evidence about adaptive behavior.

TEST THE DEFENDANT'S KNOWLEDGE

Several tests of knowledge include topics that are relevant to adaptive behavior. However, the defendant's current knowledge may be a very imprecise indicator of his or her adaptive behavior when not incarcerated. Tests of academic achievement typically do not address practical applications. Tests of vocational knowledge, interest, or aptitude are only loosely related to community functioning. The format of many tests also makes them poor predictors of the application of knowledge. For example, tests that require an oral answer, or pointing to the right answer, or pointing to a picture of the right answer are likely to be inadequate indicators of actual community functioning.

TEST THE DEFENDANT'S PERFORMANCE

Performance in the highly structured and limited environment of prison is a poor indicator of one's functioning. Many people with mental retardation perform better in the structured prison setting than in less structured settings (Bonnie & Gustafson, 2007). Therefore, observing the defendant's completion of prison chores or any other activities does not give a valid sample of adaptive behavior. An examiner may ask a defendant to complete practical tasks, such as writing his name, looking up numbers in a telephone book, or demonstrating map skills. However, the observed behavior provides only anecdotal evidence.

One may reasonably infer that a defendant who currently is unable to perform these tasks did not perform them at an earlier time.

INTERVIEW FAMILY MEMBERS, FORMER NEIGHBORS, FRIENDS, AND EMPLOYERS

People who knew the defendant well in his or her community (and especially during childhood and adolescence) can be excellent sources of adaptive behavior information if they are available (Greenspan & Switzy, 2006; Patton & Keyes, 2006; Borthwick-Duffy, 2007; Olley, 2007). The best informant is one who has known the defendant well and has no reason to be biased in the information provided. Like the defendant, family members may be motivated to make members of their family look good to avoid stigma or to report deficits in adaptive behavior in hope that a diagnosis of mental retardation will help their family member to avoid execution. The interviewer must exercise careful judgment to obtain the most objective information possible.

Independent of whether an informant is able to complete the ABAS-II, supplementary interview questions may be helpful in providing practical examples of adaptive behavior. The following are examples of some follow-up questions that one may consider.

Home Living: Did [the defendant] ever live independently (maintain his or her own home or apartment)? Whether living alone or with another person, how much assistance did [the defendant] need when performing routine household tasks (e.g., clothing care, housekeeping, property maintenance, cooking, budgeting, shopping)?

Social: Tell me more about the kind of friends that [the defendant] had. Were they a good influence on him/her? Did he/she bring them to his/her home? Did they treat him/her fairly, or did they take advantage of him/her? How did they take advantage of him/her? Did [the defendant] realize that these friends were taking advantage of him/her? Did [the defendant] have healthy, non-exploitive sexual relationships?

Community Use: Did [the defendant] vote? Was he/she registered to vote?

Self-Direction: Did [the defendant] make the major decisions in his life, or did others make these decisions for him/her? Did [the defendant] have a long-term plan for his/her life that involved work, relationships, saving money, and achieving greater independence? Would you regard [the defendant] as a responsible person who lived up to his/her obligations? Did he/she use good judgment? Explain.

Health and Safety: Did the defendant brush his/her teeth daily? Did he/she go to a dentist for preventive care or just in a dental emergency? Did he/she remove dangerous objects from his/her home or property (e.g., old prescription drugs, old refrigerators, junk cars)?

Functional Academics: Did [the defendant] have a driver's license? If not, why? If yes, how many times did he/she take the test? Did he/she receive assistance when taking the test? What type? From whom? Did [the defendant] have a bank account? What type? Did he/she deposit and withdraw money independently? Did he/she file an income tax return? Did he/she require assistance when needing to read, use money, or do tasks that required math skills?

Leisure: Did [the defendant] make good use of his/her leisure time? Did he/she have varied interests? Did he/she have leisure interests that involved others, or were his/her activities solitary in nature? Were his/her interests active (e.g., fishing, engaging in sports) or passive (e.g., watching television)? Was he/she open to new experiences?

Work: How did [the defendant] obtain employment (e.g., assistance from family, read newspaper, use employment agency)? How did employment end (e.g., quit, fired)? What was the length of his jobs? How many hours weekly did he/she work? Did he/she take classes or receive other special training to prepare for his/her work? When leaving a job, did he/she give notice or just stop showing up? Describe the responsibilities of his/her job(s). Were they repetitive, or did they require change among tasks? How did he/she respond to such changes? Did his/her work require judgment, decision-making, or problem solving? Describe. Was he/she ever promoted to a position of higher responsibility? Did he/she ever supervise anyone on the job? Did he/she call his supervisor if he/she was going to be absent from work,? What type of supervision did he/she require? How did he/she get to and from work? Did he/she require transportation assistance?

SEEK OBJECTIVE, ARCHIVAL INFORMATION

All of the previously mentioned sources of adaptive behavior information come from individuals. All sources are subject to bias of some kind and may be further limited by the informants' memories. Therefore, when possible, information from these sources should be supplemented with information collected objectively and at a time before the defendant was accused of the crime in question.

Archival information that describes functioning during childhood and adolescence may be helpful in addressing the third component of the mental retardation definition: origin in the developmental period (usually defined as before age 18). The most common example of such information is school records. If the defendant received special education services, records of classroom grades reflecting achievement as well as formal test results (e.g., of intelligence, academic achievement, adaptive behavior) that justified special education placement may have been retained. School policies differ with regard to how long such records are kept and whether the records may be purged of certain information. School systems may remove teacher comments or even remove all evidence of special education services or identification of a disability, given their desire to protect the student from stigma or because they interpret the Family Educational Rights and Privacy Act (FERPA) (20 U.S.C. § 1232g; 34 CFR Part 99) to allow or require the destruction of certain records.

Although school records may be useful, they also may be misleading and inaccurate. Patton and Keyes (2006) provided a thorough discussion of this topic. For example, students with mental retardation may not be identified at all or may be served under another classification, most often learning disabled. This label is less stigmatizing for families, and schools may elect to limit the proportion of students from minority backgrounds who are identified as having mental retardation. Patton and Keyes (2006) also offered cautions regarding the interpretation of standardized achievement tests that often appear in school records. They noted that, "These tests are group-administered achievement instruments, not intelligence tests, and the actual performance of an individual student cannot be validated" (p. 251). Interviews with educators who knew the defendant as a student may be very valuable. These interviews may provide new information and assist in interpreting school records or correcting school records that may be inaccurate.

In addition to school records, the defendant may have medical, mental health, or related records from other evaluations or social services. If the defendant received social security benefits because of a disability, these records often contain extensive information on adaptive behavior collected before the time of the crime (National Research Council, 2002).

SEEK SUBJECTIVE ARCHIVAL INFORMATION

As noted in the previous section, school records may include teacher comments, or their comments may have been removed. Although information from day care providers, coaches, scout leaders, camp counselors, and others who knew the defendant during childhood and adolescence can be valuable, they seldom are preserved in writing. Records from therapeutic programs, such as camps or residential programs, may contain comments or notes that address adaptive behavior. However, if such comments are limited to functioning in a structured program, they may not be useful for assessing typical community functioning.

CLINICAL JUDGMENT

The task of the expert witness is to review all relevant information and to use clinical judgment to reach a conclusion. Courts in the United States apply the Daubert standard (Daubert v. Merrill Dow Pharmaceuticals, 1993) that requires expert testimony to be based on objective research or science. The opinions of experts generally are respected in court if they are based on science and objective information rather than uninformed or personal opinion. For example, interpretation of scores is part of clinical judgment. However, alteration of scores without a scientific basis is not acceptable practice. "Adjustments" that raise or lower scores to make them fit one's clinical judgment or to account for possible influences, (e.g., poverty, lack of experience with test-talking, limited educational opportunities) are improper and should not be used. Consult Schalock et al. (2007) and Schalock and Luckasson (2005) for excellent discussions of the use of clinical judgment in the diagnosis of mental retardation.

CONCLUSION

Information about adaptive behavior is critical to the determination of mental retardation in *Atkins* hearings and in determining competence or level of functioning in other legal proceedings. Current, widely accepted standards for the diagnosis of mental retardation, for psychological assessment, and for ethical practice form a foundation for practice. On this foundation, the Supreme Court has required in *Atkins* that states establish procedures for a fair and scientifically sound diagnosis of mental retardation. The challenges of carrying out such an assessment and reaching a valid conclusion have been described in this chapter. These challenges can be addressed through careful and thorough assessment that relies on the best available procedures and instruments. The ABAS-II offers some unique features that contribute essential information to the assessment of adaptive behavior. The careful use of the ABAS-II provides information that can be integrated with other sources of adaptive behavior information to yield valid conclusions that are respected in the courts and are much preferred to less systematic and less scientific methods.

REFERENCES

American Academy of Psychiatry and the Law (2005). *Ethics Guidelines for the Practice of Forensic Psychiatry.* Retrieved August 1, 2007, from http://www.aapl.org/pdf/ethicsgdlns.pdf

American Association on Mental Retardation (AAMR) (1992). *Mental Retardation: Definition, Classification, and Systems of Supports*, 9th edn., Washington, DC: AAMR.

American Association on Mental Retardation (AAMR) (2002). *Mental Retardation: Definition, Classification, and Systems of Supports*, 10th edn., Washington, DC: AAMR.

American Bar Association. Task Force on Mental Disability and the Death Penalty (2006). Recommendations and report on the death penalty and persons with mental disabilities. *Mental and Physical Disability Law Reporter*, *30*, 668–677.

American Psychiatric Association (2000). *Diagnostic and Statistical Manual of Mental Disorders*, 4th edn., text rev., Washington, DC: American Psychiatric Association.

American Psychological Association (2002). Ethical principles of psychologists and code of conduct. *American Psychologist*, *57*, 1060–1073.

Atkins v Virginia, 536 U.S. 304 (2002).

Bonnie, R. J. (2004). The American Psychiatric Association's resource document on mental retardation and capital sentencing: Implementing *Atkins v. Virginia*. *Journal of the American Association of Psychiatry and the Law*, *32*, 304–308.

Bonnie, R. J. & Gustafson, K. (2007). The challenges of implementing *Atkins v. Virginia*: How legislatures and courts can promote accurate assessments and adjudications of mental retardation in death penalty cases. *University of Richmond Law Review*, *41*, 810–860.

Borthwick-Duffy, S. A. (2007). Adaptive behavior. In J. Jacobson, J. Mulick, & J. Rojahn (Eds.), *Handbook of Intellectual and Developmental Disabilities*, pp. 279–291. New York: Springer.

Brodsky, S. L. & Galloway, V. A. (2003). Ethical and professional demands for forensic mental health professionals in the post-*Atkins* era. *Journal of Ethics and Behavior*, *13*(1), 3–9.

Committee on the Revision of the Specialty Guidelines for Forensic Psychology (2006). Specialty guidelines for forensic psychology. Retrieved August 1, 2007, from American Psychology-Law Society website: http://apls.org/links/SGFP%20January%202006-pdf

Daubert v. Merrell Dow Pharmaceuticals, 509 U.S. 579 (1993).

Duvall, J. C. & Morris, R. J. (2006). Assessing mental retardation in death penalty cases: Critical issues for psychology and psychological practice. *Professional Psychology: Research and Practice*, *37*, 658–665.

Edgerton, R. B. (1967). *The Cloak of Competence: Stigma in the Lives of the Mentally Retarded.* Berkeley, CA: University of California Press.

Edgerton, R. B. (2001). The hidden majority of individuals with mental retardation and developmental disability. In A. J. Tymchuk, K. C. Lakin, & R. Luckasson (Eds.), *The Forgotten Generation: The Status and Challenges of Adults with Mild Cognitive Limitations*, pp. 3–19. Baltimore: Paul H. Brookes.

Ellis, J. W. (2003). Mental retardation and the death penalty: A guide to legislative issues. *Mental and Physical Disability Law Reporter*, *27*(1), 11–24.

Everington, C. & Keyes, D. W. (1999). Mental retardation: Diagnosing mental retardation in criminal proceedings: The critical importance of documenting adaptive behavior. *The Forensic Examiner*, July–August, 31–34.

Everington, C. & Olley, J. G. (in press). Implications of *Atkins v. Virginia*: Issues in defining and diagnosing mental retardation. *Journal of Forensic Psychology Practice.*

Finlay, W. M. & Lyons, E. (2001). Methodological issues in interviewing and using self-report questionnaires with people with mental retardation. *Psychological Assessment*, *13*, 319–335.

Fletcher, R., Loschen, E., Stavrakaki, C., & First, M. (Eds.) (2007). *Diagnostic Manual – Intellectual Disability (DM-ID): A Textbook of Diagnosis of Mental Disorders in Persons with Intellectual Disability.* Kingston, NY: NADD Press.

Greenspan, S. & Switzky, H. N. (2006). Lessons from the *Atkins* decision for the next AAMR manual. In H. N. Switzky & S. Greenspan (Eds.), *What is Mental Retardation? Ideas for An Evolving Disability in the 21st Century*, rev. edn., pp. 283–302. Washington, DC: American Association on Mental Retardation.

Harrison, P. L. & Oakland, T. (2003). *Adaptive Behavior Assessment System,* 2nd edn., San Antonio: Harcourt Assessment.

Heber, R. (1961). A manual on terminology and classification in mental retardation, 2nd edn., Monograph Suppl. *American Journal of Mental Deficiency.*

Jacobson, J. W. & Mulick, J. A. (Eds.) (1996). *Manual of Diagnosis and Professional Practice in Mental Retardation.* Washington, DC: American Psychological Association.

Jacobson, J. W., Mulick, J. A., & Rojahn, J. (Eds.) (2007). *Handbook of Intellectual and Developmental Disabilities.* New York: Springer.

Landau, R. J. (2007). Advocacy and litigation in professional practice. In J. Jacobson, J. Mulick, & J. Rojahn (Eds.), *Handbook of Intellectual and Developmental Disabilities*, pp. 245–258. New York: Springer.

National Research Council (2002). Mental retardation: Determining eligibility for Social Security benefits. Committee on Disability Determination for Mental Retardation. D. J. Reschly, T. G. Myers, & C. R. Hartel (Eds.), *Division of Behavioral and Social Sciences and Education.* Washington, DC: National Academy Press.

Olley, J. G. (2007). The assessment of adaptive behavior in adult forensic cases: Part 3. Sources of adaptive behavior information. *Psychology in Mental Retardation and Developmental Disabilities*, *33*(1), 3–6.

Olley, J. G., Greenspan, S., & Switzky, H. (2006). Division 33 *Ad Hoc* Committee on Mental Retardation and the Death Penalty. *Psychology in Mental Retardation and Developmental Disabilities*, *31*(2), 11–13.

Patton, J. R. & Keyes, D. W. (2006). Death penalty issues following *Atkins*. *Exceptionality*, *14*, 237–255.

Schalock, R. L. (Ed.) (1999). *Adaptive Behavior and Its Measurement: Implications for the Field of Mental Retardation.* Washington, DC: American Association on Mental Retardation.

Schalock, R. L. & Luckasson, R. (2005). *Clinical Judgment.* Washington, DC: American Association on Mental Retardation.

Schalock, R. L., Buntinx, W., Borthwick-Duffy, S., Luckasson, R., Snell, M., Tassé, M. J., & Wehmeyer, M. (2007). *User's Guide: Mental Retardation: Definition, Classification and Systems of Supports. Applications for Clinicians, Educators, Disability Program Managers, and Policy Makers*, 10th edn., Washington, DC: American Association on Intellectual and Developmental Disabilities.

Simon, R. I. & Shuman, D. W. (Eds.) (2002). *Retrospective Assessment of Mental States in Litigation: Predicting the Past.* Washington, DC: American Psychiatric Publishing.

Spreat, S. (1999). Psychometric standards for adaptive behavior assessment. In R. Schalock (Ed.), *Adaptive Behavior and Its Measurement: Implications for the Field of Mental Retardation*, pp. 103–108. Washington, DC: American Association on Mental Retardation.

Stevens, K. B. & Price, J. R. (2006). Adaptive behavior, mental retardation, and the death penalty. *Journal of Forensic Psychology Practice*, *6*(3), 1–29.

Switzky, H. & Greenspan, S. (Eds.) (2008) *What is Mental Retardation? Ideas for An Evolving Disability in the 21st Century*, rev. edn., Washington, DC: American Association on Mental Retardation.

Wickham, P. (2002). Misconceptions of idiocy in Colonial Massachusetts. *Journal of Social History*, *35*, 935–954.

Wickham, P. (2006). Idiocy in Virginia, 1616–1860. *Bulletin of the History of Medicine*, 80, 677–701.

INDEX

Note: Page numbers followed by *f*, *t* indicates figures and tables respectively.

D

E

F

M

N

FSC
www.fsc.org
MIX
Papier | Fördert
gute Waldnutzung
FSC® C083411

Kolibri 360 GmbH
Ferdinand-Jühlke-Straße 7
99095 Erfurt, Deutschland
produktsicherheit@kolibri360.de